Essential Reading Skills

Interactive Practice Workbook

Authors

Omie Drawhorn

Teresa Perrin

Senior Consultants

Bonnie Goonen

Susan Pittman-Shetler

Published by Essential Education

Essential Reading Skills

ISBN 978-1-940532-01-1

Eleventh printing, April 2021

For more information, contact:
Essential Education Corporation
895 NW Grant Avenue
Corvallis, OR 97330
phone: 800-931-8069

Cover Design: Karen Guard

Essential Education provides innovative, effective HSE test preparation and adult learning programs centered on the learner's needs.
For more information, please visit http://www.essentialed.com/educators/.

Table of Contents

Download supplemental learning materials from Essential Education.

Visit the Essential Education website to find additional learning materials, including new workbook sections. http://www.essentialed.com/downloads.php

Introduction

The *Essential Reading Skills* workbook will help you understand what you read at a deeper level. You will learn the DARE process for reading, which makes the connection between your purpose for reading and the way you read. By acquiring new strategies, you will become a better, more effective reader. You'll be able to tailor your reading style to the task you're doing, whether you're gathering specific information, studying, or reading for pleasure.

Reasoning is an essential part of the reading process. Truly understanding what you're reading means being able to analyze and develop your opinions about what the writer is saying. This workbook will help you understand and evaluate arguments and viewpoints as you read and compare texts.

You can use this workbook to get extra practice to supplement a class or online learning program, such as Essential Education's GED Academy™ and Essential Skills Online reading programs. If you're in a class, your teacher can help you choose appropriate sections from this workbook to supplement your learning. If you're studying on your own, you can identify the sections that are most relevant to what you're learning.

This workbook can also be used on its own as a standalone learning tool, by working through each lesson. Using this workbook, you'll solidify the foundations of your reading skills and learn to apply reasoning to career- and college-level texts.

Each lesson has four parts:

- **Connections** introduces important ideas for the lesson. Connect what you'll learn to what you already know, and learn how the concepts apply to your life.
- **Learn It!** guides you through a strategy to achieve the goal for the lesson and get more from your reading.
- **Practice It!** provides practice for the strategy you've learned. You'll also think about how to apply the strategy to varying situations.
- **Check Your Skills** gives you a check-up to see what you've learned. You'll answer question types from the 2014 GED® test as well as questions that test your mastery of the lesson.

This reading book contains practice exercises that require different levels of knowledge and thinking:

If an exercise has one star, it's checking if you can follow the procedure you've been learning. You need to apply reading skills, identify elements of a text, or complete part of a clear-cut strategy.

If an exercise has two stars, it will require more thought. You'll have to consider options and show a deeper understanding of reading.

If an exercise has three stars, it will really get you thinking about how you approach reading and how you think about what you read.

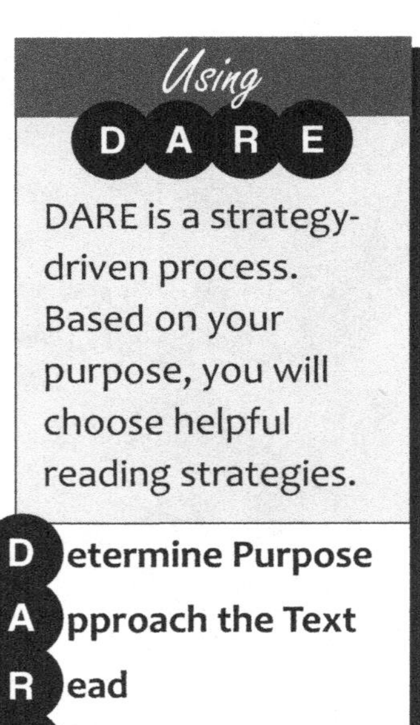

As you work through this book, keep track of ideas and concepts that are important and useful. Practice your reading skills every day. Don't limit your reading to what you're required to do. Read things that you enjoy and that interest you. It will help you become a better reader.

Reading Strategically

Introduction

Successful readers are strategic readers. Reading strategically means that you have a purpose for reading, and you adjust how you read for your specific purpose. The DARE process starts with determining your purpose, because your purpose for reading is essential in choosing a strategy.

What is your goal when you start reading? Are you looking up a phone number in a directory? Are you reading a novel because you enjoyed the movie adaptation? Are you trying to learn the customer service rules at your work? Are you looking at the online reviews of a restaurant to see if you want to eat there? Do you need to understand what your treatment options are for an ulcer? (We hope not!) In each of these circumstances, you would have a different goal, so you would use a different strategy when you read.

Reading strategies help you identify and focus on what's important. They also help you read actively so that you get more out of what you read. This section will introduce you to some fundamental strategies that you can use while reading. It will cover:

- **The DARE Process**
  Learn and practice how to use the DARE process for strategic reading.

- **Questioning**
  Practice using questioning to think about and understand what you're reading.

- **Skimming and Scanning**
  Practice finding specific information in a text and previewing what you're about to read.

- **Note-Taking and Summarizing**
  Get experience using note-taking and summarizing to learn, understand, and remember what you're reading.

- **Graphic Organizers**
  Find out how to organize information in a visual way to make sense of what you're reading.

- **Unfamiliar Words**
  Learn and try strategies for dealing with new words and unfamiliar vocabulary while you're reading.

- **Career and College Vocabulary**
  Expand your vocabulary to include commonly used words in texts for the workplace and for college classes.

- **Inferences**
  Practice making inferences beyond what's stated directly to better understand what you're reading.

- **Central Ideas**
  Learn how to identify the central focus of a text and get the big picture.

The DARE Process

Connections

Have you ever needed to...

- Read a warranty to find out if your computer repairs were covered?
- Know the details of your loan agreement to avoid fees?
- Find out how to set up a science experiment for class?

If you have, the good news is that you're just like everyone else; you need to read to do everyday tasks. We read to find information, understand ideas, and learn new things. How you read depends on what you're reading and your purpose for reading.

Being aware of the reading process helps you read more effectively. When you read, you think through your task, see what you need to do, and anticipate or deal with problems. When you plan and adjust your reading based on your purpose, you are reading strategically.

Strategic readers thoughtfully use strategies, tools, and skills to find meaning. This workbook will give you specific strategies you can use to plan your approach to reading and to understand a text. The first step to reading strategically, though, is to understand the reading process and how you can use it.

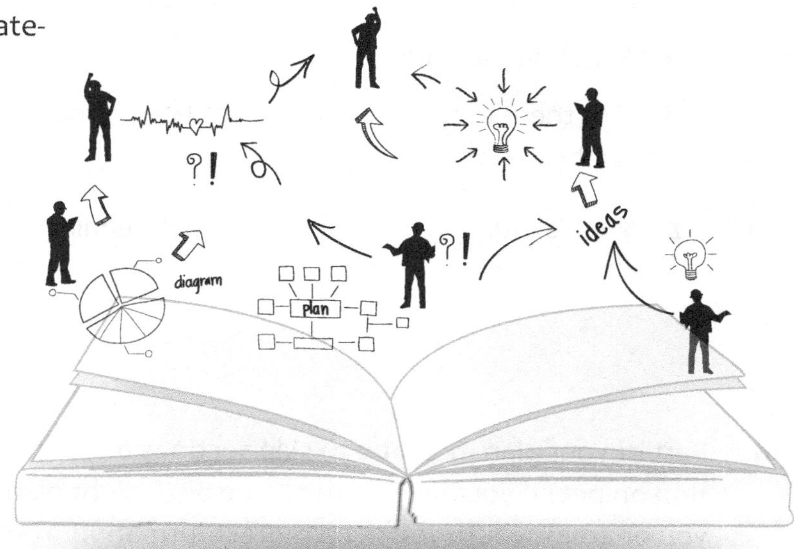

Using DARE

Every time you read, you have a purpose. When you adjust your reading to your purpose, you are reading strategically. You'll use strategies to preview the text, plan your approach, understand as you read, and evaluate after your read.

D *Determine Your Purpose*

What is your reason for reading? What do you want to understand or learn? What might make this reading easy or hard? Imagine that your purpose in reading a rental agreement is to decide whether or not to move into a new apartment.

1. What about the agreement would you need to understand to reach this goal?

As a potential tenant, you will need to understand the details of the agreement. You'll want to identify any details that will cause a problem or that you need explained more clearly. A potential problem might be the legal language of the document.

A *Approach the Text*

After you identify your purpose, you'll need an approach to meet your reading goal. Often, you will preview to get an idea of what's in the text.

To plan how to approach a text, ask yourself:

- How important are specific details?
- What's the best and easiest way to accomplish my goal?
- What do I already know?
- Are there sections, tables of content, or other features of the text that can help?

2. What is one way you could approach reading the rental agreement?

> *Using* **DARE**
>
> In sports, coaches and athletes plan the best way to win a game. Creating your **approach** to reading is the same—you need a plan to reach your goal.
>
> **D**etermine Purpose
> **A****pproach the Text**
> **R**ead
> **E**valuate

Part of your plan might be to skip sections of the text that don't apply to you, such as a section on pets if you have no pets. You also might plan to take notes of things that concern you or areas where you need more information. You might decide to make a list of specific questions you want answered and note the answers if you find them in the agreement.

R *Read*

While you read the text, carry out and evaluate your approach.

- Are you hitting stumbling blocks that you didn't anticipate?
- How can you deal with problems that arise?
- Do you understand what you're reading?
- Are you getting the information you need?

? 3. You are reading a rental agreement, and decide to skip certain sections because you don't think you need to know that information. What problem might occur? How would you resolve that problem?

You might discover that you still have unanswered questions. To solve the problem, you could go back and skim through the remaining sections to find answers to your questions.

E *Evaluate*

After you read, review what you've read. Did you get what you needed? Can you make a decision on the apartment rental?

- Review your notes.
- Think through your impressions.
- Go back to your goal.

? 4. What would you do if you read a rental agreement and at the end found that you had some unanswered questions and some new questions?

After reading a rental agreement and evaluating what you've read, you might decide that you need to talk with the apartment manager to find answers. You also might decide that next time you won't skip sections that don't seem to apply to you, but instead skim them for important information.

Answer the following questions.

1. Tom wants to know if the extended warranty he bought will cover the repairs to fix the viruses on his computer.

   Which would be the best approach for Tom to use?

   a. Read the subheads of the warranty and then read sections related to viruses

   b. Read through the whole text three times to answer his questions

   c. Read the subheads of the warranty to make educated guesses about the answer

   d. Read through the text and compare it with an Internet search about viruses

2. Sarah wants to know what steps she needs to take to complete a science experiment. She wants to make sure she follows the directions in the correct order, or the experimental results will not be reliable.

   Which would be the best approach for Sarah to use?

   a. Scan for words she doesn't know, write them down, and then read the text for definitions

   b. Read, take notes, and then read the text again while doing the experiment

   c. Skim the whole text and perform the experiment based on memory, keeping the text nearby

   d. Make a guess of what the experiment is about based on the title and then skim through the text, paying special attention to pictures

3. Hillary is reading two editorials with opposing viewpoints on an initiative to put fluoride in the city's drinking water. She isn't sure which side she supports, but she has specific questions about the effects of fluoride in the drinking water.

   Which is the best approach for Hillary to take?

   a. Skim both editorials for each side's general opinion to make a decision about which side she supports

   b. Read the headline of each editorial to identify which side has a more effective argument

   c. Write down her questions and read through each editorial looking for answers and taking notes

   d. Look through the text for words she doesn't know and write them down to look up in the dictionary

> *Reading for Understanding*
>
> What does it mean to be a **good reader**? A good reader reads with a purpose, thinks through the reading, and gains information and understanding.

Read the passage and answer the questions that follow.

Joe has been at his job for several months. He is having an ongoing conflict with a coworker because he disagreed with the coworker publicly in a meeting. The coworker now refuses to cooperate on any project and has been spreading lies about Joe around the office. Joe has never read through his workplace manual, but he needs to know what action to take. The manual is about 50 pages long and includes a variety of sections, as well as heads and bulleted lists.

Joe decides to read through the whole manual because he doesn't want to miss anything important. However, he's finding that reading the whole manual is very time consuming. Joe decides to take notes as he reads. If he comes across something that is relevant, he writes down keywords and ideas, along with the page number.

4. What potential problems do you see with Joe's approach?

5. What is effective about Joe's approach?

Read the passage and answer the questions that follow.

Sally is studying her driver's manual with the hope of getting her driver's license. She tries reading every word because she doesn't want to miss anything. Halfway through the manual she realizes she doesn't remember anything she read. Sally doesn't want to skim because there's too much information she'll miss.

6. What potential problems do you see with Sally's approach?

7. What is effective about Sally's approach?

A recent documentary about West Nile Virus has made Nate concerned about an upcoming hunting trip.

Use this passage to answer the questions that follow.

What about West Nile Virus in game birds? Should hunters be concerned about eating the game they catch?

Some game birds have tested positive for West Nile Virus (WNV). However, there is no evidence of human infection by consumption of properly cooked infected game. Hunters are likely at higher risk of infection by mosquito exposure, particularly in wetland environments. Protective measures should be taken to prevent mosquito exposure while hunting. There are extremely rare cases of laboratory workers contracting WNV through accidental exposure to infected tissues and blood. Hunters should wear gloves when dressing (cleaning) the birds to protect against accidental injury and exposure to blood. Consult with a physician immediately if an injury occurs to discuss the risk of WNV exposure. To prevent exposure to any infectious organisms carried by game species, hunters should wash hands with soap and water after handling carcasses and should thoroughly cook the meat.

Are birds the only species that is susceptible to West Nile Virus infection?

West Nile Virus (WNV) has been detected in at least 48 species of mosquitoes, over 320 species of birds, at least 2 species of reptiles, and more than 25 mammalian species, including horses and humans.

Birds are the natural host and reservoir of WNV. Although other animals are susceptible to WNV infection, only birds develop a high enough virus load to transmit the infection to an uninfected mosquito.

Source: U.S. Geological Survey, adapted from http://www.usgs.gov/faq/?q=categories/9858/2803 and http://www.usgs.gov/faq/?q=categories/9858/2792

 **8.** How should Nate approach this passage from the U.S. Geological Survey website?

 **9.** Should Nate be worried about contracting West Nile Virus? Why or why not?

Check Your Skills

Imagine you are new to a company. Word around the office is that a coworker was recently fired for inappropriate use of his cell phone. You had assumed that making personal calls wasn't a big deal. You have two young children at home and need to be available, so you decide to find out what qualifies as appropriate cell phone use.

Read the passage and answer the questions that follow.

Workplace Cell Phone Policy

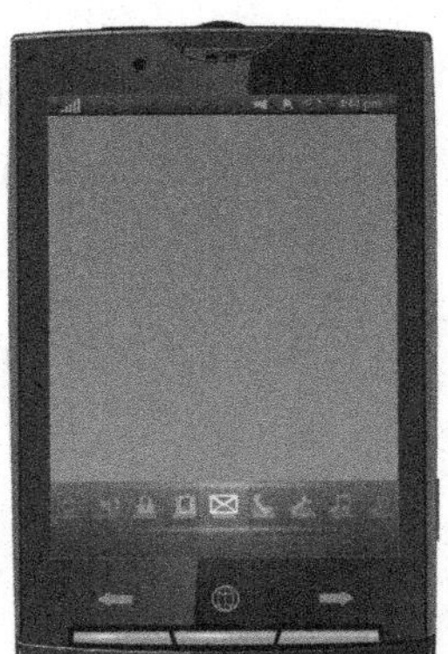

A cell phone is any personal cellular device that makes or receives phone calls, sends and receives text messages, and/or is able to access the Internet and emails.

This policy applies to both employee-owned and company-provided phones.

Driving Policy

An employee who uses a company-supplied vehicle is not allowed to use a cell phone while driving. This includes hands on or hands off, whether or not the use is personal or company-related. None of the following are allowed: placing or receiving phone calls, IMS/text messaging, visiting websites, reading or sending email, and checking for phone messages.

While you are driving your personal vehicle, business-related cell phone calls are discouraged due to statistics that point to the dangers of talking on the phone while driving.

Cell Phones at Work

Although cell phones are often used for business purposes, they can be a distraction in the workplace. Employees are asked to leave cell phones at their desk and to limit personal calls while in their workspace. With approval from a manager, in the event of an emergency or anticipated emergency, the cell phone may be carried to a meeting or other company business on vibrate mode.

Disciplinary actions will be taken against employees who violate this policy. Depending on the circumstances and violations, disciplinary actions could include termination of employment.

1. Based on the passage, which of the following is appropriate cell phone use?
   - **a.** Taking a business call on a cell phone while driving your own car
   - **b.** Taking a lengthy social call at your desk
   - **c.** Checking your personal email while driving a company car
   - **d.** Taking a brief call from your daughter's school at your desk

2. Based on the passage, which situation is likely considered an emergency?
   - **a.** A child who has a cold at home with a babysitter
   - **b.** A wife who is going into labor
   - **c.** A question from a family member or close friend
   - **d.** A call to catch up with a longtime friend

3. What information or situations are not addressed in the passage?

4. Talking on the cell phone while driving is not allowed at this company although it is legal in the company's state. Why doesn't the company allow this even though it is legal?
   - **a.** The company is concerned about employees' safety and avoiding accidents.
   - **b.** The company is concerned about their lease fees for company cars.
   - **c.** The company is concerned about employees' privacy and security.
   - **d.** The company is attempting to have more control over employees.

5. Imagine you are a supervisor. In a meeting, an employee keeps checking her cell phone and texting. You pull her aside, and she tells you that she is checking on her sick children.

   As a supervisor, based on this policy, what would you do?

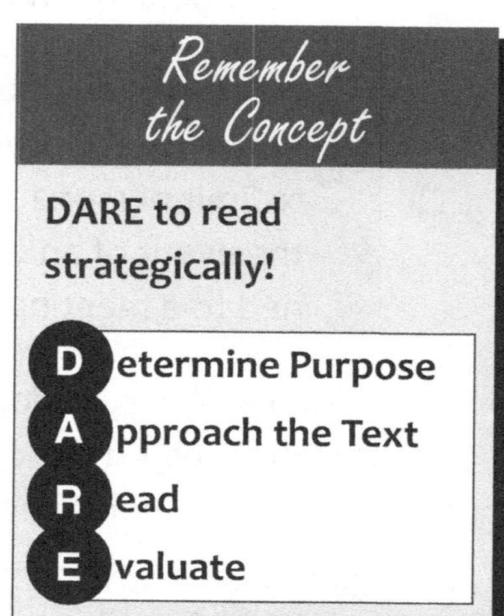

Questioning

Connections

Imagine you just got an exciting new job. You're reading through the work manual but discover you don't remember anything you just read. There's too much information! Some of it doesn't seem important, and some doesn't make sense.

Asking and answering questions throughout the reading process can help you understand better, focus your reading, and read with a purpose.

Questioning is a strategy where you ask and answer questions. By questioning before, during, and after reading, you're being an active reader. You're processing the information you're reading and cementing in your mind the things that are important. Just passing your eyes over the words doesn't help you learn or understand. Thinking actively does.

Ask Three *Whats*

Before: *What* do I want to know?

During: *What* does this mean?

After: *What* have I learned?

Asking and Answering Questions

You can use questioning before, during, and after reading to focus your reading and improve your understanding.

Ask Three Whats:

- **Before** reading, ask about what you want to know.
- **During** reading, ask about what it means.
- **After** reading, ask about what you've learned.

Don't just ask one question. Expand your ideas and ask yourself detailed questions about what you think, wonder, and want to know.

Use this passage with the questioning exercises that follow.

SSRI Drugs and Surgery Risks

Antidepressants relieve the symptoms of depression for many people. However, those who use antidepressants may want to consider the safety risks before undergoing a surgical procedure. Research suggests that taking antidepressant drugs around the time of surgery may result in the need for readmission to the hospital, blood transfusion, or even death.

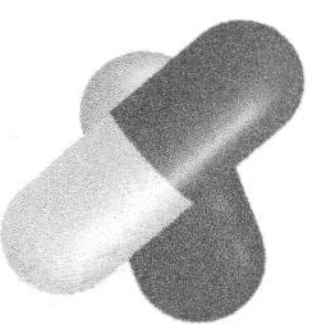

Researchers found that certain types of antidepressants known as selected serotonin reuptake inhibitors (SSRIs) were connected with these risks. Prozac and Paxil are examples of common SSRIs. People taking these medications were 10 percent more likely to experience a complication with surgery than those not taking an SSRI. The study showed an association between SSRI use and surgical risks, but it did not show that SSRIs caused bleeding or complications in other circumstances.

D *Determine the Purpose*

Sherman has been taking antidepressants for a while and is nervous about an upcoming medical procedure. He is hoping the passage will give him information about what he can do to make sure the procedure goes as smoothly as possible.

A *Approach the Text*

Sherman will use questions to help him read and understand. He asks questions before reading to prepare and plan.

? 1. What questions would you ask before you begin reading?

Sherman wants details that tell him how to be as safe as possible during his surgery. Sherman might ask, "What are SSRI drugs? Do I need to avoid them before surgery?" He might also ask, "What kinds of surgery risks are connected to SSRI drugs?"

R *Read*

As Sherman reads, he asks himself questions to find meaning and to make sure he understands. He also tries to answer the questions he asked before reading.

? 2. Read the passage. Try to answer the questions you have and ask new questions while you read.

The questions you ask while reading will depend on your thought process and understanding. As Sherman reads the first paragraph, he asks: "Do all kinds of antidepressants result in surgery risks?" "How often do people who take SSRIs have problems with surgery?" In the second paragraph, Sherman finds that only certain types of antidepressants are linked to surgery risks. He also finds that people who take SSRIs are 10 percent more likely to experience complications.

E *Evaluate*

After you read, ask questions about what you've learned.

? 3. What questions would you ask after reading?

After reading, Sherman asks what the passage means to him. Does his reading bring up new questions? Sherman asks himself, "What should I do before the medical procedure?"

Sherman doesn't see his antidepressant mentioned in the article. He decides to find out if his medicine is an SSRI, and if it is, talk to his doctor about how to minimize risks. Sherman also wonders whether his procedure qualifies as surgery and decides he needs more information.

Reading for Understanding

If you can't answer your questions while reading, try scanning for relevant sections to reread.

Use this passage to answer the questions that follow.

Advice from a Caterpillar

The Caterpillar and Alice looked at each other for some time in silence: at last the Caterpillar took the hookah out of its mouth, and addressed her in a languid, sleepy voice.

"Who are you?" said the Caterpillar.

This was not an encouraging opening for a conversation. Alice replied, rather shyly, "I—I hardly know, sir, just at present—at least I know who I was when I got up this morning, but I think I must have been changed several times since then."

"What do you mean by that?" said the Caterpillar sternly. "Explain yourself!"

"I can't explain myself, I'm afraid, sir," said Alice, "because I'm not myself, you see."

"I don't see," said the Caterpillar.

"I'm afraid I can't put it more clearly," Alice replied very politely, "for I can't understand it myself, to begin with; and being so many different sizes in a day is very confusing."

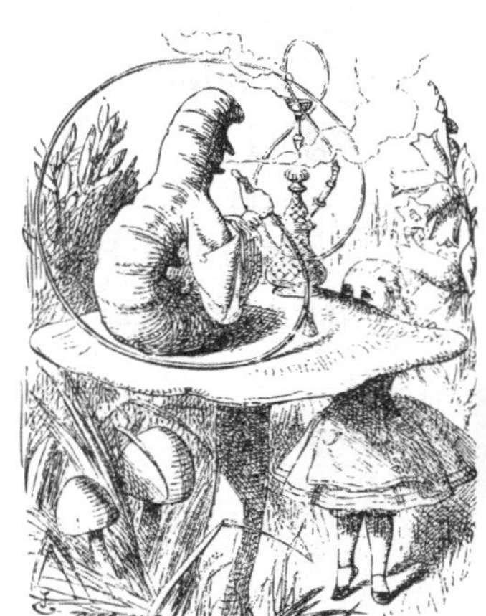

"It isn't," said the Caterpillar.

"Well, perhaps you haven't found it so yet," said Alice; "but when you have to turn into a chrysalis—you will some day, you know—and then after that into a butterfly, I should think you'll feel it a little queer, won't you?"

"Not a bit," said the Caterpillar.

From *Alice's Adventures in Wonderland* by Lewis Carroll, 1865

1. Marisa is reading the passage from *Alice's Adventures in Wonderland*. When she gets to the end, she finds she doesn't understand what Alice means when she says she hardly knows who she is. What questions can Marisa ask herself to find the meaning?

 2. Tran is reading the passage from *Alice's Adventures in Wonderland*. When he gets to the end, he wants to know what the point of the interaction between Alice and the Caterpillar was. How can he figure this out using questioning?

Maria has learned that dementia has affected many of her family members as they aged. She is interested in reading this article to see if there is anything she can do to prevent herself from developing dementia.

Use this passage to answer the questions that follow.

Mind over Matter: Study Shows the Mediterranean Diet's Connection with Improved Mental Skills

Older adults who follow the Mediterranean diet may be able to keep their memory sharp, according to a recent study. Those who follow the diet eat foods rich in omega 3 fatty acids, such as fish, chicken, and olives, and stay away from other meat and dairy products.

The researchers studied diet information in more than 17,000 people in their mid-sixties. Researchers measured memory and thinking skills, following the participants for a period of four years. In that time, seven percent of participants showed a decline of the measured skills.

Those who followed the Mediterranean diet were 19 percent less likely to develop thinking and memory problems. Participants with diabetes did not see benefits from the diet. The study found a lower rate of memory loss and declining thinking skills in people who followed a Mediterranean diet; however, a cause-and-effect relationship was not established. Further research is needed to establish whether the Mediterranean diet caused the decrease in mental problems and, if it is the cause, the reasons behind its effectiveness.

 3. Write two questions Maria could ask before she reads.

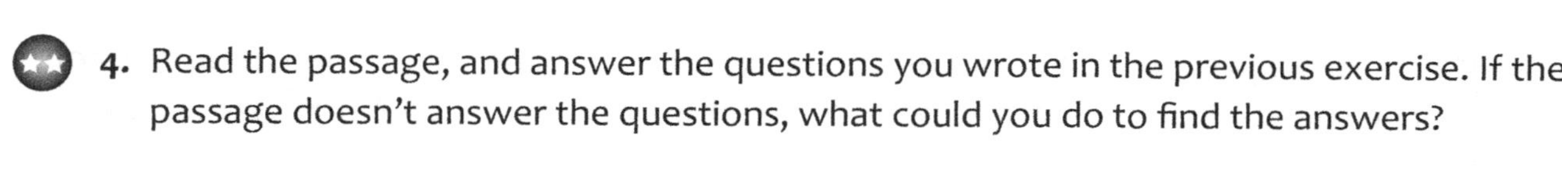

4. Read the passage, and answer the questions you wrote in the previous exercise. If the passage doesn't answer the questions, what could you do to find the answers?

5. Give an example of an additional question you asked yourself while reading.

6. Questions can help you understand the central idea of a text.

   a. Write a question to help you understand the central idea of the passage.

   b. Answer your question.

7. Questions can also help you understand important details.

   a. Write a question to help you understand an important detail in the passage.

   b. Answer your question.

8. Write a question to help you connect the passage to your life.

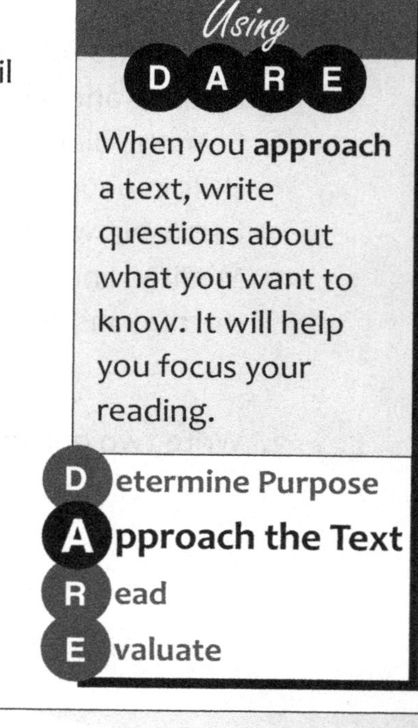

Check Your Skills

Read the passage and answer the questions that follow.

Warmer Springs Causing Loss of Snow Cover throughout the Rocky Mountains

BOZEMAN, Mont.—Warmer spring temperatures since 1980 are causing an estimated 20 percent loss of snow cover across the Rocky Mountains of western North America, according to new research from the U.S. Geological Survey.

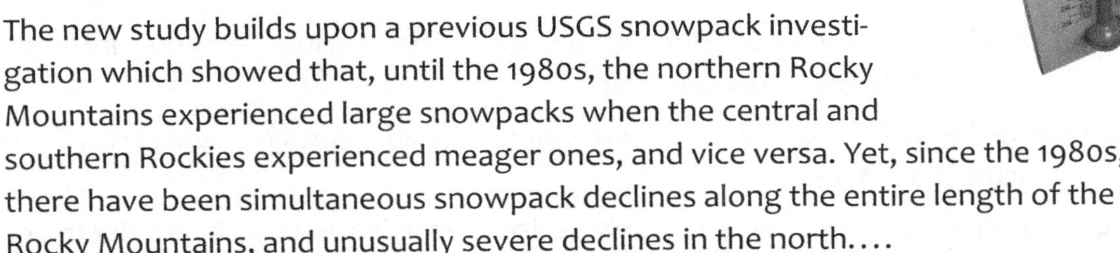

The new study builds upon a previous USGS snowpack investigation which showed that, until the 1980s, the northern Rocky Mountains experienced large snowpacks when the central and southern Rockies experienced meager ones, and vice versa. Yet, since the 1980s, there have been simultaneous snowpack declines along the entire length of the Rocky Mountains, and unusually severe declines in the north. . . .

Runoff from Rocky Mountain winter snowpack accounts for 60 to 80 percent of the annual water supply for more than 70 million people living in the western U.S., and is influenced by factors such as the snowpack's water content, known as snow water equivalent, and the timing of snowmelt.

The timing of snowmelt affects not only when water is available for crop irrigation and energy production from hydroelectric dams, but also the risk of regional floods and wildfires. Earlier and faster snowmelt could have repercussions for water supply, risk management, and ecosystem health in western watersheds.

Regional snowpack accumulation is highly sensitive to variations in both temperature and precipitation over time. Patterns and sources of these variations are difficult to discern due to complex mountain topography, the different influence of Pacific Ocean climate, like La Niña and El Niño, on winter precipitation in the northern versus southern and central Rockies, and the brevity and patchiness of detailed snow records. . . .

[Study author Julian Betancourt] said, "Regardless of the ultimate causes, continuation of present snowpack trends in the Rocky Mountains will pose difficult challenges for watershed management and conventional water planning in the American West."

Source: U.S. Geological Survey, adapted from "Warmer Springs Causing Loss of Snow Cover throughout the Rocky Mountains," http://www.usgs.gov/newsroom/article.asp?ID=3587&from=rss#.UbiV9va4F7s

1. What is the central idea of this article?
   - **a.** Warmer spring temperatures are causing a lack of snow cover in the Rocky Mountains.
   - **b.** Global warming is destroying the Rocky Mountains, a precursor of future destruction.
   - **c.** A lot of people depend on snowmelt from the Rockies for their lives and businesses.
   - **d.** The snowpack accumulation is affected by variations in temperature and precipitation over time.

2. What is the strongest piece of evidence to support the article's central idea?
   - **a.** A USGS survey each April since 1980 showed that warmer temperatures melted the snow earlier than in previous years.
   - **b.** Regardless of the causes, reduced snowpack in the Rocky Mountains will create difficult challenges.
   - **c.** The timing of snowmelt affects water for crop irrigation and hydroelectric energy production as well as regional floods and wildfires.
   - **d.** Earlier and faster snowmelt could have repercussions for water supply, risk management, and ecosystem health.

3. What is most likely to happen if the trend described in the article continues?
   - **a.** Skiers will be unable to take advantage of the snow in the Rockies and will have to go elsewhere.
   - **b.** A large portion of the people and environment in the western U.S. will be severely affected.
   - **c.** The article doesn't give enough information to predict what will happen if the trend continues.
   - **d.** The climate of the region will become known for its mild winters.

4. What does the lack of snow in the Rockies mean for the rest of the United States and the world?

Remember the Concept

Ask Three Whats:

- **Before** reading, ask about what you want to know.
- **During** reading, ask about what it means.
- **After** reading, ask about what you've learned.

Skimming and Scanning

Connections

Have you ever had to . . .

- Cram for a test?
- Read a work manual?
- Find a date in an article?

These tasks require you to go through a lot of text to get to the important information, but you don't need to read every word. You can find what you need quickly by **skimming** and **scanning**.

You can use the structure and features of a text to help you skim and scan to find specific details or locate the overall idea.

Skimming and **scanning** are similar in process but different in purpose.

Skimming gives you an overview of what's in the text. It can help you . . .

- Prepare to read by getting a preview.
- Get the big ideas quickly.
- Review after you've read.

Scanning is a way to find a specific piece of information in a lot of text. You can scan for a fact, name, date, or statistic. When you scan, use the text features and structure to predict where the information will be. Then, look for keywords to find the information you need.

A Process for Skimming

Skimming is a good way to get an overview of a text. To skim, remember GPS:

Go Quick • Predict • Stand-Outs

Use this passage for the exercises that follow.

NASA Study Projects Warming-Driven Changes in Global Rainfall

WASHINGTON—A NASA-led modeling study provides new evidence that global warming may increase the risk for extreme rainfall and drought. The study shows for the first time how rising carbon dioxide concentrations could affect the entire range of rainfall types on Earth.

Analysis of computer simulations from 14 climate models indicates wet regions of the world, such as the equatorial Pacific Ocean and Asian monsoon regions, will see increases in heavy precipitation because of warming resulting from projected increases in carbon dioxide levels. Arid land areas outside the tropics and many regions with moderate rainfall could become drier. Areas projected to see the most significant increase in heavy rainfall are in the tropical zones around the equator, particularly in the Pacific Ocean and Asian monsoon regions.

The models project for every 1 degree Fahrenheit of carbon dioxide-induced warming, heavy rainfall will increase globally by 3.9 percent and light rain will increase globally by 1 percent. However, total global rainfall is not projected to change much because moderate rainfall will decrease globally by 1.4 percent.

Source: NASA, adapted from "NASA Study Projects Warming-Driven Changes in Global Rainfall ," http://www.nasa.gov/home/hqnews/2013/may/HQ_13-119_Rainfall_Response.html

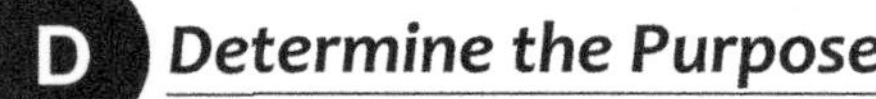

D *Determine the Purpose*

Imagine you're doing research for a school project about the effects of global warming on global rainfall. You want to preview the passage to see if it includes useful information.

1. In this example, is your purpose to find the central idea or to find specific details?

You want to determine what the passage discusses. It's more important to understand the central idea than to pick out details.

A Approach the Text

Skimming is a good plan to find the central idea. Before you begin, look for **Stand Outs**:

- Read the title.
- Look for subheads, bullets, images, or charts.

? **2.** Read the passage's title. What does the title tell you about the passage?

A title often gives you a summary. Based on the title, the passage will be about changes in rainfall that are caused by global warming.

R Read

To skim:

- **Go Quick:** Move your eyes quickly over the text to get the gist. Don't try to read every word.
- **Predict:** Predict where important information will be. Read the beginnings and ends of paragraphs and sections.
- **Stand Outs:** Pay attention to subheads, bullets, images, charts, bold words, and other emphasized elements.

Reading for Understanding

Skimming Tip: When looking for important ideas, look for words that are repeated or clue words that answer the 5Ws and H: *who, what, when, where, why,* and *how?*

? **3.** Skim the passage. What is the central idea?

The first paragraph expands on the information in the title, stating that global warming could affect all kinds of rainfall across the world. The central idea of the passage is that a study shows that global warming can increase the risk for extreme rainfall and drought.

E Evaluate

After skimming, evaluate what you learned. Skimming can give you a preview, so your next step may be to read more carefully. Or, you might not need to read further. Either you've found the information you need, or you've decided that the text isn't what you need.

? **4.** Is this passage appropriate for your research? What should be your next step?

After skimming, you can tell that this is a useful passage for your research. You may plan to read it carefully and take notes for your research.

Use this passage to answer the questions that follow.

U.S. Businesses Show First Rise in Employment Since 2008

In 2011, total employment from all U.S. business sectors was 113.4 million, an increase of 1.5 million employees from 2010, according to new statistics released today by the U.S. Census Bureau. The mining, quarrying, and oil and gas extraction sector led the way with a 12.0 percent increase in employment from 2010 to 2011.

This year is the first since 2008 in which U.S. businesses reported an increase in employment over the prior year. There were 7.4 million U.S. businesses with paid employees for 2011, a loss of 42,585 establishments from 2010. This is the fourth consecutive year of decline for the number of U.S. businesses.

"The strength of this release is that we can measure the economic activity of businesses at the local level, including changes over time," said William Bostic, the Census Bureau's associate director for economic programs. "This year's County Business Patterns report is the first since the most recent recession to show a reversal in the downward trend of employment. The growth in employment combined with the increase in annual payroll is another indication of a recovering economy."

State Highlights

North Dakota showed the largest percentage rise in the number of establishments, total number of employees and total payroll for any state in 2011. There were 22,370 establishments in North Dakota in 2011, an increase of 538 (2.5 percent) from 2010. There were 306,064 employees in North Dakota in 2011, an increase of 11,157 (3.8 percent) from 2010. Annual payroll was at $12.3 billion, up $1.7 billion (16.5 percent) from 2010.

Industry Highlights

Other industry sectors that had an increase in employment included administrative and support and waste management and remediation services (4.6 percent), educational services (3.4 percent), management of companies and enterprises (3.1 percent), and transportation and warehousing (2.4 percent).

Source: U.S. Census Bureau, adapted from "U.S. Businesses Show First Rise in Employment Since 2008 Led by Mining Sector, Census Bureau Reports," http://www.census.gov/newsroom/releases/archives/county_business_patterns/cb13-75.html

1. Skim the first three paragraphs of the passage. In your own words, explain the overall idea of the section. What clues led you to that conclusion?

2. What is the central idea of the whole passage? How do you know?

Skim this passage and answer the questions that follow.

ARCATA, Calif.—Climate change is expected to amplify both droughts and wildfires across the western United States. A new study shows that the effects of drought and fire work in combination, such that forests experiencing drought will see more dead trees in the aftermath of wildfires.

"There is a lot of research showing that climate change is already increasing wildfire frequency and fire spread," says forest ecologist Phillip van Mantgem of the U.S. Geological Survey and lead author of the study. "But what this study shows is that there is an additional risk to warming trends—namely that trees already stressed by drought may be more likely to die from fires."

Source: U.S. Geological Survey, adapted from "Hotter, Drier Climate Leads to More Tree Deaths from Fire," http://www.usgs.gov/newsroom/article.asp?ID=3649#.UfvyjGS4GRY

3. What is the central idea of the passage?

4. What do the results of the study show?

A Process for Scanning

Scanning is a useful strategy for finding specific information. You can scan a large amount of information and pull out specific details like a fact, name, date, or statistic. To scan:

- Identify a specific keyword or keywords to find.
- Predict where the information you want will appear.
- Move your eyes quickly over the text, looking for the keywords.
- When you find a keyword, stop and read that area.

Refer to "NASA Study Projects Warming-Driven Changes in Global Rainfall" on page 22 for the following exercises.

D Determine the Purpose

Imagine you're doing research for a school project about the effects of global warming on rainfall around the world. You have specific questions, and you need to find details and evidence to answer those questions.

A Approach the Text

Scanning is a good strategy to help you find specific information. Before you read, identify what you need to know and what keywords you should try to find. What will the information look like? Can you look for a number, a capitalized word, a percent, or other easily spotted words? Is there a keyword that will show you the information is nearby?

1. Imagine you want to find out which parts of the world will be most affected by climate change. What words or types of text would you try to find?

Words like *most, increase,* and *heavy rainfall* could lead you to your answer. It is a good idea to look for capitalized words such as names of countries or parts of the world. Words that look different, like numbers, titles, or capitalized words, are easier to find.

Located in the southwestern Pacific Ocean and comprised of two main islands and many smaller islands, New Zealand is a remote and unusual land. One of the last areas inhabited by man, it developed a distinctive biodiversity before Polynesians first settled there in 1250–1300 CE. Of particular interest is the variety of unique birds that have evolved on the island nation.

When scanning, it's easier to pick out words that look different, such as capitalized words and numbers.

R Read

When you scan, move your eyes quickly over the text, looking for specific information.

- Keep in mind what keywords you want to find.
- Predict where the information will be and pay attention to scanning those areas.
- When you find a keyword, stop and read through that area of the text.

? 2. Scan the passage on page 22. Which area will likely have the most significant increase in rainfall?

As you scan for the answer, look for words like *most, increase,* and *heavy rainfall.* Also look for capital letters to identify names of countries or parts of the world. You can find the answer in this sentence: "Areas projected to see the most significant increase in heavy rainfall are in the tropical zones around the equator, particularly in the Pacific Ocean and Asian monsoon regions."

E Evaluate

After you scan, plan your next steps. Did scanning help you find the answers you need? If not, why not? Could you change your approach?

? 3. How does scanning help you find information?

Scanning helps you find a specific piece of information in a text without reading through every word. It can help you find a listing in a directory, find a quote you vaguely remember, or pick out a detail you need.

Reading for Understanding

Scanning Tip: Before you read, notice how the text is arranged. Then, decide where you're most likely to find the information you need.

Scan "U.S. Businesses Show First Rise in Employment Since 2008" on page 24 to answer the following questions.

1. You need to know the percentage of new businesses in North Dakota since 2010. In your own words, explain what you found.

2. You are looking for a job in the education field and want to find out how big of an increase the industry saw in 2011. In your own words, explain what you found.

3. You want to find out which industries experienced the highest growth in employment.

   a. In your own words, explain what you found.

   b. How did you find the information?

4. Why is the information in this passage important, according to William Bostic?

5. Mary is trying to set up her new desktop computer and needs to find the answers to specific questions in the user's manual. Explain how Mary should approach the text.

Skimming is often helpful in figuring out your **approach** to the text.

Scanning is a good **approach** if your purpose is to find specific information.

Determine Purpose
Approach the Text
Read
Evaluate

Check Your Skills

Use this passage to answer the questions that follow.

LARAMIE, Wyo.—Migratory elk are coming back from Yellowstone National Park with fewer calves due to drought and increased numbers of big predators. These two changes are reducing the benefits of migration with broader implications for conservation of migratory animals, according to a new study. The new study describes a long-term decline in the number of calves produced annually by the Clarks Fork herd, a population of about 4000 elk whose migrants travel annually between Cody, Wyoming and Yellowstone National Park. Migratory elk experienced a 19 percent depression in rates of pregnancy over the four years of the study and a 70 percent decline in reproduction over 21 years of monitoring. The elk that did not migrate experienced high pregnancy and are expanding their numbers and range into private lands outside of the park.

A key finding of the study was that only 70 percent of migratory elk were pregnant, compared to 90 percent of residents. The study shows that the hotter and drier summer conditions of the last two decades, along with the long-term drought widely affecting the West, has reduced the duration of the spring period when tender new grasses are available to elk. This makes it harder for female migratory elk to find the food they need to both nurse a calf and breed. Though elk typically bear a calf every year, migratory elk that nursed a calf had only a 23 percent chance of becoming pregnant again in the following year.

Another likely cause of the declining calf numbers among migrants was predators. Migrants live alongside four times as many grizzly bears and wolves than resident elk. Resident elk don't experience the high number of predators, in part because when predators kill livestock on the resident range, they are often lethally removed by wildlife managers and ranchers.

Globally, wildlife migration is decreasing. Research and management often place blame on barriers like fences, roads, and other kinds of development that can physically impede migration corridors. While those are important, this study suggests that even in a landscape as well-protected as the Greater Yellowstone Ecosystem, subtler changes in predator management and forage quality in the migratory animals' environment will also play an important role. Migration has been understood as a strategy to gain better forage quality while also reducing exposure to predators. In this case, those benefits are instead being realized by the residents.

Source: U.S. Geological Survey, adapted from "Migration No Longer Best Strategy for Yellowstone Elk," http://www.usgs.gov/newsroom/article.asp?ID=3611&from=rss_home#.Ub058fa4F7s

1. Which sentence most directly indicates the central idea of the passage?
   - **a.** Migratory elk are coming back from Yellowstone National Park with fewer calves due to drought and increased numbers of big predators.
   - **b.** A key finding of the study was that only 70 percent of migratory elk were pregnant, compared to 90 percent of residents.
   - **c.** The new study by the Wyoming Cooperative Fish and Wildlife Research Unit describes a long-term decline in the number of calves produced annually by the Clarks Fork herd.
   - **d.** The study shows that the hotter and drier summer conditions of the last two decades, from the long-term drought widely affecting the West, has reduced the duration of the spring period when tender new grasses are available to elk.

2. Which answer most accurately describes the central idea of the second paragraph?
   - **a.** The study shows that the hotter and drier summer conditions of the last two decades has reduced the spring.
   - **b.** Only 70 percent of migratory elk were pregnant, compared to 90 percent of residents.
   - **c.** Migratory elk that nursed a calf had only a 23 percent chance of becoming pregnant again in the following year.
   - **d.** Another likely cause of the declining calf numbers among migrants was predation.

3. What happens when predators kill livestock on the resident range?
   - **a.** They are often lethally removed by wildlife managers and ranchers.
   - **b.** They are moved to another location where they are no longer a threat.
   - **c.** The ranchers evacuate the ranch out of fear.
   - **d.** The ranchers move their animals off the property.

4. What does this study tell us about migration on a global level?
   - **a.** Migrating wildlife have discovered how to thrive.
   - **b.** Migrating wildlife is a fairly new phenomenon.
   - **c.** Wildlife are migrating more and more infrequently.
   - **d.** Migrating wildlife is staying steady.

Remember the Concept

Skim with GPS:

- Go Quick
- Predict
- Stand-Outs

Scan for keywords to find a specific detail.

Note-Taking and Summarizing

Connections

Have you ever tried to...

- Study for a test but didn't know what was important?
- Explain what you just read but couldn't remember it?
- Read a textbook but didn't feel you learned anything?

It's one thing to read words on a page, but understanding and remembering can be tough. **Taking notes** or **summarizing** allows you to find and focus on the important information. These strategies help you...

- Understand better.
- Remember more.
- Focus on what you're reading.

Note-taking means writing down and organizing information, then restating it in your own words. The notes you take depend on why you are reading and what you are hoping to learn. Keep in mind that regardless of the purpose, note-taking always involves figuring out what's important. Note-taking also helps you learn and remember details.

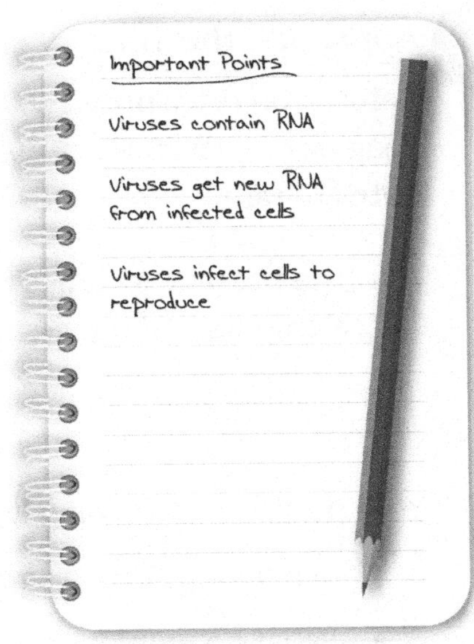

When you **summarize,** you identify the main ideas. You pick out the most important parts of what you read and restate them in your own words. When you reduce what you read to the main points, you'll be able to better understand and remember the information.

Taking Notes through Preview → Note → Review

Writing down information, organizing it, and restating it in your own words helps you understand and remember. A good note-taking strategy is to:

Preview → Note → Review

Use this passage for the exercises that follow.

An Online Presence

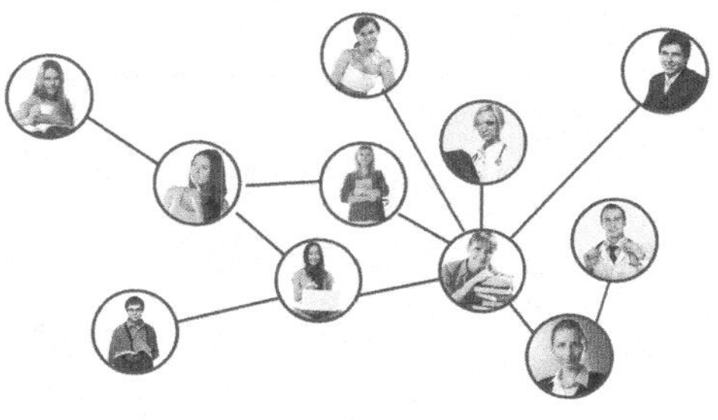

One of the first things many employers will do after you apply to a job is plug your name into Google or look for your LinkedIn profile. LinkedIn gives employers a good idea of your work history, who you might know in common, and what your additional skills are. However, your profile needs to match what you have included on your résumé. If they don't match, employers might get the impression that you left out important information. It's becoming common practice for managers to request LinkedIn pages instead of résumés, and it could be beneficial to create a LinkedIn profile and include a link to it on your résumé.

D *Determine the Purpose*

Imagine you're looking for a job in your career field. You've heard how important networking and creating an online presence are and want to know how they can help you. Keep your purpose in mind when you select important information for your notes.

A *Approach the Text*

Before you read, **preview**. Look at the table of contents, first sentence, heads, subheads, images, or charts. Then, write down questions you have. This will help you decide what notes to take.

? **1.** The passage includes the head "An Online Presence" and an image. Preview these elements and the first sentence. Then write two questions about the reading.

Your purpose for reading is to learn to network and build an online presence. You might ask:

- What steps do I take to create an online presence?
- What do employers look for in an online presence?

R Read

As you read, **note** answers to your questions, important ideas, helpful examples and details, and unfamiliar vocabulary and definitions.

? **2.** Note three important ideas and details from the passage.

You might choose to take notes on the following ideas and details:

- Employers plug your name into Google or look for your LinkedIn profile.
- LinkedIn gives employers a good idea of your additional skills.
- Your profile needs to match what you have on your résumé.

E Evaluate

After you take notes, **review**.

- Organize your notes.
- Rewrite or summarize them in your own words.
- Evaluate them.

Did you find the information you needed? What helpful ideas have you found? How can you use them?

? **3.** Restate the information that you found in the passage in a way that will be useful to you.

You could restate your ideas as a to-do list:

- Create a LinkedIn page.
- Include skills on LinkedIn.
- Compare my LinkedIn profile to my résumé.

Try Using a Simple Table to Preview → Note → Review

Preview	Note	Review
Questions?	Answers Important points	Organize Restate

Read the passage and answer the questions that follow.

Infants of Women Who Take Vitamin C Have Better Lung Function

Mothers who smoke during pregnancy risk their children developing lung problems, but a new study shows that if mothers take vitamin C during pregnancy, they could prevent these problems. Researchers found that if a pregnant woman can't quit smoking, taking vitamin C may help protect the baby's lungs.

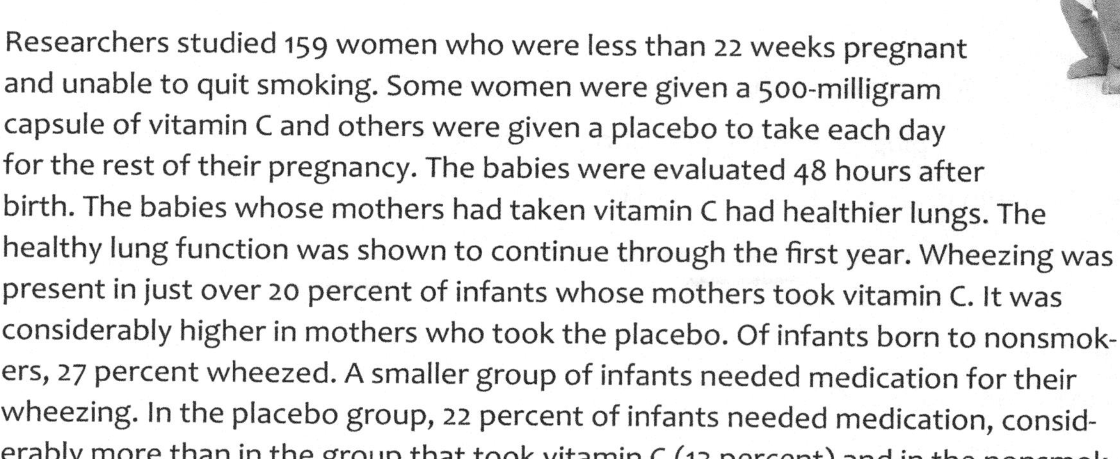

Researchers studied 159 women who were less than 22 weeks pregnant and unable to quit smoking. Some women were given a 500-milligram capsule of vitamin C and others were given a placebo to take each day for the rest of their pregnancy. The babies were evaluated 48 hours after birth. The babies whose mothers had taken vitamin C had healthier lungs. The healthy lung function was shown to continue through the first year. Wheezing was present in just over 20 percent of infants whose mothers took vitamin C. It was considerably higher in mothers who took the placebo. Of infants born to nonsmokers, 27 percent wheezed. A smaller group of infants needed medication for their wheezing. In the placebo group, 22 percent of infants needed medication, considerably more than in the group that took vitamin C (13 percent) and in the nonsmoking group (10 percent).

1. Imagine that you are pregnant but just can't seem to quit smoking. You want your baby to be as healthy as possible. Preview the text. What questions do you have?

Preview

2. Read the passage. Take notes on your reading, including answering your questions.

Note

 3. Review your notes.

Review

 4. If you were a smoker and an expecting mother, what would you do to make sure your baby is as healthy as possible?

 5. Eva is taking notes on the American Revolution from an online article. She will be using the information to write a history paper. She isn't sure what notes to take, so she starts writing down every detail that includes a statistic or a number. When she's done and goes back over her notes, she isn't sure what the statistics actually mean.

a. What steps should Eva follow to take effective notes?

b. What did Eva do correctly?

 6. Ron is trying to understand the safety procedures that he must follow at his job by reading the safety manual. He wants to remember the important information, so he has decided to take notes. He writes down the technical terms that are in bold.

a. What steps should Ron follow to take effective notes?

b. What did he do correctly?

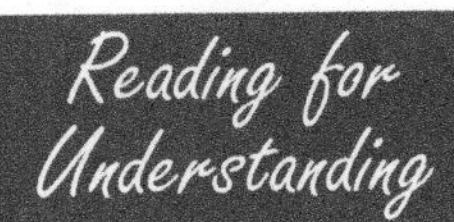

Using a graphic organizer in your notes can give you a visual of how ideas and details relate.

Using the 5Ws and H to Summarize

A summary is a brief statement of the important ideas and details of a text in your own words. Summarizing helps you improve your understanding, remember what you read, and inform others about what you read.

Use this passage for the exercises that follow.

Cedarville has an 11 percent unemployment rate, and that makes looking for jobs a challenge. Experts say that networking is key to making contacts and finding a new job. In addition to finding internships, expand your professional network by contacting professionals in your desired career field and building relationships with them. Join the local Chamber of Commerce, attend social mixers and industry events, and look into other professional organizations to make contacts in your field of choice. Branching out of your usual social circle can help you stay up to date on your field of interest and make valuable contacts that can help you along in your career.

D *Determine the Purpose*

Imagine your friend is hunting for a job and is curious about networking. She asks you if you have any helpful information. You want to review the passage and email her a summary.

A *Approach the Text*

Before you read, think about how to gather information for your summary. One way to summarize is to ask and answer the 5Ws and H:

Who?	What?	When?	Where?	Why?	How?

1. How do the 5Ws and H help you create a summary?

Asking, "Who, what, when, where, why, and how?" helps you find out what's happening. It helps you identify important ideas, and that's what should be in a summary.

R **_Read_**

As you read the text, look for answers to the 5Ws and H. After you've finished reading, set aside the text and answer the questions in your own words.

? **2.** Read the passage, and answer the following questions.

Who?

What?

When?

Where?

Why?

How?

The 5Ws and H help you find the most important information in a text. You might answer:

- **Who:** People looking for jobs
- **What:** Networking
- **When:** Now
- **Where:** Cedarville (or anywhere the jobseeker lives)
- **Why:** To help build contacts, find a job that's right for you, and stay up to date
- **How:** Join a local Chamber of Commerce, contact professionals in your field

E **_Evaluate_**

After reading, write your summary. Include the important ideas and details from the passage, keeping in mind your purpose.

? **3.** Write a one-sentence summary of the passage.

An effective summary is written in your own words. A summary includes the central idea of the passage and important details and keeps in mind your purpose. A sample summary is:

Networking by joining a Chamber of Commerce or contacting professionals in your field helps you form connections so you can find a job and stay up-to-date in your field.

Read the passage and answer the questions that follow.

Parents Sucking Pacifiers May Benefit Infants' Immune Systems

The results of a new study have many parents shaking their heads. Most parents want to keep their infants healthy, but the study suggests that parents pop their infants' pacifiers into their own mouths before giving them back to their babies. The reason? To protect infants from developing allergies.

Researchers found that transferring oral bacteria from adults to infants helps train the immune system to ignore germs that aren't a threat to the body. Children whose parents sucked on their pacifiers to clean them were less likely to suffer from eczema, asthma, and sensitivity to allergens.

The immune system needs to learn to recognize when foreign material poses a threat to the body and distinguish between threatening and nonthreatening microbes. If your immune system never comes across any germs, it will attack harmless particles, like foods, cat dander, or dust mites.

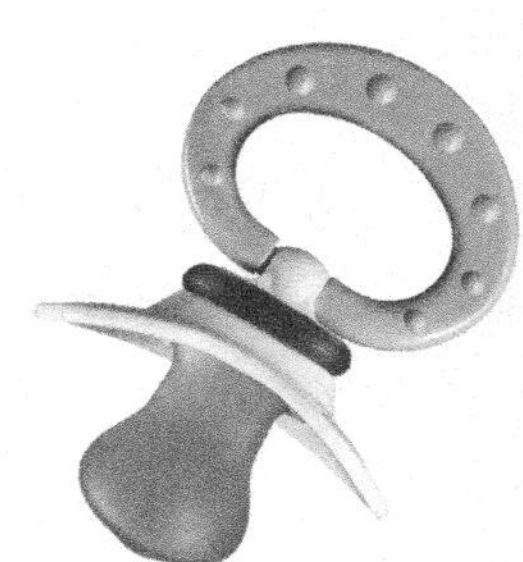

A report shows that the number of American children with allergies has seen a large increase. Around 17 percent of children have breathing-related allergies, and 13 percent report allergies that affect the skin.

1. Answer the 5Ws and H to help you write your summary.

2. Use the answers to the 5Ws and H to write a one-sentence summary.

3. Review the passage "Infants of Women Who Take Vitamin C..." on page 36. Explain the process you would use to summarize the passage. What steps would you take?

Check Your Skills

Imagine you are doing research for a paper about earthquakes and their relationship to aftershocks.

Read the passage and answer the questions that follow.

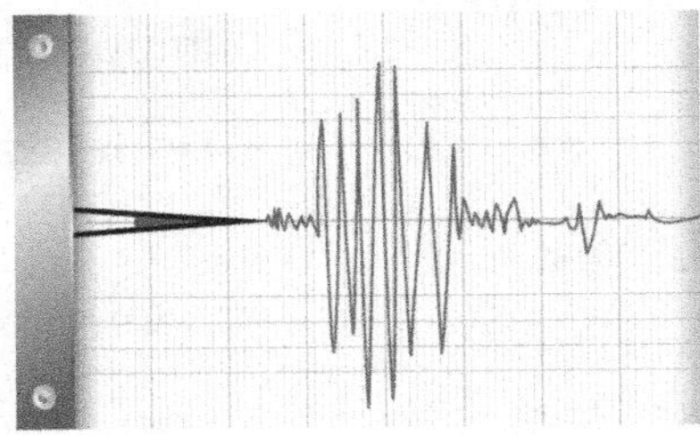

Aftershock from 2011 Earthquake in Virginia

A magnitude 2.3 earthquake struck Louisa, Virginia, on May 15, 2013 at 7:01 A.M. local time.

Wednesday's earthquake was an aftershock from the magnitude 5.8 earthquake of August 23, 2011. That previous earthquake startled tens of millions of people in the eastern U.S. and southeastern Canada, and damaged schools and houses in the epicentral area.

Since the 2011 earthquake, more than 450 aftershocks have been recorded. These events were catalogued by the USGS National Earthquake Information Center (NEIC), using data from portable seismographs that were deployed by several organizations immediately after the earthquake.

More than 50 of the aftershocks were large enough to be felt, and 38 were the size of today's earthquake, or larger. Scientists expect that these aftershocks will continue for many months.

Earthquakes in this area are not unprecedented, as they are within the Central Virginia seismic zone. This zone has been identified on USGS seismic hazard maps for decades as an area of elevated earthquake risk.

Although earthquakes are less frequent in the East, their damaging effects can extend over a much larger area as compared to the western United States. The difference between seismic shaking in the East versus the West is due in part to the geologic structure and rock properties that allow seismic waves to travel farther without weakening.

> ***Reading for Understanding***
>
> When you summarize, answer the 5Ws and H to identify the important ideas.

Source: U.S. Geological Survey, adapted from "Magnitude 2.3 Earthquake in Virginia," http://www.usgs.gov/blogs/features/usgs_top_story/magnitude-2-3-earthquake-in-virginia/

1. What is important about the 2013 earthquake in Virginia?
   - **a.** This event was catalogued by the USGS.
   - **b.** In the East, earthquakes' damaging effects can extend over a large area.
   - **c.** The earthquake was an aftershock from a 5.8 earthquake in 2011.
   - **d.** This zone has been identified as an area of elevated earthquake risk.

2. What is different about East Coast earthquakes versus West Coast earthquakes?
   - **a.** Earthquakes can damage a larger area on the East Coast.
   - **b.** Earthquakes are usually stronger on the East Coast.
   - **c.** Most earthquakes on the East Coast are aftershocks.
   - **d.** Earthquakes are just as frequent in the East, but they tend to be small.

3. How does this earthquake compare with the other aftershocks?
   - **a.** It was one of the smaller aftershocks.
   - **b.** It was one of 50 aftershocks large enough to be felt.
   - **c.** It caused more devastation than other aftershocks.
   - **d.** It caused scientists more surprise than other aftershocks.

4. Select the best summary of the text.
   - **a.** An earthquake in Virginia in May 2013 was large enough to be felt and occurred on the East Coast, where earthquakes may affect large areas.
   - **b.** The difference between seismic shaking in the East versus the West is due in part to the geologic structure and is tracked by the USGS.
   - **c.** Scientists expect aftershocks, which the USGS tracks, to go on for many months.
   - **d.** On May 15, 2013, on of many aftershocks of a widespread 2011 earthquake was felt in Louisa, Virginia, a town in the Central Virginia seismic zone.

Remember the Concept

Taking notes or summarizing helps you:

- See what's important
- Understand better
- Remember more
- Focus on what you're reading

Graphic Organizers

Connections

Have you ever . . .

- Made a pro and con list to make a decision?
- Mapped out the events in a story?
- Created or read a timeline of historical events?

These are all examples of **graphic organizers.** A graphic organizer is a visual diagram that shows the relationships among a number of ideas. You can use a graphic organizer to make new connections and better understand the meaning of what you read.

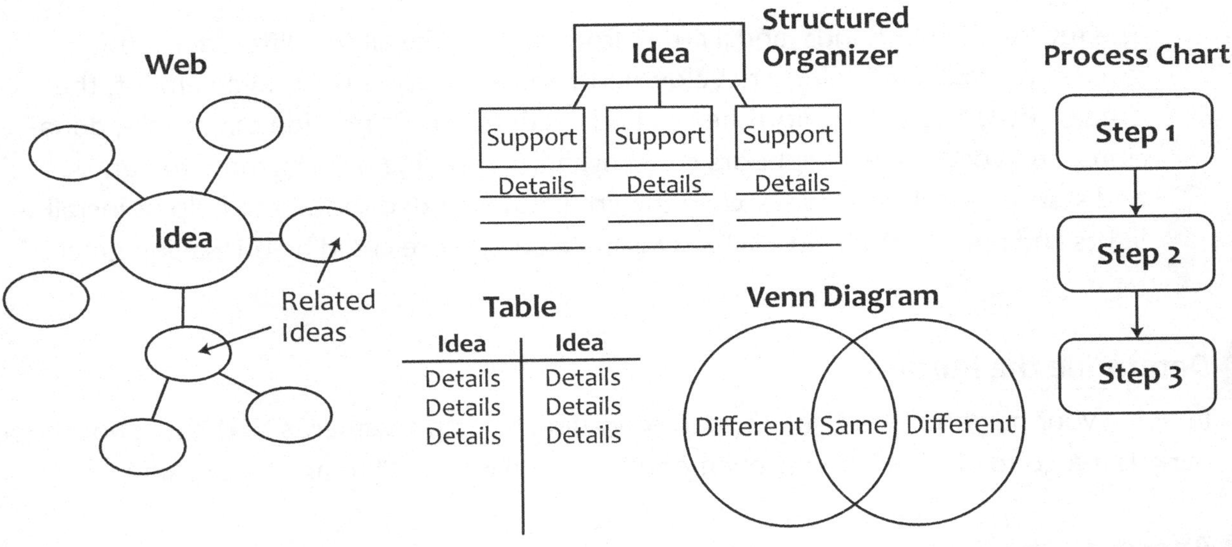

Graphic organizers help you . . .

- Organize and remember information.
- Understand how ideas are related.
- Relate new information to what you already know.

Using a Graphic Organizer

Graphic organizers show information in different ways for different tasks. First, **choose** the best organizer or your purpose. Then, **complete** the organizer as part of your reading plan. Finally, **evaluate** the organizer and draw conclusions.

Use this passage for the exercises that follow.

Our neighborhood park needs major improvements. The neighborhood is filled with children and pets that need a place to exercise and play. Some homes are not equipped with backyards and the park provides a place to barbecue and relax.

The park currently does not provide a safe environment for children. Police investigate criminal complaints in the area, and the local newspaper has run a series of articles about the drug culture in the park. There are no working lights in the park, which lends itself to suspicious behavior. The grass is overgrown, and the fields aren't ideal for playing. The playground equipment is rusted and cracking. No parent wants to risk an injury on their child.

The park would be the perfect place for kids to play sports. In a world where children rely more and more on video games and the Internet for entertainment, we need to give them a reason to get outside. It is the only green space in the area, and the ballfield is just waiting to be used.

The future is in our hands, and a little effort could make all the difference. City grants are available for local development, and with city council involvement, the dream could become reality. The city and residents could provide tax dollars, donations, and volunteers. Neighbors could organize cleaning parties, mow the grass, and start a neighborhood watch in the area, but we need the city to help us install lights and upkeep the fields. What was once an eyesore could be our saving grace.

D *Determine the Purpose*

Imagine your neighbor gave you this letter arguing for improvements to the neighborhood park. Is it a good idea? What improvements does she want? What are her arguments?

A *Approach the Text*

To form an opinion, you can identify and evaluate important ideas and support. A structured overview organizer is a good choice. First, find the central idea by skimming the passage and write it in the top box. You will track supporting ideas and details in the space below the central idea.

? 1. Write the central idea of the passage in the structured overview organizer.

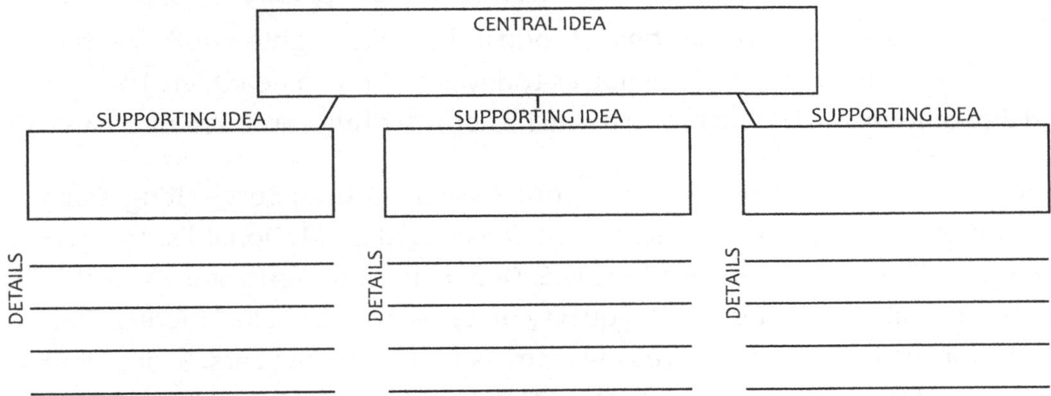

In the passage, the central idea is stated at the beginning: to clean up and improve the park.

R *Read*

As you read, complete your organizer with supporting ideas and details.

? 2. Read through the passage, and complete the graphic organizer.

E *Evaluate*

After you read, review the graphic organizer. Look at the ideas and make changes or notes. Do the ideas and organization make sense?

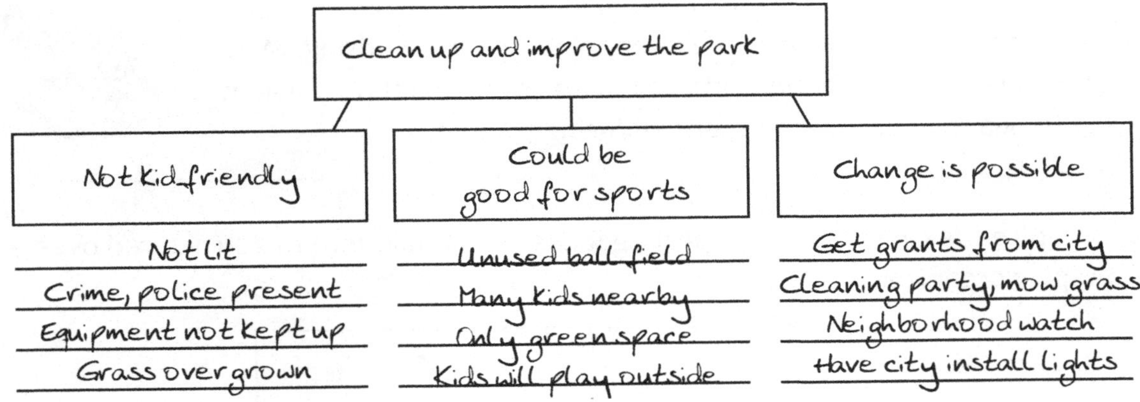

? 3. What do you understand better by using this graphic organizer?

Seeing how ideas and details are related can help you understand what the author is saying and why. You can clearly explain why improvements should be made at the park.

Practice It!

Read the passage and complete the exercises that follow.

Despite pressure for the fast food industry to "lighten up" over the years, a new study shows that choices today aren't much healthier. The nutritional quality of items on the fast food menu has only slightly improved over 14 years.

The study used data from eight fast food chains—Arby's, Burger King, Dairy Queen, Jack in the Box, Kentucky Fried Chicken (KFC), McDonald's, Taco Bell, and Wendy's. The researchers used the U.S. Department of Agriculture's Healthy Eating Index to evaluate the nutritional quality of items on the chains' menus. The overall score for the eight chains increased from 45 to 48 over 14 years. Scores for meat, saturated fat, and calories from fat and added sugars improved. Scores remained the same for legumes, total grains, whole grains, total vegetables, dark green and orange vegetables, fruit, and oils. Scores for dairy and sodium got worse.

The overall nutritional quality score of 48 was not impressive, researchers said. The score was below that of the average American diet (55), which is considered far from ideal. Researchers said that because fast food is such a large part of Americans' diets, the restaurants are well positioned to help improve the diet quality in the U.S. by improving nutritional values of menu items. Researchers also said that the improvements on the menu were likely related to legislative efforts, but there is much more room for improvement. The study authors noted that more than one-quarter of American adults eat fast food two or more times a week.

Experts are calling the increase disappointing and surprising. Many of these restaurants report adding healthier menu options, switching to healthier cooking fats, and reducing sodium.

1. Organize the central idea, supporting ideas, and details into this structured overview graphic organizer.

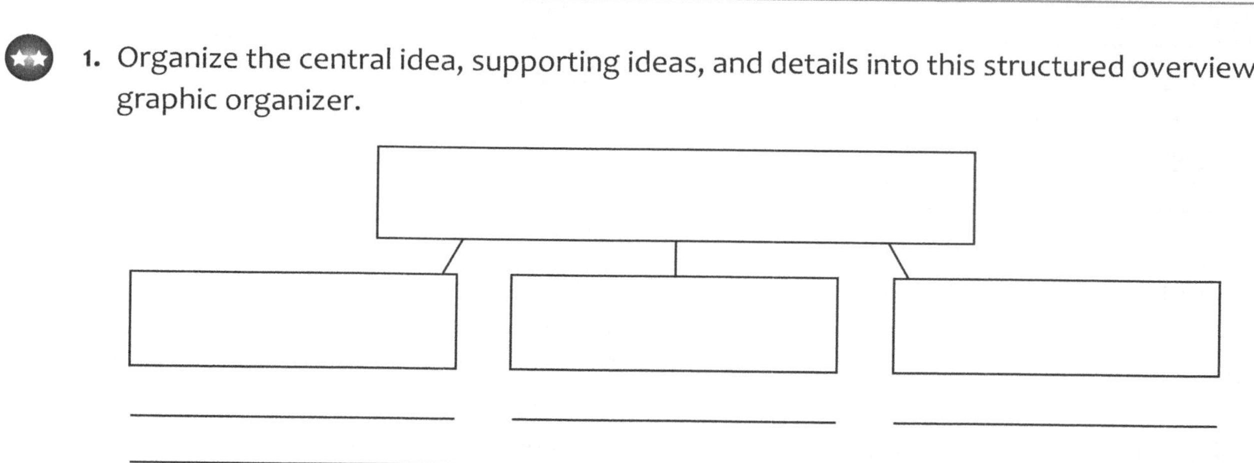

2. Based on the information in your graphic organizer, explain how smaller ideas relate to an overall idea in a text. What role do the details play in a text?

3. What conclusions can you draw about fast food in America, based on this passage? Is there anything that doesn't make sense?

4. Create a word web about the idea "fast food" based on the passage. Fill in the circles with related ideas, and add more circles if you need them. How does this graphic organizer affect your ideas? How does it compare to the structural overview?

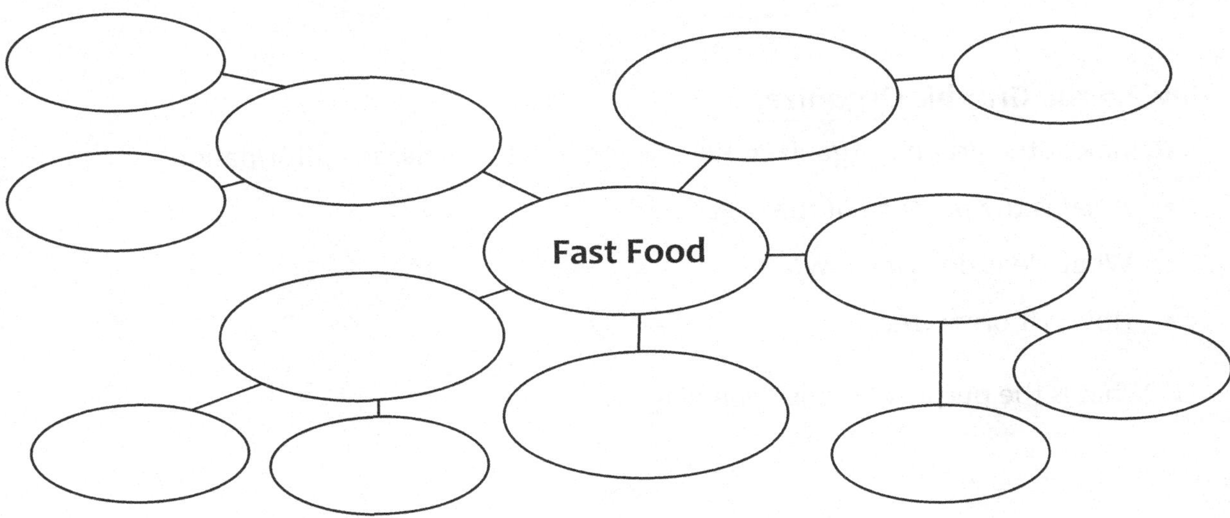

Evaluating Information in a Graphic Organizer

Evaluating is an important step when you're using a graphic organizer. Interpreting the results of a graphic organizer helps you draw conclusions about what you read. It allows you to think of information in a new way.

A **Venn diagram** is a type of graphic organizer that helps you make comparisons between characters, themes, ideas, topics, settings, and arguments. Each circle contains qualities that describe one person or idea. The qualities they share go in the overlapping area.

Jack and Ralph in *Lord of the Flies* by William Golding

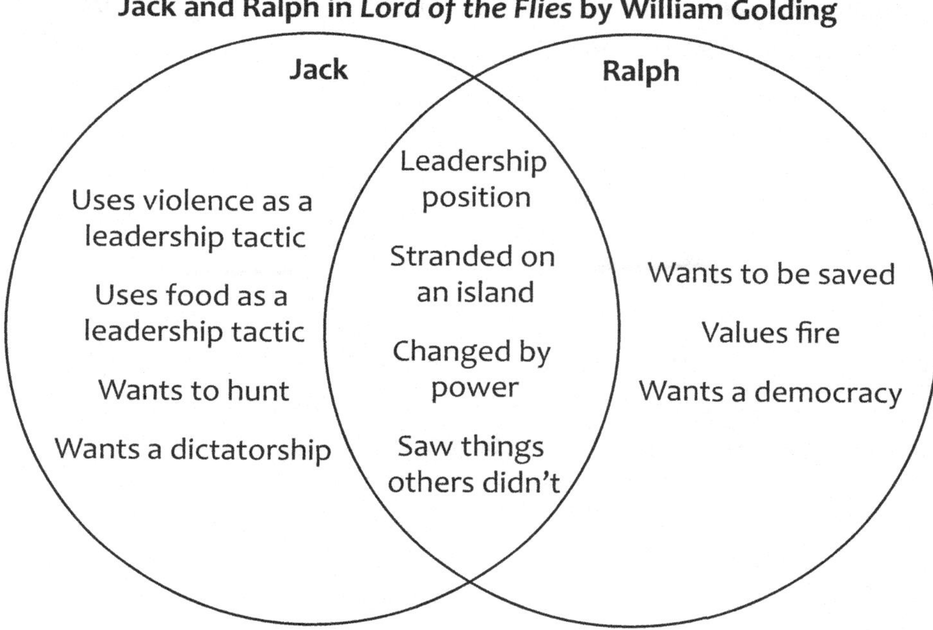

Review the Graphic Organizer

First, look at the graphic organizer. Review the heads, labels, and information.

- What is the purpose of the organizer?
- What ideas does it show?
- How is it organized?

?

1. What is the purpose of this Venn diagram?

The purpose of this diagram is to compare two characters from the book *Lord of the Flies* by William Golding.

Ask Questions

Next, ask and answer questions:

- What are the relationships between information?
- What inferences you can make?
- What does the graphic organizer make you wonder?

In this Venn diagram, your questions should help you compare the characters and draw conclusions about their personalities.

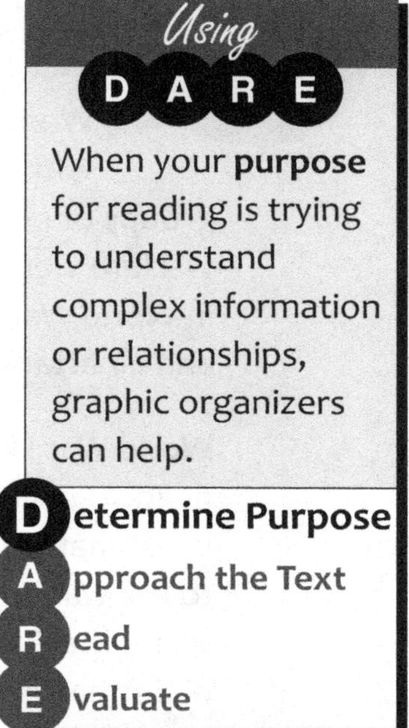

2. Write a question about the characters in the Venn diagram, and use the diagram to answer it.

You could ask a comparison question, such as: Which character is more likely to solve a problem with violence? By reviewing the diagram, you can see that Jack uses violence as a leadership tactic.

Draw Conclusions

After asking and answering questions, pull together what you've learned into a bigger idea. Based on your comparisons, you might conclude that one character is a better leader. What else do you notice about the characters based on their similarities and differences? What does this tell you about leaders and power? These questions don't have one right answer, but they should be supported with evidence.

3. Which character would make a better leader and why?

You could answer the question this way: Ralph would make a better leader because he doesn't use violence or bribery to bring people to his side. He has a goal of being saved and values a democracy, where everybody has a voice.

Practice It!

Read the passage and answer the questions that follow.

World War I and World War II had similar roots and causes. Both began with threats to power and revolved around conflicts of entire nations and groups of people, rather than between governments. However, the methods of warfare were very different between the two wars. Armies used trench warfare in World War I, but by World War II military technology had expanded to bombing and air attacks on civilians and military groups.

World War I left approximately 10 million military personnel dead, 7 million civilians dead, 21 million total wounded, and 7.7 million imprisoned or missing. In World War II, estimated deaths ranged from 50 to 80 million. Up to 55 million civilians died due to the war, including 13 to 20 million from war-related disease and famine. In World War I, the Ottoman Empire committed genocide against Armenians. In World War II, German Nazis committed genocide against Jews and other minorities.

1. Create a Venn diagram comparing World War I and World War II, based on the passage.

2. What factors might have caused the higher death toll in World War II?

3. What connections do you see between the two World Wars?

Check Your Skills

Read the passage and answer the questions that follow.

A study found that it's generally a bad idea to grocery shop while hungry. People who hit the grocery store when hungry tend to reach for higher-calorie foods and more of them. This affects not only their meal that night, but their meals for the rest of the week.

The study found that when people are hungry, they think high-calorie foods can provide them with more energy. Candy, salty snacks, and red meat are higher-calorie foods hungry people bought in the study. Vegetables, fruits, and chicken breasts were lower-calorie choices. Researchers are now investigating whether having a snack before food shopping makes people more likely to choose lower-calorie foods.

Researchers speculate that, based on the study results, dieting by skipping meals might not be a good idea. Study results indicate that when the body is deprived of food, the body doesn't know the difference between dieting and famine. It goes into survival mode because it does not know when there will be another meal.

In the study, researchers performed two experiments. In the first, people were told not to eat for five hours before the study. A portion of the 68 participants snacked on crackers at the beginning of the study. Then, all the participants shopped in a simulated online grocery store. The participants who had not eaten crackers tended to choose higher-calorie foods such as regular ice cream over low-fat ice cream, the researchers found. In the second experiment, researchers followed 82 actual shoppers during the course of the day at times when they were most likely to be full or hungry. They found that hungry shoppers bought more high-calorie products compared to shoppers who weren't hungry.

Nutritionists say that it is important to eat at regular intervals. This signals the body that fuel is readily available, so the body's metabolism continues at normal levels. Enough energy is available for biological functions and daily activities.

1. Create a Venn diagram to compare the passage about fast food on page 44 with the passage on page 49.

2. Becca is trying to make some healthier choices in her life. After reading both articles, what conclusions might she draw? Select all correct answers.
   - ❑ Eating fast food and shopping while hungry are two unwise choices that many Americans make.
   - ❑ When you are hungry, you tend to make unwise food choices.
   - ❑ Grocery stores hold some of the blame for shoppers' unhealthy choices.
   - ❑ Americans are too lazy to make wise eating choices.

3. Based on the passages, what can Becca do to prevent herself from making unhealthy choices? Select all correct answers.
   - ❑ Have a snack before grocery shopping
   - ❑ Never eat out at restaurants
   - ❑ Eat more meals at home
   - ❑ Have a friend do her grocery shopping for her
   - ❑ Skip a meal here and there

4. Using your Venn diagram from the first exercise, write a short comparison of the information in the two articles. What did each article emphasize about healthy eating? What advice did it give consumers? What makes eating healthily a challenge?

Remember the Concept

Graphic organizers show information visually. They help you:

- Make new connections.
- Understand better.

Unfamiliar Words

Connections

While reading a book for school or a document for work, how often do you come across a word you don't understand? Do you continue to read and hope you still get the meaning? Do you try to understand it? Do you give up and put the book down?

Understanding words is fundamental to reading. You can't make sense of what you're reading if you can't make sense of the words.

Looking up words in a dictionary isn't always practical, and it isn't always the best way to really understand a word's meaning. By using **context clues** and **word parts,** you can understand unfamiliar words while you're reading.

Context clues are clues in nearby words and sentences that help you find a word's meaning.

Context = What's Nearby

Word parts are the root word, prefixes, and suffixes that make up a word.

- A **root word** forms the base or main part of a word.
- A **prefix** comes before the root and changes the meaning of the word.
- A **suffix** comes after the root and changes the meaning of the word.

Word Meaning = Prefix Meaning + Root Meaning + Suffix Meaning

Using Context Clues

If you come across a word you don't know, you can use context clues in nearby words to find the meaning. Read around the word to see if the rest of the sentence and paragraph can help you.

Look for Examples

When you identify a word you don't know, look for examples that show what the word might mean, and use them to try to understand the word. **Signal words** are words that give you clues about what's nearby.

Signal words for examples: *such as, for example, including*

?

1. Many early pioneers who headed west faced **tribulations**, such as starvation, illness, and extreme weather.

   What examples of tribulations are in this sentence?

This sentence includes examples of tribulations: starvation, illness, and extreme weather. Based on the examples of tribulations in the sentence, you can guess that tribulations are severe problems.

Look for Synonyms

A **synonym**, a word with a similar meaning to the unknown word, can also be a context clue. You'll often find a synonym of the unfamiliar word in the same sentence or paragraph.

Signal words for synonyms: *as, is, or, are*

?

2. Cell phones have become **ubiquitous**; you can see and hear them everywhere.

   Which word in the sentence is a synonym for *ubiquitous*?

Everywhere is a synonym for *ubiquitous*. The second half of the sentence explains what the author means by *ubiquitous*.

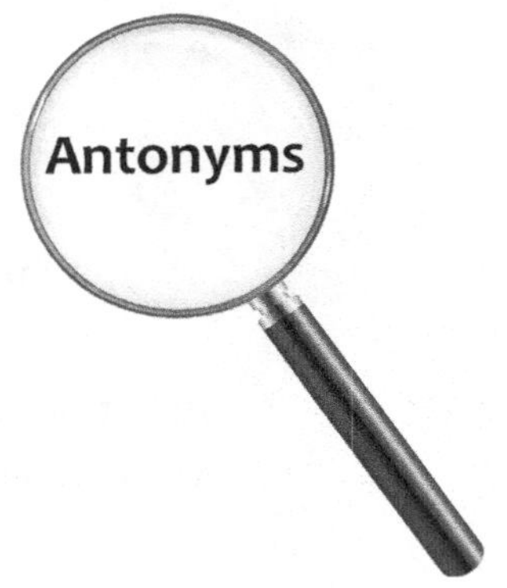

Look for Antonyms

An **antonym** is a word with a meaning that's opposite of the unknown word. Antonyms are often found in nearby text.

Signal words for antonyms: *however, than, but, yet, on the other hand, in contrast*

? 3. A memo that is brief and to the point is more likely to be read than one that is **verbose** and **rambling.**

In this sentence, what are the antonyms for *verbose* and *rambling*?

The word *than* signals that a word of opposite meaning is coming. *Brief* and *to the point* are antonyms of *verbose* and *rambling*. *Verbose* and *rambling* mean the opposite: *long* and *not keeping to the point.*

Check Your Meaning Using Substitution

After you have an idea of what an unknown word might mean, check your idea. Substitute your meaning for the unknown word in the sentence. Does it make sense? If it does, you've got the right meaning.

? 4. Many early pioneers who headed west faced **tribulations**, such as starvation, illness, and extreme weather.

Replace the word *tribulations* with your definition. Does the meaning make sense?

Here is an example of a definition substituted for the word:

> Many early pioneers who headed west faced **severe problems,** such as starvation, illness, and extreme weather.

The definition makes sense, so it's probably correct.

Practice It!

Use context clues to determine the meaning of the words in the passages.

Most surprising of all, germs can survive on an inanimate object and will eventually be picked up by the next person who touches that object. Think about how many objects we touch each day. We don't even think about germs as we touch tabletops, doorknobs, toilets, light switches, or money, to name a few.

1. What does the word *inanimate* mean? Write your own definition.

2. How did you reach that conclusion?

3. Write your own sentence using the word *inanimate*.

After the altercation with his former best friend, he was asked to pay for the damage the fight had caused and not to return to the location.

4. What does the word *altercation* mean? Write your own definition.

5. How did you reach that conclusion?

6. Write your own sentence using the word *altercation*.

Read the passage. Show your understanding of the vocabulary in the passage by answering the questions that follow.

Joe balked at the idea that he needed to tip the waitress 20 percent. She had given him slow service in the restaurant all night, despite the fact that there were only two other couples in the restaurant. Joe wanted to show his date that he had impeccable taste in restaurants, but he feared that he had disappointed her with the food and service.

7. Who do you know that has impeccable taste? How do they show it?

8. Have you ever balked at something a politician, an actor, a family member, or a friend said? What was it? Why did you react that way?

9. Write a question that uses the word *balked*. Answer the question, showing your understanding of the word.

10. Write a question that uses the word *impeccable*. Answer the question, showing your understanding of the word.

Using Word Parts

By breaking up an unknown word into parts—roots, prefixes, and suffixes—it can be easier to find the word's meaning.

Break Apart the Word

If an unknown word has multiple syllables, chances are there are parts of the word that might look familiar. Separate the word by prefix, root, and suffix. Have you heard any of the word parts before?

? **1.** Break up the word *justify* into word parts. Can you recognize any of the parts on their own?

Prefix	Root	Suffix

The word justify has no prefix. The root is *just-* and the suffix is *-ify*.

Determine the Meaning of Word Parts

Chances are you probably have heard the word *just* before, either by itself or as part of other words. The ending *-ify* is also a common suffix. Think about other words you know with similar endings. They probably also have similar meanings.

? **2.** Based on words you know, guess the meaning of each of these word parts.

just-

-ify

The root *just-* can be found in words like *justice* and *unjust*, which are about being fair and reasonable. "Fair and reasonable" might be a good definition of the root *just-*. The suffix *-ify* is found at the end of words such as *fortify* (to make secure) or *clarify* (to show or make clear) and means "to make or show."

Determine the Meaning of the Word

If you put the meaning of the word parts together, you can get a good idea of what the word means.

Word Meaning = Prefix Meaning + Root Meaning + Suffix Meaning

? 3. Based on the root and suffix, what does the word *justify* mean?

If you combine the two word parts, *justify* means to make or show to be fair or reasonable. You might guess it means to show that something's reasonable.

Check Your Meaning Using Substitution

After you have an idea of what an unknown word might mean, it's time to check your idea. Substitute your meaning for the unknown word in the sentence to see if it makes sense. If it does, you've got the correct meaning.

? 4. She **justified** her overreaction by saying that she had not gotten enough sleep the previous night.

Replace the word *justified* with your definition. Does the meaning make sense?

> **Reading for Understanding**
>
> Anytime you think you might know what a word means, you can insert a similar word in its place. Does the similar word make sense?

You might put in your definition like this:

She **[showed to be reasonable]** her overreaction by saying that she had not gotten enough sleep the previous night.

The wording sounds a little strange, but the meaning makes sense if you rearrange the words:

She showed that her overreaction was reasonable.

Answer the following questions.

1. Divide the words below into their parts (prefixes, roots, and suffixes), and think through the meaning of each word part. Combine the meanings of each part to guess the meaning of the word.

	Word	Prefix	Root	Suffix
Word Parts	Ex: Amorphous	a-	-morph-	-ous
Definitions	Having the quality of no shape	None, without	Shape	Having a quality
Word Parts	Ambidextrous			
Definitions				
Word Parts	Transformation			
Definitions				
Word Parts	Nonconformity			
Definitions				

2. The money he had left in his bank account would be **insufficient** to pay for fixing the leak in his roof.

   a. Analyze the word parts of the word *insufficient*.

   b. Write a definition of the word *insufficient*.

3. The police determined that the arsonist was a **pyromaniac**.

   a. Analyze the word parts of the word *pyromaniac*.

   b. Write a definition of the word *pyromaniac*.

Check Your Skills

Read the passage and answer the questions that follow.

Researchers have found a connection between heading, using the head to hit a soccer ball, and changes in the brain. The more heading people do, the more likely their thinking and memory will be affected. Doctors discovered more structural abnormalities in the brains of people who frequently used heading in soccer. Research also showed that these people are more likely to perform poorly on cognitive tests, especially tests involving memory.

Doctors are hesitant to say that heading caused the changes, however. They acknowledge a connection but won't confirm that heading is directly the cause of brain changes. To know for certain, doctors say they would need to perform a longitudinal study that observes people over a period of decades.

Soccer is the world's most popular sport, and heading is a common technique. In official games, players head the ball between six and 12 times, and often more. In this top level of play, the ball can move at velocities of 50 miles per hour or more. Doctors say it is not surprising that this might result in changes to the brain.

1. According to the text, what does *heading* mean?

a. To head out or leave
b. To use your head to hit a ball
c. To use your brain to think
d. Something that causes brain problems

2. What does *longitudinal* mean in this passage?

a. Observing over long periods of time
b. To move straight up and down
c. To move from side to side
d. Observing different items sequentially

3. Which word or phrase most directly shows you the definition of *longitudinal*?
   a. "for certain, they would need"
   b. "head the ball between six and 12 times"
   c. "observes people over a period of decades"
   d. "especially tests involving memory"

4. What does *velocities* mean in this passage?
   a. Speeds
   b. Travels
   c. Organizations
   d. Rules

5. Which word or phrase most directly shows you the definition of *velocities*?
   a. "top level of play"
   b. "of 50 miles per hour or more"
   c. "head the ball an average of six to 12 times"
   d. "longitudinal study"

6. Which word is a synonym for *abnormalities*?
   a. Interesting facts
   b. Irregularities
   c. Regular changes
   d. Diseased areas

7. Which word is most closely related to the word *abnormality*?
   a. Abs
   b. Mality
   c. Normal
   d. It

Remember the Concept

- Read around a word for **context clues.**
- Break up a word to analyze **word parts.**

Career and College Vocabulary

Connections

Imagine you've just begun college classes. Your economics teacher assigns you a chapter to read.

After reading, you are expected to demonstrate knowledge of the latest economic crisis. As you start to read, you quickly get lost. You don't know the meanings of some important words.

You might have the same experience reading an employee manual or a financial newspaper. In a career or college environment, you need to be prepared to deal with more complex vocabulary. If you're familiar with common college-level words, you can focus on finding meaning without getting tripped up on individual words.

Academic vocabulary includes words that are critical in school, and these same words are just as important in the workplace.

Many people fall behind in reading because they don't learn academic vocabulary in their everyday lives. By learning strategies to understand and remember academic vocabulary, you can increase your ability to read career and college texts.

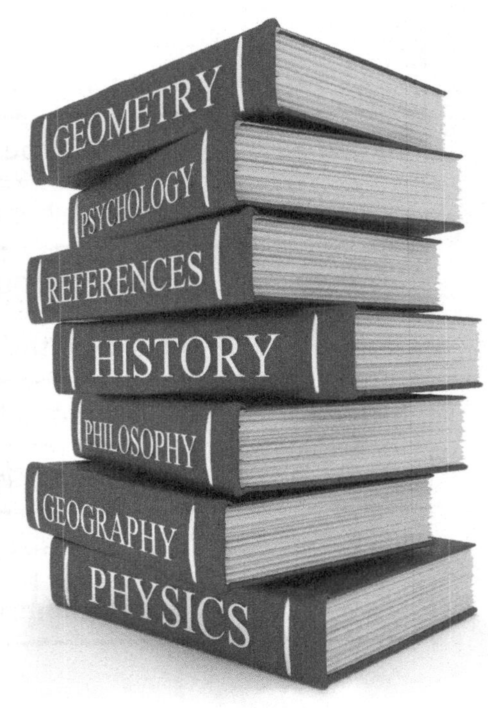

Understand to Remember!

Increasing your understanding of a word makes it easier to remember and recall.

Academic Vocabulary Words

Use this selection of academic vocabulary words for the following exercises.

Economy	The way a country manages its money and resources (such as workers and land) to produce, buy, and sell goods and services
	The President announced his plan to help the *economy* and bring down the unemployment rate.
Income	Money received from work or investments
	When he started his new job, his *income* increased.
Issue	An important topic for debate or discussion
	She felt that the most important *issue* on the ballot was a local tax for public schools.
Policy	A plan of action that is proposed or enforced
	The governor opposed a change to the current unemployment *policy*.
Process	A series of steps or actions that result in a change or complete a task
	She followed a complicated *process* to make a layer cake.
Research	The study of materials and sources to establish facts and reach new conclusions
	She found several helpful sources for her *research* paper.
Require	To cause to be necessary
	To receive her diploma, she was *required* to take four years of English.
Section	A piece, i.e., one part after something is divided
	He divided the orange into *sections*.
Structure	The way something is organized, constructed, or built
	The company is *structured* with a president and three department heads.
Vary	To differ in size, amount, degree, or nature from something else
	The eggplants in the produce section tend to *vary* in size.

Using a Word Web

Using a word web helps you gain a deeper understanding of the meaning of a word. As you explore connections with other words, it's easier to see how the word is connected to your world.

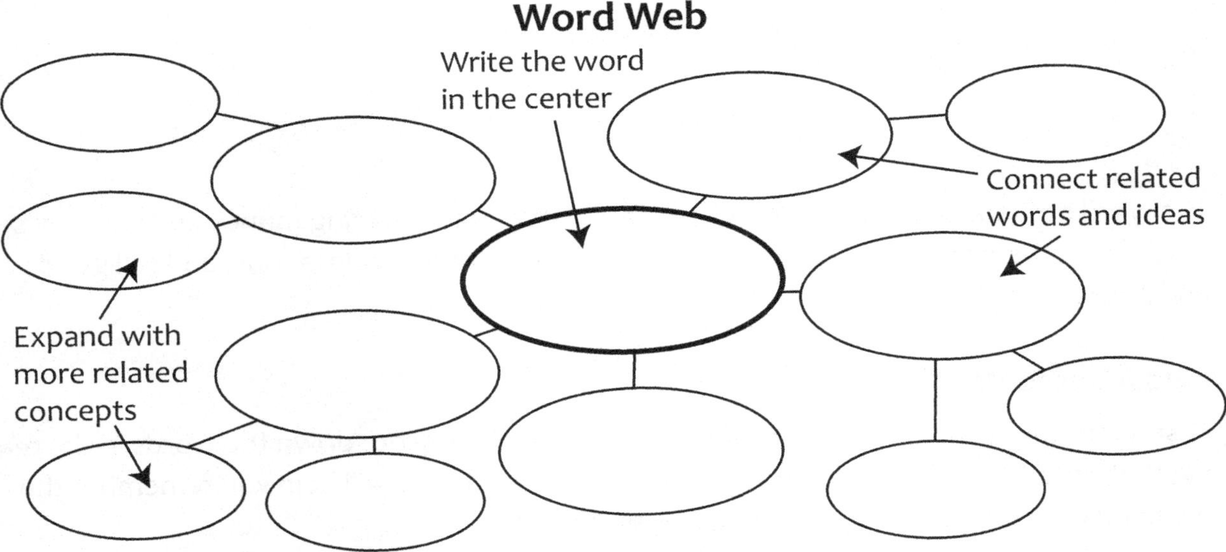

Use this passage for the exercises that follow.

E-Commerce and the Electronic Economy

The growth of information technology is changing our society and our economy. Today, computers, tablets, and smartphones let us communicate over the Internet in new ways. Consumers and businesses have been quick to recognize the potential benefits of conducting business online. Many consumers now routinely use the Internet to find and evaluate sellers and service providers, to compare prices at both online and brick-and-mortar stores, and to research products and services.

Businesses use the Internet even more extensively for tracking production, marketing products, communicating internally, and reaching new customers. This electronic revolution is spurring additional investments in hardware, software, facilities, services, and human capital. Ultimately, the Internet may change the structure and performance of the American economy as much as the introduction of the computer a generation ago.

Find the Definition

When you come across an unknown word, find its meaning. You can look it up in a dictionary, use context clues, or use word parts to find meaning.

1. What is the meaning of the word *economy* in the passage?

The word *economy* means a country or area's system for managing money and resources (such as workers and land). It's the system that lets people produce, buy, and sell goods and services.

Find Related Words

First, write the word in the center of the word web. Next, write down the words in the reading that are related to or help you understand the word. This will help you remember the meaning of the word and apply it in other situations.

2. In the bubbles connected to the center of the word web, write five words from the passage that help you understand the word *economy*.

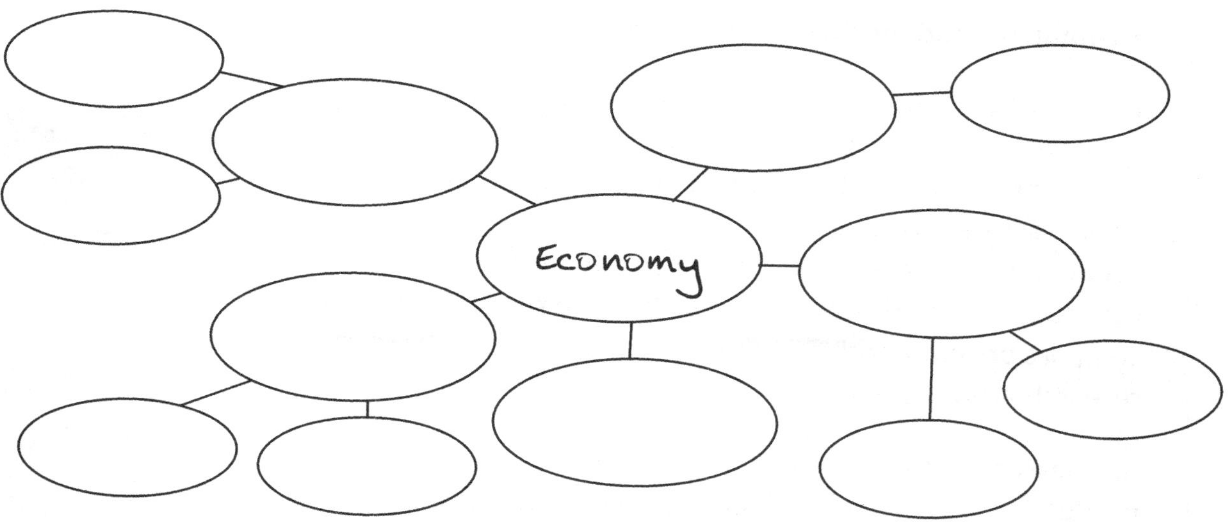

Five words you might choose are:

E-commerce Business Investments Production Services

Explain the Connection

How do the words you selected relate to the meaning of economy? Explaining the connection will help you remember and understand the word's meaning better.

Using your prior knowledge and the text, add more words to the word web related to each concept to help you build your understanding of the words and their relationships.

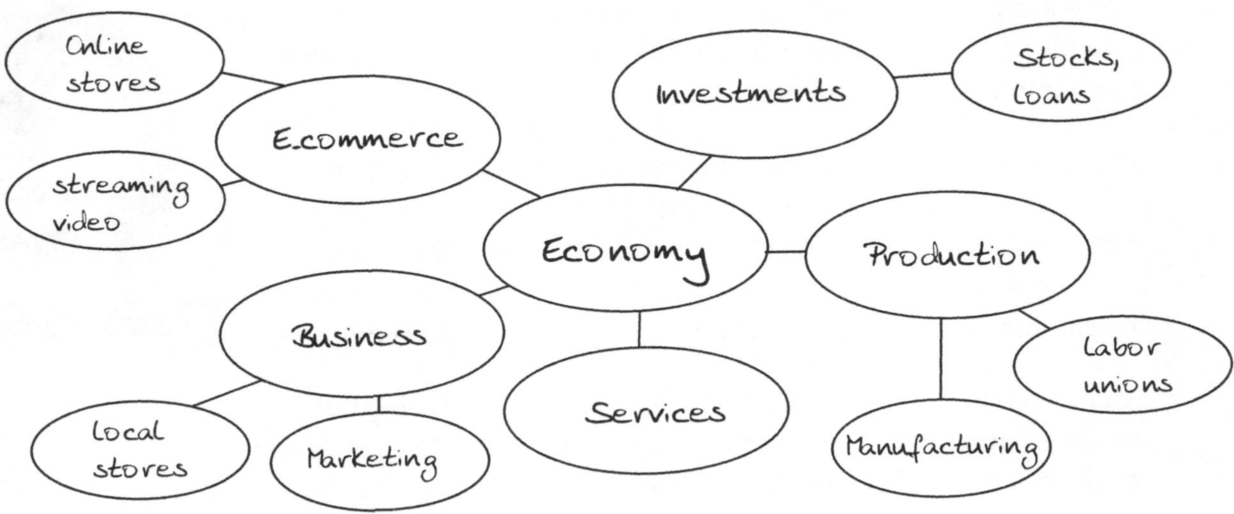

? **3.** Explain the connection between *economy* and *e-commerce.*

An economy is how a country or area manages its money and resources. It is the system that moves money and resources. E-commerce is one way people buy and sell in the economy. With e-commerce, businesses sell products and services online. The economy is shifting to include more customers using e-commerce to purchase goods and services.

Evaluate What You Learned

Did the word web help you gain a better understanding of the word *economy*?

? **4.** How did the word web help you understand *economy*?

A word web can help you understand an unknown word by asking you to look beyond the definition. You gain an understanding of how the economy relates to different situations and affects the world around you.

Practice It!

Read the passage and answer the questions that follow.

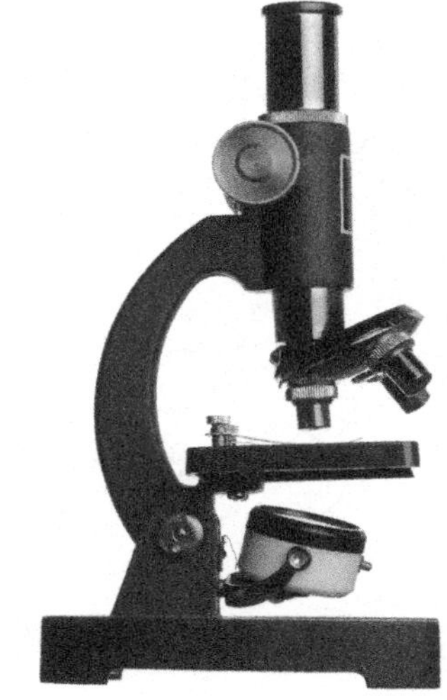

Scientific research often measures something, such as how often people speak to strangers, how many insects of a specific color live in a particular place, how quickly bacteria reproduce in certain circumstances, or what the temperature is inside volcanos. These sorts of measurements help scientists make general statements about the world: why insects are a particular color or what causes bacteria to thrive.

It usually doesn't make sense to measure a whole population or group, so scientists measure samples. Measurements are then made on those samples. The data is collected and analyzed, and researchers draw conclusions. If the sampling was done correctly, the sample accurately reflects the rest of the population or group.

Scientists base their research and studies on research questions. An observation might lead a researcher to ask a question, or the results of a reseacher's study may lead to further questions. A review of published research on a given topic may also point out an area that has not been investigated.

1. Use the passage and your prior knowledge to complete this word web.

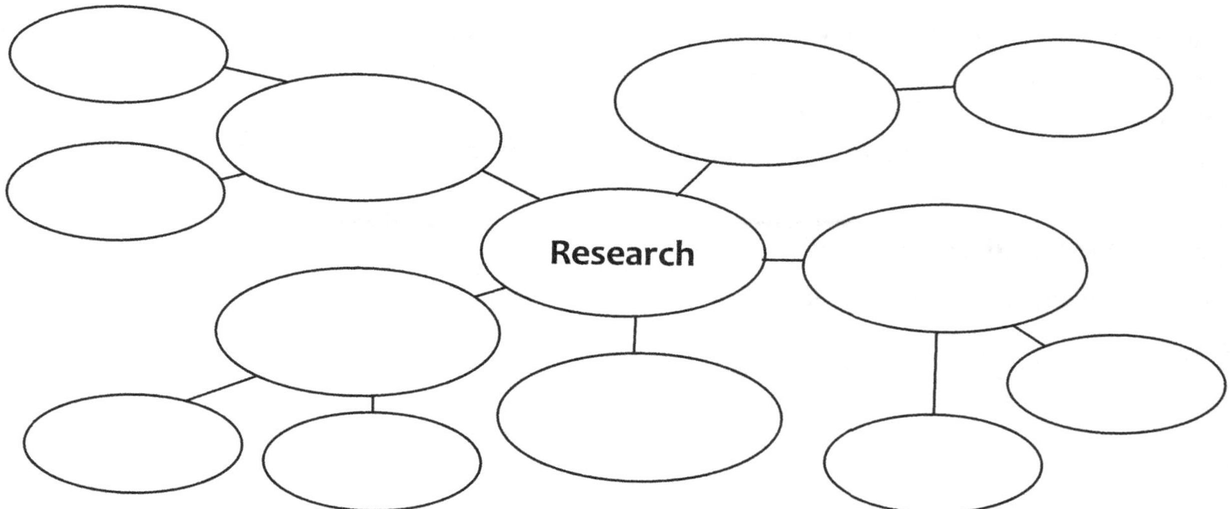

2. Write two sentences that use the word *research*. Use at least two words from your word web.

3. Select the best synonym of the word *research* from the following words.
   a. Study
   b. Select
   c. Building
   d. Necessary

4. Explain the connection of the word *research* to three words in your word web.

5. Based on your examination of the word *research*, what are two important things to keep in mind when doing research?

6. Write a paragraph using at least five of the vocabulary terms defined at the beginning of the lesson. All of the words must be used correctly, and you must demonstrate that you know what each of the word means through its usage.

Reading for Understanding

To remember the meaning of a new vocabulary word, relate the word to something meaningful to you.

Check Your Skills

Read the passage and answer the questions that follow.

Mark analyzed every aspect of last night's date to predict whether Karla would call him back. He had no particular order or method, no data or research. He simply recalled her reactions to jokes he made and the expression on her face when he said, "See you soon?"

For any other date, Mark would not have cared, but in a sea of bad dates, this one was significant. He wished he knew what Karla was thinking so he could decide how to proceed. Mark was still waiting for Karla to respond to his phone call. It had been one full day.

1. How is Mark analyzing the date?
   - **a.** By doing scientific research
   - **b.** By recalling his date's reactions
   - **c.** By asking his friends to ask her
   - **d.** By comparing the date to other dates

2. When you have a method for doing something, you have a ____________ in place.
   - **a.** Procedure
   - **b.** Thesis
   - **c.** Collection
   - **d.** Question

3. Review the word *significant* in the passage. Which of the following events is generally the most significant?
   - **a.** Flossing your teeth
   - **b.** Telling your neighbor hello
   - **c.** Witnessing the birth of your first child
   - **d.** Deciding what to wear in the morning

4. Which word is the most accurate synonym for *proceed* as it is used in the passage?
   - a. Move
   - b. Advance
   - c. Decide
   - d. Data

5. Based on the passage, how does Mark feel about his date?

Read the passage and answer the questions that follow.

Amy stayed late in the lab even though she was not required to do so. She had discovered that the way her research was structured was all wrong. The process Amy was using was incorrect, and she had a lot of work to do to fix the problems.

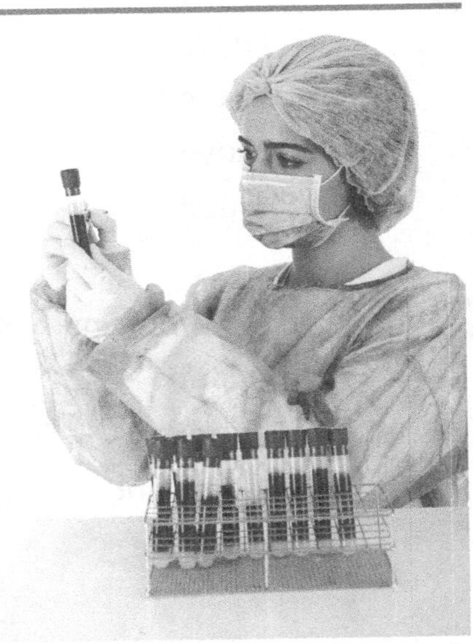

Amy wanted to find a cure for the disease that had plagued her family for years. Maybe she could find an escape for them and eventually for herself. The severity of the disease varied among sufferers, and Amy had no way of knowing how it would eventually affect her. She began to section off a portion of the lab to continue her research.

6. Why is Amy in the lab even though she is not required to be there?
   - a. To find a cure for a disease that affects her family
   - b. To keep herself busy since work is the most important thing to her
   - c. To fix an experiment that Amy did incorrectly the first time
   - d. To make sure that she understands the background for her research

7. What is a synonym for *structured* in this passage?
   a. Framed and held up
   b. Made with wood beams
   c. Set up
   d. Finished

8. Rewrite this sentence, replacing the words in bold with synonyms.
   "She started to **section** off a part of the lab to do her **research**."

9. What is a synonym for *varied* in this passage?
   a. Ravaged
   b. Differed
   c. Enjoyed
   d. Valued

10. What is a synonym for *process* in this passage?
   a. Variation
   b. Paperwork
   c. Understand
   d. Procedure

Remember the Concept

Understand to Remember!

The more deeply you understand a word, the better you'll remember it.

Inferences

Connections

Have you ever...

- Decided what gift would be best for a friend?
- Picked a meeting place that your friends would like?
- Formed a first impression about somebody?

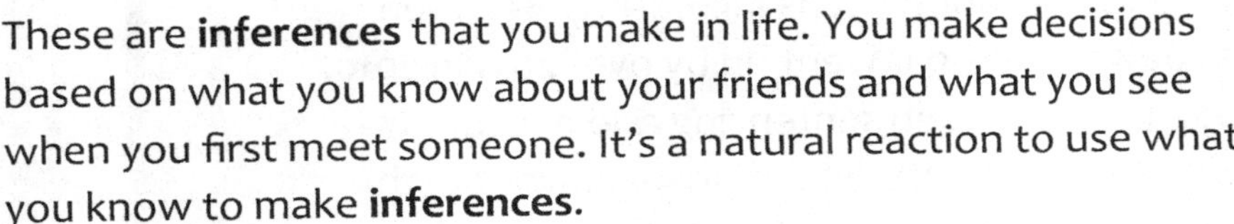

These are **inferences** that you make in life. You make decisions based on what you know about your friends and what you see when you first meet someone. It's a natural reaction to use what you know to make **inferences**.

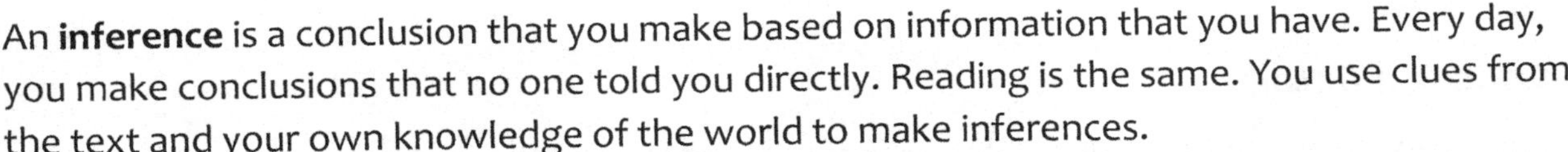

An **inference** is a conclusion that you make based on information that you have. Every day, you make conclusions that no one told you directly. Reading is the same. You use clues from the text and your own knowledge of the world to make inferences.

- Some information in a text is stated clearly.
- Other information is implied through details in the text.

You use information in the text along with own personal experience to make an inference. Have you heard of "reading between the lines" or "making an educated guess"? That's the same as making an inference.

Inference = What You Know + Clues from the Text

Making Inferences Using an Inference Chart

An inference chart helps you analyze details and your own knowledge to make and understand inferences.

Use this passage for the exercises that follow.

Let's examine the facts. Death row inmates cost the taxpayers millions of dollars each year. It costs far more to prosecute a death penalty case than it does to imprison a convict for life without the possibility of parole. Just maintaining security on death row is incredibly expensive, even without taking into account the cost of countless appeals.

Did you know that U.S. prisoners on death row often wait years before they're executed? The time between sentencing and execution keeps increasing. Between the years 2008 and 2009 it went up by over 20%. In 2010, the average time between sentencing and execution was almost 15 years. Nearly 25% of prisoners on death row die of natural causes, meaning that the state has paid a premium price for a sentence of life in prison.

Choose a Detail

First, choose a significant detail. If you want to understand the author's perspective, find a detail that seems to show the author's feelings or beliefs.

?

1. Select a detail that shows the author's perspective and write it in the chart.

Detail or Clue	What I Already Know	Inference

You might choose the statement: "Death row inmates cost the taxpayers millions of dollars each year."

Review What You Already Know

Identify what you know that can help you make an inference.

? 2. What do you know that can help you make an inference from the detail in the chart? Add it to the chart.

Detail or Clue	What I Already Know	Inference
"Death row inmates cost the taxpayers millions of dollars each year."		

You might realize that people are often critical of government spending for programs they oppose politically.

Make an Inference

Review details and background knowledge to make an inference.

? 3. State your inference in the chart.

Detail or Clue	What I Already Know	Inference
"Death row inmates cost the taxpayers millions of dollars each year."	People are often critical of government spending for programs they oppose politically.	

You might conclude that the author is opposed to the death penalty.

? 4. Add another inference to the chart, using the same passage.

Detail or Clue	What I Already Know	Inference
"Death row inmates cost the taxpayers millions of dollars each year."	People are often critical of government spending for programs they're against politically.	The author is opposed to the death penalty.

Read the passage and answer the questions that follow.

Company Policy on the Use of Technology

Internet Use

Internet use on company time must be for only business-related purposes. As you use the Internet, be careful of the sites you visit. Confidential company information could be compromised. By visiting an insecure site, you could download a virus or spyware that would damage the system and allow people outside the company to access private information.

Company computers are not allowed to view any pornographic, inappropriate, or non-business-related sites. Doing so can lead to action against you, and depending on the case, an end to employment with us.

Email Use

Email should be used for company business only. Do not reveal private company information to people outside the company. Also, remember that non-business related emails (even to coworkers) waste company time. Viewing pornography or sending pornographic jokes or stories via email is considered sexual harassment and will be addressed according to our sexual harassment policy.

Any emails that discriminate against employees based on race, gender, nationality, or religion will be dealt with according to the harassment policy. These emails are not allowed. Sending non-business emails will result in disciplinary action that may lead to an end of employment.

Company Owns Employee Email

Keep in mind that the company owns any email sent through the company email account and any document stored on a company computer. Management has the right to look at any emails or files on your computer at any time. Please do not consider any emails, Internet use, or documents that are created or stored at work to be private.

Reading for Understanding

Never lose sight of the text. Base your inferences on the facts. Notice when a conclusion doesn't have support in the reading.

1. Complete the following inference chart.

Detail or Clue	What I Already Know	Inference
"you could download a virus or spyware that would damage the system and allow people outside the company to access private information"		
"Any emails that discriminate against employees based on race, gender, nationality, or religion will be dealt with according to the harrassment policy."		
"Keep in mind that the company owns any email sent through the company email account and any document stored on a company computer."		

2. Curtis has been sending personal emails to coworkers on company time. Based on the description of what is acceptable work email and Internet use, what inferences can you make about what will happen to Curtis if he is caught?

3. Becca is applying for a job at a different company and saves her job application on her work computer. What could be the consequences of this? What should Becca do differently, if anything? Explain your reasoning.

4. Which of the following sites can you infer would be appropriate to visit at work? Select all that apply.
   - ❑ A website that allows you to download music for free
   - ❑ Websites that belong to the company's competitors
   - ❑ Google, to perform company research
   - ❑ Twitter, to see what your coworkers are posting in their personal accounts
   - ❑ Twitter, to see what your company and its competition are posting in their business accounts

5. Dwayne is very anxious about whether his new sneakers have been shipped from the manufacturer yet. What is the company's policy about Dwayne checking the website to see if it has shipped? What details in the text support your answer?

6. Try writing text that causes the reader make an inference. Sarah is really nervous about the test today. Write three to five sentences that give the reader clues about how Sarah feels and why, without actually telling the reader that Sarah is nervous.

Using a Chart to Support Your Inference

When you make an inference, it's important to know what information led you there. It helps you prove you've made a good inference. You can use an inference chart to help define the reasons for an inference.

Susan left in the middle of the film and exited into a dark, empty street. As she looked for a taxi, she noticed the gray-coated man at the bus stop.

Holding her breath, Susan backed up under the cover of the marquee. Had he seen her? She was lucky. He was looking away. Now he turned his face to the theater doorway, and her heart raced as she hid in the shadows.

Susan had nowhere to go but back inside the theater. As soon as he glanced away, she ducked through the glass doors and past the attendant, into the dark, anonymous theater seats. What now?

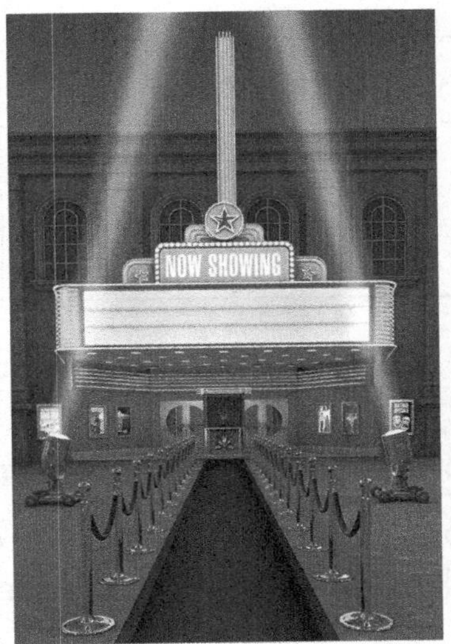

Make Your Inference

We all make inferences every day. You probably normally infer things about what you're reading, but you might not always be able to clearly state why.

1. How does Susan feel when she sees the man? Write your inference in the chart.

Detail or Clue	What I Already Know	Inference

Though the text doesn't say how Susan feels when she sees the man, you probably infer from her actions that she is afraid.

Identify Supporting Details

Now, find a detail that leads you to believe that Susan is afraid. When a character's feelings aren't explicitly stated, you can infer how she is feeling through descriptions of her actions and words.

? **2.** List one detail that shows you how Susan is feeling.

Detail or Clue	What I Already Know	Inference
		Susan feels afraid.

One supporting detail is that Susan hides when she sees the man.

Connect to What You Already Know

If you've ever been afraid, you can relate to Susan's actions when she sees the man. By thinking about your own experience, you can often relate to what others are experiencing.

? **3.** What do you already know that can help explain Susan's actions? Write it in the chart.

Detail or Clue	What I Already Know	Inference
Susan hides when she sees the man.		Susan feels afraid.

An example of what you know might be that people hide when they're afraid or don't want to be seen.

? **4.** Using the passage, find another supporting detail for an inference.

Detail or Clue	What I Already Know	Inference
Susan hides when she sees the man.	People hide when they're afraid or don't want to be seen.	Susan feels afraid.

This passage is from *The Picture of Dorian Gray* by Oscar Wilde. In this passage, the painter has just finished his portrait of Dorian Gray.

Read the passage and answer the questions that follow.

As the painter looked at the gracious and comely form he had so skillfully mirrored in his art, a smile of pleasure passed across his face, and seemed about to linger there. But he suddenly started up, and closing his eyes, placed his fingers upon the lids, as though he sought to imprison within his brain some curious dream from which he feared he might awake.

"It is your best work, Basil, the best thing you have ever done," said Lord Henry languidly. "You must certainly send it next year to the Grosvenor. The Academy is too large and too vulgar. Whenever I have gone there, there have been either so many people that I have not been able to see the pictures, which was dreadful, or so many pictures that I have not been able to see the people, which was worse. The Grosvenor is really the only place."

"I don't think I shall send it anywhere," he answered, tossing his head back in that odd way that used to make his friends laugh at him at Oxford. "No, I won't send it anywhere."

Lord Henry elevated his eyebrows and looked at him in amazement... "Not send it anywhere? My dear fellow, why? Have you any reason? What odd chaps you painters are! You do anything in the world to gain a reputation. As soon as you have one, you seem to want to throw it away. It is silly of you, for there is only one thing in the world worse than being talked about, and that is not being talked about. A portrait like this would set you far above all the young men in England, and make the old men quite jealous, if old men are ever capable of any emotion."

"I know you will laugh at me," he replied, "but I really can't exhibit it. I have put too much of myself into it."

Lord Henry stretched himself out on the divan and laughed.

"Yes, I knew you would; but it is quite true, all the same."

From *The Picture of Dorian Gray* by Oscar Wilde, 1890

Reading for Understanding

Consider the alternatives. Don't just accept the first inference that comes to mind. Consider details in the text and possible explanations.

1. Use the details from the passage and your background knowledge to finish filling out the chart.

Detail or Clue	What I Already Know	Inference
		Basil likes the painting he's just finished.
		Basil and Lord Henry are friends.
		Basil is a successful artist.

2. Based on the passage, what kind of relationship does Basil have with Lord Henry?

3. What does Lord Henry mean when he says that "there is only one thing in the world worse than being talked about, and that is not being talked about"?

4. How are Basil's feelings about the painting different from Lord Henry's? What details led you to that conclusion?

Check Your Skills

Read the passage and answer the questions that follow.

A recent study has established a connection between autism and attention deficit/hyperactivity disorder (ADHD) in children. Nearly 30 percent of children with autism also show signs of ADHD. That figure is three times higher than it is in the general population.

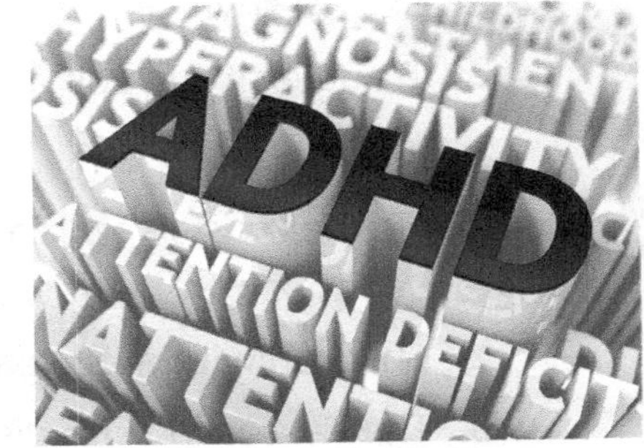

Doctors say that they don't know what causes ADHD in most cases. That is similar to autism, where the cause is usually unknown. Both disorders affect the brain and its functioning, and something that affects the brain and causes one developmental issue is also likely to cause another developmental issue.

Children in the study with both autism and ADHD had a harder time learning and socializing than children with just autism. Children with autism who aren't seeing improvements in their treatment, where they need to focus on specific skills, may benefit from undergoing ADHD treatments.

Common symptoms of children with ADHD include not being able to wait their turn, interrupting others, fidgeting with items when eating, or not being able to go slower.

Out of 62 children with autism aged four to eight, 18 (29 percent) also showed signs of ADHD.

The director of the Center for Autism Spectrum Disorders called the connection "not surprising." In children who are severely autistic, ADHD can be more of a challenge to identify. However, if parents and teachers notice that attention or activity problems are getting in the way of a child's ability to make progress, they shouldn't hesitate to seek help, the director noted.

1. Which of the following is the most accurate conclusion based on this study?
   - **a.** A child with autism is more likely to have ADHD than other children.
   - **b.** A child with autism is less likely to have ADHD than other children.
   - **c.** Autism may cause ADHD.
   - **d.** ADHD may cause autism.

2. Based on the text, what are the symptoms of ADHD? Select all that apply.
   - ❑ Lack of concentration
   - ❑ Fatigue
   - ❑ Interrupting
   - ❑ Severe shyness
   - ❑ Trouble sitting still

3. What is the most likely reason that the director says that the increased occurrence of ADHD in those with autism is "not surprising"?
   - **a.** Children with autism are susceptible to many other health concerns.
   - **b.** The causes of both disorders are unknown, so the same thing causes both.
   - **c.** Earlier studies have shown the same thing.
   - **d.** Symptoms of the two conditions resemble each other.

4. Which of the following is the most likely reason that ADHD is harder to spot in children with severe autism?
   - **a.** Children with severe autism won't cooperate for the study.
   - **b.** Children with autism are better at hiding their ADHD.
   - **c.** The symptoms of autism can be similar to those of ADHD.
   - **d.** In some cases, children with ADHD won't show symptoms.

5. In undiagnosed cases, which probably is **not** a sign that parents should treat their child with autism for ADHD?
   - **a.** They notice their child can't focus in school or social settings.
   - **b.** Treatment for autism isn't working.
   - **c.** Their child's grades are in trouble.
   - **d.** A child is more helpful with chores.

Remember the Concept

Inference = What You Know + Clues from the Text

Central Ideas

Connections

Have you ever...

- Struggled to understand a political speech?
- Felt an author was trying to say something, but you weren't sure what?
- Read through an office memo without getting the real point?

These texts have different purposes, but they all are communicating a **central idea.** The central idea is the most important point in what you are reading—the author's overall point.

Understanding a **central idea** isn't always easy. Sometimes the central idea is stated simply, but many times you'll have to infer it. The central idea can often be found at the beginning of a text, but other times you'll have to read further to find it.

Looking at the topic and the author's ideas will lead you to the central idea.

Central Idea = Topic + Author's Ideas

Finding a Central Idea

Central Idea = Topic + Author's Ideas

Use this passage for the exercises that follow.

Per Student Public Education Spending Decreases in 2011 for First Time in Nearly Four Decades

The year 2011 marked the first decrease in per student public education spending since the U.S. Census Bureau began collecting data on an annual basis in 1977, according to new statistics released May 21, 2013. The 50 states and the District of Columbia spent $10,560 per student in 2011, down 0.4 percent from 2010. The top spenders were New York ($19,076), the District of Columbia ($18,475), Alaska ($16,674), New Jersey ($15,968) and Vermont ($15,925). The amount of money spent by public elementary and secondary school systems totaled $595.1 billion in 2011, down 1.1 percent from 2010. This is the second time expenses have shown a year-to-year decrease, the first time being 2010.

Source: U.S. Census Bureau, adapted from "Per Student Public Education Spending Decreases in 2011 for First Time in Nearly Four Decades, Census Bureau Reports," http://www.census.gov/newsroom/releases/archives/governments/cb13-92.html

Find the Topic

First, ask: What's the topic? To find the topic, use three or fewer words to describe the subject. Use words that are as specific as possible.

1. What is the topic of this passage?

The paragraph is about public education spending. You might choose different words, but the meaning should be the same. Remember to use specific words, not general ones!

Find the Author's Ideas

Second, ask: What are the author's ideas about the topic? Make a list of three to five important ideas in the reading to identify what the author is saying about the topic.

? **2.** Make a list of three important ideas about the topic in the passage.

Three important ideas you might choose are:

- This is the second time expenses have shown a year-to-year decrease.
- The year 2011 marked the first decrease in per student public education spending since 1977.
- The 50 states and the District of Columbia spent $10,560 per student in 2011.

Summarize the Central Idea

Finally, put together the topic with the author's ideas. What do they have in common? What is the author's overall message or argument?

? **2.** What is the central idea—the author's overall message or argument?

You should be able to state the central idea in one sentence. In this case, you could say, "The amount of money spent per student is lower than it's been since 2007."

Reading for Understanding

Heads or titles may contain the topic or the central idea. Also look for repeated words that may show the topic.

Read the passage and answer the questions that follow.

Stop Whining about Garbage Pickup

I am sick of people whining about every-other-week garbage pickup. People keep complaining about how impossible it is to live without weekly pickup. They endlessly grumble about piles of trash and the smell it makes. Some people say that less frequent service is unfair for larger families or those with infants and toddlers. I happen to have my own family, and a little one in diapers, and I do just fine with every-other-week pickup. If families would reduce what they buy, reuse and repair items, and compost organic waste, it wouldn't be an issue. Households could make many changes to reduce the amount of waste they produce. It's time to start encouraging change for the better. It is useless to insist that current habits are reasonable, sustainable, or responsible.

1. What is the topic of the passage?
   - **a.** Whiny neighbors
   - **b.** Composting
   - **c.** Garbage pickup
   - **d.** Large families

2. What are three important ideas the author states about the topic?

3. What is the central idea of the passage?

Read the passage and answer the questions that follow.

It has come to our attention that some 1999 Volkswagen Jettas manufactured between February and April of 1999 may have defective driver's side air bags. In several instances, the airbag did not deploy properly during a collision, resulting in unnecessary injuries and trauma. If you have a car manufactured in 1999, call the dealership to determine if your car may be affected. If your car may have defective airbags, schedule an appointment with the local dealership, and your airbag will be repaired free of charge. Please call your dealership with your VIN number handy so we can look your car up for you, or visit us online with questions or concerns.

4. What is the central idea?

5. Explain the process you used to find the central idea.

6. Give a detail that supports the central idea, and explain how it relates to the central idea.

Reading for Understanding

To understand the author's ideas, ask what all the details have in common. When put together, what do they show?

7. Rose is trying to find the central idea of a newspaper article so she can explain the article to a friend. The article has heads, subheads, and a photo. Walk Rose through the process of finding the central idea. What steps should she take, and how will they help?

8. Sarah is trying to find the central idea in a section of her employee procedures manual. She sees various examples, but she fails to see what the examples have in common. Walk Sarah through the process of finding the central idea. What steps should she take, and how will they help?

Reading for Understanding

Summarizing a text and using graphic organizers can also help you find the central idea.

Check Your Skills

Read the passage and answer the questions that follow.

I believe our city is thoughtful and intelligent, but the debate about fluoridation leaves me embarrassed about how little scientific knowledge our community has. There is no need to keep chemicals out of the water. We already add chemicals such as ammonia, chlorine, and sodium hydroxide to our water. Don't forget, water is also a ***chemical:*** dihydrogen oxide. Chemicals are all around us. Everything we consume is composed of chemicals. Iron, calcium, potassium, and other chemicals are essential for human health.

The benefits and safety of fluoride are scientifically accepted. If we vote against fluoridation despite the scientific evidence, fear and ignorance will have triumphed over scientific fact, and public health will suffer. I hope and believe we are smarter than that.

1. What is the author's central idea?
   - **a.** Objections to fluoridation of water are unscientific and incorrect.
   - **b.** Adding fluoride to the water causes excessive harm according to studies.
   - **c.** Our water needs chemicals such as iron, calcium, and dihydrogen oxide.
   - **d.** Thoughtful communities should have a say over what goes into the water.

2. What is one of the author's arguments for her central idea?
   - **a.** Politicians support fluoride's use in local water.
   - **b.** Chemicals are not necessarily harmful.
   - **c.** Fluoride in water will help lower-income families.
   - **d.** Fluoride's use in local water will enhance the economy.

3. How does the author use the word *chemical* to support the central idea?
   - **a.** To scare readers about substances they don't understand
   - **b.** To compare fluoride to other commonly accepted substances
   - **c.** To show the reader she is intelligent and can use scientific words
   - **d.** To emphasize the idea that scientists support the use of fluoride

Read the passage and answer the questions that follow.

Astronomers search for potentially habitable planets using a handful of criteria. Ideally, they want to find planets just like Earth, since we know without a doubt that life took root here. The hunt is on for planets about the size of Earth that orbit at just the right distance from their star—in a region termed the habitable zone.

NASA's Kepler mission is helping scientists in the quest to find these worlds, sometimes called Goldilocks planets after the fairy tale because they orbit where conditions are "just right" for life. Kepler and other telescopes have confirmed a handful so far, all of which are a bit larger than Earth—the Super Earths. The search for Earth's twin, a habitable-zone planet as small as Earth, is ongoing.

Source: NASA, adapted from "In the Zone: How Scientists Search for Habitable Planets," http://www.nasa.gov/mission_pages/kepler/news/kepler20130717.html#.Uem1nz64GRZ

4. What is the author's central idea?
   - **a.** Scientists are looking for habitable planets.
   - **b.** Habitable planets are called Goldilocks planets.
   - **c.** On a habitable planet, conditions are just right for life.
   - **d.** Scientists have yet to find a habitable planet.

5. What details does the author give about the central idea? Select all correct answers.
   - ❑ Scientists want to find planets similar to Earth.
   - ❑ Planets at the right distance from a star are more likely to support life.
   - ❑ NASA's Kepler telescope helps scientists find planets.
   - ❑ Super Earths have not been found as of yet.

Remember the Concept

Central Idea = Topic + Author's Ideas

Reading Nonfiction Texts

Nonfiction texts describe facts, opinions and beliefs, or experiences. Nonfiction is defined by what it's not; it's not a fictional story. Most writing you encounter, from a memo to a cereal box to a newspaper, is nonfiction.

- **Informational nonfiction** provides information. A magazine article, a workplace manual, or a pamphlet from your doctor's office is an informational text. Informational texts are common because they accomplish an important task: conveying information.
- **Narrative nonfiction** tells a nonfiction story, conveying real-life events while often using elements of fictional storytelling. Biographies, true crime books, and survival stories are examples of narrative nonfiction.
- **Persuasive nonfiction** makes an argument. It attempts to persuade the reader to have a specific opinion or take a specific action. Examples of persuasive nonfiction include speeches, editorials, and advertisements. Thinking critically about persuasive nonfiction is essential to making good choices.

Your approach to reading nonfiction will depend on your purpose, and you'll use the DARE process to **determine your purpose, approach the text, read,** and **evaluate.** If your goal is to understand a complex topic, you will choose strategies that help you understand the details and how they are connected. If your goal is to make a decision about a proposed tax, you will need to evaluate information an arguments. If your goal is to read about an exciting climb to the top of Mount Everest, you'll want to immerse yourself in the characters and descriptive detail.

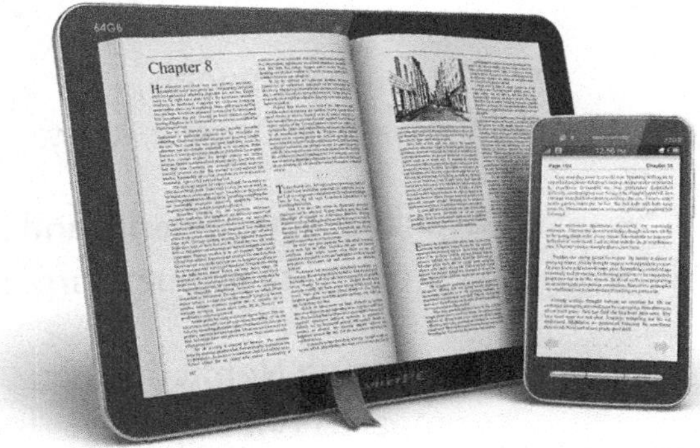

This section will give you strategies to approach nonfiction. It covers:

- **Text Structure**
  Learn about common ways that nonfiction texts are organized.
- **Text Features**
  Find out how to use features such as subheads and lists to navigate a text.
- **Visual Elements**
  Examine how to learn more from illustrations, photos, charts and graphs, and other visual elements.
- **Author's Purpose**
  Identify the author's purpose to understand the text better.
- **Reading in Science**
  Learn how to approach science texts to learn more effectively.
- **Reading in Social Studies**
  Approach social studies texts by understanding the author's perspective, especially in primary source texts written in other places or times.
- **Tone**
  Recognize and understand the author's tone or attitude.
- **Details in Nonfiction**
  Learn strategies to identify, understand, and remember details in nonfiction.
- **Arguments**
  Examine persuasive texts to identify the author's argument.
- **Claims and Evidence**
  Identify the claim of an argument and the evidence that supports that claim.
- **Fallacies**
  Find out how to recognize faulty logic in persuasive nonfiction.
- **Persuasive Appeals**
  Examine emotional, logical, and credibility-based appeals in arguments.
- **Evaluating Arguments and Evidence**
  Learn how to evaluate arguments and evidence in persuasive nonfiction.
- **Comparing Nonfiction**
  Compare nonfiction texts to gain a better understanding of both.

Text Structure

Connections

Have you ever...

- Looked up the answer to a question in a book?
- Flipped to the end of a story to take a sneak peek?
- Used a how-to guide to complete a project?

If you've done any of these things, you've used **structure**—the way the text is organized. If you understand how text is organized, you'll know where to look for information. You'll also know what to expect next, and that helps you comprehend as you read.

A **structure** is a pattern in a text. Regardless of your purpose for reading, understanding the structure will help you make sense of what you read. Some common structures are:

Structure	What Is It?	Keywords
Descriptive	Describes what something is like	*looks like, smells like, sounds like, feels like,* adjectives
Chronological	Organizes information by time, in the order things happened	*first, second, next, last, then, later, finally*
Statement & Support	Gives an idea, then gives details to support it	*for example, one reason, shows it's true*
Comparison	Compares similarities and differences of two or more things	*similarity, difference, like, unlike, on the other hand, as well, also*
Why? Cause & Effect	Shows reasons things happen; may be several causes or effects	*cause, effect, as a result, because, consequently*
Problem & Solution	Presents a problem and a proposed solution	*problem, solution, solve, address the problem*

Using Structure to Find Meaning

Structure can help you find meaning because you can anticipate what you will read. You can skim to identify structure and use structure to find information.

Use this passage for the exercises that follow.

Preventing Heat Illness in the Workplace

Heat illness can be deadly. Every year, thousands of workers become sick from heat, and some die. These illnesses and deaths are preventable.

Who is affected? Workers exposed to hot and humid conditions are at risk of heat illness, especially those doing heavy work tasks or using bulky protective clothing and equipment. Some workers might be at greater risk than others if they have not built up a tolerance to hot conditions.

What is heat illness? The body normally cools itself by sweating. During hot weather, especially with high humidity, sweating isn't enough. Body temperature can rise to dangerous levels if precautions are not taken. Heat illnesses range from heat rash and heat cramps to heat exhaustion and heat stroke. Heat stroke requires immediate medical attention and can result in death.

How can heat illness be prevented? Remember three simple words: water, rest, shade. Employers should educate their workers on how drinking water often, taking breaks, and limiting time in the heat can help prevent heat illness. They should include these prevention steps in worksite training and plans. Employers should also teach employees to gradually build up to heavy work in hot conditions because this helps you build tolerance to the heat—or become acclimated. They should take steps that help workers become acclimated, especially workers who are new to working outdoors in the heat or have been away from work for a week or more. Lastly, during the first week of work, employers should gradually increase workloads and allow more frequent breaks. You should plan for an emergency and know what to do—acting quickly can save lives!

Source: U.S. Department of Labor, Occupational Safety & Health Administration, adapted from "Welcome to OSHA's Campaign to Prevent Heat Illness in Outdoor Workers," http://www.osha.gov/SLTC/heatillness/index.html

Determine Your Purpose

Imagine temperatures have been climbing into the mid-90s, and you spend most of your time working outdoors. You want to know how you can take safety precautions.

A Approach the Text

Examining the structure can help you create a plan to find the information you need.

? 1. Read the title and skim the passage for keywords or patterns. Based on what you can tell about the structure, make a plan to find the information you want.

By skimming the text, you can see that the passage follows a **problem and solution** structure. The first paragraph describes the overall problem. The other three paragraphs start with questions that tell you what's ahead. The question states a problem or issue, and the paragraph answers it. You are probably most interested in how heat illness can be prevented, so a good plan would be to read the paragraph that asks, "How can heat illness be prevented?"

R Read

Next, you'll carry out your reading plan to find the information you need.

? 2. How can you take precautions in high heat?

If you carry out your plan to read the last paragraph, you'll learn that to stay cool, you can drink a lot of water. You should also take breaks and limit your time in the sun.

E Evaluate

After you read, evaluate. Did you answer the question, "What should you do to prevent heat illness?" Did your approach work well? What's your next step?

? 3. How did the structure help you understand the passage?

Structure helps you understand what you're reading by organizing the information and letting you know what's important. If you understand the structure, you'll better understand what the author is saying.

In this passage, the problem and solution structure helps you find information easily. It also can help you understand the important ideas the author is trying to communicate.

Reading for Understanding

A paragraph often begins with a topic sentence that explains what's coming.

Practice It!

Read the passage and answer the questions that follow.

CORVALLIS, Ore.—The first-ever estimate of how fast frogs, toads, and salamanders in the United States are disappearing from their habitats reveals they are vanishing at an alarming and rapid rate. According to the study, even the species of amphibians presumed to be relatively stable and widespread are declining. And these declines are occurring in amphibian populations everywhere, from the swamps in Louisiana and Florida to the high mountains of the Sierras and the Rockies.

The study by USGS scientists and collaborators concluded that U.S. amphibian declines may be more widespread and severe than previously realized, and that significant declines are notably occurring even in protected national parks and wildlife refuges. "Amphibians have been a constant presence in our planet's ponds, streams, lakes and rivers for 350 million years or so, surviving countless changes that caused many other groups of animals to go extinct," said USGS Director Suzette Kimball. "This is why the findings of this study are so noteworthy; they demonstrate that the pressures amphibians now face exceed the ability of many of these survivors to cope."

On average, populations of all amphibians examined vanished from habitats at a rate of 3.7 percent each year. If the rate observed is representative and remains unchanged, these species would disappear from half of the habitats they currently occupy in about 20 years. The more threatened species, considered "Red-Listed" in an assessment by the global organization International Union for Conservation of Nature, disappeared from their studied habitats at a rate of 11.6 percent each year. If the rate observed is representative and remains unchanged, these Red-Listed species would disappear from half of the habitats they currently occupy in about six years.

Brian Gratwicke, amphibian conservation biologist with the Smithsonian Conservation Biology Institute, said, "This is the culmination of an incredible sampling effort and cutting-edge analysis pioneered by the USGS, but it is very bad news for amphibians. Now, more than ever, we need to confront amphibian declines in the U.S. and take actions to conserve our incredible frog and salamander biodiversity."

Source: U.S. Geological Survey, adapted from "USGS Study Confirms U.S. Amphibian Populations Declining at Precipitous Rates," http://www.usgs.gov/newsroom/article.asp?ID=3597#.Ub87efa4F7s

1. Read the first and last paragraphs of the passage. Which of the following text structures does the passage use?
   a. Cause and effect
   b. Comparison
   c. Problem and solution
   d. Chronological

2. Explain how the passage follows this structure.

3. Which of the following problems is described in this article?
   a. Frogs, salamanders, and toads are quickly disappearing from their habitats.
   b. Frogs, salamanders, and toads aren't experiencing any changes.
   c. The study of frogs, salamanders, and toads is being challenged by others.
   d. There is no problem discussed in the article.

4. Which of the following solutions is proposed in the article?
   a. There is nothing that can be done to stop amphibian declines.
   b. Amphibians need to build up their strength to cope with change.
   c. We need to confront the problem and take action on conservation.
   d. Amphibians need to be moved to a new location to stop the decline.

5. Which of the following text structures is used in the second paragraph?
   a. Descriptive
   b. Comparison
   c. Chronological
   d. Problem & Solution

6. What is the central idea of the second paragraph?

Reading for Understanding

Notice that a written work can contain more than one type of structure.

Text Structures
 Descriptive
 Chronological
 Statement & Support
 Comparison
 Cause & Effect
 Problem & Solution

 7. Shae is reading about the Great Depression. Her book starts with the events leading up to the Great Depression and ends with the effects of the Depression on our world today.

   a. What text structures are likely used in the text? Explain your thinking.

   b. How can Shae use the text structures to find information about the New Deal put in place at the end of the Great Depression?

 8. Marcus is reading a memo that explains the process employees should use to acquire new clients and how this process resolves commonly reported problems.

   a. What text structures are likely used in the memo? Explain your thinking.

   b. How can Marcus use text structures to find information about how to initiate contact with a client?

 9. Mary is trying to decide whether to vote to pass a levy to bring in funds for a new high school. She is reading an article about what has happened in other cities where new high schools have been built.

   a. What text structures are likely used in the article? Explain your thinking.

   b. How can Mary use text structures to find information about how the new high school will impact the students and the community?

Check Your Skills

Read this passage from a project proposal and answer the questions that follow.

Project Proposal

Objective: The students of the Hillsdale School District would benefit from the formation of an after-school program during the 2013–2014 school year. The increase in crime in Hillsdale and its connection to underage youth is a problem that needs a solution. There are many parents who work late and students who are left on their own at the end of the school day. With nothing to do and no one to supervise them, some students don't make wise choices. An after-school program would provide an outlet for students to find new hobbies and passions, meet new people, and get homework help as needed. The program would also be part of the district's efforts to reduce accelerating dropout rates.

Goals

- To reduce the dropout rate, improve grades, and improve understanding of subject matter.
- To provide students with a place to go after school and help them find new interests and hobbies through classes and field trips.
- To provide a resource for students who need extra assistance.

Considerations

- **The cost of the program:** Costs are undetermined but include start up costs, administrative costs, advertising costs, paid employees, and location costs.
- **The scale of the program:** What hours would it operate? How many classes or activities would it offer? Would the classes be free of charge?

Solutions

- Proceed with a cost analysis. Potential ways to reduce costs:
    - Use volunteers along with paid staff members. Salary and wages to be determined.
    - Find teaching students to donate their time teaching a class. A small stipend is also a possibility.
    - Operate out of a church, school, or low- or no-cost facility.

1. What is the author proposing?
    - a. The formation of an after-school program
    - b. The expansion of a homework club
    - c. A request for tutors for the after-school program
    - d. Funding for publicity for the program

2. Why did the author create the proposal?
    - a. To reduce the dropout rate
    - b. To provide teachers with additional work
    - c. To raise money for students
    - d. To provide students with more time to study.

3. Create a pro and con chart for the after-school program using ideas and details from the passage.

Pro	Con
Students will have a place to go after school.	

4. Based on the pro and con chart, what would you recommend? Is more information needed?

5. What potential problems do you see with the project?

Text Structures

- Descriptive
- Chronological
- Statement & Support
- Comparison
- Cause & Effect
- Problem & Solution

Remember the Concept

Understand structure to find meaning.

- Skim the passage to identify structure.
- Use the structure to find information.
- Evaluate structure during and after reading.

Text Features

Connections

Have you ever...

- Used a table of contents to find the chapter you needed?
- Thumbed through a book to look at the pictures and charts?
- Glanced at the headlines in the paper to choose an article?

Tables of contents, charts and pictures, and headlines are all **text features.** If you know how to use them, you can find information quickly and easily.

There are many types of text features:

- Titles and heads
- Bold or italicized words
- Bullets and numbered lists
- Pictures, tables, charts, and graphs
- Indexes
- Tables of contents

DAILY NEWS

World - Business - Finance - Lifestyle - Travel - Sport - Weather

THE INSIDE STORY

World leaders meet in London to discuss the global economy.

Have scientists made a major breakthrough in the never ending search for a cure?

Can you live without technology, discover how computers have changed our lives.

Climate change - Does recycling really make a difference or is history just repeating itself?

Working hard for a better lifestyle, but is it damaging your longterm health, read what the experts say.

Anything that's formatted to stand out is a text feature. If you're looking for something specific, text features can help you navigate to what you need. Text features also help you preview and process information so you can comprehend what you read. Text features:

- Organize the text in a logical way.
- Present information quickly.
- Make the text more understandable.
- Show which parts are most important.

PPL: Preview → Predict → Learn with Text Features

Text features are useful tools for readers. You can use them to preview the text, predict what will happen, and learn from your reading.

Preview → Predict → Learn

Use this passage for the exercises that follow.

A Call to Action: Parents and Children Need to 'Pool Safely in Pools and Spas'

In anticipation of the thousands of gatherings around public and private pools over the Independence Day holiday, the U.S. Consumer Product Safety Commission (CPSC) is reminding parents and children alike of the steps they should take to stay safe when spending time in the water.

The July 4th holiday has traditionally seen an increase in the number of pool and spa drownings, compared to an average week over the rest of the summer. According to data compiled from media reports by *USA Swimming*, during the last three years over the week of July 4th an average of 26 children drowned in pools and spas. In 2012, 30 pool or spa-related drownings were reported involving children younger than 15 over the week of the July 4 holiday (June 30 through July 6).

Staying Close, Being Alert, and Watching Children in and around the Pool

Never leave a child unattended in a pool or spa and always watch your children closely around all bodies of water. Designate a water watcher to supervise children in the pool or spa. This person should not be reading, texting, using a smart phone or otherwise distracted.

- Teach children basic water safety tips.
- Keep children away from pool drains and other openings to avoid entrapments.
- Have a telephone close by when you or your family are using a pool or spa.
- Look for a missing child in the pool or spa first.
- Share safety instructions with family, friends, and neighbors.

Learning and Practicing Water Safety Skills

- Learn how to swim and teach your child how to swim.
- Learn how to perform CPR on children and adults. Update those skills regularly.
- Understand the basics of life-saving so that you can assist in a pool emergency.

Having the Appropriate Equipment for Your Pool or Spa

- Install a four-foot or taller fence around the perimeter of the pool and spa and use self-closing and self-latching gates; ask your neighbors to do the same at their pools.
- Install and use a lockable safety cover on your spa.
- Have lifesaving equipment such as life rings, floats or a reaching pole available and easily accessible.

Source: U.S. Consumer Product Safety Commission, PoolSafely.gov, adapted from "A Call to Action: Parents and Children Need to 'Pool Safely' in Pools and Spas over the July 4th Holiday," http://www.poolsafely.gov/news/call-action-parents-children-pool-safely-pools-spas-july-4th-holiday/

D Determine the Purpose

Imagine you plan to take your nieces to the pool over the Fourth of July weekend. You're nervous about possible accidents, so you decide to read a pamphlet online about pool safety. You want to know specifically how you can keep your nieces safe in the public pool.

A Approach the Text

To approach the text, you'll **Preview** and **Predict**. Use text features to preview what you're going to read. Based on what you know, predict where you'll find information. Identify the areas that will be most important to read.

?

1. Preview the passage using the text features. Predict where you'll find the information you need.

By previewing the title and heads, you can identify important parts of the passage where you can find information about staying safe in the pool. The section on having equipment for your pool won't be as important, since you are going to a public pool. The information is organized into bullets. You should expect that each bullet will give an important detail.

Even if you're not narrowing down the sections you need to read, previewing prepares you to read, focus, and understand.

R Read

Now it's time to **Learn**. As you read, put your plan into action. Pay close attention to the sections that you expect to be relevant. Were you able to predict what to expect?

? **2.** What can you do to be safe when you bring your nieces to the pool?

After reading, you might decide to prepare by talking to your nieces about water safety and taking a CPR class. You might also plan to stay near the children at the pool, keep your phone handy, and pay attention while your nieces are in the water.

E Evaluate

Complete the **Learn** step by evaluating what you've read.

- Did you answer your questions?
- Do you have new questions to investigate?
- How did the text features help you find the answer?
- How did previewing and predicting help you learn?

Preview → Predict → Learn

? **3.** How did the text features help you understand the passage?

Text features let you preview what you'll read. You can predict what information you'll find and where you'll find it. By using text features, you can find information quicker and understand better as you read.

Using D A R E

When you **determine your purpose,** identify the information you need. Text features will help you locate the ideas and details you seek.

Determine Purpose
Approach the Text
Read
Evaluate

Use PPL to read and answer questions about this passage.

1. Read the title and heads, and predict the topic of the passage.

Texas Cities Lead Nation in Population Growth

Eight of the 15 fastest-growing large U.S. cities and towns for the year ending July 1, 2012 were in Texas, according to population estimates released today by the U.S. Census Bureau. The Lone Star State also stood out in terms of the size of population growth, with five of the 10 cities and towns that added the most people over the year.

Fastest Growth Rate

The fastest-growing municipalities are spread across Texas, from the High Plains of West Texas to the Houston suburbs. San Marcos, along the Interstate 35 corridor between Austin and San Antonio, had the highest rate of growth among all U.S. cities and towns with at least 50,000 people. Its population rose 4.9 percent between 2011 and 2012. Completing the top five nationwide were Midland and Cedar Park, both in Texas; South Jordan, Utah; and Clarksville, Tenn. No state other than Texas had more than one city on the list of the 15 fastest-growing large cities and towns. However, all but one were in the South or West.

Most People Added

The Texas cities that added the most people included Houston, San Antonio, Austin, Dallas, and Fort Worth. New York topped the list and was the only city among the top 15 outside the South or West. It added 67,058 people over the year. Three cities were in California: Los Angeles, San Diego and San Jose.

Other highlights:

- Of the 19,516 incorporated places in the United States, only 3.7 percent (726) had populations of 50,000 or more in 2012.
- Nine areas surpassed the 50,000-population mark between 2011 and 2012, including four in the West, four in the South, and one in the Northeast.
- Two local governmental units dropped below the 50,000 threshold between 2011 and 2012.

Source: U.S. Census Bureau, adapted from "Texas Cities Lead Nation in Population Growth, Census Bureau Reports," http://www.census.gov/newsroom/releases/archives/population/cb13-94.html

2. Why did the author choose to use the subheads "Fastest Growth Rate" and "Most People Added"?

3. Why did the author choose to list some of the information in bullet points instead of in a paragraph?

4. The passage uses many numbers and percentages. What does that tell you about the content?

Reading for Understanding

Watch for things that stand out:

- Different fonts
- Bold and italic print
- Colored print
- Bullets
- Titles, heads, and subheads
- Labels and captions

5. You are reading a book for history class to find information about the first Europeans in America, and you preview the chapter titles. Which of the following chapters would you choose to read?

   a. "The Native Americans"

   b. "The Earliest Settlers"

   c. "A Growing Country"

   d. "The Roots of a Conflict"

6. You are skimming through a website and see the following heads: "The Events of October 12," "For the Disaster Victims," "How to Help," and "Prepare for Future Tornadoes." Predict the website's topic.

   a. Disaster victims

   b. Natural disaster prevention

   c. First aid

   d. A recent tornado

Check Your Skills

Imagine you have just started a new job and need to review the safety section in the employee handbook before orientation.

Read the passage and answer the questions that follow.

Emergency Procedures

Emergency Evacuation Map

An evacuation map for the building is posted in the lower hallway by the front office. It shows the location of exits, fire extinguishers, first aid kits, and where to assemble outside the building.

Fire Emergency

Fire extinguishers are located on each floor of the building next to the staircase. To use the fire extinguisher, remember the acronym PASS.

Pull the pin at the top of the extinguisher. The pin releases a locking mechanism and will allow you to discharge the extinguisher.

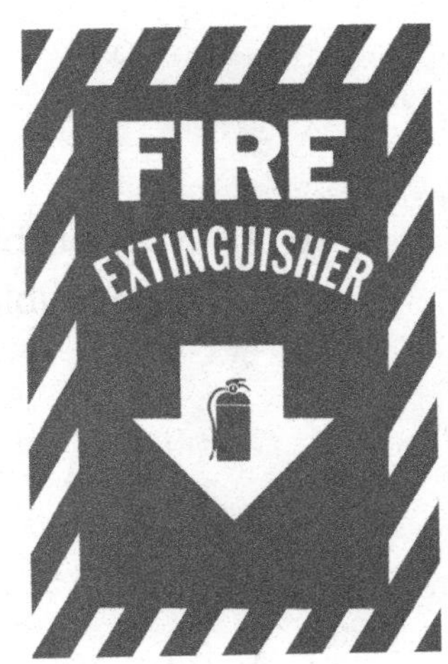

Aim at the base of the fire, not the flames.

Squeeze the lever slowly to release the chemicals in the extinguisher and put out the fire. If you release the handle, the discharge will stop.

Sweep from side to side. Using a sweeping motion, move the fire extinguisher back and forth until the fire is completely extinguished. Operate the extinguisher from a safe distance several feet away from the fire. Then move towards the fire once it starts to diminish. Be sure to read the instructions on your fire extinguisher. Different fire extinguishers recommend operating them from different distances.

If you discover a fire:

- Tell another person immediately, and call 911 and a supervisor.
- Put small fires out with a fire extinguisher.
- Do not continue to fight the fire if the fire grows or there is thick smoke.
- Evacuate all employees in the vicinity of a fire that cannot be quickly extinguished.
- After evacuation, go to the designated assembly point outside the building.

Hazardous Chemicals

Hazardous chemicals are used at this location.

Safe use and emergency actions to take following an accidental exposure.

We use a limited number of chemicals. You will receive a separate orientation as part of our chemical hazard communication program on the hazards of these chemicals before you work with them or work in an area where they are used.

---

1. According to the passage, what should you do if you discover a small fire?
   a. Try to extinguish the fire with a fire extinguisher.
   b. Evacuate the building immediately.
   c. Take cover under a desk or in another secure place.
   d. Check the rest of the building for additional fires.

2. You are nervous about remembering how to use a fire extinguisher. What acronym should you remember?

3. What problem could having a fire evacuation map only on the first floor cause? What is a possible solution to this problem?

4. Based on the information in the document, which of the following is the best assumption about chemical use at the company?
   a. Employees are never exposed to chemicals.
   b. Employees are in contact with some chemicals.
   c. Management doesn't take chemical safety very seriously.
   d. Employees are trusted to use their instincts around dangerous chemicals.

Remember the Concept

Text features help you find information quickly and understand effectively.

Preview → Predict → Learn

Visual Elements

Connections

Have you ever...

- Looked at a chart to understand poll results?
- Read a editorial cartoon that illustrated an article in a magazine?
- Looked at photographs to follow a recipe on a blog?

Visual elements, like pictures, charts, diagrams, and illustrations, can be found in almost every kind of text. Human beings are visual creatures! Sometimes it's easier to understand a concept if you have a picture or illustration to go along with it.

Visual elements are images. Many types of visual elements can be found in texts:

- Diagrams
- Illustrations
- Maps
- Charts, graphs, and tables
- Photographs
- Cartoons

Often, visual elements will have labels and captions to read, but the main point is what you see.

Charts, graphs, timelines, photographs, and editorial cartoons show information in a visual way that's easy to understand and analyze.

Previewing Visual Elements

Examine visual elements and connect them to the text to get more information and increase your understanding.

- **Connect** to what you know.
- **Look** at features.
- **Draw conclusions** about the visual element.
- **Relate** to the text.

Use this passage for the exercises that follow.

Births to Unmarried Mothers and Age

As of 2011, 62 percent of women age 20 to 24 who gave birth in the previous 12 months were unmarried, according to a report released by the U.S. Census Bureau. This compares with 17 percent among women age 35 to 39.

Rose Kreider, a family demographer with the Census Bureau and one of the report's authors said, "The American Community Survey provides the nation with extensive data on the characteristics of recent mothers with a high level of geographic detail."

In 2011, 4.1 million women reported that they had given birth in the last year. Of these women, 36 percent were unmarried at the time of the survey, an increase from 2005 when an estimated 31 percent of recent births were to unmarried women.

Percent of Births to Unmarried Women

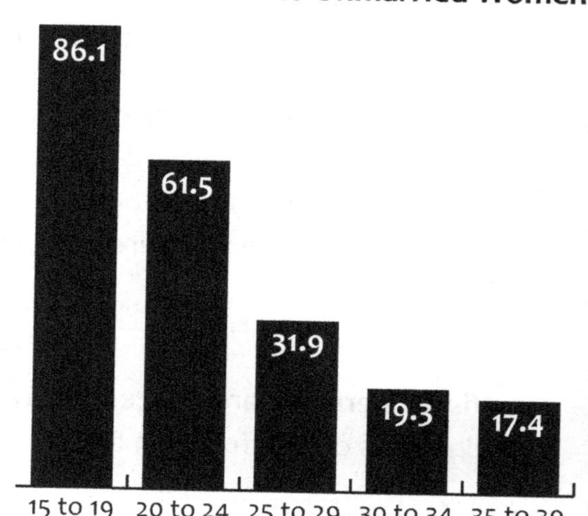

Source: Social and Economic Characteristics of Currently Unmarried Women with a Recent Birth: 2011, from American Community Survey. U.S. Census Bureau. http://www.census.gov/newsroom/releases/pdf/cb13-80_fig1.pdf

"The increased share of unmarried recent mothers is one measure of the nation's changing family structure," Kreider said. "Nonmarital fertility has been climbing steadily since the 1940s and has risen even more markedly in recent years."

The American Community Survey asks the question on fertility for a variety of reasons, including to help project the future size of the population and to carry out various programs required by law, such as researching matters on child welfare.

Source: U.S. Census Bureau, adapted from "About 6 in 10 Recent Moms in Their Early 20s are Unmarried, Census Bureau Reports," http://www.census.gov/newsroom/releases/archives/american_community_survey_acs/cb13-80.html

Connect to What You Know

When you come across a chart, photograph, or other visual element, think about what you already know.

- Have you seen anything like this in the past?
- What information do you expect to find?
- How does it relate to what you're reading?

1. What kind of information do you expect to see in a bar graph?

A bar graph compares two or more statistics. By showing the numbers visually as bars, they are easy to compare. You can see which numbers are higher or lower.

Look for Features

To understand what the visual element is about, look for features and visual clues. What does the visual element show, and how does it show it?

Titles, heads, bold or italicized words, labels, captions, pictures, directional arrows, and icons can give you clues about what it means.

2. What information is shown in the chart? What do the chart's features tell you?

The title is "Percent of Births to Unmarried Women." The chart shows what percentage of new mothers are unmarried.

Labels at the bottom of the bars show that mothers in the study are categorized by age group. The labels in white within the bars give the percentage of the mothers in each age group who were unmarried.

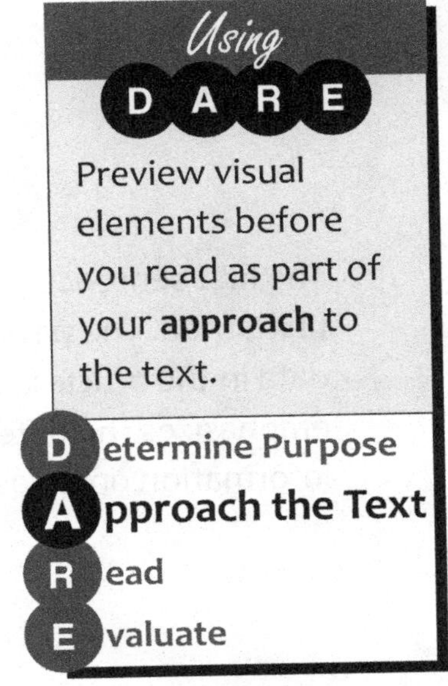

Draw Conclusions

Draw conclusions about the graphic.

- If there's a photograph, what does it mean? Why is it shown?
- If there's a chart, what's it pointing out about the data?
- If there's a diagram, what can you say about it?

3. What conclusion can you draw about the data in this chart?

You can conclude that the percentage of babies born to unmarried women is lower among older women. The percentage of unmarried mothers also seems to level off around age 30 to 40.

Relate It to the Text

Read the text and relate it to the visual element.

- Does the text give more detailed information?
- Can you find your conclusion in the text?
- Is there another conclusion?

4. How does the passage relate to the chart?

The first sentence of the passage tells you that 62 percent of mothers aged 20 to 24 are unmarried. The passage compares this number to lower statistics for older women. The data in the article is also given in the chart. By comparing high and low statistics, the article emphasizes the difference between age groups. The passage also provides background information on measuring births of unmarried mothers.

Read the passage and answer the questions that follow.

International Migration Is Projected to Become Primary Driver of U.S. Population Growth for First Time in Nearly Two Centuries

International migration is projected to surpass natural increase (births minus deaths) as the principal driver of U.S. population growth by the middle of this century, according to three new series of population projections released today by the U.S. Census Bureau. This scenario would mark the first time that natural increase was not the leading cause of population increase since at least 1850, when the census began collecting information about residents' country of birth. The shift in what drives U.S. population growth is projected to occur between 2027 and 2038, depending on the future level of international migration.

Net International Migration and Natural Increase (Births minus Deaths): 2012 to 2060 ***Middle Series Projections***

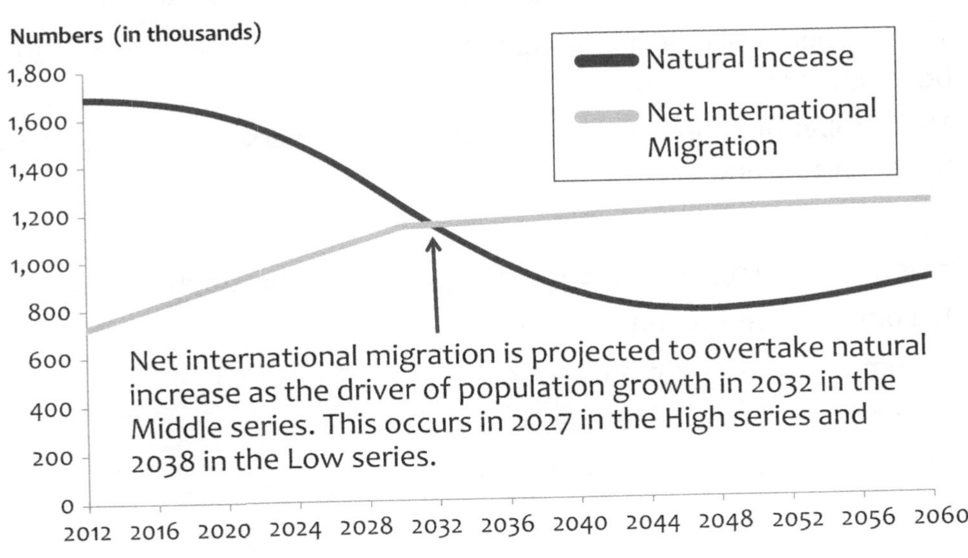

Source: U.S. Census Bureau, 2012 National Projections.
http://www.census.gov/newsroom/releases/pdf/NetMigration_NaturalIncrease%5B1%5D.pdf

"Our nation has had higher immigration rates in the past, particularly during the great waves of the late 19th and early 20th centuries," said Thomas Mesenbourg, the Census Bureau's senior adviser. "This projected milestone reflects the mix of our nation's declining fertility rates, the aging of the baby boomer population and continued immigration."

"Projections of international migration are challenging to produce, because it is difficult to anticipate future social, political, and economic conditions and how they may influence migration into or out of the United States," notes Census Bureau demographer Jennifer Ortman. "Developing this range of alternative projections shows how differing levels of net international migration alter the pace at which the U.S. population grows, ages, and diversifies."

Higher international migration would mean a faster growing, more diverse, and younger U.S. population. The December 2012 series projected net international migration to increase from 725,000 in 2012 to 1.2 million in 2060. In contrast, the alternative measures are considerably different.

Source: U.S. Census Bureau, "International Migration is Projected to Become Primary Driver of U.S. Population Growth for First Time in Nearly Two Centuries," http://www.census.gov/newsroom/releases/archives/population/cb13-89.html

1. Connect the graph to what you know and look at the features. What does the graph show?
   - **a.** International migration versus increase in population from births between 2012 and 2060
   - **b.** The birth rate in the United States versus the death rate between 2012 and 2060
   - **c.** The number of people migrating to the United States versus the death rate between 2012 and 2060
   - **d.** The number of people born in the United States versus the rest of the world between 2012 and 2060

2. Which of the following best describes the purpose of the graph?
   - **a.** To compare information
   - **b.** To summarize information
   - **c.** To put events in chronological order
   - **d.** To show the cause and effect of an event

3. What can you conclude about the information on the graph?

4. How does the conclusion relate to the information in the text?

Use this editorial cartoon to answer the questions that follow.

Prohibition, which banned alcohol in the United States from 1920 to 1933, was known as "The Noble Experiment" because of its noble goals, including keeping families together and reducing violence.

"Yes, it's a noble experiment."

5. Connect the cartoon to what you know and look at the features. What are the characters in the cartoon doing, and how are they labeled?

6. What can you conclude about the author's meaning?

7. How does the caption add to or change the meaning?

8. How does the cartoon relate to the introductory text?

Use this editorial cartoon to answer the questions that follow.

Prohibition was expected to decrease crime, because alcohol can contribute to violent behavior. Instead, it increased crime, because illegal alcohol became a profitable criminal business.

9. What is the author's point of view about Prohibition?

10. How did you think through the cartoon's meaning to understand it?

11. Write a paragraph comparing the editorial cartoon above with the one on page 115. How are the author's points of view similar and different? How do the cartoons express differing opinions?

Reading for Understanding

A diagram is an important visual element in science. Use diagrams to understand processes and systems.

Check Your Skills

Use this graph to answer the questions that follow.

Percent Voting in Presidential Elections by Race and Hispanic Origin: 1996 to 2012

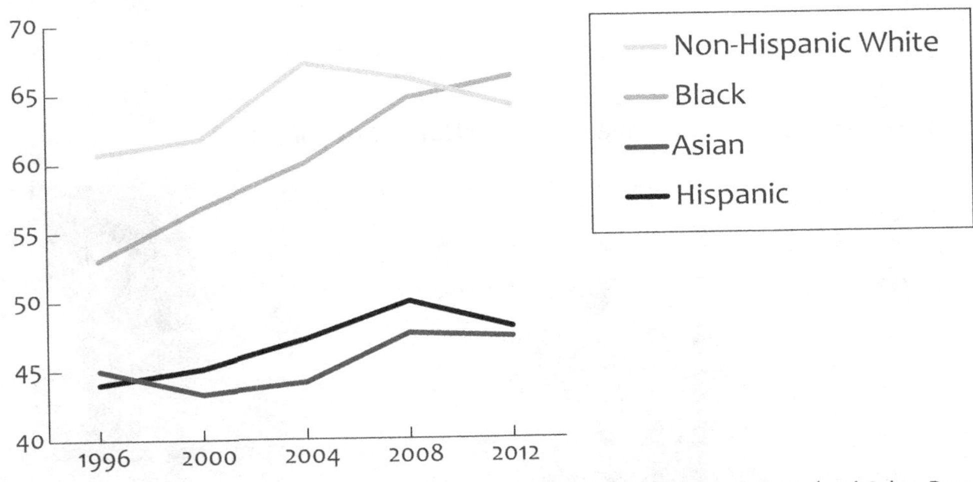

Source: The Diversifying Electorate—Voting Rates by Race and Hispanic Origin in 2012 (and Other Recent Elections), from Current Population Survey.

U.S. Census Bureau, http://www.census.gov/newsroom/releases/pdf/cb13-84_figure.pdf

1. Which statement best describes what the graph shows?
   - **a.** The percentage of people in different age groups who voted in the Presidential elections between 1996 and 2012
   - **b.** The candidates who were most popular with voters and the years that they ran for office
   - **c.** The winners of the last presidential election and the percentage of people who voted for them
   - **d.** The percentage of people of different races who voted in Presidential elections between 1996 and 2012

2. Which of the following conclusions can you draw from the graph?
   - **a.** Black voter turnout has climbed steadily since 1996.
   - **b.** Hispanic voters trailed behind the Asian vote in the 2012 election.
   - **c.** Non-Hispanic white voters always have the highest turnout.
   - **d.** Asian and Hispanic voters have not increased since 1996.

3. If you were writing an article about the information in this graph, what would be your central idea? What else would you emphasize? Explain your reasoning.

Examine the photograph and answer the questions that follow.

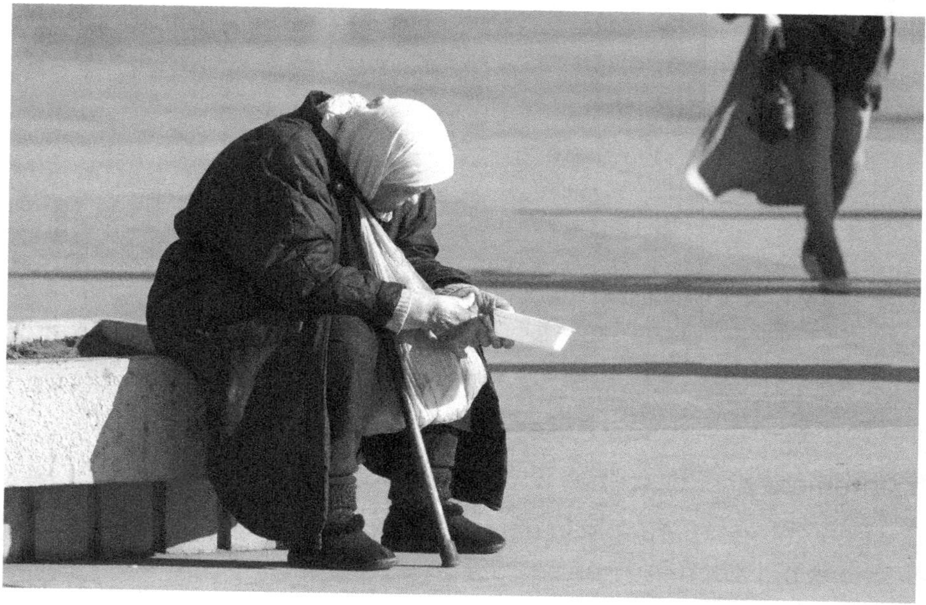

4. Which of the following best describes this photograph?
   - **a.** A woman is begging on the streets.
   - **b.** A woman is peacefully sitting in a plaza.
   - **c.** A woman is looking for someone.
   - **d.** A woman has just purchased some food.

5. Which of the following texts might accompany this photo? Select all correct answers.
   - ❑ A newspaper article about homelessness
   - ❑ A history text about life during World War II
   - ❑ A workplace text about company dress code
   - ❑ A social studies text about life in a foreign country

Remember the Concept

- Connect to what you know
- Look at features
- Draw conclusions
- Relate to the text

Author's Purpose

Connections

Have you ever...

- Suspected that what looked like an article was really an ad?
- Read an editorial with skepticism because of who the author was?
- Skipped reading a blog post because it seemed to be promoting a product?

There's a purpose behind everything you read. Sometimes the purpose is clear, like selling a product or describing a new work policy. Sometimes it's harder to determine.

The **author's purpose** is the author's goal in writing. The author's perspective and opinions relate to the purpose.

- A company-wide memo or email written by a supervisor will be different from one written by a client.
- A letter to the editor supporting a candidate written by the campaign's supervisor will be different from one written by a concerned citizen.
- A historical speech will be different from a historical diary entry.

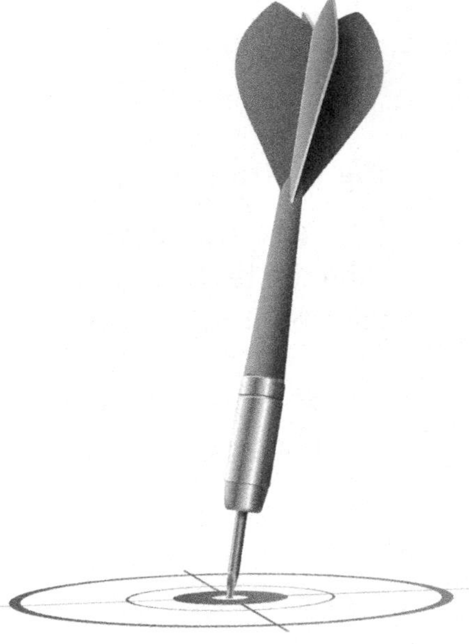

Big Picture & Details to Find Purpose

Authors write for different purposes. If you are aware of why the author wrote something, you can better understand the text and how it's useful to you. To find the purpose, look at the **big picture and details.**

Use this cover letter for the exercises that follow.

Dear Sue Randall,

My name is Mary Peterson, and I would like to apply for the paralegal job opening at Kelly, Kelly, & Stevens. I was excited to read about the position. I have several years of relevant experience in a variety of fields including insurance and finance, and I recently completed my paralegal training. Growing up, I was glued to television shows about the legal field and was fascinated by the legal process. I have always had a passion for the law and hope to start law school next year.

In addition to my extensive office experience and paralegal training, I have strong communication, customer service, and administrative skills. My broad background makes me an excellent candidate for this position.

Thank you for your consideration. I look forward to hearing from you to arrange an interview.

Sincerely,

Mary Peterson

Big Picture: Preview the Text

First, get the big picture. To begin to understand the author's purpose, skim the text. What do the titles, heads, images, and central ideas tell you about the purpose?

1. Skim this passage. What does skimming tell you about the author's purpose? Fill in the Big Picture in the graphic organizer.

An overview of the author's purpose can help you plan how you will **approach** a text.

Determine Purpose
Approach the Text
Read
Evaluate

Big Picture & Details

Big Picture: Skim and use your background knowledge to get an overview. What's the big picture?

Details: Look for details to expand and support your ideas.

Detail Meaning	Detail Meaning
Detail Meaning	Detail Meaning

The format tells you that the passage is a letter. Letters are usually addressed to somebody specific for a particular reason. If the letter is professional, the author often begins by stating the purpose of the letter. By reading the opening sentence you can get a general idea of why the author is writing. Mary Peterson is applying for a paralegal job at a law firm.

Details: Examine Word Choice and Examples

Now that you've got the big picture, hone in on details to support your ideas. Look for specific words and examples that reveal how an author feels about a subject.

?

2. What words show the author's feelings? Add two words as details in the **big picture and details** graphic organizer.

Big Picture & Details

Big Picture: Skim and use your background knowledge to get an overview. What's the big picture?

Mary Peterson is applying for a paralegal job at a law firm

Details: Look for details to expand and support your ideas.

Detail Meaning	Detail Meaning
Detail Meaning	Detail Meaning

The words *excited* and *passion* show the feelings the author is trying to convey. She's trying to show how excited she is about the job.

? **3.** Add to the organizer one additional detail that helps reveal the author's purpose.

Big Picture & Details

Big Picture: Skim and use your background knowledge to get an overview. What's the big picture?

Mary Peterson is applying for a paralegal job at a law firm

Details: Look for details to expand and support your ideas.

Detail excited Meaning thrillled, shows enthusiasm	Detail passion Meaning great desire or love; shows personal commitment
Detail Meaning	Detail Meaning

You might focus on this sentence: "Growing up, I was glued to television shows about the legal field and was fascinated by the legal process." The author's fascination with the law from childhood shows a personal interest in the position.

Evaluate to Find the Author's Purpose

Review the **big picture and details**. Use the combined information to draw a complete picture of the author's reason for writing.

Big Picture & Details

Big Picture: Skim and use your background knowledge to get an overview. What's the big picture?

Mary Peterson is applying for a paralegal job at a law firm

Details: Look for details to expand and support your ideas.

Detail excited Meaning thrillled, shows enthusiasm	Detail passion Meaning great desire or love; shows personal commitment
Detail Fascinated with law from childhood Meaning Personal interest in the job	Detail Meaning

? **4.** What is the author's purpose?

The author is applying for a job and wants to convince Susan Randall that she is the best candidate because of her enthusiasm for the job and personal commitment to the law.

Read the passage and answer the questions that follow.

About Kemp's Ridley Sea Turtles

The Kemp's ridley turtles are considered the smallest sea turtle in the world, with adults reaching about 2 feet long and weighing up to 100 pounds. They are found in the Gulf of Mexico and the Atlantic seaboard and feed primarily on crab species living on the seafloor of shallow waters. Their name comes from a fisherman named Richard Kemp of Key West, Florida, who provided the specimen used to describe the species in 1880. They are related to olive ridleys, another small sea turtle found around the world.

Kemp's ridley sea turtles are listed in the U.S. and internationally as endangered throughout their range due to dramatic population declines in the 20th Century. The vast majority of Kemp's ridleys converge on three major sites in the state of Tamaulipas, Mexico every year to nest. In the early 1960s, a film was discovered that showed an estimated 40,000 females nesting at one particular site—Rancho Nuevo—on one day.

Threats to Kemp's ridleys once included egg collection, overhunting, and unintentional capture during fisheries operations. Today, most of their nesting occurs on protected lands. Nonetheless, nesting habitat is still sometimes disturbed by natural and human events such as hurricanes, oil spills, or erosion. Also, activities that affect the seafloor (what scientists call benthic habitat) can disturb their feeding habitat. This includes bottom trawling and dredging. Another known threat is incidental capture, or unintentional by-catch, in fishing gear.

Although conservation efforts began in the 1960s, the number of nesting females continued to decline. By 1978, the U.S. and Mexico started a multi-agency effort to safeguard Kemp's ridleys from extinction by encouraging nesting at Padre Island National Seashore in Texas. Biologists have since been monitoring nesting activity, and there has been an increase in the number of nests since 1985.

Source: National Park Service, adapted from "Endangered Sea Turtle Feeding Grounds Discovered in Gulf," http://www.nps.gov/news/release.htm?id=1484

1. Preview the passage. What is the central idea, the big picture of what the author is trying to say?
   a. Kemp's ridley sea turtles are endangered.
   b. Kemp's ridley sea turtles are fascinating creatures.
   c. Kemp's ridley sea turtles need your help.
   d. Kemp's ridley sea turtles are related to olive ridleys.

2. Read the following details from the passage.

   The Kemp's ridley turtles are considered the smallest sea turtle in the world, with adults reaching about 2 feet long and weighing up to 100 pounds.

   Kemp's ridley sea turtles are listed in the U.S. and internationally as endangered throughout their range due to dramatic population declines in the 20th century.

   Although conservation efforts began in the 1960s, the number of nesting females continued to decline.

   What does the author hope to do through these details?
   a. Entertain the reader
   b. Inform the reader
   c. Persuade the reader
   d. Raise questions for the reader to consider

3. Consider the **big picture and details** of this passage.

   a. What is the author's purpose in writing this passage? How do you know?

   b. In what kind of publication would you find this passage, and who might read it?

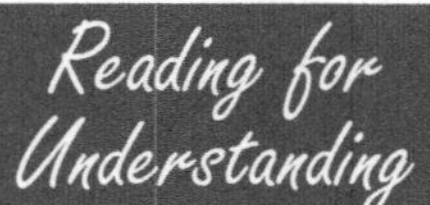

The facts, details, and examples that authors select depend on their purpose for writing.

Read the passage and answer the questions that follow.

It's an Unfair Tax

As a small farm owner, I am horrified that the latest proposed ballot measure includes a hidden tax. Those who support it claim that it will raise money for schools, but they leave out important information: how the money is raised.

An income tax should be a tax on earned income, i.e., a tax on profit generated by the business. Instead, this proposal would change the law so that farms and other small businesses would be expected to pay a tax on our gross income, even if we don't make a profit. This is a travesty. Where will small businesses get the money to pay tax on income that's already been spent on expenses? Prices will need to go up, and that means we will lose business. Agriculture is one of the reasons our state is thriving, but we farmers can't survive this. I wish I could pick up my farm and move it.

Sarah McPherson

4. Complete the following **big picture and details** graphic organizer.

Big Picture & Details

Big Picture: Skim and use your background knowledge to get an overview. What's the big picture?

Details: Look for details to expand and support your ideas.

Detail Meaning	Detail Meaning
Detail Meaning	Detail Meaning

5. Based on the **big picture and details**, what is the author's purpose?

Check Your Skills

IN CONGRESS. July 4, 1776.

The unanimous Declaration of the ... States of America,

The Declaration of Independence is one of the founding documents of the United States. It was written when the United States was in the midst of the Revolutionary War, the fight for independence from Great Britain. In June 1776, a five-man committee including Thomas Jefferson, John Adams, and Benjamin Franklin drafted the Declaration as a formal statement of the colonies' intention to start a new nation. It was formally adopted on July 4, a date now celebrated as the beginning of American independence.

Read the passage and answer the questions that follow.

From the Declaration of Independence

When in the Course of human events, it becomes necessary for one people to dissolve the political bands which have connected them with another, and to assume among the powers of the earth, the separate and equal station to which the Laws of Nature and of Nature's God entitle them, a decent respect to the opinions of mankind requires that they should declare the causes which impel them to the separation.

We hold these truths to be self-evident, that all men are created equal, that they are endowed by their Creator with certain unalienable Rights, that among these are Life, Liberty and the pursuit of Happiness.—That to secure these rights, Governments are instituted among Men, deriving their just powers from the consent of the governed,—That whenever any Form of Government becomes destructive of these ends, it is the Right of the People to alter or to abolish it, and to institute new Government, laying its foundation on such principles and organizing its powers in such form, as to them shall seem most likely to effect their Safety and Happiness.

Source: The Declaration of Independence, available at the National Archives: http://www.archives.gov/exhibits/charters/declaration_transcript.html

> This passage is from a **primary source**—a text written during a historical period being studied.

1. Which of the following best states the author's purpose?
   - **a.** To convince France that the revolutionaries are in the right
   - **b.** To explain why the people are separating from the government
   - **c.** To argue against any form of government as limiting people's rights
   - **d.** To persuade the people not to overthrow the government

2. Describe the reasons the author gives for making this declaration.

> **Reading for Understanding**
>
> The **author's purpose** is often directly related to the author's **tone,** which is the author's attitude about a subject.

3. Explain what the author probably hopes to accomplish. Who might the author hope to influence?

The first 10 amendments to the U.S. Constitution are known as the Bill of Rights. It is one of the founding documents of the United States. The Bill of Rights added specific guarantees of rights to the Constitution and also declared that these were not meant to limit the rights of the people. The following passage is the introduction to the Bill of Rights.

Read the passage and answer the questions that follow.

Introduction to the Bill of Rights

The Conventions of a number of the States, having at the time of their adopting the Constitution, expressed a desire, in order to prevent misconstruction or abuse of its powers, that further declaratory and restrictive clauses should be added: And as extending the ground of public confidence in the Government, will best ensure the beneficent ends of its institution.

Resolved by the Senate and House of Representatives of the United States of America, in Congress assembled, two thirds of both Houses concurring, that the following Articles be proposed to the Legislatures of the several States, as amendments to the Constitution of the United States, all, or any of which Articles, when ratified by three fourths of the said Legislatures, to be valid to all intents and purposes, as part of the said Constitution.

> This passage is from a **primary source**—a text written during a historical period being studied.

Source: The Bill of Rights, available at the National Archives: http://www.archives.gov/exhibits/charters/bill_of_rights_transcript.html

 4. Why was the Bill of Rights written?

a. To introduce tactics for fighting against an oppressive government
b. To add constitutional amendments that protect the rights of the American people
c. To express complaints by individual states about the federal government
d. To introduce tactics to protect the government against its people

 5. When the Constitution was written, some representatives did not want to include specific rights, for fear that the Constitution would be interpreted as recognizing only those rights. What is the opposing viewpoint that led to the Bill of Rights?

 6. Which of the following statements most strongly supports the purpose for the Bill of Rights?

a. "The conventions of a number of the States, having at the time of their adopting the Constitution, expressed a desire,"
b. "in order to prevent misconstruction or abuse of its powers, that further declaratory and restrictive clauses should be added"
c. "Resolved by the Senate and House of Representatives of the United States of America, in Congress assembled, two thirds of both Houses concurring,"
d. "all, or any of which Articles, when ratified by three fourths of the said Legislatures, to be valid to all intents and purposes, as part of the said Constitution."

Remember the Concept

Look at the **big picture and details** to understand the author's purpose.

Reading in Science

Connections

Have you ever...

- Read about a new treatment for cancer in the newspaper?
- Tried to make a decision about a proposition for school lunch reform?
- Been asked to sign a petition about climate change?

Science is an important part of everyday life. Science affects health care decisions, political initiatives, and the technology we use. Reading about these issues means reading about science.

Comprehending science texts is easier if you have a basic understanding of science ideas like:

- **Systems** and **processes**
- **Hypotheses** and **conclusions**

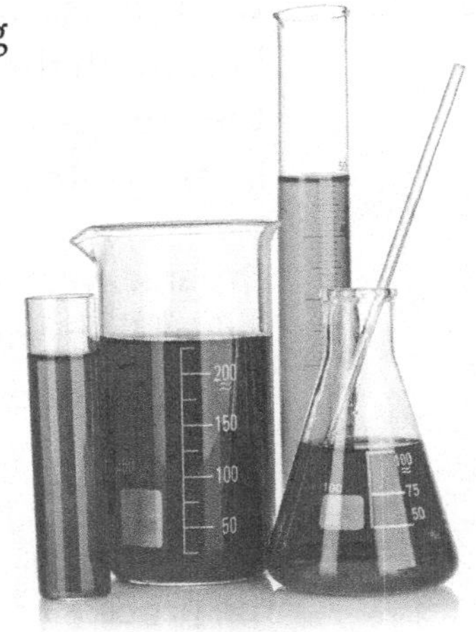

Systems and Processes

A **system** is a set of elements that work together in an interrelated way. A **process** is a series of steps that lead to an end result. Systems and processes are important ways to describe the natural world.

Hypotheses and Conclusions

A **hypothesis** is an idea a scientist believes might be true. Scientists try to prove or disprove hypotheses through gathering evidence. A **conclusion** is also an idea that could be true or false, but it's based on experimental results. Based on experimental evidence, scientists draw conclusions. Not every conclusion from a single study is true. However, If a conclusion has enough evidence from many sources, it can become accepted scientific theory.

Diagramming Scientific Systems and Processes

Sometimes recognizing and grasping a process or system can be a challenge. Diagramming, or creating a visual representation, can help you break down a system or process and understand how the parts are related.

Use this passage for the exercises that follow.

Weathering

Weathering is the natural process that breaks down rock. There are three types of weathering: mechanical, chemical, and organic.

Mechanical weathering physically breaks up rock. One example is known as frost action or frost shattering. In frost shattering, water gets into openings or cracks in bedrock. If it gets cold enough for the water to freeze, it expands, and the cracks are forced open slightly wider. Over time, pieces of rock can split off a rock face, and big boulders can be broken into smaller rocks and gravel.

Chemical weathering changes the chemical composition of rocks and minerals. One well-known example of chemical weathering is water dissolving limestone (calcium carbonate) through the process of carbonation. In this process, atmospheric carbon dioxide leads to solution weathering. Rain combines with the carbon dioxide from the atmosphere to form a weak acid. The acid then reacts with limestone creating chemical weathering of the limestone. Calcium bicarbonate is created as a byproduct of the chemical weathering process.

Organic weathering is also known as biological weathering or bioweathering. It involves both mechanical and chemical weathering brought on by plants or animals. Examples of organic weathering are plants' roots breaking up rocks, acids from lichens dissolving rock, or animals digging through soil and rocks.

Once rock has been weakened and broken up by weathering, erosion occurs. In the process of erosion, rocks and sediments are picked up and moved to another place by water or ice, wind, gravity, or other forces.

Determine the Purpose

Imagine you are preparing for a presentation about weathering for your geology class. You need to understand weathering. You know rock breaks down, but how and why?

A Approach the Text

To diagram a **system**, skim the text to get an overview of the system and plan a diagram.

A **process** can be diagrammed in steps. Start by skimming the text to determine the beginning and ending of the process.

? **1.** Skim the passage, and identify the beginning and ending of the weathering process.

At the beginning of the weathering process there is solid rock. At the end, it has eroded.

R Read

As you read, identify steps in the process or parts and relationships of a system. Create a diagram showing the order and relationships of the elements you've identified. It can help to break up a complicated process or system into smaller parts. This passage describes several types of weathering. You may wish to diagram each type of weathering process separately.

? **2.** Read the passage. Complete the diagram to show the process of frost shattering.

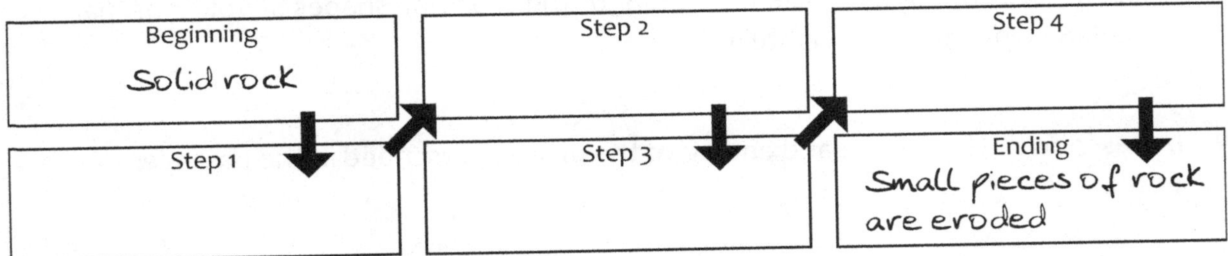

E Evaluate

After you read, evaluate the diagram. Can you fully understand the process or system? What conclusions can you make? What questions do you still have?

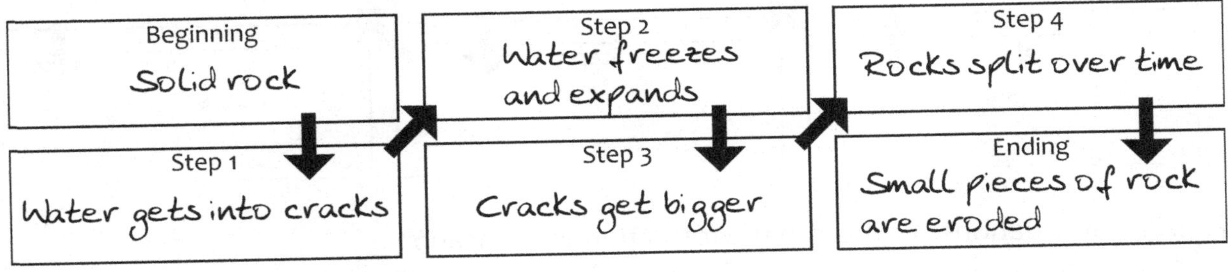

? **3.** How are all of the weathering processes similar?

In all the processes, rock is dissolved, worn away, or broken down into smaller pieces.

Read the passage and answer the questions that follow.

Volcanoes form when magma, molten and semi-molten rock beneath the Earth's surface, rises and leaks into the crust. Magma may come from melted material in the Earth's crust that has been forced further beneath the Earth's surface, or subducted. Magma also may come from deeper in the interior of the Earth. In both cases, the rock turns into magma because of the intense heat.

When a volcano begins to form, magma, rising from lower reaches, gathers in a reservoir in a weak portion of the overlying rock. This reservoir is known as a magma chamber. Sometimes, the magma will erupt onto the surface, becoming lava. When the lava cools, it forms volcanic rock, such as basalt or rhyolite. Lava flows and volcanoes vary, and complex factors, including the gases and minerals in the magma and the amount of pressure that is built up, determine the end results.

When magma rises, strong earthquakes occur, and the volcanic cone may enlarge just before an eruption. Scientists monitor the changing shapes of volcanos, particularly when they anticipate an eruption.

1. Describe the beginning and ending of the process described in the passage.

2. Diagram the process of the formation of a volcano.

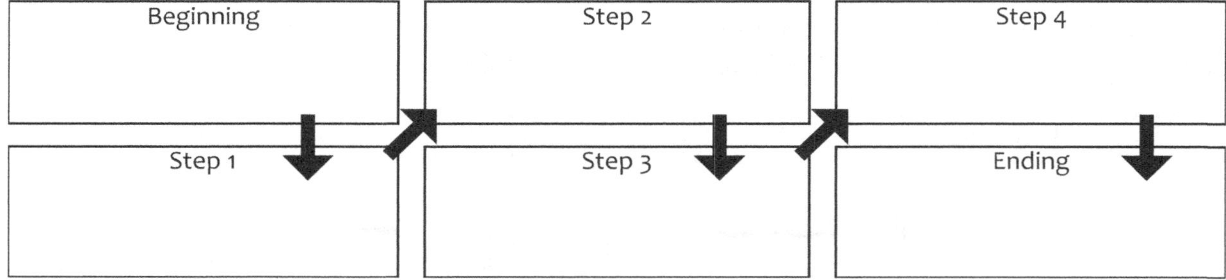

3. What variations are there in the formation of a volcano?

4. What additional questions do you have about volcanoes after reading the passage?

Read the passage and answer the questions that follow.

Water Cycle

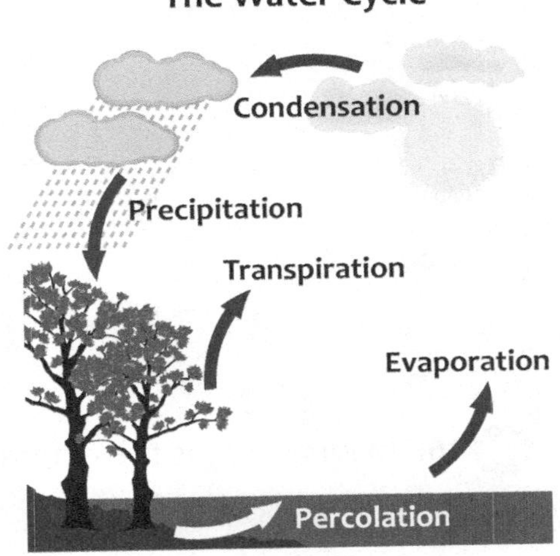

Water is constantly in motion. Sometimes it moves quickly, like a fast-flowing river, but sometimes it moves quite slowly, like in underground aquifers, glaciers, and deep ocean currents.

Water moves through Earth's systems in a cyclic fashion taking many forms as it travels. This process is known as the hydrologic or water cycle. The water cycle is often shown as a simple circular cycle (as in the accompanying diagram) in which water evaporates from the ocean, is carried over land, falls as rain, and then travels back to the ocean through rivers.

Although a drawing of the water cycle oversimplifies the actual movement of water, the diagram is a useful tool. The actual path any given water molecule follows in a complete water cycle can be varied and complex and may not follow the exact path shown by a diagram.

Water cycle diagrams do not show the amount of time that a water molecule may take as it travels through the water cycle. For instance, water starting in the Antarctic may take over 250 years to travel along the bottom of the Pacific Ocean before it re-surfaces near Alaska. Water can also remain frozen in a glacier or ice sheet for thousands of years before re-melting.

Water may also change state, back and forth, from a liquid, gas, and solid (condensing, evaporating, etc.) as it travels through the cycle. Water even travels underground, where it seeps through the spaces between grains of soil, sometimes coming to the surface as artesian springs, where water will flow to the surface without pumping because of natural pressure from below.

Living organisms also move water around. Water is either directly consumed as liquid or extracted from food and then carried within bodies. It leaves the organism as a gas during respiration, is excreted, or may evaporate from the skin as perspiration. Plants are the major biotic movers of water. Their roots collect water for distribution throughout the plant. Some of the water will be used in photosynthesis, but most travels to the leaves where it is easily evaporated.

Source: National Oceanic and Atmospheric Administration, adapted from "Water Cycle," http://www.education.noaa.gov/Freshwater/Water_Cycle.html

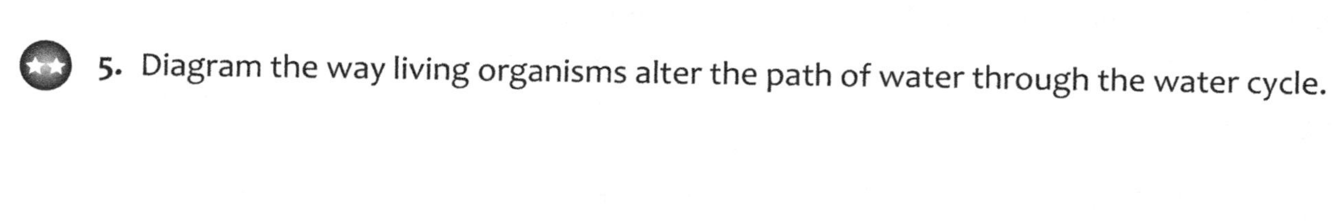

5. Diagram the way living organisms alter the path of water through the water cycle.

6. In what way is the diagram of the water cycle in the passage incomplete?

7. How can diagramming help you understand the water cycle?

8. Which of the following statements is true?
   a. Each drop of water follows the same exact path in the water cycle, but the speed may vary.
   b. Each drop of water follows a unique path through the water cycle, and its speed may vary.
   c. Each drop of water follows the same exact path in the water cycle at a consistent speed.
   d. Each drop of water follows a unique path through the water cycle but at a consistent speed.

9. What changes or additions would you make to the diagram to clarify it?

> *Reading for Understanding*
>
> Words in bold or italics, heads, and graphs or diagrams can help you understand systems and processes. Try using **PPL: Preview → Predict → Learn** to increase your understanding.

Distinguishing Fact from Opinion

Some opinions are matters of values and perspective, but science uses **hypotheses** and **conclusions**. Hypotheses and conclusions are either true or false and can be shown to be true or false through experiment.

Use the passage for the exercises that follow.

Wolf Harassment Has Little Impact on Elk

LARAMIE, Wyo. (Released: 6/11/2013 2:00:00 PM)—The mere presence of wolves, previously shown to affect the behavior of elk in the greater Yellowstone ecosystem, is not potent enough to reduce the body condition and reproductive rates of female elk, according to new research published today.

The research, led by recent University of Wyoming Ph.D. graduate Arthur Middleton, provides the most comprehensive evidence to date refuting the idea that wolves are capable of reducing elk calf recruitment indirectly through predation risk.

The detailed movement data on both wolves and elk allowed the researchers to identify each time one of the collared elk encountered a collared wolf. The elk herd, one of several migratory herds in the greater Yellowstone area, spends summers in Yellowstone National Park and moves into the Sunlight Basin during winter. The researchers also recaptured GPS-collared elk at the end of winter and the end of summer each year to assess their annual fat dynamics and pregnancy rates using ultrasonography.

Source: U.S. Geological Survey, adapted from "Wolf Harassment Has Little Impact on Elk," http://www.usgs.gov/newsroom/article.asp?ID=3613#.Ucy37D64EgQ

Identify the Purpose

Knowing the purpose of a text will help you determine the role of fact and opinion.

1. Skim the passage to identify its purpose, and predict how it will use fact and opinion.

The author's purpose is to inform the reader of the results of a study about wolves' impact on elk. You are likely to find facts and conclusions based on the author's purpose.

Identify Facts and Opinions

As you read, be aware of what is fact, opinion, conclusion, or hypotheses.

- Is it a proven statement beyond a doubt? (Fact)
- Is it something someone believes but can't be proven? (Opinion)
- Is it based on values? (Opinion)
- Does it contain signal words like *think, believe, best, worst, should*? (Opinion)
- Is it an idea that could be true, based on evidence and logic? (Conclusion)
- Is it a statement that is yet to be proven true or false? (Hypothesis)

? **2.** Does the first paragraph of the passage describe a fact, opinion, hypothesis or conclusion?

The first paragraph tells about the study's results. Because it is based on the results of research, it is a conclusion. It is possible that other studies could prove it incorrect. However, if future studies continue to support the conclusion, it could eventually be considered a fact.

Evaluate as You Read

As you read, evaluate the facts, opinions, hypotheses, and conclusions.

- How do they affect the text?
- How are they related to each other?
- Are they well supported?

? **3.** Read the whole passage. What are the relationships between facts, opinions, hypotheses, and conclusions in the passage?

Most of the information in the passage is either fact or conclusion. The facts that are presented support the conclusion.

Reading for Understanding

Value words (words that contain a judgment) usually represent opinions. Look for words like *best, worst, better, worse, great, terrible, lovely,* and *disgusting.*

This passage is part of a statement by NASA Administrator Charles Bolden as he spoke before the U.N. Committee on the Peaceful Uses of Outer Space

Read the passage and answer the questions that follow.

Vienna, Austria, June 17, 2013

But there is something intrinsically unifying about humankind's exploration of the heavens. Beyond the scientific and economic benefits of launching into space, there is the great possibility that when viewed from orbit, our borderless Earth inspires a sense of both oneness and wonder. As the great British astronomer Sir Fred Hoyle said in 1948, "Once a photograph of the Earth, taken from outside is available, a new idea as powerful as any in history will be let loose." How very true!

President Obama has also made space exploration a key element of America's commitment to building a more peaceful world.

In his speech at NASA's Kennedy Space Center in Florida three years ago he said, "No longer are we racing against an adversary; in fact, what was once a global competition has long since become a global collaboration."

Source: NASA, from "NASA Administrator Charles Bolden, U.N. Committee on the Peaceful Uses of Outer Space," http://www.nasa.gov/pdf/755792main_13_06_17_Bolden_final_UNCOPUOS_Speech.pdf

1. Which is most likely the purpose of this passage?
   - **a.** To persuade that countries should collaborate on space exploration
   - **b.** To complain about NASA's recent efforts in space exploration
   - **c.** To entertain with stories of space exploration
   - **d.** To question the U.N. Committee's efforts to encourage collaboration

2. Is the first sentence a fact, opinion, hypothesis, or conclusion? Explain your reasoning.

3. What is the speaker's main point? How do the facts, opinions, conclusions, and hypotheses in this passage work together to show the main point?

Read the passage and answer the questions that follow.

SACRAMENTO, Calif. — A study on frogs in remote Sierra Nevada mountain habitats including Yosemite National Park and Giant Sequoia National Monument, detected concentrations of pesticides in frog tissue that potentially came from California's Central Valley sources.

Two fungicides, commonly used in agriculture, pyraclostrobin and tebuconazole, and one herbicide, simazine, were the most frequently detected compounds, and this is the first time these compounds have ever been reported in wild frog tissue. DDE, a byproduct of the pesticide DDT, was another compound frequently found in frogs collected — though this is not surprising since DDE is one of the most widely detected compounds globally, even decades after DDT was banned in the United States.

"One notable finding was that among sites where pesticides were detected in frog tissue, none of those compounds were detected in the water samples and only a few were detected in the sediment samples," adds Smalling. "This suggests that frogs might be a more reliable indicator of environmental accumulation for these types of pesticides, than either water or soil."

Source: U.S. Geological Survey, adapted from "Pesticide Accumulation in Sierra Nevada Frogs," http://www.usgs.gov/newsroom/article.asp?ID=3650&from=rss_home

4. Describe the author's purpose.

5. Read the first sentence of the passage. Does it describe a fact, opinion, hypothesis, or conclusion? How do you know?

6. How does the author use facts, opinions, hypotheses, and conclusions?

Check Your Skills

Read the passage and answer the questions that follow.

Production of Digestive Juices

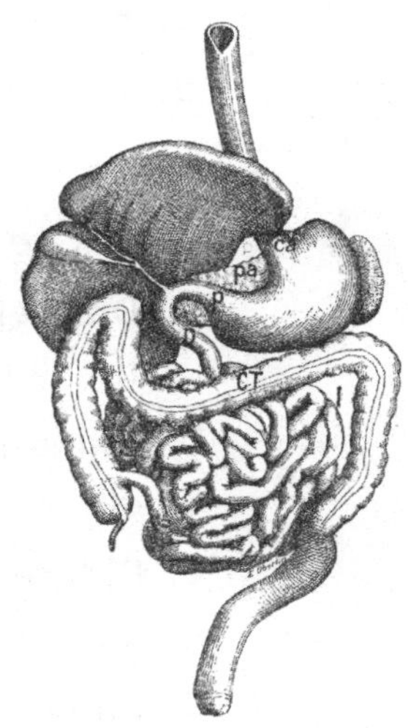

The digestive glands that act first are in the mouth—the salivary glands. Saliva produced by these glands contains an enzyme that begins to digest the starch from food into smaller molecules. An enzyme is a substance that speeds up chemical reactions in the body.

The next set of digestive glands is in the stomach lining. They produce stomach acid and an enzyme that digests protein. A thick mucus layer coats the mucosa and helps keep the acidic digestive juice from dissolving the tissue of the stomach itself. In most people, the stomach mucosa is able to resist the juice, although food and other tissues of the body cannot.

After the stomach empties the food and juice mixture into the small intestine, the juices of two other digestive organs mix with the food. One of these organs, the pancreas, produces a juice that contains a wide array of enzymes to break down the carbohydrate, fat, and protein in food. Other enzymes that are active in the process come from glands in the wall of the intestine.

The second organ, the liver, produces yet another digestive juice—bile. Bile is stored between meals in the gallbladder. At mealtime, it is squeezed out of the gallbladder, through the bile ducts, and into the intestine to mix with the fat in food. The bile acids dissolve fat into the watery contents of the intestine, much like detergents that dissolve grease from a frying pan. After fat is dissolved, it is digested by enzymes from the pancreas and the lining of the intestine.

Source: National Institutes of Health, adapted from "Your Digestive System and How It Works," http://digestive.niddk.nih.gov/ddiseases/pubs/yrdd/

1. What is the role of digestive juices in the digestive system?
   - **a.** Digestive juices dissolve fat away from the food that moves through the system.
   - **b.** Digestive juices dissolve and break down food that moves through the system.
   - **c.** Digestive juices assist chewing and swallowing and digest food in the stomach.
   - **d.** Digestive juices produce stomach acid and thick mucus to protect the stomach.

2. Some people develop stomach ulcers, small holes in the stomach lining. Based on the passage, which of the following is likely happening in people with ulcers?
   - **a.** Not enough protein is being digested in the stomach.
   - **b.** There is not enough digestive juice being produced.
   - **c.** Bile is interfering with the gallbladder's function.
   - **d.** The mucus layer is unable to fully protect the stomach.

3. Why is it necessary to have multiple types of digestive juices?
   - **a.** Different digestive juices break down food in different ways as it moves through the digestive system.
   - **b.** Different digestive juices do essentially the same things, but they are produced in different parts of the system.
   - **c.** Different digestive juices break down different specific types of foods, like meats, dairy, vegetables, or fruit.
   - **d.** Different digestive juices have differing functions, such as breaking down food, protecting the organs, and helping new cells to grow.

4. Which of the following is not a fact?
   - **a.** "An enzyme is a substance that speeds up chemical reactions"
   - **b.** "The next set of digestive glands is in the stomach lining."
   - **c.** "In most people, the stomach mucosa is able to resist the juice."
   - **d.** "much like detergents that dissolve grease from a frying pan."

5. Which of the following is a conclusion you can draw based on this article?
   - **a.** The digestive process is not well understood.
   - **b.** Breaking down food requires multiple stages.
   - **c.** The digestive process is the same in all animals.
   - **d.** Breaking down food is not a necessary function.

6. According to the information in the passage, which of the following is the first element of food that begins to digest?
   - **a.** Protein
   - **b.** Fat
   - **c.** Starch
   - **d.** Fiber

Remember the Concept

Diagram to understand systems or processes.

Check for facts and opinions in science writing.

Reading in Social Studies

Connections

Have you ever...

- Listened to a political speech?
- Read a diary or autobiography from another time period?
- Voted on an economic issue?

Politics, history, and economics are just a few aspects of social studies that affect your everyday life. In social studies, you'll often read texts from different times and places. These texts may present very different perspectives or points of view than you have.

A **primary source** is a text that was written or created in the time and place you're studying. A **secondary source** is a text written about another time and place, often citing and analyzing primary sources. An author's perspective is especially important when you are reading a primary source document.

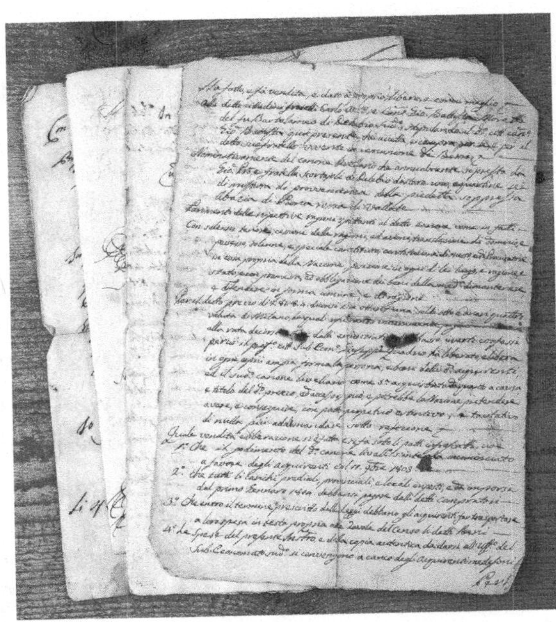

The author's perspective includes his or her values, beliefs, background, and reasons for writing. The author may have been affected by what is happening in the world. Likewise, the author's culture and knowledge may affect how he responds within the text. Understanding the author's perspective will give you insight into the text you're reading.

Determining Author's Perspective

An author's perspective is a specific viewpoint—a way to think about the topic. It is related to the purpose, and also to the author's cultural and political background, interests, experiences, and values. You can examine the author's perspective by looking at the **big picture and details**.

Use this passage for the exercises that follow.

The Emancipation Proclamation

President Abraham Lincoln issued the Emancipation Proclamation on September 22, 1862, as the United States was facing a third year of the Civil War. It was an order as Commander in Chief to the military and executive branch. The proclamation declared "that all persons held as slaves" within the rebellious states "are, and henceforth shall be free." The following is an excerpt from the proclamation.

By the President of the United States of America:

A Proclamation.

And by virtue of the power, and for the purpose aforesaid, I do order and declare that all persons held as slaves within said designated States, and parts of States, are, and henceforward shall be free; and that the Executive government of the United States, including the military and naval authorities thereof, will recognize and maintain the freedom of said persons.

And I hereby enjoin upon the people so declared to be free to abstain from all violence, unless in necessary self-defence; and I recommend to them that, in all cases when allowed, they labor faithfully for reasonable wages.

And I further declare and make known, that such persons of suitable condition, will be received into the armed service of the United States to garrison forts, positions, stations, and other places, and to man vessels of all sorts in said service.

And upon this act, sincerely believed to be an act of justice, warranted by the Constitution, upon military necessity, I invoke the considerate judgment of mankind, and the gracious favor of Almighty God.

> This historical passage is from a **primary source.** The introduction is a **secondary source.**

Source: The National Archives, adapted from "The Emancipation Proclamation," http://www.archives.gov/exhibits/featured_documents/emancipation_proclamation/

Big Picture

Before you read the text, examine your background knowledge. Do you know anything about the author or subject matter? What can that tell you about the author's perspective? Skim the text, making sure to read any context or background information like location and time period.

?

1. Skim the passage and think about your background knowledge. Fill in the Big Picture on the graphic organizer.

Big Picture & Details

Big Picture: Skim and use your background knowledge to get an overview. What's the big picture?

Details: Look for details to expand and support your ideas.

Detail Meaning	Detail Meaning

President Abraham Lincoln created this document during the Civil War. It declared all slaves in the rebelling southern states free. The word *emancipation* means the act of freeing. You might assume that there are complex political issues behind this document, from keeping the country united to the moral stance of abolitionists, who strongly opposed slavery.

Details: Examine the Author's Word Choice

Authors' words communicate their perspective. In a conversation, your words show your feelings and viewpoint. Authors' words do the same thing when they write.

?

2. Add one word that shows the author's perspective to the graphic organizer.

Big Picture & Details

Big Picture: Skim and use your background knowledge to get an overview. What's the big picture?

Lincoln is declaring the military should free Southern slaves in the Civil War, may be many political reasons

Details: Look for details to expand and support your ideas.

Detail Meaning	Detail Meaning

You might choose the word *order* or *declare* because they show Lincoln's demand to end slavery. He is not asking or recommending. He is ordering and declaring that slaves are free.

Details: Examine Facts and Examples

Locate a detail that shows an author's perspective, and then find its meaning. What does it tell you about the author?

3. Add a fact, example, or piece of evidence that shows the author's perspective to the graphic organizer.

Big Picture & Details

Big Picture: Skim and use your background knowledge to get an overview. What's the big picture?

Lincoln is declaring the military should free Southern slaves in the Civil War, may be many political reasons

Details: Look for details to expand and support your ideas.

Detail declare Meaning state strongly, certain, formal	Detail Meaning

You might choose "act of justice" or "gracious favor of Almighty God" as details that show Lincoln's values.

Determine Author's Perspective

You can make inferences about an author's beliefs, feelings, and values. Examine the **big picture and details** to define the author's perspective.

Big Picture & Details

Big Picture: Skim and use your background knowledge to get an overview. What's the big picture?

Lincoln is declaring the military should free Southern slaves in the Civil War, may be many political reasons

Details: Look for details to expand and support your ideas.

Detail declare Meaning state strongly, certain, formal	Detail "act of justice" Meaning justice is valued, important

4. Review the **big picture and details.** What can you say about Lincoln's perspective?

The document is a rule issued by the President to set military policy. It's a strong political action against the South, framing the war as one about slavery. Lincoln also refers to justice, the Constitution, human kindness, and God. As a reader, you can infer that these are values that influenced the document.

The following passage is from the majority opinion on Brown v. Board of Education, a U.S. Supreme Court case that resulted in the desegregation of public schools in 1952. A majority opinion explains the reasons for the ruling agreed on by the majority of justices.

Use this passage to answer the questions that follow.

Opinion

MR. CHIEF JUSTICE WARREN delivered the opinion of the Court...

We come then to the question presented: Does segregation of children in public schools solely on the basis of race, even though the physical facilities and other "tangible" factors may be equal, deprive the children of the minority group of equal educational opportunities? We believe that it does.

In Sweatt v. Painter, supra, in finding that a segregated law school for Negroes could not provide them equal educational opportunities, this Court relied in large part on "those qualities which are incapable of objective measurement but which make for greatness in a law school." In McLaurin v. Oklahoma State Regents, supra, the Court, in requiring that a Negro admitted to a white graduate school be treated like all other students, again resorted to intangible considerations: "...his ability to study, to engage in discussions and exchange views with other students, and, in general, to learn his profession." Such considerations apply with added force to children in grade and high schools. To separate them from others of similar age and qualifications solely because of their race generates a feeling of inferiority as to their status in the community that may affect their hearts and minds in a way unlikely ever to be undone....

We conclude that, in the field of public education, the doctrine of "separate but equal" has no place. Separate educational facilities are inherently unequal. Therefore, we hold that the plaintiffs and others similarly situated for whom the actions have been brought are, by reason of the segregation complained of, deprived of the equal protection of the laws guaranteed by the Fourteenth Amendment. This disposition makes unnecessary any discussion whether such segregation also violates the Due Process Clause of the Fourteenth Amendment.

Source: Brown v. Board of Education, 347 U.S. 483 (1954) (USSC+), available at The National Center for Public Policy Research, http://www.nationalcenter.org/brown.html

This historical passage is from a **primary source**—a text written during a historical period being studied.

1. Complete the graphic organizer with the **big picture and details** about the author's perspective.

Big Picture & Details

Big Picture: Skim and use your background knowledge to get an overview. What's the big picture?

Details: Look for details to expand and support your ideas.

Detail Meaning	Detail Meaning
Detail Meaning	Detail Meaning

2. Describe Chief Justice Warren's perspective as the author of this decision.

3. What is the reason Warren gives to overturn "separate but equal" in education?
   - **a.** Separate schools are impossible to maintain.
   - **b.** Separate schools don't provide equal education.
   - **c.** Separate schools are too costly and unnecessary.
   - **d.** Separate schools have tangible equal factors.

4. Chief Justice Warren writes, "To separate them from others of similar age and qualifications solely because of their race generates a feeling of inferiority as to their status in the community that may affect their hearts and minds in a way unlikely ever to be undone." What does this quote show that Chief Justice Warren values?
   - **a.** Special treatment of minority races
   - **b.** Government regulation
   - **c.** Children's psychological well-being
   - **d.** Religious freedom

The following passage is from Susan B. Anthony's 1873 speech after she was arrested, tried, and fined $100 for voting in the 1872 Presidential Election.

Read the passage and answer the questions that follow.

Friends and Fellow Citizens: I stand before you tonight under indictment for the alleged crime of having voted at the last presidential election, without having a lawful right to vote. It shall be my work this evening to prove to you that in thus voting, I not only committed no crime, but, instead, simply exercised my citizen's rights, guaranteed to me and all United States citizens by the National Constitution, beyond the power of any State to deny.

The preamble of the Federal Constitution says:

"We, the people of the United States, in order to form a more perfect union, establish justice, insure domestic tranquility, provide for the common defense, promote the general welfare, and secure the blessings of liberty to ourselves and our posterity, do ordain and establish this Constitution for the United States of America."

It was we, the people; not we, the white male citizens; nor yet we, the male citizens; but we, the whole people, who formed the Union. And we formed it, not to give the blessings of liberty, but to secure them; not to the half of ourselves and the half of our posterity, but to the whole people—women as well as men. And it is a downright mockery to talk to women of their enjoyment of the blessings of liberty while they are denied the use of the only means of securing them provided by this democratic-republican government—the ballot.

For any State to make sex a qualification that must ever result in the disfranchisement of one entire half of the people is to pass a bill of attainder, or an *ex post facto* law, and is therefore a violation of the supreme law of the land. By it the blessings of liberty are for ever withheld from women and their female posterity. To them this government has no just powers derived from the consent of the governed. To them this government is not a democracy. It is not a republic. It is an odious aristocracy; a hateful oligarchy of sex; the most hateful aristocracy ever established on the face of the globe; an oligarchy of wealth, where the right govern the poor. An oligarchy of learning, where the educated govern the ignorant, or even an oligarchy of race, where the Saxon rules the African, might be endured; but this oligarchy of sex, which makes father, brothers, husband, sons, the oligarchs over the mother and sisters, the wife and daughters of every household—which ordains all men sovereigns, all women subjects, carries dissension, discord and rebellion into every home of the nation.

Source: "Is it a Crime for a Citizen of the United States to Vote?" by Susan B. Anthony, available at http://law2.umkc.edu/faculty/projects/ftrials/anthony/anthonyaddress.html

This historical passage is from a **primary source**.

5. Describe Susan B. Anthony's perspective.

6. Select and explain two powerful details that show Anthony's beliefs, feelings, or values.

7. What does Anthony mean when she says, "To them this government has no just powers derived from the consent of the governed"?

8. Imagine you are researching women's fight for the right to vote. How might you use the information in this passage?

Check Your Skills

Read the passage and answer the questions that follow.

The following is an excerpt from the first Fireside Chat with former President Franklin Delano Roosevelt on March 12, 1933. It was given after the nation's banks closed to stop mass withdrawals by people worried about bank failures.

I want to talk for a few minutes with the people of the United States about banking—with the comparatively few who understand the mechanics of banking but more particularly with the overwhelming majority who use banks for the making of deposits and the drawing of checks. I want to tell you what has been done in the last few days, why it was done, and what the next steps are going to be. I recognize that the many proclamations from State capitals and from Washington, the legislation, the Treasury regulations, etc., couched for the most part in banking and legal terms, should be explained for the benefit of the average citizen. I owe this in particular because of the fortitude and good temper with which everybody has accepted the inconvenience and hardships of the banking holiday. I know that when you understand what we in Washington have been about I shall continue to have your cooperation as fully as I have had your sympathy and help during the past week. . . .

Because of undermined confidence on the part of the public, there was a general rush by a large portion of our population to turn bank deposits into currency or gold—a rush so great that the soundest banks could not get enough currency to meet the demand. The reason for this was that on the spur of the moment it was, of course, impossible to sell perfectly sound assets of a bank and convert them into cash except at panic prices far below their real value. . . .

It was then that I issued the proclamation providing for the nationwide bank holiday, and this was the first step in the Government's reconstruction of our financial and economic fabric.

This historical passage is from a **primary source.**

Source: President Franklin Delano Roosevelt, First Fireside Chat, available at: http://historymatters.gmu.edu/d/5199/

1. Which of the following describes President Roosevelt's message in the passage?
   - a. President Roosevelt is explaining why the banks have closed.
   - b. President Roosevelt is giving a lesson on banking to the people.
   - c. President Roosevelt is blaming the people for the failure of the banks.
   - d. President Roosevelt is angry at the banks for closing.

2. Why does President Roosevelt thank the listeners for their strength and patience?
   - a. He is paying an underhanded compliment to his opponents.
   - b. He is being sarcastic and pointing out the harm of panicking.
   - c. He wants the listeners to accept future bank closures.
   - d. He wants the listeners to be supportive of his policies.

3. Who is the main audience President Roosevelt is speaking to in this Fireside Chat?
   - a. The American people
   - b. The banking industry
   - c. President Roosevelt's friends and family
   - d. The world

4. What is President Roosevelt's purpose for speaking?
   - a. To explain banking to the public
   - b. To calm the public's fears about the bank failure
   - c. To entertain with stories about the Great Depression
   - d. To deceive the public into taking his side

5. Which best describes President Roosevelt's interest in the banking failure?
   - a. He thinks the banks deserve to fail because of the downfall of the economy.
   - b. He wants to protect the people from the knowledge that more banks could fail.
   - c. He wants to bail the banks out with government money.
   - d. He wants to work with the banks to reconstruct the economy.

Remember the Concept

The author's perspective can help you understand how to read a text and how the author's values, background, and biases can affect a text.

Tone

Connections

Have you ever noticed without being told that…

- A friend is mad at you?
- Your brother liked his gift?
- The boss is impressed with your work?

Even if your friends, family, and coworkers don't tell you how they feel, you can usually understand their tone of voice. Just as we express our feelings through tone when we speak, an author chooses words and details that express an attitude.

Tone is the author's attitude toward a subject. It is closely related to the author's purpose. For example, if you are reading a social studies textbook, chances are, the author's purpose is to inform. Because the author's purpose is to inform, the text will be written in a matter-of-fact tone, leaving out emotion and opinion.

Words That Might Describe Tone

Amused	Angry	Cheerful	Clear	Formal
Gloomy	Horrified	Humorous	Informal	Ironic
Light	Matter-of-fact	Optimistic	Pessimistic	Playful
Pompous	Resigned	Sad	Serious	Witty

Determining Tone through Word Choice

To determine the author's tone, examine word choice.

Ask yourself:

- What connotations do the words have?
- What do the words tell you about how the author feels?

Use a **Words → Meaning → Purpose** table to get meaning from word choice.

Words	Meaning	Purpose

Use this passage for the exercises that follow.

I rarely ever eat the lunches provided at work. The lunches taste awful, and the smell of grease makes me sick to my stomach. It's outrageous that they can serve lunches like that with the obesity crisis in this country.

Determine the Purpose

A coworker hands you a letter that is being passed around your office. You aren't sure how to react to the information. What is the author's intention? One key to intention is tone, so you decide to examine the tone to help you understand the reason for the letter.

Approach the Text

Before reading, think about how you will approach the text. Skim to get an overview and prepare for reading. What is it the subject? What is the central idea?

1. What is the central idea of the passage?

The author is saying that he dislikes the lunches at work. That gives you a starting point to understand tone. Since the author dislikes the lunches, the tone might be negative. You might plan to look for word choices and examples that show a negative attitude as you read.

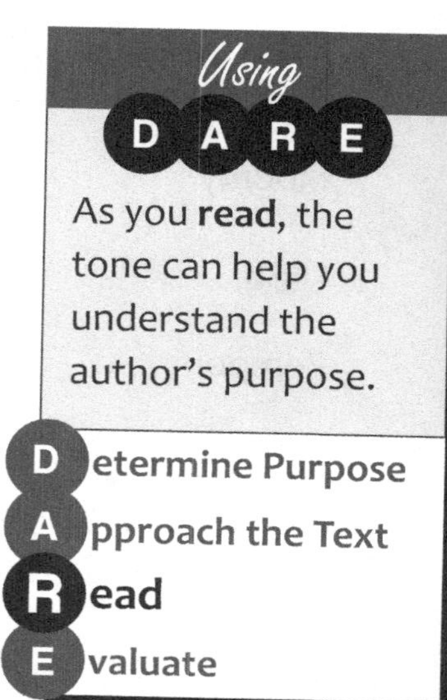

R **_Read_**

As you read, examine the author's word choice by using a **Words → Meaning → Purpose** table. What words and details show the author's attitude? Write down the words, their meaning, and the author's purpose in using them.

? **2.** Choose three words from the passage to complete the table.

Words	Meaning	Purpose

The author uses strong words and phrases in the passage, such as *can't stand, awful, sick to my stomach,* and *outrageous.* The author also connects lunches at work with obesity. You might fill out the chart like this:

Words	Meaning	Purpose
Awful	Bad, terrible	Shows how bad lunches taste
Outrageous	Ridiculous, unbelievably bad	Shows outrage
Obesity	Condition of being extremely overweight	Shows lunches are unhealthy

E **_Evaluate_**

How do the words and examples lead you to the tone? What do the words you chose have in common? Can you think of one word that shows the author's attitude? How can understanding the tone affect the way you read a text?

? **3.** In one word, describe the tone of the passage.

Based on the words and examples, you could describe the tone as angry or disgusted. Understanding the author's tone can help you can understand the purpose of the letter. The author is emotional about the topic. Your next question might be, is the anger and disgust warranted?

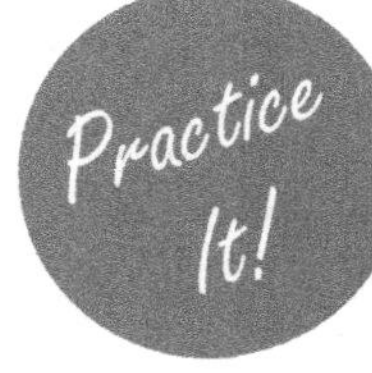

Answer the following questions about tone.

1. Imagine you are driving to school or work. You see an aggressive driver weaving in and out of traffic, narrowly missing other cars. In one word, describe the tone of each of your fellow drivers, based on these quotations.

a. "Oh no! I hope he doesn't hit me. This always happens to me. No matter where I go, something like this happens."

b. "That jerk! Who does he think he is? If he tries cutting me off, he's in for it."

c. "That driver seems like he's taking some chances. I'm going to slow down so that there is space between his car and ours."

> *Reading for Understanding*
>
> To understand tone, try to mentally "hear" the emotion behind the words and the attitude of the author.

2. Julie is reading a cover letter from a job applicant. She is impressed by the letter. Which of the following is the most likely tone of the letter?
   a. Upbeat, positive
   b. Humorous, entertaining
   c. Sarcastic, rude
   d. Demanding, forceful

3. Which of the following is the most likely purpose of the job applicant's cover letter?
   a. To inform Julie's company about his or her life and background
   b. To persuade Julie's company to bring him or her in for a job interview
   c. To entertain Julie with a funny story about why she might apply for the job
   d. To ask Julie specific questions about the company and the job opening

4. How can knowing the author's purpose help you find the tone?

5. How would a letter to the editor with an angry tone be different from one on the same topic with a reasoning, persuasive tone?

Read the passage and answer the questions that follow.

Letter to the Editor

The article on emergency preparedness did a great job explaining to individuals how to prepare in different situations. On a larger level, the tornado in Oklahoma showed again how important a large-scale emergency plan is in providing immediate aid and assistance. We were unprepared, but the kindness of friends, family, neighbors, and strangers is helping us through this difficult time. As a native Oklahoman, I would like to thank everyone who has donated time and money for those families struggling to put their lives back together after this devastating tornado. Your kindness makes all the difference.

6. Choose three words from the passage that indicate tone to complete the **Words** → **Meaning** → **Purpose** table.

Words	Meaning	Purpose

7. In one word, describe the author's tone.

8. What examples and evidence show the author's tone?

9. Based on the tone, how does the author feel about relief efforts in Oklahoma?

Read this company-wide email and answer the questions that follow.

Change in Policy

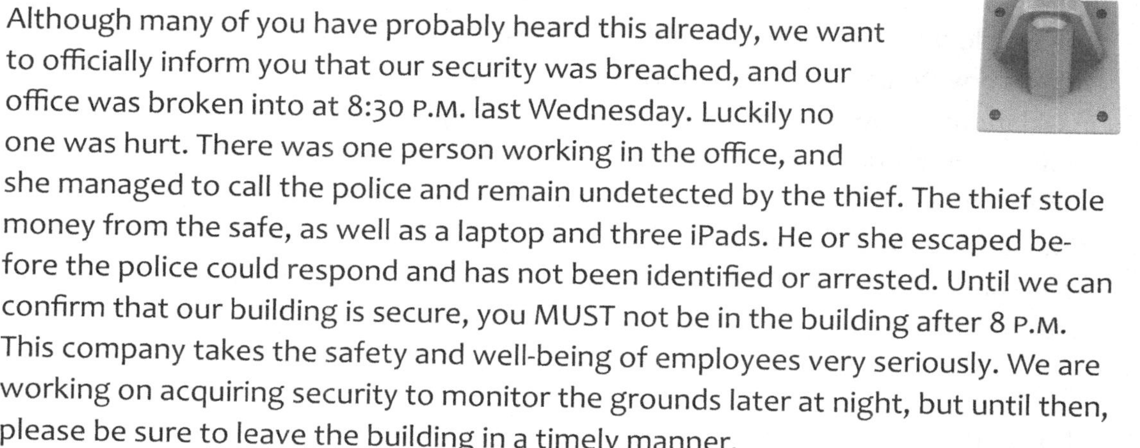

This email is to notify you of a change in our after-hours policy. Effective Monday, we can no longer allow employees on the premises after 8 P.M. due to security concerns. Your safety is of the utmost concern to us, and recent events have caused us to look more closely at our practices.

Although many of you have probably heard this already, we want to officially inform you that our security was breached, and our office was broken into at 8:30 P.M. last Wednesday. Luckily no one was hurt. There was one person working in the office, and she managed to call the police and remain undetected by the thief. The thief stole money from the safe, as well as a laptop and three iPads. He or she escaped before the police could respond and has not been identified or arrested. Until we can confirm that our building is secure, you MUST not be in the building after 8 P.M. This company takes the safety and well-being of employees very seriously. We are working on acquiring security to monitor the grounds later at night, but until then, please be sure to leave the building in a timely manner.

10. Choose three words from the passage that indicate tone to complete the table.

Words	Meaning	Purpose

11. In one word, describe the author's tone.

12. Besides word choice, how does the author show tone?

Check Your Skills

The following passage is from "My Views on Foreign Policy: We Ought to Stay Out of the War," a radio speech delivered by Joseph P. Kennedy, Ambassador to Great Britain, on January 18, 1941.

Read the passage and answer the questions that follow.

Shortly after I came home from London I spoke over the radio for the re-election of President Roosevelt. I declared then that my sincere judgment was that we ought to stay out of war—that we could stay out of war. I urged that we give England all possible aid. I feel the same way about it today.

Since then there have appeared many false statements regarding my views on foreign policy. Moreover, there is a growing confusion and a reliance upon emotion which strikes me as altogether unnecessary and extremely harmful.

Tonight I hope to set forth as clearly as possible my views on some phases of the great issue confronting the American people. It is my earnest desire that I may be of some assistance in helping my fellow-citizens to form a clearer understanding of the burning issue of our foreign policy.

The saddest feature of recent months is the growth of intolerance. Honest men's motives are being attacked. Many Americans, including myself, have been subjected to deliberate smear campaigns merely because we differed from an articulate minority. A few ruthless and irresponsible Washington columnists have claimed for themselves the right to speak for the nation. The reputation of the American press for fairness is being compromised by the tactics of these men.

Source: Joseph P. Kennedy, "My Views on Foreign Policy: We Ought to Stay Out of the War," available at: http://www.ibiblio.org/pha/policy/1941/1941-01-18a.html

This historical passage is from a **primary source**—a text written during a historical period being studied.

1. Which of the following is the purpose of this passage?
   - **a.** To explain what an outrage the war is and to convince others to oppose the war
   - **b.** To persuade listeners that the author is against the war but supports his country and Europe
   - **c.** To entertain Americans with stories of war and get them to embrace the current war
   - **d.** To point fingers at other politicians for supporting the war and for misleading Americans

2. What is Kennedy's attitude toward a "reliance upon emotion"?
   - **a.** Maintaining connection with emotions keeps politicians honest.
   - **b.** Basing policy on pure emotion is a bad idea.
   - **c.** Emotions are the most reliable indicator of how you really feel.
   - **d.** Policy that is devoid of emotion is a bad idea.

3. Select the answer that best describes the tone of this passage.
   - **a.** Melancholy
   - **b.** Cheerful
   - **c.** Frightened
   - **d.** Defensive

4. How does Kennedy feel about the press? How do you know?

5. Based on this passage, what was the general feeling about World War II in the United States in 1941?
   - **a.** Supportive
   - **b.** Strongly against
   - **c.** Neutral
   - **d.** Angry

Remember the Concept

The author's **tone** expresses an attitude through **word choice** and **details.**

Details in Nonfiction

Connections

Have you ever...

- Followed a recipe?
- Learned a new procedure for your job?
- Voted on a change to the tax structure?

The details are important! The big picture alone rarely gives you enough information. If you're following directions, you need to know specifics. If you're trying to understand the effects of a new law or make up your mind about a controversial topic, you need the details. Details tell you exactly what's happening.

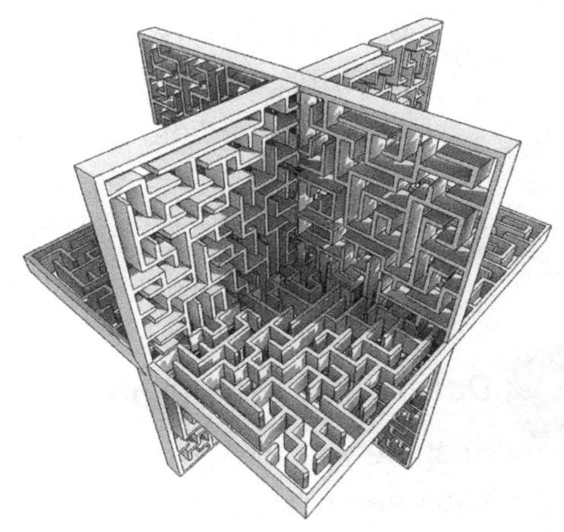

Details support, explain, or develop a central idea. Much of the meaning is in the details. The more complex an idea is, the more you need details to understand it.

There are many types of details. A detail can be a fact, example, anecdote, reason, statistic, or quotation.

The details of a topic can be complicated and numerous, making them hard to remember. To understand and remember details:

- Organize them.
- Identify relationships and patterns among them.
- Connect them to what you know.
- Restate or recall them.

Creating an Outline

By organizing ideas and details into an outline, you can see relationships and understand at a deeper level. Details help you understand a topic more fully.

Read the passage and use it for the exercises that follow.

A new U.S. Geological Survey study shows that the nation's aquifers are decreasing at an accelerating rate. The study evaluates long-term cumulative depletion in 40 separate aquifers (underground water storage areas) in the United States, bringing together reliable information from previous references and from new analyses.

"Groundwater is one of the nation's most important natural resources. It provides drinking water in both rural and urban communities. It supports irrigation and industry, sustains the flow of streams and rivers, and maintains ecosystems," said Suzette Kimball, acting USGS Director. "Because groundwater systems typically respond slowly to human actions, a long-term perspective is vital to manage this valuable resource in sustainable ways."

To outline the scale of groundwater depletion across the country, here are two startling facts drawn from the study's wealth of statistics. First, from 1900 to 2008, the Nation's aquifers, the natural stocks of water found under the land, decreased by more than twice the volume of water found in Lake Erie. Second, groundwater depletion in the U.S. in the years 2000–2008 can explain more than 2 percent of the observed global sea-level rise during that period.

Source: U.S. Geological Survey, adapted from "Deficit in Nation's Aquifers Accelerating," http://www.usgs.gov/newsroom/article.asp?ID=3595#.UcHUWT64F7s

D *Determine the Purpose*

Imagine you are working on a project about acquifiers for your environmental biology class. You need to understand the details of the passage for your project.

?

1. Why is it important to understand the details in this passage?

The details will give you a better understanding of the topic and may suggest more questions that you can investigate.

A Approach the Text

Creating an outline will help you identify important details that support the central idea. Before you read and start outlining, skim the text to determine the central idea.

Central Idea = Topic + Author's Ideas

? **2.** What is the central idea of the passage? Start your outline with the central idea.

I. Central Idea

____

You might state the central idea this way: A new study by the U.S. Geological Survey shows that underground reserves of water, called aquifers, are depleting rapidly.

R Read

As you read, find supporting ideas and details that explain the central idea.

- What supporting ideas show that aquifers are decreasing?
- What details further explain the supporting ideas?

? **3.** Complete the outline by identifying two supporting ideas and details that explain them.

I. Central Idea

A new USGS study shows that aquifers are depleting rapidly.

a. Supporting Idea

____

1. Detail

____

2. Detail

____

b. Supporting Idea

____

1. Detail

____

2. Detail

____

There are several possible ways to outline this passage, but the supporting ideas should explain or further develop the central idea and reflect the information in the passage.

E Evaluate

Evaluate your outline, and reorganize it or add to it as needed. Do you understand the information? Is it organized well, so that you understand the details? Can you see the relationship between the details and central idea? What conclusions can you draw from the outline?

I. Central Idea
A new USGS study shows that aquifers are depleting rapidly.

a. Supporting Idea
Groundwater is important as a natural resource.

1. Detail
Groundwater gives communities drinking water.

2. Detail
Groundwater is important for irrigation and industry.

b. Supporting Idea
The amount of groundwater reserves is decreasing.

1. Detail From 1900 to 2008, aquifers decreased more than than twice the volume of Lake Erie.

2. Detail Groundwater decrease explains more than two percent of sealevel rise between 2000 and 2008.

?

3. Explain how you know that the amount of water in the aquifers is dropping. Use specific details.

According to the study, between 1900 and 2008 the nation's aquifers decreased by more than twice the volume of water found in Lake Erie.

Reading for Understanding

Note-taking is another strategy that helps you identify and remember important details.

Read the passage and answer the questions that follow.

Message from the Director: Diversity Matters

Statement to the Workforce from D/CIA Brennan about Diversity, March 12, 2013

I believe diversity is critical to the success of our mission at the CIA. We need a workforce with a broad range of ethnic and cultural backgrounds, language expertise, and educational and life experiences to ensure diversity of thought and to operate effectively worldwide. And we are fortunate that our Nation offers such a tremendous variety of talented women and men—the first requirement of a truly global intelligence service.

But hiring a diverse workforce is not enough—we will not reap the benefits of that diversity unless we also foster a culture of inclusion. Engaged employees are not only more productive, they also bring the full range of views, ideas, and talents of our dedicated workforce to our vital mission.

To be sure, diversity is not only about mission. It is also about our bedrock belief as Americans in equality of opportunity. I am committed to hiring and retaining a diverse workforce across all Directorates and in leadership positions. I have asked the CIA's Executive Diversity and Inclusion Council and the Center for Mission Diversity and Inclusion to complete the Agency's first strategic plan since 2007 for this mission-critical area.

Our people are what make this Agency great. I call on every one of you to help foster a culture of inclusion, one in which we all benefit from the skills, experiences, and viewpoints of an ever more diverse workforce. That is how we will become an employer of choice across all communities—and how we will continue to succeed as an Agency.

John O. Brennan

Source: CIA, adapted from "Message from the Director: Diversity Matters," https://www.cia.gov/news-information/press-releases-statements/2013-press-releases-statements/message-from-director-diversity-matters.html

1. What is the central idea of the passage?

2. Outline the passage.

   I. Central Idea

   ____

   a. Supporting Idea

   ____

   1. Detail

   ____

   2. Detail

   ____

   3. Detail

   ____

   b. Supporting Idea

   ____

   1. Detail

   ____

   2. Detail

   ____

   3. Detail

   ____

3. Explain how Brennan uses details and supporting ideas. What additional details could Brennan include?

4. Brennan says the people of the CIA make the agency great. What reason does he give?

5. Which of the following summaries most effectively uses the passage's ideas and details?
   a. The CIA is committed to hiring a diverse workforce and creating a culture of inclusion.
   b. Engaged employees and an equal opportunity workforce will improve the CIA.
   c. Everyone benefits from a diverse workforce, so it is essential to hire more diverse employees.
   d. The availability of diverse talent in the U.S. is key to the success of the CIA as a global intelligence service.

Read the passage and answer the questions that follow.

3D Printing: Food in Space

NASA and a Texas company are exploring the possibility of using a 3D printer on deep space missions in a way where the "D" would stand for dining. 3D printing an additive manufacturing process that makes an object from a digital model by laying down thin layers of a material.

NASA has awarded a Small Business Innovation Research (SBIR) Phase I contract to Systems and Materials Research Consultancy of Austin, Texas to study the feasibility of using additive manufacturing for making food in space. Systems and Materials Research Consultancy will conduct a study for the development of a 3D printed food system for long duration space missions. Phase I SBIR proposals are very early stage concepts that may or may not mature into actual systems.

As NASA ventures farther into space, whether redirecting an asteroid or sending astronauts to Mars, the agency will need to make improvements in life support systems, including how to feed the crew during those long deep space missions. NASA's Advanced Food Technology program is interested in developing methods that will provide food to meet safety, acceptability, variety, and nutritional stability requirements for long exploration missions, while using the least amount of spacecraft resources and crew time. The current food system wouldn't meet the nutritional needs and five-year shelf life required for a mission to Mars or other long duration missions. Because refrigeration and freezing require significant spacecraft resources, current NASA provisions consist solely of individually prepackaged shelf stable foods, processed with technologies that degrade the micronutrients in the foods.

Additionally, the current space food is selected before astronauts ever leave the ground. Crew members don't have the ability to personalize recipes or prepare foods themselves. Over long duration missions, a variety of acceptable food is critical to ensure crew members continue to eat adequate amounts of food, and consequently, get the nutrients they need to maintain their health and performance.

3D printing is just one of the many transformation technologies that NASA is investing in to create the new knowledge and capabilities needed to enable future space missions while benefiting life here on Earth.

Source: NASA, adapted from "3D Printing: Food in Space," http://www.nasa.gov/directorates/spacetech/home/feature_3d_food_prt.htm

 **6.** Outline the passage.

 **7.** Evaluate the potential usefulness of 3D printing as a technology for space travel. Use details to support your ideas.

Check Your Skills

Read the passage and answer the questions that follow.

CORPUS CHRISTI, Texas—The favored feeding grounds of the endangered Kemp's ridley sea turtle coincide with some Gulf of Mexico waters that are subject to oil spills, extensive commercial fishing and oxygen depletion. These first-of-their-kind details on foraging locations and migration patterns of the Kemp's ridley sea turtle are from a new National Park Service and U.S. Geological Survey study, providing resource managers new information on how best to manage the species.

Scientists do not know why the turtles feed where they do, how human influences may affect turtle health or behavior, or whether human impacts on their chosen feeding areas might change their future foraging behavior. The researchers identified the feeding grounds of the Kemp's ridley, considered the most endangered and smallest hard-shelled sea turtle in the world, by analyzing 13 years of satellite-tracking data.

Donna Shaver, chief of the National Park Service's Sea Turtle Science and Recovery Division at Padre Island National Seashore, said, "Protecting feeding grounds for adult female sea turtles is important for the recovery of the species and this new information is important for future planning and restoration decisions."

Cooperative efforts between Mexico and several U.S. agencies have helped increase the population of this species of sea turtle. Species support includes protection of nesting turtles and their eggs on nesting beaches and reducing threats from fishing. The number of Kemp's ridleys nesting in the region has increased from 702 nests in 1985 to about 22,000 in 2012.

Source: U.S. Geological Survey, adapted from "Endangered Sea Turtle Feeding Grounds Discovered in Gulf," http://www.usgs.gov/newsroom/article.asp?ID=3602#.UcHq0T64F7s

1. What is the central idea of this passage?
   a. Scientists do not know why the endangered sea turtles feed in the Gulf of Mexico.
   b. Researchers analyzed 13 years of satellite data to find the feeding grounds of the sea turtles.
   c. Endangered sea turtle feeding grounds were discovered in the Gulf of Mexico.
   d. Cooperative efforts between Mexico and several U.S. agencies have helped increase the population of this species of sea turtle.

2. Which of the following is the most effective summary of the passage?
   a. For the first time, researchers have found the endangered Kemp's ridley sea turtles' feeding grounds in the Gulf of Mexico, an area that is known for commercial fishing, oil spills, and oxygen depletion.
   b. The number of Kemp's ridley sea turtles nesting on the shores of the Gulf of Mexico has increased from 702 nests in 1985 to about 22,000 in 2012.
   c. Protecting feeding grounds for adult female sea turtles is important for the recovery of the species, and information about feeding grounds helps in making better planning and restoration decisions.
   d. Cooperative efforts between Mexico and several U.S. agencies have helped increase the population of this species of sea turtle and continued efforts are needed for their survival.

3. What reason does Donna Shaver give to explain why protecting the feeding grounds is important?
   a. It is important because it will keep commercial fishermen out of the area.
   b. It is important for the recovery of many diverse species.
   c. It is important because scientists want to keep the feeding grounds in that area.
   d. It is important for recovery of the Kemp's ridley species.

4. Why is it significant that researchers were able to gather the information in the passage?
   a. It is the first information of its kind.
   b. It is the most recent information out there.
   c. It is vastly different from another study in the same year.
   d. It changes all the researchers' ideas about Kemp's ridley turtles.

5. How big was the sea turtle population in 2012? What can be done to increase this population?

Remember the Concept

Details help you thoroughly understand what you're reading.

Make an **outline** to find and understand the details.

Arguments

Connections

Think about the last time you had an argument. You probably had strong feelings about your position. What were your reasons?

We often think of an argument as an emotional experience where people's feelings get out of control, but the word *argument* applies to any claim (your point) and the evidence given in support of that claim.

An **argument** can be . . .

- A rational discussion where a person advances and supports a point of view.
- An explanation of the reasoning behind an idea.

To understand an argument, identify what the author is saying and why. Is the author making a point or supporting a conclusion? Is there solid evidence for what the author is saying?

Arguments can be found in many places:

- Speeches
- Letters to the editor
- Scientific articles
- Advertisements
- Cover letters
- Memos
- Historical documents
- Emails

It's important to recognize when an author is making an argument, so you can evaluate the author's purpose and reasons.

Identifying an Argument

You can identify an argument by examining the central idea, purpose, tone, and structure. Then, evaluate to determine the author's argument.

Use this passage for the exercises that follow.

I am concerned about the dress code in our office. I agree that we work in a professional place of business, but our workplace is friendly and personable. The current dress code doesn't match our personality as an office. We do see clients on a daily basis, but we would look no less professional, and maybe even less stuffy, if we made some changes to the dress code.

When the temperature creeps up to 90 degrees, men are often uncomfortable wearing suits or long-sleeved shirts. On a well-groomed employee, a polo shirt or short-sleeved button-down shirt can look as professional as a suit. Many of our clients visit our offices in jeans and t-shirts. A less formal dress code may make those clients more comfortable in our offices.

Determine the Central Idea

To identify an argument, find the central idea of the text.

Central Idea = Topic + Author's Ideas

?

1. What is the central idea of the passage?

The central idea is that the dress code at the author's office needs to be less rigid.

Determine the Author's Purpose and Tone

The central idea gives you the big picture. Next, look at the details, including word choice, to identify purpose and tone.

?

2. What is the author's purpose in this passage?

The author is writing to convince the management to make a change to the dress code.

3. What is the tone of the passage?

The author uses words like *concerned, stuffy,* and *uncomfortable*. You might describe the tone as unhappy.

Identify Text Structure

To examine the text structure, skim through the text. An argument usually follows one of several text structures:

- **Statement and Support:** Does the author state a claim and support it with evidence?
- **Problem and Solution:** Does the author identify a problem and suggest a solution?
- **Comparison:** Does the author draw a comparison between her proposed idea and an opposing idea or position?
- **Cause and Effect:** Does the author analyze cause and effect to make an argument?

4. Which one of the following text structures is used in the passage?
   a. Cause and effect
   b. Problem and solution
   c. Comparison
   d. Chronological

The text follows a problem and solution format. The author describes and explains the problem—uncomfortable clothing in hot weather. Then, the author presents a solution—allowing polo shirts and other short-sleeved shirts.

Draw a Conclusion: What Argument, If Any, Is Presented?

After examining the central idea, purpose, tone, and structure, evaluate the author's argument. What argument is the writer presenting?

5. Describe the author's argument in this passage.

The author is unhappy with the dress code and makes an argument that the management should change it. The author tries to persuade the audience by pointing out problems and suggesting solutions.

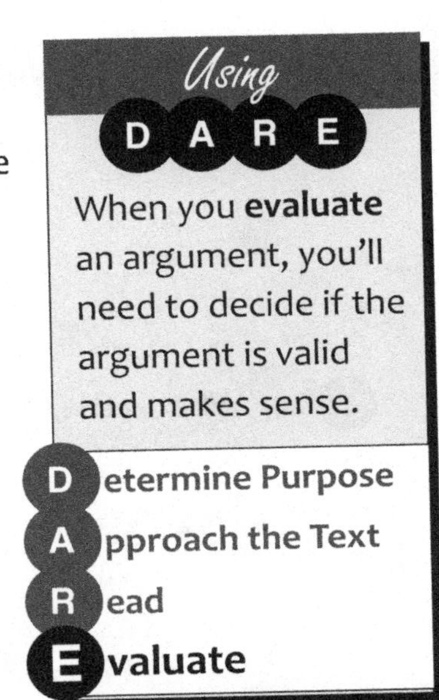

Practice It!

Read the email and answer the questions that follow.

After yesterday's meeting I just had a few thoughts I wanted to get down in email. I strongly believe that working on commission works against our clients. Our clients should be our highest priority. If we are trying to sell them the most expensive product whether or not they need it, then we don't have their best interest in mind. We should receive a high enough wage that taking advantage of our clients shouldn't even cross our mind.

I took a phone call from a very upset young woman who had paid top dollar for our most expensive treatment. She had found out elsewhere that she didn't need it. Now she will be taking her business elsewhere.

1. What is the central idea?

2. What is the author's purpose?

3. What is the author's tone?

4. What is the text structure?

5. Describe the argument in the passage.

6. How do the central idea, purpose, tone, and structure help you understand the argument?

Read the passage and answer the questions that follow.

Statement from the White House

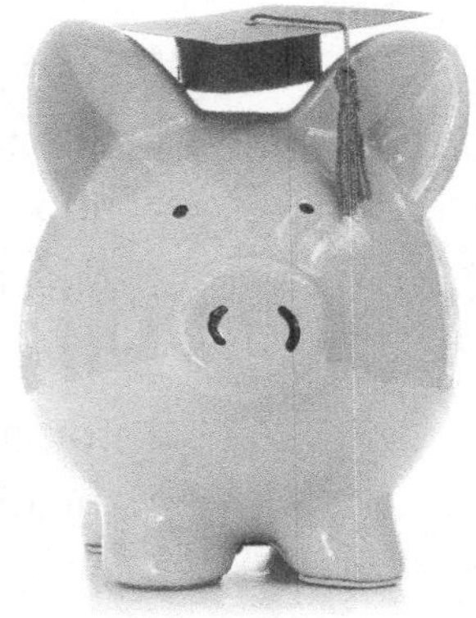

Last year the President worked with Republicans and Democrats in Congress to secure a one-year extension to keep the student loan interest rate from doubling to 6.8 percent. Without Congressional action, interest rates on new subsidized student loans will double once again on July 1 of this year. To keep rates from doubling, the President proposed that Congress enact a long-term solution. The solution includes cutting rates this year on nearly all new loans and ensuring that all students have access to affordable repayment options. It would not charge students a higher interest rate to pay for deficit reduction.

The comprehensive solution put forward by the President allows borrowers to benefit from the low interest rates currently available in the marketplace and guarantees these rates over the life of their loans. In the future, fixed rates would be determined each year, and the plan would ensure that borrower's rates are in line with the government's own cost of borrowing. Additionally, the President's plan guarantees that student loans remain affordable by allowing all students—past, present, and future—to cap their payments at 10 percent of income.

Source: The White House Blog, adapted from "If Congress Doesn't Act, Rates for New Federal Student Loans Will Double," http://www.whitehouse.gov/blog/2013/05/31/if-congress-doesnt-act-rates-new-federal-student-loans-will-double

7. Describe the argument in the passage.

8. How does the author use text structure to attempt to persuade the reader?

9. What reasons might someone give in opposition to this argument?

10. Which of the following people are reading texts that make an argument? Select all correct answers.

- ❑ Sofia is reading an email from a client who complains that her bill was inaccurate and explains why.
- ❑ Alex is reading a workforce policy on harassment and notices new changes that have been made to the policy.
- ❑ Tomas is reading a science textbook that explains migration patterns of geese and the history of the study of migration patterns.
- ❑ Jin is reading a scientific journal article stating that earlier studies are inaccurate and a recent study should be taken more seriously.
- ❑ Jesse is reading a news article informing readers of changes in trash pick-up.

11. Molly is reading a historical essay and trying to plan how to approach the reading. How can she tell whether the essay is making an argument?

Check Your Skills

This passage is from a speech by U.S. President Harry Truman on March 12, 1947 that introduces the Truman Doctrine. While the speech does not mention the USSR by name, Truman makes it clear that the U.S. will intervene to support any nation being threatened by a takeover by an armed minority.

Read the passage and answer the questions that follow.

The United States has received from the Greek Government an urgent appeal for financial and economic assistance. Preliminary reports from the American Economic Mission now in Greece and reports from the American Ambassador in Greece corroborate the statement of the Greek Government that assistance is imperative if Greece is to survive as a free nation.

I do not believe that the American people and the Congress wish to turn a deaf ear to the appeal of the Greek Government.

Greece is not a rich country. Lack of sufficient natural resources has always forced the Greek people to work hard to make both ends meet. Since 1940, this industrious and peace-loving country has suffered invasion, four years of cruel enemy occupation, and bitter internal strife.

When forces of liberation entered Greece they found that the retreating Germans had destroyed virtually all the railways, roads, port facilities, communications and merchant marine. More than a thousand villages had been burned. Eighty-five per cent of the children were tubercular. Livestock, poultry and draft animals had almost disappeared. Inflation had wiped out practically all savings.

As a result of these tragic conditions, a military minority, exploiting human want and misery, was able to create political chaos which, until now, has made economic recovery impossible.

Source: From "The Truman Doctrine," a speech by Harry S. Truman on March 12, 1947, available at http://avalon.law.yale.edu/20th_century/trudoc.asp

1. What is Truman's central idea in this passage?
   a. The U.S. must mind its own business.
   b. Greece is a peaceful country.
   c. The U.S. must step in to save Greece.
   d. Greece is not a rich country.

2. How does Truman portray Greece in his speech? Select all that apply.
   - ❑ Helpless
   - ❑ Angry
   - ❑ Hard-working
   - ❑ Happy-go-lucky
   - ❑ Peaceful
   - ❑ Spiteful

3. How does Truman's portrayal of Greece fit with his purpose?
   a. Truman's portrayal of Greece attempts to gain support against the Germans.
   b. Truman's portrayal of Greece raises awareness about the history of struggles of the people of Greece.
   c. Truman's portrayal of Greece shows that Greece is insignificant in world affairs.
   d. Truman's portrayal of Greece evokes sympathy to gain support for aiding the Greeks.

4. Why would the invading German army destroy Greek railways, roads, port facilities, and communications?
   a. To defend themselves against Greece
   b. To settle a personal argument
   c. To gain control over Greek natural resources
   d. To maintain control over the area

5. Who might oppose Truman's argument and why?

Remember the Concept

To understand an argument, examine:

- Central Idea
- Purpose
- Tone
- Structure

Claims and Evidence

Connections

Have you ever . . .

- Been unable to decide if you agree with an editorial?
- Had a tough time choosing how to vote on a proposition?
- Found it difficult to believe a product's advertisements?

Every time you make a choice or listen to an opinion, you're evaluating an argument. To evaluate an argument effectively, it helps to identify the **claim**—the author's point—and the **evidence**—how the author supports the claim.

Arguments center around a **claim**, which the author attempts to show is true.

A **claim** is . . .

- Not a factual statement.
- Argued as either true or false.
- Backed up with **evidence.**

A claim alone is not enough to persuade a reader. If someone makes a claim, you'll likely ask, "Why?" Evidence gives you reasons to help you decide whether an argument is valid. Evidence includes data and examples that connect to and support the claim.

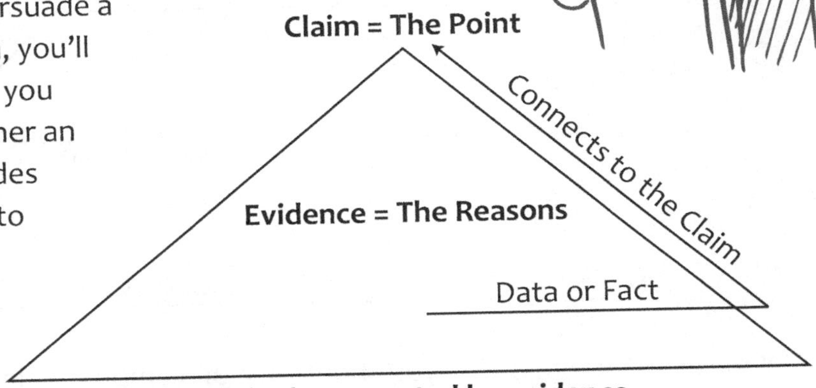

Claim = The Point

Connects to the Claim

Evidence = The Reasons

Data or Fact

A claim is supported by evidence.

The Claims and Evidence Pyramid

Identifying the claim and evidence in an argument helps you to more effectively evaluate the author's stance.

Use this passage for the exercises that follow.

When I was attending college, living off campus was the most freedom I'd ever felt. I spent my freshman and sophomore years living in the dorms. I found the experience cramped, uncomfortable, and miserable. Luckily, I found a quaint but affordable apartment of my own during my junior and senior year. Living off campus gave me the independence and freedom I had craved for so long. I could be myself without worrying about what others thought. I could concentrate on my studies and see people I wanted to see. Having my own kitchen and bathroom provided me with the convenience I needed at a fraction of the cost of living in a dorm. It was a sanctuary I could retreat to when I needed to regroup after a particularly tough day. It also introduced me to life off campus, which is nonexistent while living in the dorms. I was exposed to the life and vibrancy of the larger community.

D — *Determine the Purpose*

Imagine you are trying to decide whether to live on or off campus at college. Your sister sent you the above email. Evaluate what she's saying to determine if you agree with her advice.

A — *Approach the Text*

To find out what your sister is claiming and why, identify her claim and evidence. A good plan is to skim the text to identify the claim. When you're reading, look for specific evidence.

?

1. Skim the text and write the claim at the top of the pyramid:

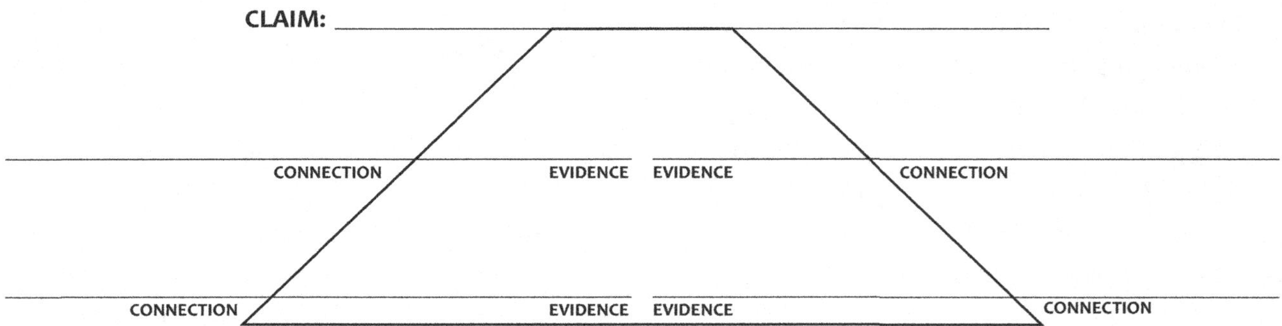

Your sister's claim is that you should live off campus. A claim is often stated toward the beginning of a text. Here, the claim isn't stated directly, but you can infer it by skimming.

R *Read*

As you read, identify the evidence that supports the claim. An effective argument includes evidence that is relevant, sufficient, and credible. Look for:

- Examples
- Reasons
- Facts
- Anecdotes
- Statistics

After you find supporting evidence, look for the link between the evidence and the claim. Why does this evidence help prove the claim?

2. Complete the pyramid with evidence from the passage.

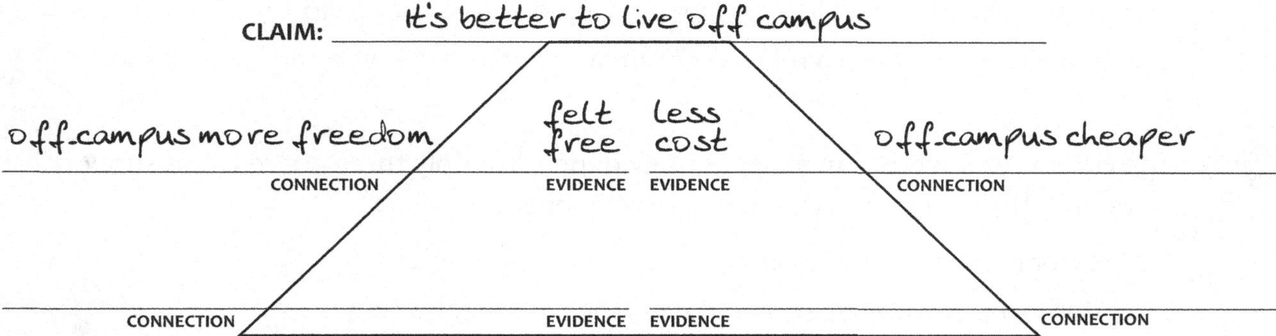

E *Evaluate*

Evaluate the claims and evidence. Does the evidence make sense? Are you convinced?

CLAIM: It's better to live off campus

off-campus more freedom
CONNECTION
felt free
EVIDENCE
less cost
EVIDENCE
off-campus cheaper
CONNECTION

off-campus privacy
CONNECTION
concentrate on studying
EVIDENCE
kitchen and bathroom
EVIDENCE
off-campus convenience
CONNECTION

3. In the passage, is the evidence convincing?

The evidence is reasonably convincing. However, it is only one person's experience. Maybe your sister got a great deal on rent in a nice place, or maybe prices have risen. Maybe you have different priorities and want to be near your classes, meet other students, and experience campus life. Still, there is a clear claim and relevant evidence in her letter.

Answer the following questions about claims and evidence.

1. Label each sentence as either C (claim) or E (evidence).

   ___ Everyone should try to eat as healthily as possible.

   ___ A healthy diet will help you feel better and lose weight.

   ___ A healthy diet is linked to fewer health problems and a longer life.

2. Label each sentence as either C (claim) or S (support).

   ___ Affordable day care centers often lack trained staff and adequate safety procedures.

   ___ It's hard for working parents to find quality, affordable day care.

   ___ Quality day care can cost $15,000 to $20,000 a year per child.

   ___ Not all parents have a relative or family friend nearby who can lend a hand.

3. The claim is followed by five pieces of evidence, but only three are relevant support. Select the three most relevant pieces of evidence.

   Claim: Our company should hire three more employees.

   - ❑ Many of our employees have experience in other markets.
   - ❑ We are understaffed, and employees are working overtime to make it work.
   - ❑ Our profits are growing, and if we make cuts, we will have enough in the budget for more employees.
   - ❑ Our company is a relaxed place to work where the employees enjoy their work.
   - ❑ With overtime pay, we waste money and overwork staff.

4. Based on the following support, what is the author's claim?

   Corporations often choose the cheapest way to get rid of waste products, which means releasing them into the air, waterways, and dump sites.

   In one case, a corporation dumped 43.6 million pounds of 82 chemical substances into a waterway in New York.

   Corporations often get away with dumping without so much as a "slap on the wrist."

Claims and Evidence

Read the passage and answer the questions that follow.

The latest proposal by the city council to tax bicycles is simply crazy. Some residents are concerned that expanding the use of bicycles in the city could threaten their own modes of transportation. This makes no sense. There is no reason why bikes, cars, busses, and pedestrians can't all coexist.

More people riding bicycles means less car traffic, fewer road repairs, and a diminished need for parking spaces. In a world of skyrocketing obesity and diabetes, bicycles promote a healthier lifestyle, which leads to fewer health care costs. In addition, the 50-plus bicycle shops in the city bring jobs and a significant amount of money into the local economy through the cycling community and tourists.

If we follow the logic of the city council, I assume an anti-walking campaign with taxes on shoes will be the next great idea from city government.

5. Fill out the pyramid with the claim, evidence, and connections.

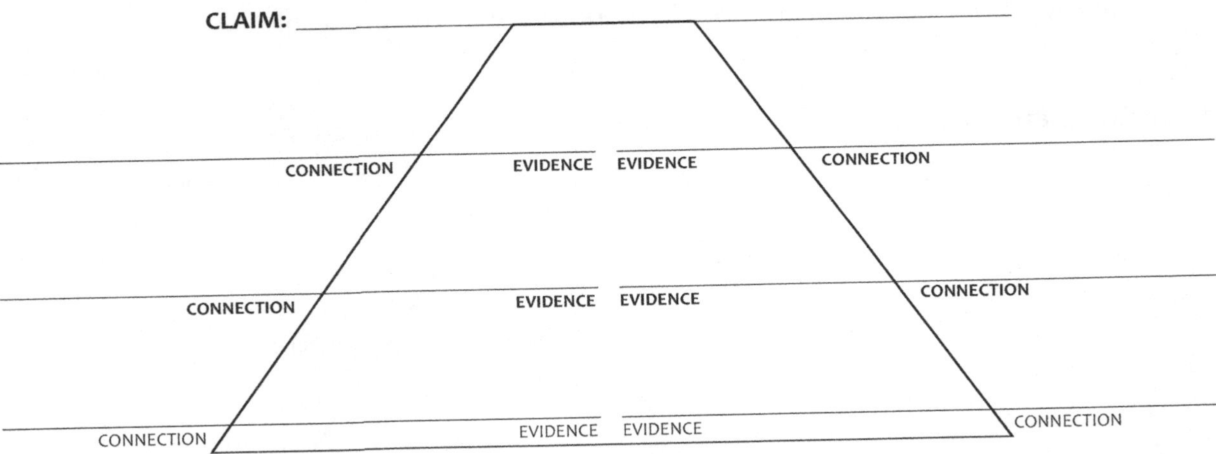

6. Does the evidence provide enough relevant support for the claim? Why or why not?

7. What evidence could you provide to support a tax on bicycles?

Read the passage and answer the questions that follow.

There are entirely too many overlapping layers of government in this state—particularly for those who live in metropolitan areas. The San Francisco Bay Area includes multiple city governments, several county governments, regional governments such as the Association of Bay Area Governments and the Metropolitan Transportation Commission, numerous school districts, and special districts of various kinds. Now, the governments fight with each other for taxes and attempt to shift their costs to each other.

The San Francisco taxpayers are taking on the burden of providing for the homeless and mentally ill from all over the region, both in and out of the city. The mayor of San Francisco refused to pay for a mental health facility that he felt the county should fund before reversing his original decision and deciding to fund it. We have a jail that has stood unused for 10 years because the county cannot afford to staff it, but other jails are overcrowded. People in different counties pay different property taxes, despite owning similar houses. Different qualities of education are available to children who live in adjoining towns. We need to learn how to work together toward a solution.

> **Reading for Understanding**
>
> A writer often states his or her claim up front. However, sometimes you will need to infer the claim from examples and details.

8. Complete the pyramid with the claim, evidence, and connections.

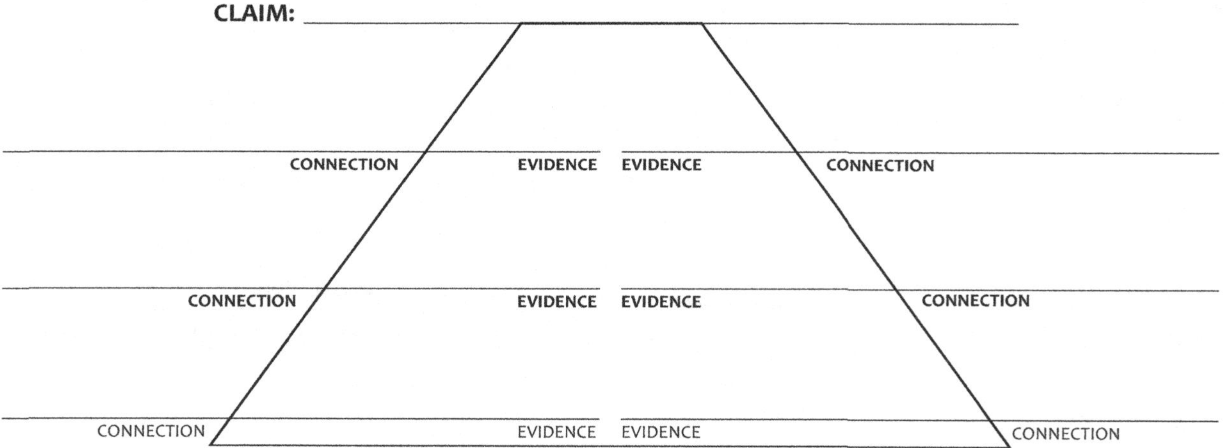

9. Does the evidence provide enough relevant support for the claim? Why or why not?

Check Your Skills

Read the passage and answer the questions that follow.

> This passage is from a **primary source**—a text written during a historical period being studied.

Not to Humiliate but to Win Over

Another thing that we had to get over was the fact that the nonviolent resister does not seek to humiliate or defeat the opponent but to win his friendship and understanding. This was always a cry that we had to set before people that our aim is not to defeat the white community, not to humiliate the white community, but to win the friendship of all of the persons who had perpetrated this system in the past. The end of violence or the aftermath of violence is bitterness. The aftermath of nonviolence is reconciliation and the creation of a beloved community. A boycott is never an end within itself. It is merely a means to awaken a sense of shame within the oppressor but the end is reconciliation, the end is redemption.

Then we had to make it clear also that the nonviolent resister seeks to attack the evil system rather than individuals who happen to be caught up in the system. And this is why I say from time to time that the struggle in the South is not so much the tension between white people and Negro people. The struggle is rather between justice and injustice, between the forces of light and the forces of darkness. And if there is a victory it will not be a victory merely for fifty thousand Negroes. But it will be a victory for justice, a victory for good will, a victory for democracy.

Another basic thing we had to get over is that nonviolent resistance is also an internal matter. It not only avoids external violence or external physical violence but also internal violence of spirit. And so at the center of our movement stood the philosophy of love. The attitude that the only way to ultimately change humanity and make for the society that we all long for is to keep love at the center of our lives. Now people used to ask me from the beginning what do you mean by love and how is it that you can tell us to love those persons who seek to defeat us and those persons who stand against us; how can you love such persons? And I had to make it clear all along that love in its highest sense is not a sentimental sort of thing, not even an affectionate sort of thing.

Source: From "The Power of Non-violence," a speech by Martin Luther King, Jr., June 04, 1957, available at: http://teachingamericanhistory.org/library/document/the-power-of-non-violence/

1. What is King's main argument in this speech?
    a. Nonviolence defeats the opponent without humiliation and through love.
    b. Nonviolence has its benefits, but doesn't convince anyone of anything.
    c. Love is not a sentimental thing, but a way to fight oppression.
    d. There is a time and a place for nonviolence, but this time is not one of them.

2. Which of the following reasons does King give to support his claim?
    a. Winning is important no matter what the cost.
    b. Violence creates bitterness.
    c. Nonviolence causes problems for protestors.
    d. Humiliating the white community is the ultimate goal.

3. King says he fights against injustice instead of fighting against white people. What is the connection between this point and the claim?
    a. It is a way to humiliate the opponent through shame.
    b. It is a violent approach that breaks down the community.
    c. It is a nonviolent approach that promotes eventual unity.
    d. It is a way to bring about eventual reversal of race roles.

4. How does King use the idea of love to support his main argument?
    a. He says non-violent protest is founded on the same principles as romantic love.
    b. He says non-violent protest is founded on a special doctrine of loving only your enemies.
    c. He says non-violent protest means to love fellow protestors through the hard times.
    d. He says non-violent protest means to love your opposition as fellow humans.

5. Give one piece of evidence to support the opposing claim that nonviolence is ineffective.

Remember the Concept

Claim = The Point

Evidence = The Reasons

A claim is supported by evidence.

Fallacies

Connections

Have you ever . . .

- Heard an argument that didn't make sense?
- Questioned whether "it's popular" was a good reason to buy a soda?
- Been insulted during an argument?

To make an informed decision or to argue against someone's claim, you need to spot when an argument is flawed and why.

Fallacies are mistakes in reasoning. There are many types of fallacies, such as:

Circular Logic	Using a claim as the proof of the claim ***Example:*** Ellway is great because he's the best senator we've had.
Slippery Slope	Saying that a situation will escalate without evidence ***Example:*** If kids watch movies on finals' day, soon they'll just watch movies all year!
Straw Man	Setting up a poor opposing argument that's easy to knock down ***Example:*** People say pizza is bad because it's messy. Just use a napkin!
Bandwagon	Saying that something is good or right because it's popular ***Example:*** Use Soapy Soap because 9 out of 10 households use it!
False Dilemma	Setting up a false choice that you must do either *one thing* or *another thing* when there may be many other choices ***Example:*** It's either raise taxes or destroy schools. We don't want to destroy schools!
Generalization	Making a general statement as if it's always true from a limited sample ***Example:*** John was rude to me. All boys are rude!
Personal Attacks	Attacking the opponent instead of attacking the argument ***Example:*** Carlos is just a child, so what he's saying can't be true.

Is the Evidence PALE?

To identify a fallacy, identify the claim and evidence. Is the evidence PALE?

- **Personal attacks:** Does it attack a person instead of the issue?
- **Assumptions:** Does it make assumptions without reasons?
- **Logic Errors:** Does the logic make sense?
- **Emotion:** Does it make emotional appeals without reasons to back it up?

Imagine your sister has received a parking ticket that she believes is unfair. She asks you to review her letter to the city about the ticket and look for any problems with her argument.

Use this passage for the exercises that follow.

To Whom It May Concern,

The ticket I received last week for parking next to a fire hydrant is unwarranted. The $150 I am being forced to pay for the ticket is not the only charge I am facing. When I arrived to retrieve my car from the tow lot, I was forced to pay $183 for the return of my vehicle. So, when you add those two numbers up, you are charging nearly $350 for parking near a fire hydrant. That astronomical number is more than I had to pay for rolling through a stop sign last year.

The hydrant is also not clearly marked. When I parked in the "illegal spot," I was meeting a friend at a restaurant nearby and running late. I saw the spot and failed to notice the hydrant.

It's not like anyone died or was even hurt. I fail to see why I should have to pay. Ticketing people for parking near hydrants is completely pointless. Obviously, people who work for the city are money-hungry jerks. Just because the city is trying to meet a quota to raise money doesn't mean I should be affected.

Soon, people won't be able to park anywhere without fear of being towed. People will end up parking inside a paid lot to make sure their cars won't be towed.

> ***Reading for Understanding***
>
> Fallacies are sometimes intentional and meant to distract you from the lack of evidence and support for an argument.

Identify the Claim and Evidence

Identify the claim and evidence so that you can check for fallacies.

?

1. Identify the claim and two pieces of evidence the author uses to support the claim.

The claim is that the parking ticket is unfair. The author gives several pieces of evidence. You might choose these: "Obviously, people who work for the city are money-hungry jerks." and "Soon, people won't be able to park anywhere without fear of being towed. People will end up parking inside a paid lot to make sure their cars won't be towed."

Is It PALE?

Examine each piece of evidence. Is it PALE? Check for personal attacks, assumptions, logic errors, and emotion.

?

2. "Obviously, people who work for the city are money-hungry jerks."
   What problem does this evidence have?

This statement is a personal attack. It doesn't make an argument about the ticket.

?

3. "Soon, people won't be able to park anywhere without fear of being towed. People will end up parking inside a paid lot to make sure their car won't be towed."
   What is the logic error in this evidence?

The argument says the city will soon tow you for parking anywhere. This is a "slippery slope." There is no evidence that the city will expand its reasons for towing.

Evaluate

Evaluate the support for the claim overall. After you identify any fallacies, does the argument still hold together?

?

4. How does the use of fallacies affect the argument?

The author's reasoning doesn't effectively argue against the ticket. Most of the evidence contains fallacies. The author states that the hydrant isn't clearly marked but lacks evidence.

Use your understanding of fallacies to answer the following questions.

1. Herbert argues that people who aren't in support of the recycling ordinance are lazy and unconcerned about the environment. Is this a fallacy? Why or why not?

2. Raymond says that people who want to raise money for the local paper think that's the only source for news, but there are lots of other news sources. Is this a fallacy? Why or why not?

3. Allie argues that if smoking is made illegal in bars in the city, soon smoking anywhere will be illegal. Is this a fallacy? Why or why not?

4. Sonia argues that if city money is spent on the park, it will reduce funds for other purposes. Is this a fallacy? Why or why not?

5. Van argues that it's obvious Carlos Hadden is the best candidate for city council, since he's ahead in the polls by 15 points. Is this a fallacy? Why or why not?

Using D A R E

Determine Purpose: Look for fallacies when you're evaluating an argument.

Approach the Text: Skim to identify the claim.

Read: Identify evidence and look for fallacies.

Evaluate: Evaluate the evidence and the whole argument.

 **6.** Which of the following is a better argument? Explain your reasoning.

Our mayor's opinions about local crime are worthless. Last week, her own son was arrested for disturbing the peace.

Vote Lei Sanchez because she is tough on crime. She hired 12 new police officers last year.

 **7.** Which of the following is a better argument? Explain your reasoning.

The swimming pool is bad idea. Children will hang out there and neglect their studies.

The swimming pool is a good idea. It will help children get more exercise and provide recreation for the community.

 **8.** Which of the following is a better argument? Explain your reasoning.

The new apartment manager never seems to be here. When I call him about a problem, he never gets back to me. I think we need to find someone to replace him.

A week after our new apartment manager took over, the elevator stopped working. He's obviously a terrible supervisor, or this wouldn't have happened.

 **9.** Which of the following is a better argument? Explain your reasoning.

The police in our area are understaffed. I don't think I've ever seen a police officer near my house or on my block.

The police in our area are understaffed. Crimes have gone up, but the number of police is down by five percent.

Read the passage and answer the questions that follow.

I'm a stay-at-home dad. I get to spend all my time with my children. I make sure they do their homework, finish their chores, spend time outdoors, and have creative play. In households where both parents work, children don't get these opportunities. A parent who works can't take the time to give their children the attention they need. It doesn't matter which parent stays home, but children need someone who's there all the time.

I know it can be tough to survive on one income, but having children requires sacrifices. If you aren't willing to live without more expensive vacations, a new car, or cable TV for the benefit of your children, you're not making the right choices.

Consider your children's futures. A two-parent household shouldn't have two working parents. Someone should stay home and make sure the children get the right start in life.

10. Identify the claim and evidence in the passage.

11. What fallacies are there in the passage?

12. Evaluate the argument in the passage. How effective and convincing is the argument? Why?

Check Your Skills

Read the passages and answer the questions that follow.

Pilar's Position

I agree that we need to be sympathetic to all people, but those who give money to panhandlers are basically funding their alcohol, cigarette, and drug addictions. Panhandling shows a lack of goals and initiative on the part of those asking for handouts. If we continue to give panhandlers money, we are just enabling them, and the homelessness problem in the city will only increase.

As a longtime resident, I can't enjoy the city nearly as much with the current atmosphere. I can't go to work without fear of harassment. My parents no longer look for accommodations downtown when visiting because of the street kids. By confronting the problem, the mayor is showing how much he values this city. I applaud his efforts.

Olena's Position

I'm concerned about reports of "aggressive panhandling" in the media. I've lived in the city for almost 20 years, and I haven't seen a problem. The homeless on our streets are people like you and me. I've met some who lost their jobs during the recession. Without anyone to help bail them out, they ended up on the street trying to make ends meet. Others are veterans who have mental health problems. They ended up on the streets because of their service to our country.

I firmly believe that the homeless should be given the same human decency as the rest of us. Most of us are just one or two paychecks away from the streets. Think about how easily you could be homeless, too, and it will become easier to think of the homeless as human beings.

1. Which of the following statements best supports Pilar's position?
   - a. There are more than 1.6 million homeless children in the U.S. each year, according to the National Center on Family Homelessness.
   - b. Federal governments, state governments, and organizations each have their own definitions of homelessness.
   - c. A large number of factors, including poverty, domestic violence, and foreclosure, contribute to homelessness.
   - d. The U.S. Conference of Mayors in 2005 stated that 30% of homeless people suffer from addiction.

2. Which of the following statements best supports Olena's position?
   - a. Not all panhandlers are homeless, and often homeless people do not panhandle.
   - b. A 1996 study concluded that 40% of homeless men served in the armed forces.
   - c. People who live in poverty are most at risk of becoming homeless.
   - d. Five percent of the urban homeless population are unaccompanied minors, according to the National Law Center on Homelessness and Poverty, 2004.

3. Which of the following assumptions does Pilar's statement make?
   - a. That panhandlers are mostly minorities
   - b. That panhandlers are all from the same background
   - c. That panhandlers will use their money to buy food
   - d. That panhandlers are addicted to drugs, alcohol, or cigarettes

4. Which of the following assumptions does Olena's statement make?
   - a. That panhandlers avoid Olena's area because of the good lighting
   - b. That people who complain about aggressive panhandlers don't consider them human
   - c. That people who complain about aggressive panhandlers don't understand the language of panhandling
   - d. That panhandlers are all from the same background

5. Compare the two arguments. Which argument is more effective and why?

Remember the Concept

To find fallacies, ask: Is the argument PALE?

- Personal attacks
- Assumptions
- Logic errors
- Emotion

Persuasive Appeals

Connections

Have you ever...

- Given in to your little sister because she acted so sad?
- Gotten an email from your mom trying to get you to visit?
- Bought a new product because its commercials were convincing?

These are all examples of persuasive arguments. In persuasive arguments, authors or speakers use different types of **persuasive appeals** or methods of persuading their audience. Recognizing how an argument is attempting to persuade you can help you evaluate that argument.

There are three types of persuasive appeals used in arguments to support claims and respond to opposing arguments. A convincing argument will often use a combination of all three types of appeals.

- **Logos** relies on logic and reason to persuade by constructing logical arguments. A strong argument needs to be supported by logic.
- **Pathos** appeals to an audience's needs, values, and emotions. Appeals to emotions and values are important to capture the attention and sympathy of an audience.
- **Ethos** shows the character, credibility, or reliability of the author or speaker. A strong argument has authority behind it. The source should not be biased or uninformed.

Understanding a Persuasive Appeal

To identify persuasive appeals, remember:

- **Logos** = Logic
- **Pathos** = Emotion
- **Ethos** = Character

Use this passage for the exercises that follow.

The people of Dearborne need to give their opposition to the proposed Franklin's store a rest.

Yes, there are possible issues, including questions about the company's treatment of employees. This is not a question about large retail stores. It's a question of labor law and enforcement, and so it should be dealt with separately. What good does it do to stop one offender from opening a store? Shouldn't we focus on enforcing good laws on all businesses in the community?

The main argument against the store is its effect on the rest of the community. Dearborne is not a small town, and its businesses are already accustomed to competition. Franklin's will be forced to compete with rival discounters who already exist in the city. One more large shopping center won't change the character of the bustling town. Dearborne was growing before Franklin's decided to try to open another location. Businesses and developments are cropping up all the time. Dearborne will certainly continue to grow after the retailer opens.

People should accept that it's too late to contest the business. Site work has begun, and the store is scheduled to open next spring. The opponents of the store need to realize that a crackdown on large retailers like Franklin's easily could hurt other businesses. The best way to ensure that Franklin's thrives is to protest it, making it difficult for new competitors to open in Dearborne.

Determine the Purpose

Imagine that many of your neighbors and friends are up in arms about the thought of a Franklin's moving into town. You aren't sure what to think, and a friend tells you to read this letter to the editor to gain a better understanding.

A Approach the Text

Understanding persuasive appeals can help you better identify and evaluate an author's evidence. Before reading, skim the text to find the claim and evidence.

? 1. Underline the claim and one piece of evidence the author uses.

You'll find the claim in the first sentence: "The people of Dearborne need to give their opposition to the proposed big box store a rest." You might underline the following evidence: "Franklin's will be forced to compete with rival discounters who already exist in the city. One more strip shopping center won't change the character of the bustling town."

R Read

As you read, examine the support. Determine how the author uses the evidence to persuade you. Identify logos, pathos, and ethos in the argument.

? 2. Read the third paragraph. How does the author use pathos, ethos, or logos?

There are several uses of logos and pathos. The author uses logos when he says that the Franklin's won't cause the town to grow because it was already growing. He uses pathos by appealing to the common value of enjoying life in a small town.

E Evaluate

Once you've identified persuasive appeals, evaluate their effect on the argument.

- **Logos:** Is the logic sound and reasonable?
- **Pathos:** Is there logic to back up emotional appeals? Are appeals to values balanced?
- **Ethos:** Is the author credible?

? 3. In this passage, is logos, ethos, and pathos effective and appropriate?

The passage uses primarily logos and some pathos. The logical arguments seem reasonable, and the pathos is not overblown and is balanced by logic.

An effective argument should be balanced between logos, ethos, and pathos. Every argument needs hard evidence to be persuasive. An argument's source needs to be credible. Emotional appeals capture attention and open minds.

Use your understanding of logos, pathos, and ethos to answer the following questions.

1. In the following scenario, which kinds of persuasive appeals are used? Explain your reasoning.

Your coworker Lia asks you to read a letter she wrote to the boss. Lia is hoping to bring her son to work with her two afternoons a week. In the letter, Lia says that her sister was babysitting for her but recently moved away. Lia can't afford to put her son in daycare every afternoon. If she can't bring her son to work, she will have to pay for daycare, and then she won't be able to pay rent.

2. In the following scenario, which kinds of persuasive appeals are used? Explain your reasoning.

You are watching a mayoral debate on television. The incumbent candidate, who has been mayor for the past four years, explains that she is best for the job because of her proven track record of supporting schools and local businesses.

3. Mark is trying to convince people to contribute to his Kickstarter campaign to help get his organic, local produce stand off the ground. The produce would be affordable so that more people could afford to eat local and organic food. Which persuasive appeal would be most effective in Mark's argument?
   - **a.** An explanation of the set up of the produce stand
   - **b.** A specific example of how produce goes from the fields to the stores
   - **c.** A specific example of a person who couldn't afford organic produce otherwise
   - **d.** An explanation of how Mark intends to use the donations for the stand

The following passage is from a television broadcast on January 17, 1961, when President Dwight D. Eisenhower made his farewell address to the nation—his last public speech.

Read the passage and answer the questions that follow.

Three days from now, after a half century of service of our country, I shall lay down the responsibilities of office as, in traditional and solemn ceremony, the authority of the Presidency is vested in my successor. . . .

General of the Army Dwight D. Eisenhower, 1947

America is today the strongest, the most influential and most productive nation in the world. Understandably proud of this pre-eminence, we yet realize that America's leadership and prestige depend, not merely upon our unmatched material progress, riches and military strength, but on how we use our power in the interests of world peace and human betterment.

Throughout America's adventure in free government, such basic purposes have been to keep the peace, to foster progress in human achievement, and to enhance liberty, dignity and integrity among peoples and among nations. To strive for less would be unworthy of a free and religious people. Any failure traceable to arrogance or our lack of comprehension or readiness to sacrifice would inflict upon us a grievous hurt, both at home and abroad. . . .

Crises there will continue to be. In meeting them, whether foreign or domestic, great or small, there is a recurring temptation to feel that some spectacular and costly action could become the miraculous solution to all current difficulties. A huge increase in the newer elements of our defenses; development of unrealistic programs to cure every ill in agriculture; a dramatic expansion in basic and applied research—these and many other possibilities, each possibly promising in itself, may be suggested as the only way to the road we wish to travel.

But each proposal must be weighed in light of a broader consideration; the need to maintain balance in and among national programs—balance between the private and the public economy, balance between the cost and hoped for advantages—balance between the clearly necessary and the comfortably desirable; balance between our essential requirements as a nation and the duties imposed by the nation upon the individual; balance between the actions of the moment and the national welfare of the future. Good judgment seeks balance and progress; lack of it eventually finds imbalance and frustration.

Source: Military-Industrial Complex Speech, by Dwight D. Eisenhower, 1961, available at: http://coursesa.matrix.msu.edu/~hst306/documents/indust.html

This historical passage is from a **primary source.**

4. What is Eisenhower's claim in this passage?

Reading for Understanding

Logos, pathos, and ethos can help you identify the author's purpose.

5. Explain the use of logos in this passage.

6. Explain the use of pathos in this passage.

7. Explain the use of ethos in this passage.

8. How persuasive is this passage? Explain your reasoning.

9. Provide a counterargument to this passage using pathos and logos.

Check Your Skills

This passage is from a commencement speech on human rights and foreign policy given at Notre Dame University on May 22, 1977 by President Jimmy Carter.

Read the passage and answer the questions that follow.

It is a new world, but America should not fear it. It is a new world, and we should help to shape it. It is a new world that calls for a new American foreign policy—a policy based on constant decency in its values and on optimism in our historical vision.... Our policy must reflect our belief that the world can hope for more than simple survival and our belief that dignity and freedom are fundamental spiritual requirements. Our policy must shape an international system that will last longer than secret deals. We cannot make this kind of policy by manipulation. Our policy must be open; it must be candid; it must be one of constructive global involvement, resting on five cardinal principles.

I've tried to make these premises clear to the American people since last January. Let me review what we have been doing and discuss what we intend to do. First, we have reaffirmed America's commitment to human rights as a fundamental tenet of our foreign policy. In ancestry, religion, color, place of origin, and cultural background, we Americans are as diverse a nation as the world has even seen. No common mystique of blood or soil unites us. What draws us together, perhaps more than anything else, is a belief in human freedom. We want the world to know that our Nation stands for more than financial prosperity.

This does not mean that we can conduct our foreign policy by rigid moral maxims. We live in a world that is imperfect and which will always be imperfect—a world that is complex and confused and which will always be complex and confused.

Source: University of Notre Dame Address at Commencement Exercises by Jimmy Carter, May 22, 1977, available at http://www.presidency.ucsb.edu/ws/?pid=7552

1. President Carter says, "Our policy must reflect... our belief that dignity and freedom are fundamental spiritual requirements." What does this statement show?
   - **a.** His experience when President as a foreign policy maker
   - **b.** His shared values with other Americans
   - **c.** The positive consequences of his foreign policy
   - **d.** The logical consequences of opponents' foreign policy proposals

2. Which quotation from the passage best defines the foreign policy Carter is proposing?
   a. "We want the world to know that our Nation stands for more than financial prosperity."
   b. "What draws us together, perhaps more than anything else, is a belief in human freedom."
   c. "It is a new world, but America should not fear it."
   d. "...a policy based on constant decency in its values and on optimism in our historical vision."

3. How does Carter connect foreign policy to Americans' emotions in the speech?
   a. He speaks about the dangers of living without a stronger foreign policy.
   b. He speaks about the freedom that draws Americans and the human race together.
   c. He uses a specific example of a country that needs the compassion of the United States.
   d. He appeals to America's sense of adventure by saying that it's a new world, not to be feared.

4. Carter states, "It is a new world, and we should help to shape it." What does this quotation imply?
   a. That Americans can spread their values through foreign policy
   b. That Americans can redefine national boundaries in the new world
   c. That Americans can shape the makeup of parliaments and congresses in other nations
   d. That Americans can define the policy of the United Nations

5. How does Carter build trust and likability in the passage?
   a. Carter refers to a new and exciting world.
   b. Carter shows that he believes in the people.
   c. Carter talks about his position as President.
   d. Carter tells them that to refuse to change is to live in fear.

Remember the Concept

A convincing argument will often use a combination of ethos, logos, and pathos.

Logos = Logic

Pathos = Emotion

Ethos = Character

Evaluating Arguments and Evidence

Connections

Suppose you are reading an argument that advises consumers to shop for local and organic produce. What might convince you?

- Reasons why local and organic produce is healthier.
- A cost comparison and reasons why organic food is worth the cost.
- An explanation of how to find affordable organic produce.
- Stories about people whose health has improved by eating organic.

Evaluating evidence is essential when reading argumentative texts. You evaluate arguments to decide whether to buy a product or service, follow a piece of advice, or take a particular position on an issue. What makes an argument convincing and valid?

When you evaluate an argument, consider:

How much evidence is there? Does the argument cover many points of view and give multiple pieces of evidence? Does it only make one point?

What kind of evidence is there? Is there logic as well as emotion? Is the author credible? Are there fallacies in the argument?

What conclusions are drawn from the evidence? Does the argument make assumptions? Do the conclusions follow logically from the evidence?

Evaluating an Argument

To evaluate an argument, put together what you know about:

- Claims and evidence
- Fallacies
- Logos, pathos, and ethos

Use the passage for the exercises that follow.

I'm not anti-government or anti-law enforcement, but the huge amount of overtime pay being handed out at the Sheriff's Office infuriates me. The situation supports the anti-government argument that government employees think they have a blank check signed by the public. Government workers live in a bubble protected from the realities of supply and demand that affect the rest of the world.

There is no way this over-spending would happen in the private sector. If a manager spent hundreds of thousands of dollars on overtime pay instead of simply hiring more employees to avoid time-and-a-half wages, that manager would be replaced. But in government, nothing changes.

In the private sector, the owners are financially responsible for the company. They realize that overtime pay comes directly out of their pockets. In the public sector, we all pay the costs, but we're not running the organization. I'm not suggesting that everything be privatized, but we have to build some accountability into government.

Determine the Claim and Evidence

Identify the claim, the point that the author is arguing, and the evidence that supports it.

1. What is the claim in this passage?

The author's claim is that there needs to be accountability for spending in government.

2. Identify evidence that the author presents.

One piece of evidence the author gives is overspending on overtime in the Sheriff's Office.

Check for Fallacies

Fallacies are errors in reasoning. Ask yourself, is the evidence PALE? Look for personal attacks, assumptions, logic errors, and emotion.

? 3. Does the argument contain logical fallacies?

One example of a logical fallacy is "government employees think they have a blank check." This is a personal attack. The author also writes "in government nothing changes." This is a generalization without support. The idea that government doesn't change is an assumption.

Examine the Use of Persuasive Appeals

How does the author use logos, pathos, and ethos? Are the appeals to logic, emotion, and values effective and appropriate?

? 4. How does the author use persuasive appeals in this argument?

The author claims not to be anti-government or anti-law enforcement, which is an appeal to ethos. Appeals to the common value of saving money and to anti-government sentiments are pathos. The author uses a logical argument to connect wasting money with the lack of accountability in the government.

Evaluate the Argument

After examining the claim and evidence, fallacies, and persuasive appeals, how does the argument hold up? Is there enough strong, valid evidence to support the claim?

? 5. Is the argument effective? Why or why not?

The argument relies on only one example of government spending. Multiple examples would be more convincing. The argument would also benefit from a more specific explanation of the accountability the author wants.

The mix of emotional and logical appeals might be convincing, but the author makes some generalizations that show bias. The statements that all government employees are careless with the public's money and that government never changes weaken the argument.

Practice It!

Read the passage and answer the questions that follow.

I know I'm overweight. I know I need to be healthier. But I'm not going on a diet; that's the worst thing I could do. Many of my friends, coworkers, and acquaintances have gone on diets. They lose weight and then fall back into poor eating habits. They gain back all the weight they lost and more. Although diets have short-term benefits, they are harmful to our bodies in the long run. Do you want to struggle and starve to lose weight, only to gain more weight and be less healthy in the long run? Of course not!

Diets give you rigid rules to follow about what you can and can't eat, and they limit you to miniscule amounts of calories per day. That makes diets hard to follow, and worse, a low-calorie diet can slow your metabolism. Your body may interpret low calorie intake as starvation. The body's reaction is to conserve energy. When you inevitably break your hard-to-stick-with diet, you flood your slowed-down, energy conserving body with foods—usually all the wrong ones. Of course you gain weight!

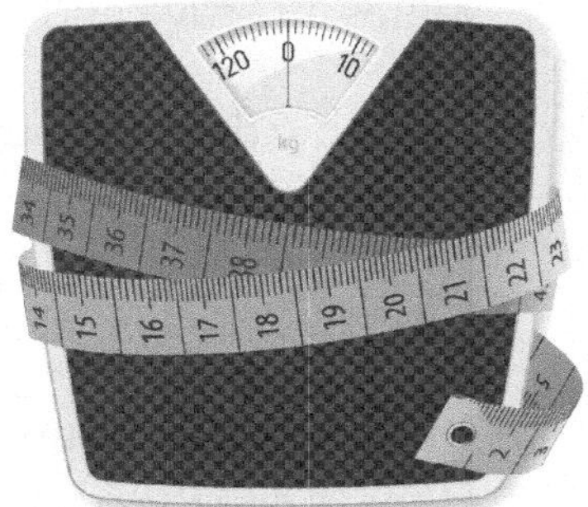

The key is not to diet, but instead to start eating more balanced, healthy foods, including fresh vegetables, whole grains, and nuts. Alongside sensible nutrition changes, start exercising. Make small changes, and soon you'll start seeing improvements. That's what I plan to do.

1. What is the author's claim?

2. What evidence does the author provide to support the claim?

3. Does the author's argument contain any fallacies? If so, explain them.

4. Explain how the author uses pathos, logos, and ethos.

5. Evaluate the argument's effectiveness.

Read the passage and answer the questions that follow.

With the advent of new technology, jobs will be lost. Our economy will be out of balance. It's time to start taking action now to prevent a painful period of adjustment. We should begin shortening the work week and securing a living wage and benefits for our workforce.

Think about the self-driving car—a car driven entirely by a computer program. This new technology already exists and has proven to be reliable. Trucking and taxi companies will switch to self-driving cars, and thousands of drivers will lose their jobs. The whole shipping and transportation industry will be disrupted.

Think about 3D printing technology. Already there are home 3D printers that can create small plastic objects from digital files. Someday, we won't need to ship items across the country or go to the store to pick up what we want. We'll simply download files over the Internet and print our own shoes, cups, or bird feeders. Manufacturing employees will lose their jobs.

Humanity needs to recognize that we don't have to work as hard anymore to provide the same quality of life. Casting thousands of workers into poverty won't help anyone. The solution is to change our idea of work. We don't need 40-hour work weeks and a minimum wage that won't buy the basic necessities. We need more free time and the money to take advantage of the self-driving cars and 3D printers that are on the way.

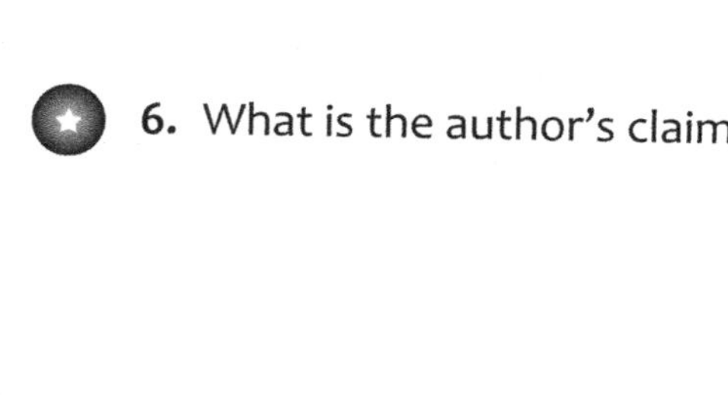

6. What is the author's claim?

7. What evidence does the author provide to support the claim?

8. Does the author's argument contain any fallacies? If so, explain them.

9. Explain how the author uses pathos, logos, and ethos.

10. Evaluate the argument's effectiveness.

Check Your Skills

On June 12, 1987, President Ronald Reagan made a speech in Berlin, near the wall that had divided East Germany and West Germany since the early 1960s. This passage is an excerpt from that speech, in which President Reagan called on General Secretary Gorbachev of the USSR to tear down the Berlin Wall.

Read the passage and answer the questions that follow.

In the 1950s, Khrushchev predicted: "We will bury you." But in the West today, we see a free world that has achieved a level of prosperity and well-being unprecedented in all human history. In the Communist world, we see failure, technological backwardness, declining standards of health, even want of the most basic kind—too little food. Even today, the Soviet Union still cannot feed itself. After these four decades, then, there stands before the entire world one great and inescapable conclusion: Freedom leads to prosperity. Freedom replaces the ancient hatreds among the nations with comity and peace. Freedom is the victor.

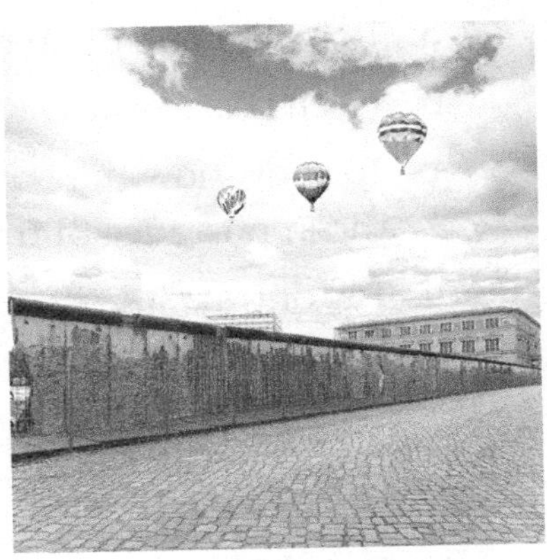

The remains of the Berlin Wall in Berlin, Germany

And now the Soviets themselves may, in a limited way, be coming to understand the importance of freedom. We hear much from Moscow about a new policy of reform and openness. Some political prisoners have been released. Certain foreign news broadcasts are no longer being jammed. Some economic enterprises have been permitted to operate with greater freedom from state control. Are these the beginnings of profound changes in the Soviet state? Or are they token gestures, intended to raise false hopes in the West, or to strengthen the Soviet system without changing it? We welcome change and openness; for we believe that freedom and security go together, that the advance of human liberty can only strengthen the cause of world peace.

There is one sign the Soviets can make that would be unmistakable, that would advance dramatically the cause of freedom and peace. General Secretary Gorbachev, if you seek peace, if you seek prosperity for the Soviet Union and Eastern Europe, if you seek liberalization: Come here to this gate! Mr. Gorbachev, open this gate! Mr. Gorbachev, tear down this wall!

Source: From Speech at the Brandenburg Gate, West Berlin, Germany, by Ronald Reagan, June 12, 1987, available at http://www.historyplace.com/speeches/reagan-tear-down.htm

Remember the Concept

How much evidence is there?

What kind of evidence is there?

What conclusions are drawn from the evidence?

1. What value does Reagan most appeal to in this passage?
   - a. Openness
   - b. Prosperity
   - c. Competitiveness
   - d. Freedom

2. Reagan quotes Khrushchev as saying "We will bury you." Why does Reagan refer to this quote?
   - a. To be fair and open-minded toward Soviet ideas
   - b. To emphasize how Khrushchev was wrong
   - c. To show how the Soviets are coming to understand the importance of freedom
   - d. To contrast Khrushchev with Gorbachev

3. Reagan asks if indications of change in Moscow are "token gestures." Why?
   - a. To question the sincerity of the actions of the Soviet Union
   - b. To belittle the accomplishments of Gorbachev in the Soviet Union
   - c. To acknowledge the gestures the Soviet Union has made toward change
   - d. To show how little Gorbachev values the release of political prisoners

4. "Even today, the Soviet Union still cannot feed itself."

   Which of the following best describes this quotation?
   - a. An emotional appeal to assist the Soviet Union in embracing freedom
   - b. A logical fallacy that plays on two meanings of the phrase "feed itself"
   - c. Part of a logical argument that Soviet Communism is inferior
   - d. A disparaging comment making a personal attack on Gorbachev

5. Which of the following is a possible counterargument to the first paragraph of the passage?
   - a. South Africa has the largest economy in Africa, despite high unemployment.
   - b. India has a growing economy under a parliamentary government.
   - c. Brazil has the sixth largest world economy, despite problems with poverty.
   - d. China has a growing economy under a Communist government.

Comparing Nonfiction

Connections

Comparing texts helps you . . .

- Decide what to buy.
- Choose your position on an issue.
- Understand conflicting opinions.

When you compare, you look at similarities and differences. You build deeper understanding and uncover surprising relationships.

To make a comparison, you need:

- **Frame of reference:** What qualities are you comparing? In nonfiction, you might compare the authors' ideas, perspective, arguments, purpose, tone, or structure.
- **Grounds for comparison:** Why are you making this comparison? Your purpose will determine what kind of comparison you make. If you're trying to decide on a candidate for mayor, you might compare arguments for and against the opponents. If you're learning about a historical period, you might compare two authors' perspectives from that time.

Comparing with a Graphic Organizer

A graphic organizer, such as a Venn diagram or T-chart, can help you identify similarities and differences. Then, you can evaluate those comparisons.

Use these letters for the exercises that follow.

To Whom It May Concern:

My name is Katherine Perez, and I am applying for the graphic designer position at Signs & Banners. I am artistic, detail-oriented, and agreeable. My goal is to make the client happy by providing artwork that satisfies us both.

For six years, I have been a stay-at-home mom. During that time I participated in community and school art projects, including deigning the mural outside the gymnasium at Mead Elementary. I also earned an associate's degree in graphic design at Carbridge Community College, where I mastered the technical requirements of this position. I am attaching a few sample signs and banners that I created. Now that my children are in school, I am ready to take on a full-time position.

Signs & Banners is known for its friendly service and high-quality artwork. I was impressed with the holiday banners your company created for the city last year. I would love to work in a professional, creative, team environment where I can learn more and contribute to the company. Please feel free to call me any time.

Sincerely,

Katherine Perez

To Whom It May Concern:

My name is Emem Hendricks, and I would like the job of graphic designer. I have loved to draw since I was a boy. I created and published my own graphic novel, and I won a third-place prize for one of my drawings at the state fair last year. I know that I would be good at working with clients and making signs and banners. I am attaching some sample artwork so that you can see my style.

I am fast, professional, lively, and humorous. I am available to begin immediately, as my current job does not require notice. I enjoy socializing, playing sports, and staying active—so I will be a good addition at the office! I will also be happy to work outside when it's required, to evaluate the locations of signage.

I look forward to the opportunity to put my creativity and artistic talent to work. Please call me at your convenience.

Sincerely,

Emem Hendricks

D *Determine the Purpose*

Imagine you are trying to help your boss make a decision about which candidate to call in for a job interview. Your boss asks you to compare their cover letters.

? 1. What is the purpose of comparing the cover letters?

By comparing, you can understand which candidate is more likely to be a good choice for the position.

A *Approach the Text*

Before you read, think about what qualities you will compare. Based on the qualities you want to compare, make a plan for comparison.

? 2. What qualities would you compare in these cover letters for a receptionist position?

In these cover letters, you might want to compare:

- The authors' tones to understand the authors' attitudes toward the job.
- The authors' arguments why they would be good for the job.
- The authors' backgrounds, skills, and qualifications.

You might decide to use a T-chart to make a side-by-side comparison.

Reading for Understanding

Look for details, quotations, and words that show the similarities and differences between the passages.

R Read

As you read, note details related to the elements you want to compare, and start filling out the T-chart.

3. List relevant qualities of each applicant's letter on the T-chart.

K. Perez	E. Hendricks
Currently not employed	Currently employed

Perez describes her schooling, art experience, and willingness to work with clients. She also projects a confident image in her tone. She has researched the company. Perez explains specifically why she wants to work in the office, mentioning banners that the company created. Her art samples are signs and banners, appropriate to the job.

Hendricks mentions examples of his personal art (a graphic novel and drawing), but he gives no technical qualifications. Hendricks describes his personal traits but doesn't provide evidence that he knows what's involved in making signs. He also doesn't explain why he wants to work at this particular business.

Both authors are applying for the same position and encourage the office to call.

E Evaluate

When you compare, it's important to draw conclusions. By evaluating a comparison, you can make a decision or gain a deeper understanding of what you've read.

4. Which applicant would you recommend for the job, based on the cover letters? Why?

The first cover letter is stronger because of its details and its confident tone. The second cover letter is vague and doesn't provide an effective argument why the applicant would be good for the job. The first cover letter is more persuasive.

Practice It!

Use the advertisements and Venn diagram to answer the questions that follow.

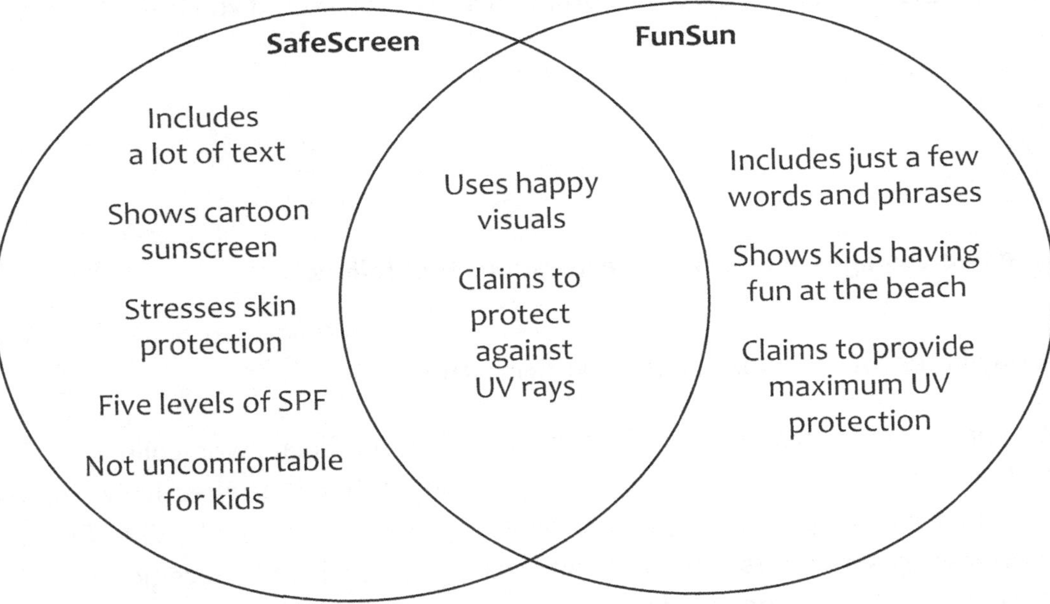

1. What is being compared in this Venn diagram?
   a. The number of products each advertisement sold
   b. The information and visuals in the advertisements
   c. The customer reactions to the advertisements
   d. The quality of the writing in each advertisement

2. What is the primary difference between the two advertisements?

3. What similarity between the advertisements will likely attract viewers?

4. What changes could be made to the advertisements to make them more effective?

5. If you were the consumer, which brand of sunscreen would you buy? Why?

Read the two passages and answer the questions that follow.

A Day in the Life of a CIA Logistics Officer: Ann

As a professional logistician at the CIA, I ensure CIA officers, who collect, analyze and report intelligence to US policymakers, can do their jobs effectively. Some of my duties include purchasing a wide variety of equipment used by CIA officers, coordinating shipments worldwide and managing stock and strategic supply items in support of the Agency's worldwide mission.

Since the world is ever changing, my assignments can change dramatically within weeks, days or even minutes. Often times, the success of the mission depends on me—like all DS professionals—being flexible, agile and organized.

I have traveled around the world to provide direct support to our officers. While overseas, I have contributed to a variety of mission requirements, such as managing finances, travel coordination and procurements.

I applied to the CIA because I wanted to serve the public and felt I could make a contribution to the CIA's mission. What I found is an exciting job that takes me all over the world, keeps me on my toes, teaches me new skills and exposes me to different people, ideas and values. I truly believe that I have made a difference as a CIA logistics officer supporting our global mission.

Source: CIA, adapted from "A Day in the Life of a CIA Logistics Officer: Ann, Logistics Officer, three years with the CIA," https://www.cia.gov/news-information/featured-story-archive/2013-featured-story-archive/cia-logistics-officer.html

A Day in the Life of a CIA Data Scientist: Cameron

Four years ago, Cameron, a data scientist, left his job in the private sector to embark on a career at the CIA.

In his previous job, Cameron analyzed large sets of disparate data to help companies make smart, profitable decisions. Once he arrived at the CIA, he quickly found that his skills clearly transferred to the intelligence profession, where his work for the Directorate of Science & Technology now informs actions and decisions that protect our nation.

On one level, Cameron sees similarities between his former and current jobs. He says, "In both positions, I use algorithms, systems, math, computers, and people to rapidly find actionable intelligence in large, complicated data sets." But some parts of the jobs diverge. He says, "There's a tactical aspect to working at the CIA that didn't exist in my previous jobs. Now I'm looking at data around specific events or threats. I'm trying to glean insights that can prevent something harmful from happening, or I'm trying to find out why or how something did happen."

Cameron points to his colleagues as one of the reasons he finds working at the CIA so rewarding. "The people here are dedicated, hard working, reliable, and industrious," he says. "They're even more results-oriented than people I worked with in the private industry because the stakes are much higher."

Cameron acknowledges that data scientists fetch higher salaries in the private sector, but he looks at the value of his work through a different prism now. He says, "On any given day, the rewards of working here are immeasurable. I've seen the intelligence I provided play out in world events. That's mind-blowing. We're working to save the lives of our family, friends and neighbors. You can't put a value on that."

Source: CIA, adapted from "A Day in the Life of a CIA Data Scientist," https://www.cia.gov/news-information/featured-story-archive/2013-featured-story-archive/cia-data-scientist.html

6. Create a Venn diagram or T-chart to compare the jobs of a CIA Data Scientist and a CIA Logistics Officer.

7. Molly is an organized, detail-oriented person. She has experience with accounting and working as an executive assistant. Is she more qualified to be a logistics officer or a data scientist? Why?

8. Which position is most likely a higher pressure position? Explain your reasoning.

9. Compare Cameron's job in the private sector and his job at the CIA.

10. What are the main differences between the data scientist and logistics officer positions?

11. What characteristics do a data scientist and a logistics officer need to succeed?

Check Your Skills

Read the letters to the editor and answer the questions that follow.

Contributing to Society

We underestimate the potential of teachers. Last Sunday, the newspaper ran a story about Miss Orowitz, a high school teacher. Miss Orowitz extends herself beyond what we expect from a teacher. Noel, a sophomore, revealed that Miss Orowitz arrives early every day to assure that students don't need to stand out in the cold. She provides snacks for hungry students. She has the courage to have down-to-earth conversations about critical topics with Noel and her other students.

Miss Orowitz positively affects her students' lives by going the extra mile and helping her students see the possibility of a better life. My question is, since our children are so important, why are the simple, kind actions that Miss Orowitz takes the "extra mile"? Why doesn't our school system pick up Miss Orowitz's banner and train all our teachers to act as mentors and helpers? Teachers can do much more than give standardized tests! We would decrease suspensions, violence, conflicts, and most important of all—dropout rates.

Marina Hines

Value Our Teachers!

Last week, this paper published a letter from Marina Hines calling for schools to train teachers to act as mentors and helpers.

I have been a teacher for 21 years. Throughout these years, I have fed students, lent them jackets, bought metro passes, counseled them, supported them, exposed them to new ideas, attended their weddings and occasionally funerals, and guided them toward better futures.

I know I am not alone. Teaching is more than just a job. We care. We extend ourselves beyond the limit each day. Miss Orowitz is not one teacher standing out in a crowd. She represents all the caring teachers who go unrecognized throughout our school districts. Maybe the reason Hines thinks we don't exist is that we're too focused on caring for our students to look for recognition.

Mark Vasquez

1. What is Hines' central idea?
   a. The school system should train teachers to mentor students and help at-risk students.
   b. The school system can't train teachers to work with at-risk students because it is instinctual.
   c. The school system needs to pay teachers more money so they can go the extra mile for students.
   d. The school system makes teachers responsible for saving students from all risky behavior.

2. What is Vasquez's central idea?
   a. Teachers need to be paid more money.
   b. Teachers already have to intervene too often in their students' lives.
   c. Teachers already go above and beyond without receiving recognition.
   d. Teachers deserve raises for all that they do.

3. Compare the two letters to the editor. Which has the stronger argument? Provide evidence from both letters to support your conclusions.

Remember the Concept

Compare similarities and differences using graphic organizers.

Draw conclusions when you compare texts.

Reading Fiction Texts

When you read fiction, your purpose is typically enjoyment. Your choice of books and stories will be based on your personal tastes. As you approach the reading, you may preview books and stories to find ones that you'll enjoy. People who read for pleasure are often the best readers. Reading for pleasure helps you improve your reading comprehension, vocabulary, and speed.

Fiction is a creative venture. Authors let their imaginations and their understanding of the human condition guide their stories and books. When we share fiction, we share thoughts and ideas about human nature.

Fiction texts have many of the same elements as television shows and movies. The reader is emotionally invested in the plot and characters. When you study fiction texts as literature, you try to find more meaning in them. This can help you enjoy them more. You can examine common themes and how they relate to humanity and the world. You can explore genres and how different works of literature are related to each other. You can look at how authors use language and symbolism to convey meaning.

This section will cover important elements of fiction:

- **Theme and Author's Purpose**
  Learn to identify the message that the author is trying to convey in a book or story.

- **Support for a Theme**
  Examine the text to find support for the theme and understand the theme in greater depth.

- **Details in Fiction**
  Identify important details and how they relate to the plot, characters, and theme of a work of fiction.

- **Word Choice**
  Evaluate the author's word choice and what specific words add to the text.

- **Figurative Language**
  Learn how to recognize figurative language and identify its meaning.

- **Characters**
  Analyze characters and their interactions to understand their motivations and significance to the text.

- **Story Structure and Conflict**
  Find the important elements of the story's structure and understand how those elements relate to the dramatic conflict.

- **Setting, Tone, Genre, and Style**
  Examine the author's style through setting, tone, genre, and other elements of style that affect a book or story.

- **Point of View**
  Identify the point of view in a fiction text and how it affects your experience of the text.

- **Comparing Fiction**
  Compare fiction texts to evaluate meaning and understand themes, characters, and other literary elements.

Theme and Author's Purpose

Connections

Have you ever...

- Left a movie with a new idea about the world?
- Wondered why a character was so cruel?
- Wished a tragedy in a book didn't have to happen?

Authors write with a purpose in mind. Through the characters, plot, setting, and other details in a book or story, the author is communicating a universal message about life and our world—the **theme**.

A **theme** is a message about life contained in a literary work. Usually, the theme is not stated directly. You infer the theme through events, symbolism, characters' actions, and dialogue.

Theme = Message

The **author's purpose** is the author's reason for writing or relationship with what they are writing. The theme an author chooses depends on his or her purpose for writing.

Understanding the theme and the author's purpose can make reading more interesting and relevant. You form connections with the characters, events, and ideas by relating to your own world. Different works convey themes in different ways. You can often identify the theme through:

- Important symbols.
- Repeated ideas.
- Significant issues.

What the Characters Learn

Literary works use many different techniques to show a theme. A common one is through the conflict and the characters. To identify a theme, look for a problem and what the characters learn from the problem.

The Red Badge of Courage by Stephen Crane tells the story of Henry Fleming, a solider who is drawn to the glory of war. In this passage, Henry has yet to fight and is becoming anxious.

Use this passage for the exercises that follow.

There was a more serious problem. He lay in his bunk pondering upon it. He tried to mathematically prove to himself that he would not run from a battle.

Previously he had never felt obliged to wrestle too seriously with this question. In his life he had taken certain things for granted, never challenging his belief in ultimate success, and bothering little about means and roads. But here he was confronted with a thing of moment. It had suddenly appeared to him that perhaps in a battle he might run. He was forced to admit that as far as war was concerned he knew nothing of himself.

A sufficient time before he would have allowed the problem to kick its heels at the outer portals of his mind, but now he felt compelled to give serious attention to it.

A little panic-fear grew in his mind. As his imagination went forward to a fight, he saw hideous possibilities. He contemplated the lurking menaces of the future, and failed in an effort to see himself standing stoutly in the midst of them. He recalled his visions of broken-bladed glory, but in the shadow of the impending tumult he suspected them to be impossible pictures.

He sprang from the bunk and began to pace nervously to and fro. "Good Lord, what's th' matter with me?" he said aloud.

He felt that in this crisis his laws of life were useless. Whatever he had learned of himself was here of no avail. He was an unknown quantity. He saw that he would again be obliged to experiment as he had in early youth. He must accumulate information of himself, and meanwhile he resolved to remain close upon his guard lest those qualities of which he knew nothing should everlastingly disgrace him.

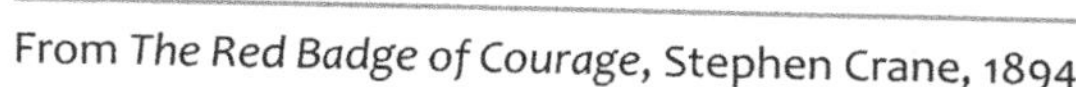
From *The Red Badge of Courage*, Stephen Crane, 1894

Identify the Problem

As you read, look for an important problem that the characters face.

?

1. What is the problem in this passage?

Henry is afraid that he will run when it comes time to fight. The problem relates to courage.

> **Reading for Understanding**
>
> The theme helps you get more out of your reading. You'll understand important details and ideas about the characters if you understand the theme.

Identify What the Character Learns

It's common for stories or novels to revolve around a problem and its resolution. When a problem is resolved, a character often learns a lesson in the process. In this passage, the problem is not yet fully resolved, but Henry decides to learn about himself, a temporary resolution.

?

2. What does Henry learn from the resolution of the problem?

At this point, Henry discovers that what he knows about himself so far is incomplete and useless in his current situation. He must learn more about himself in order to resolve the problem.

Determine the Universal Message

To find the theme, think about how the problem applies to humanity and the world. Does the character learn a lesson that can apply to humanity as a whole? What is the author trying to say? A theme is more than a simple idea, such as *justice* or *revenge*. In this passage, the theme relates to *courage*. What is the author saying about courage?

?

3. What is the theme of the passage?

You might state the theme in a number of ways, such as: "Courage requires facing the truth about yourself." or "Courage requires learning about yourself."

The full title of Mary Shelley's famous novel, commonly known as *Frankenstein*, is *Frankenstein; or, The Modern Prometheus*. In the title, Shelley compares Dr. Victor Frankenstein to the Greek mythical figure Prometheus, who created man. *Frankenstein* tells the story of Dr. Victor Frankenstein and the monster that Frankenstein created.

Read the passage and answer the questions that follow.

The different accidents of life are not so changeable as the feelings of human nature. I had worked hard for nearly two years, for the sole purpose of infusing life into an inanimate body. For this I had deprived myself of rest and health. I had desired it with an ardour that far exceeded moderation; but now that I had finished, the beauty of the dream vanished, and breathless horror and disgust filled my heart. Unable to endure the aspect of the being I had created, I rushed out of the room and continued a long time traversing my bed-chamber, unable to compose my mind to sleep. At length lassitude succeeded to the tumult I had before endured, and I threw myself on the bed in my clothes, endeavouring to seek a few moments of forgetfulness. But it was in vain; I slept, indeed, but I was disturbed by the wildest dreams. I thought I saw Elizabeth, in the bloom of health, walking in the streets of Ingolstadt. Delighted and surprised, I embraced her, but as I imprinted the first kiss on her lips, they became livid with the hue of death; her features appeared to change, and I thought that I held the corpse of my dead mother in my arms; a shroud enveloped her form, and I saw the grave-worms crawling in the folds of the flannel. I started from my sleep with horror; a cold dew covered my forehead, my teeth chattered, and every limb became convulsed; when, by the dim and yellow light of the moon, as it forced its way through the window shutters, I beheld the wretch—the miserable monster whom I had created. He held up the curtain of the bed; and his eyes, if eyes they may be called, were fixed on me. His jaws opened, and he muttered some inarticulate sounds, while a grin wrinkled his cheeks. He might have spoken, but I did not hear; one hand was stretched out, seemingly to detain me, but I escaped and rushed downstairs. I took refuge in the courtyard belonging to the house which I inhabited, where I remained during the rest of the night, walking up and down in the greatest agitation, listening attentively, catching and fearing each sound as if it were to announce the approach of the demoniacal corpse to which I had so miserably given life.

From *Frankenstein; or, The Modern Prometheus*, Mary Shelley, 1818

1. What happens in the passage?
   - a. The narrator sees his dead wife Elizabeth.
   - b. The narrator realizes he has created a monster.
   - c. The narrator must run to keep from being killed by the monster.
   - d. The narrator cannot go inside his own home.

2. What is the problem?
   - a. The narrator tried to bring his wife back to life, and instead, brings back a monster.
   - b. The narrator tried in vain to bring a man back to life with no success.
   - c. The narrator is losing his sense of reality and doesn't know what is real anymore.
   - d. The narrator wanted to bring a man back to life and now must deal with the consequences.

3. What does the narrator likely learn from his experience?
   - a. He should have considered the consequences of bringing something dead back to life.
   - b. He should have considered the feelings of the dead before messing with the laws of nature.
   - c. He has wasted a lot of time and energy failing to bring something dead back to life.
   - d. He needs to be sure he has no doubts about doing something before he does it.

4. Which of the following is the best statement of a theme of this work?
   - a. There is often more to people than meets the eye.
   - b. Bringing the dead back to life is never a good idea.
   - c. The pursuit of knowledge can be destructive.
   - d. Make sure you can live your life with no regrets.

5. Write a short paragraph that relates the theme to your own life or the present-day world.

The short story "Clay" by James Joyce is about Maria, a woman who works in a laundry. In the following passage, Maria visits Joe, a boy she helped raise.

Read the passage and answer the questions that follow.

She decided to buy some plumcake but Downes's plumcake had not enough almond icing on top of it so she went over to a shop in Henry Street. Here she was a long time in suiting herself and the stylish young lady behind the counter, who was evidently a little annoyed by her, asked her was it wedding-cake she wanted to buy. That made Maria blush and smile at the young lady; but the young lady took it all very seriously and finally cut a thick slice of plumcake, parcelled it up and said:

"Two-and-four, please."

She thought she would have to stand in the Drumcondra tram because none of the young men seemed to notice her but an elderly gentleman made room for her. He was a stout gentleman and he wore a brown hard hat; he had a square red face and a greyish moustache. Maria thought he was a colonel-looking gentleman and she reflected how much more polite he was than the young men who simply stared straight before them.

The gentleman began to chat with her about Hallow Eve and the rainy weather. He supposed the bag was full of good things for the little ones and said it was only right that the youngsters should enjoy themselves while they were young. Maria agreed with him and favoured him with demure nods and hems. He was very nice with her, and when she was getting out at the Canal Bridge she thanked him and bowed, and he bowed to her and raised his hat and smiled agreeably, and while she was going up along the terrace, bending her tiny head under the rain, she thought how easy it was to know a gentleman even when he has a drop taken.

Everybody said: "O, here's Maria!" when she came to Joe's house. Joe was there, having come home from business, and all the children had their Sunday dresses on. There were two big girls in from next door and games were going on. Maria gave the bag of cakes to the eldest boy, Alphy, to divide and Mrs. Donnelly said it was too good of her to bring such a big bag of cakes and made all the children say:

"Thanks, Maria."

But Maria said she had brought something special for papa and mamma, something they would be sure to like, and she began to look for her plumcake. She tried in Downes's bag and then in the pockets of her waterproof and then on the hallstand but nowhere could she find it. Then she asked all the children had any of them eaten it—by mistake, of course—but the children all said no and looked as if they did not like to eat cakes if they were to be accused of stealing. Everybody had a solution for the mystery and Mrs. Donnelly said it was plain that Maria had left it behind her in the tram. Maria, remembering how confused the gentleman with the greyish moustache had made her, coloured with shame and vexation and disappointment. At the thought of the failure of her little surprise and of the two and fourpence she had thrown away for nothing she nearly cried outright.

But Joe said it didn't matter and made her sit down by the fire. He was very nice with her.

From "Clay" by James Joyce, 1914

6. What problem does Maria face with the cake? Why?

7. What other problem can you infer that Maria faces, based on her encounters in the bakery and on the train?

8. How does Maria resolve her problems?

9. What might Maria learn from her problems and the resolution?

10. What theme can you infer from the passage?

11. Relate the theme of the passage to your own life.

12. In a full paragraph, compare the themes in the passages from "Clay" on page 226 and *The Red Badge of Courage* on page 222.

Reading for Understanding

Understanding theme and purpose can add to the reader's enjoyment and fulfillment because it makes the reading more interesting.

Check Your Skills

"The Story of the Bad Little Boy," by Mark Twain, tells the story of a mischievous boy named Jim.

Read the passage and answer the questions that follow.

Once [Jim] stole the teacher's pen-knife, and, when he was afraid it would be found out and he would get whipped, he slipped it into George Wilson's cap—poor Widow Wilson's son, the moral boy, the good little boy of the village, who always obeyed his mother, and never told an untruth, and was fond of his lessons, and infatuated with Sunday-school. And when the knife dropped from the cap, and poor George hung his head and blushed, as if in conscious guilt, and the grieved teacher charged the theft upon him, and was just in the very act of bringing the switch down upon his trembling shoulders, a white-haired improbable justice of the peace did not suddenly appear in their midst, and strike an attitude and say, "Spare this noble boy—there stands the cowering culprit! I was passing the school-door at recess, and unseen myself, I saw the theft committed!" And then Jim didn't get whaled, and the venerable justice didn't read the tearful school a homily and take George by the hand and say such a boy deserved to be exalted, and then tell him to come and make his home with him, and sweep out the office, and make fires, and run errands, and chop wood, and study law, and help his wife to do household labors, and have all the balance of the time to play, and get forty cents a month, and be happy. No; it would have happened that way in the books, but it didn't happen that way to Jim. No meddling old clam of a justice dropped in to make trouble, and so the model boy George got thrashed, and Jim was glad of it because, you know, Jim hated moral boys. Jim said he was "down on them milk-sops." Such was the coarse language of this bad, neglected boy.

From "The Story of the Bad Little Boy" by Mark Twain, 1875

1. Which conclusion can you make about Jim?
   a. Jim gets in trouble a lot but he is misunderstood.
   b. Jim is a model student who gets unfairly blamed.
   c. Jim sometimes is a good boy but his friends get him into trouble.
   d. Jim is a troublemaker who doesn't get caught.

2. Which conclusion can you make about George?
   a. George often misbehaves and usually gets caught.
   b. George never does anything wrong but gets punished unfairly.
   c. George often joins Jim in his misbehavior.
   d. George and Jim never do anything wrong but both get punished.

3. Which of the following is the author's message?
   a. Stories portray unrealistic ideas of justice and good versus evil.
   b. Justice is always served in one way or another.
   c. The wrong people always get punished.
   d. Most people aren't all good or all bad.

4. Which quotation from the passage most directly relates to the theme?
   a. "Once [Jim] stole the teacher's pen-knife..."
   b. "...the good little boy of the village, who always obeyed his mother, and never told an untruth."
   c. "...when the knife dropped from the cap, and poor George hung his head and blushed, as if in conscious guilt."
   d. "And then Jim didn't get whaled, and the venerable justice didn't read the tearful school a homily."

5. What can you infer from this quotation: "when the knife dropped from the cap, and poor George hung his head and blushed"?
   a. George has hidden guilt about something.
   b. George blushes because he realizes he looks guilty.
   c. George has a deep fear of even small knives.
   d. George blushes because he believes someone will save him from the awkward situation.

Remember the Concept

Theme = Message

Find the theme by:

- Asking what the character learns.
- Looking for repeated ideas or symbols.

Support for a Theme

Connections

Have you ever…

- Connected a character's behavior with a bigger idea?
- Found a movie quote meaningful?
- Seen a parallel between two scenes that might have a greater meaning?

Finding support for a theme can help you understand why events are important and how the author's message can apply to specific situations.

Supporting a theme with details is important. It helps you show that your idea of the theme is correct, and it helps you understand the theme more deeply.

Support for a theme can include…

- Something a character does.
- The way a character responds.
- How characters interact.
- A detail given by the narrator.
- The way events are connected.

Connecting Support with a Theme

Finding support for a theme is about explaining specific details in the text. You can use an **evidence-explanation table** to look at how details support a theme.

Sister Carrie by Theodore Dreiser is a novel about a young girl who moves to the big city of Chicago.

Use this passage for the exercises that follow.

When a girl leaves her home at eighteen, she does one of two things. Either she falls into saving hands and becomes better, or she rapidly assumes the cosmopolitan standard of virtue and becomes worse. Of an intermediate balance, under the circumstances, there is no possibility. The city has its cunning wiles, no less than the infinitely smaller and more human tempter. There are large forces which allure with all the soulfulness of expression possible in the most cultured human. The gleam of a thousand lights is often as effective as the persuasive light in a wooing and fascinating eye. Half the undoing of the unsophisticated and natural mind is accomplished by forces wholly superhuman. A blare of sound, a roar of life, a vast array of human hives, appeal to the astonished senses in equivocal terms. Without a counsellor at hand to whisper cautious interpretations, what falsehoods may not these things breathe into the unguarded ear! Unrecognised for what they are, their beauty, like music, too often relaxes, then weakens, then perverts the simpler human perceptions.

Caroline, or Sister Carrie, as she had been half affectionately termed by the family, was possessed of a mind rudimentary in its power of observation and analysis. Self-interest with her was high, but not strong. It was, nevertheless, her guiding characteristic. Warm with the fancies of youth, pretty with the insipid prettiness of the formative period, possessed of a figure promising eventual shapeliness and an eye alight with certain native intelligence, she was a fair example of the middle American class—two generations removed from the emigrant.

From *Sister Carrie* by Theodore Dreiser, 1900

Find Words Related to the Theme

After you've read the text and identified a theme, you'll want to back up your theme with evidence. Scan the text for keywords related to the theme. If the theme is related to justice, look for words with a similar meaning or examples of justice.

?

1. The novel's theme is related to chasing the American dream. What keywords in the passage relate to the theme?

There are many keywords you might choose, such as *cosmopolitan, forces, allure, cultured, gleam, blare, roar, self-interest, fancies, eventual,* or *American.*

Find Phrases That Support the Theme

Read the sentence or paragraph containing the keyword. What does the whole phrase containing the keyword mean? Choose phrases or sentences that seem to say something about the theme.

?

2. List three phrases on the left-hand side of the **evidence-explanation table**.

Evidence	Explanation

Here are some possible phrases you could choose:

- "Either she falls into saving hands and becomes better"
- "Assumes the cosmopolitan standard of virtue and becomes worse"
- "Large forces which allure with all the soulfulness of expression possible"
- "The gleam of a thousand lights"
- "Persuasive light in a wooing and fascinating eye"
- "A blare of sound, a roar of life, a vast array of human hives"
- "Self-interest with her was high"

Explain the Connection

Look at each phrase. How does it connect to the theme? What does it say about the theme? Add the explanation to the table.

? **3.** In the right-hand column of the table, explain how each phrase connects to the theme.

Evidence	Explanation
"Assumes the cosmopolitan standard of virtue and becomes worse"	
"Large forces which allure with all the soulfulness of expression possible"	
"The gleam of a thousand lights"	

Draw a Conclusion That Expands the Theme

Read over the table. Does the information give you a deeper understanding of the theme? Would you revise or further develop the theme based on the support?

Evidence	Explanation
"Assumes the cosmopolitan standard of virtue and becomes worse"	Adopting the city life means losing your morals.
"Large forces which allure with all the soulfulness of expression possible"	The American dream may mean leaving your simple life for one that has more allure.
"The gleam of a thousand lights"	This relates to the glitz and glamour that many traveling to the city were seeking.

? **4.** How would you state the theme, and what does the evidence show about it?

The theme is about chasing the American dream. You might state the theme as: "The American dream means a loss of innocence." The evidence shows that the American dream is not necessarily wholesome, nor does it come easy. It draws you in with excitement, but you may have to sacrifice the things you value as you search for your dream.

The story "The Happy Prince" by Oscar Wilde is about a swallow and the statue of a prince, who both perish through giving to the poor.

Read the passage and answer the questions that follow.

"Swallow, Swallow, little Swallow," said the Prince, "far away across the city I see a young man in a garret. He is leaning over a desk covered with papers, and in a tumbler by his side there is a bunch of withered violets. His hair is brown and crisp, and his lips are red as a pomegranate, and he has large and dreamy eyes. He is trying to finish a play for the Director of the Theatre, but he is too cold to write any more. There is no fire in the grate, and hunger has made him faint."

"I will wait with you one night longer," said the Swallow, who really had a good heart. "Shall I take him another ruby?"

"Alas! I have no ruby now," said the Prince; "my eyes are all that I have left. They are made of rare sapphires, which were brought out of India a thousand years ago. Pluck out one of them and take it to him. He will sell it to the jeweller, and buy food and firewood, and finish his play."

"Dear Prince," said the Swallow, "I cannot do that"; and he began to weep.

"Swallow, Swallow, little Swallow," said the Prince, "do as I command you."

So the Swallow plucked out the Prince's eye, and flew away to the student's garret. It was easy enough to get in, as there was a hole in the roof. Through this he darted, and came into the room. The young man had his head buried in his hands, so he did not hear the flutter of the bird's wings, and when he looked up he found the beautiful sapphire lying on the withered violets.

"I am beginning to be appreciated," he cried; "this is from some great admirer. Now I can finish my play," and he looked quite happy.

From "The Happy Prince" by Oscar Wilde, 1888

1. The theme of the passage is about the goodness of unselfish love and giving. What keywords in the passage relate to the theme?

2. Read the sentences containing the keywords. Choose three phrases or sentences that support the theme, and use them to complete the evidence-explanation table.

Evidence	Explanation

3. How does the evidence-explanation table affect your understanding of the theme?

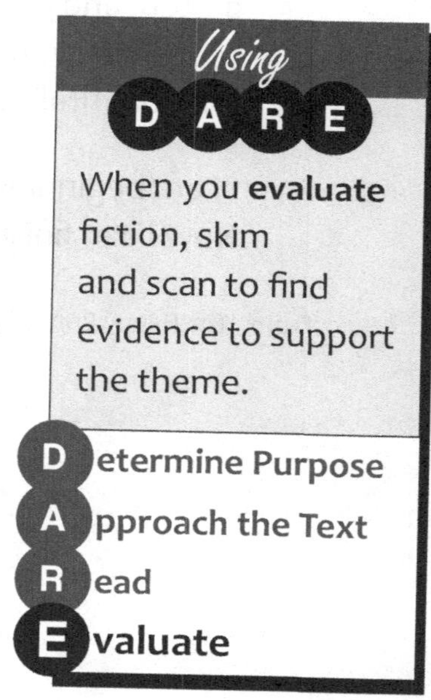

Support for a Theme

The novel *Middlemarch: A Study of Provincial Life* by George Eliot follows the lives of a large cast of characters in the fictional town of Middlemarch, England. Dorothea Brooke is an attractive and idealistic young woman who lives in the town.

Read the passage and answer the questions that follow.

"It was himself he blamed for not speaking," said Dorothea. "What he said of you was, that he could not be happy in doing anything which made you unhappy—that his marriage was of course a bond which must affect his choice about everything; and for that reason he refused my proposal that he should keep his position at the Hospital, because that would bind him to stay in Middlemarch, and he would not undertake to do anything which would be painful to you. He could say that to me, because he knows that I had much trial in my marriage, from my husband's illness, which hindered his plans and saddened him; and he knows that I have felt how hard it is to walk always in fear of hurting another who is tied to us."

Dorothea waited a little; she had discerned a faint pleasure stealing over Rosamond's face. But there was no answer, and she went on, with a gathering tremor, "Marriage is so unlike everything else. There is something even awful in the nearness it brings. Even if we loved some one else better than—than those we were married to, it would be no use"—poor Dorothea, in her palpitating anxiety, could only seize her language brokenly—"I mean, marriage drinks up all our power of giving or getting any blessedness in that sort of love. I know it may be very dear—but it murders our marriage—and then the marriage stays with us like a murder—and everything else is gone. And then our husband—if he loved and trusted us, and we have not helped him, but made a curse in his life—"

Her voice had sunk very low: there was a dread upon her of presuming too far, and of speaking as if she herself were perfection addressing error. She was too much preoccupied with her own anxiety, to be aware that Rosamond was trembling too; and filled with the need to express pitying fellowship rather than rebuke, she put her hands on Rosamond's, and said with more agitated rapidity,—"I know, I know that the feeling may be very dear—it has taken hold of us unawares—it is so hard, it may seem like death to part with it—and we are weak—I am weak—"

From *Middlemarch: A Study of Provincial Life* by George Eliot, 1874

4. The theme of the passage is about the imperfection of marriage. What keywords in the passage relate to the theme?

5. Read the sentences containing the keywords. Choose four phrases or sentences that support the theme, and use them to complete the evidence-explanation table.

Evidence	Explanation

6. How does the evidence-explanation table affect your understanding of the theme?

Reading for Understanding

Finding support for a theme can help you understand why events are important and how the author's message can apply to specific situations.

Check Your Skills

The novel *Jane Eyre* by Charlotte Brontë follows the life of a young orphaned girl.

Read the passage and answer the questions that follow.

I reflected. Poverty looks grim to grown people; still more so to children: they have not much idea of industrious, working, respectable poverty; they think of the word only as connected with ragged clothes, scanty food, fireless grates, rude manners, and debasing vices: poverty for me was synonymous with degradation.

"No; I should not like to belong to poor people," was my reply.

"Not even if they were kind to you?"

I shook my head: I could not see how poor people had the means of being kind; and then to learn to speak like them, to adopt their manners, to be uneducated, to grow up like one of the poor women I saw sometimes nursing their children or washing their clothes at the cottage doors of the village of Gateshead: no, I was not heroic enough to purchase liberty at the price of caste.

"But are your relatives so very poor? Are they working people?"

"I cannot tell; Aunt Reed says if I have any, they must be a beggarly set: I should not like to go a begging."

"Would you like to go to school?"

Again I reflected: I scarcely knew what school was: Bessie sometimes spoke of it as a place where young ladies sat in the stocks, wore backboards, and were expected to be exceedingly genteel and precise: John Reed hated his school, and abused his master; but John Reed's tastes were no rule for mine, and if Bessie's accounts of school-discipline (gathered from the young ladies of a family where she had lived before coming to Gateshead) were somewhat appalling, her details of certain accomplishments attained by these same young ladies were, I thought, equally attractive. She boasted of beautiful paintings of landscapes and flowers by them executed; of songs they could sing and pieces they could play, of purses they could net, of French books they could translate; till my spirit was moved to emulation as I listened. Besides, school would be a complete change: it implied a long journey, an entire separation from Gateshead, an entrance into a new life.

From *Jane Eyre* by Charlotte Brontë, 1847

1. Which quotation from the passage most directly supports the theme that the poor are misunderstood?
    a. "They think of the word only as connected with ragged clothes, scanty food, fireless grates, rude manners, and debasing vices."
    b. "Again I reflected: I scarcely knew what school was."
    c. "John Reed hated his school, and abused his master; but John Reed's tastes were no rule for mine."
    d. "But are your relatives so very poor? Are they working people?"

2. "I could not see how poor people had the means of being kind." What can you infer from this statement?
    a. The narrator doesn't have any concept of kindness.
    b. The narrator associates kindness with material possessions.
    c. The narrator admires people for being kind, although they are poor.
    d. The narrator has experienced kindness from many people.

3. Which adjective might the narrator use to describe her relatives?
    a. Sorrowful
    b. Well intentioned
    c. Nonexistent
    d. Undesirable

4. What does the narrator associate with begging?
    a. Being uneducated and ill-mannered
    b. Having to be out in the sun all day
    c. Being hungry
    d. Making a lot of money without working

5. Based on the details in the passage, what does the author likely believe?
    a. Income is more important than character.
    b. The rich are successful due to hard work.
    c. You can be hard-working but still be poor.
    d. The poor are unsuccessful because they are lazy.

Remember the Concept

To identify and expand on a theme, you need support.

- Find evidence.
- Explain the evidence.

Details in Fiction

Connections

Have you ever...

- Skipped past a long description and later realized you missed something important?
- Described a character as heroic, evil, or kind?
- Read a fascinating prediction about the next season of your favorite show?

In fiction, details help an author communicate a theme, describe the setting and characters, and develop the plot.

Small things sometimes carry a lot of meaning. Smelling a flower could show that a character is romantic. An old photo could symbolize lost memories. A description of a clocktower could represent the passage of time.

Details explain and elaborate on the answers to the 5Ws and H: Who? What? When? Where? Why? How? They give you the complete picture. Details:

- Convey deeper meaning in symbols and metaphors
- Build a picture to show setting and character
- Provide the key to understanding a complicated plot

Using Details to Make Inferences

As a reader, you infer ideas through details. Details are used to develop characters, setting, plot, and theme. They can be found in the text through description, dialogue, and narration.

Inference = Detail + What You Already Know

The short story "The Gift of the Magi" by O. Henry is set in the early 1900s. It tells the story of a young couple, James and Della Dillingham, who buy each other Christmas gifts on their limited budget.

Use the passage for the exercises that follow.

In the vestibule below was a letter-box into which no letter would go, and an electric button from which no mortal finger could coax a ring. Also appertaining thereunto was a card bearing the name "Mr. James Dillingham Young."

The "Dillingham" had been flung to the breeze during a former period of prosperity when its possessor was being paid $30 per week. Now, when the income was shrunk to $20, though, they were thinking seriously of contracting to a modest and unassuming D. But whenever Mr. James Dillingham Young came home and reached his flat above he was called "Jim" and greatly hugged by Mrs. James Dillingham Young, already introduced to you as Della. Which is all very good.

Della finished her cry and attended to her cheeks with the powder rag. She stood by the window and looked out dully at a gray cat walking a gray fence in a gray backyard. Tomorrow would be Christmas Day, and she had only $1.87 with which to buy Jim a present. She had been saving every penny she could for months, with this result. Twenty dollars a week doesn't go far. Expenses had been greater than she had calculated. They always are. Only $1.87 to buy a present for Jim. Her Jim. Many a happy hour she had spent planning for something nice for him. Something fine and rare and sterling—something just a little bit near to being worthy of the honor of being owned by Jim.

From "The Gift of the Magi" by O. Henry, 1905

Preview the Text

Skim the text. Read the title, first paragraph, and topic sentences to identify who and what the text describes. This will help you identify which details are important.

? 1. Who are the major characters in this passage? What is the main problem?

By skimming the passage, you can see that James and Della are important characters. Della wants to buy a present for her husband Jim, but she doesn't have enough money.

Locate Important Details

As you read, what details jump out as important? What seems meaningful?

? 2. Read the first paragraph. Write down two specific details that seem important in the first column of the table.

Detail	What I Already Know	Inference

Here are two details you might choose:

- When income goes down, they think of using "D" instead of "Dillingham."
- James is "greatly hugged" by Della.

Review What You Already Know

What do you know already that can help you make an inference?

? 2. What do you know that can help you make an inference from the details? Add what you know to the chart.

Detail	What I Already Know	Inference
When income goes down, they think of using "D" instead of "Dillingham."		
James is "greatly hugged" by Della.		

You might know:

- When you make less money, you tend to scale back.
- When you are greatly hugged it usually means you are loved.

> **Reading for Understanding**
>
> Evaluating details will help you identify important ideas and how they contribute to the theme and character development.

Make Inferences Using the Details

Details convey important information about the characters, the plot, and the theme. Think about what the details say about each of these elements.

3. What inference can you make about the characters based on each detail? Fill in the right-hand side of the table with inferences about the characters.

Detail	What I Already Know	Inference
When income goes down, they think of using "D" instead of "Dillingham."	When you make less money, you tend to scale back.	
James is "greatly hugged" by Della.	Being hugged usually means you are loved.	

You might infer that the Dillinghams are poorer than they once were and feel that Dillingham is too distinguished of a name for them now. That indicates a lack of pride. You could also infer that although they don't have a lot of money, Della loves James.

4. Try making another inference from the passage.

Detail	What I Already Know	Inference
When income goes down, they think of using "D" instead of "Dillingham."	When you make less money, you tend to scale back.	The Dillinghams are poorer than they once were and are not proud.
James is "greatly hugged" by Della.	Being hugged usually means you are loved.	Although they don't have a lot of money, Della loves James.

The novel *Little Women* by Louisa May Alcott is the story of four sisters who grow up during the Civil War.

Read the passage and answer the questions that follow.

"Really, girls, you are both to be blamed," said Meg, beginning to lecture in her elder-sisterly fashion. "You are old enough to leave off boyish tricks, and to behave better, Josephine. It didn't matter so much when you were a little girl, but now you are so tall, and turn up your hair, you should remember that you are a young lady."

"I'm not! And if turning up my hair makes me one, I'll wear it in two tails till I'm twenty," cried Jo, pulling off her net, and shaking down a chestnut mane. "I hate to think I've got to grow up, and be Miss March, and wear long gowns, and look as prim as a China Aster! It's bad enough to be a girl, anyway, when I like boy's games and work and manners! I can't get over my disappointment in not being a boy. And it's worse than ever now, for I'm dying to go and fight with Papa. And I can only stay home and knit, like a poky old woman!"

And Jo shook the blue army sock till the needles rattled like castanets, and her ball bounded across the room.

"Poor Jo! It's too bad, but it can't be helped. So you must try to be contented with making your name boyish, and playing brother to us girls," said Beth, stroking the rough head with a hand that all the dish washing and dusting in the world could not make ungentle in its touch.

"As for you, Amy," continued Meg, "you are altogether too particular and prim. Your airs are funny now, but you'll grow up an affected little goose, if you don't take care. I like your nice manners and refined ways of speaking, when you don't try to be elegant. But your absurd words are as bad as Jo's slang."

"If Jo is a tomboy and Amy a goose, what am I, please?" asked Beth, ready to share the lecture.

"You're a dear, and nothing else," answered Meg warmly, and no one contradicted her, for the 'Mouse' was the pet of the family.

From *Little Women* by Louisa May Alcott, 1868

1. Who are the major characters in the passage?

Reading for Understanding

To find important ideas, identify significant details and determine what they have in common.

2. What is happening in the passage?

3. Choose three details from the passage, and make three inferences from them using the inference chart.

Detail	What I Already Know	Inference

4. What conclusions can you draw about the conflicts the characters will face?

5. Scott is trying to understand how the setting of the film *The Matrix* affects the plot. Before viewing the movie, how can he plan to use details to do this?

6. Susie is reading *Ender's Game* by Orson Scott Card for her literature class. She needs to write a character analysis of the main character, Ender Wiggin. What should she do while reading to identify details for her character analysis?

7. Walter is reading *The Help* by Kathryn Stockett for his book club. He wants to identify a major theme. What strategy should he use to identify details related to the theme?

Check Your Skills

In this passage from *Great Expectations* by Charles Dickens, Pip, the narrator, has been summoned to visit his wealthy neighbor.

Read the passage and answer the questions that follow.

Though she called me "boy" so often, and with a carelessness that was far from complimentary, she was of about my own age. She seemed much older than I, of course, being a girl, and beautiful and self-possessed; and she was as scornful of me as if she had been one-and-twenty, and a queen.

We went into the house by a side door, the great front entrance had two chains across it outside,—and the first thing I noticed was, that the passages were all dark, and that she had left a candle burning there. She took it up, and we went through more passages and up a staircase, and still it was all dark, and only the candle lighted us.

At last we came to the door of a room, and she said, "Go in."

I answered, more in shyness than politeness, "After you, miss."

To this she returned: "Don't be ridiculous, boy; I am not going in." And scornfully walked away, and—what was worse—took the candle with her.

This was very uncomfortable, and I was half afraid. However, the only thing to be done being to knock at the door, I knocked, and was told from within to enter. I entered, therefore, and found myself in a pretty large room, well lighted with wax candles. No glimpse of daylight was to be seen in it. It was a dressing-room, as I supposed from the furniture, though much of it was of forms and uses then quite unknown to me. But prominent in it was a draped table with a gilded looking-glass, and that I made out at first sight to be a fine lady's dressing-table.

Whether I should have made out this object so soon if there had been no fine lady sitting at it, I cannot say. In an arm-chair, with an elbow resting on the table and her head leaning on that hand, sat the strangest lady I have ever seen, or shall ever see.

From *Great Expectations* by Charles Dickens, 1861

1. Select the adjectives that best describe the girl and write them in the character web.

Considerate Rude Soft-spoken Stuck up Shy Bossy Disdainful

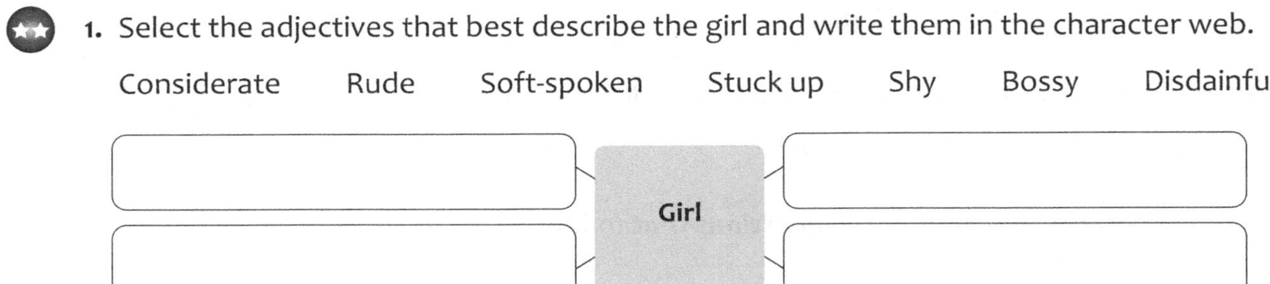

2. Which of the following can you infer from this quotation from the passage: "the great front entrance had two chains across it outside"?
   - **a.** The house often has guests.
   - **b.** The house is rundown.
   - **c.** The house is big but unwelcoming.
   - **d.** The house has to be shut up because the tenants are ill.

3. Which detail helps you understand the narrator's character?
   - **a.** "Though she called me 'boy' so often..."
   - **b.** "The only thing to be done being to knock at the door."
   - **c.** "I answered, more in shyness than politeness."
   - **d.** "In an arm-chair... sat the strangest lady I have ever seen, or shall ever see."

4. Which adjective describes the narrator in this passage?
   - **a.** Polite
   - **b.** Timid
   - **c.** Adventurous
   - **d.** Rude

5. Why is the narrator scared?
   - **a.** He is afraid of the girl.
   - **b.** He is frightened that his family will catch him there.
   - **c.** He is frightened by the strange woman.
   - **d.** He is afraid that he is being followed.

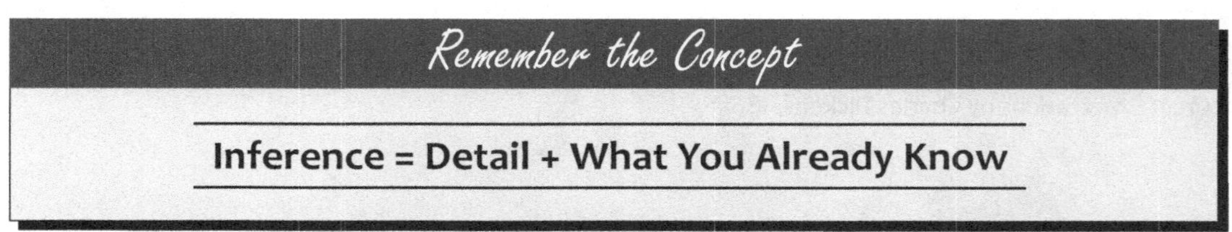

Word Choice

Connections

Have you ever...

- Pictured clearly a character's home?
- Known exactly how a character was feeling?
- Finished a story and felt depressed or hopeful?

Authors choose their words carefully. They use words that enhance meaning and help you picture what's happening. The feelings and ideas associated with a word provide you with an understanding of the writer's meaning.

The words an author chooses are intentional and serve a purpose in a text. Choosing just the right word helps convey meaning. The more vivid the words are, the more they bring a story to life.

Words help an author enhance meaning in a story through:

- Tone
- Point of view
- Voice
- Setting
- Character development
- Theme
- Plot

Three Sides of Word Meaning

You can analyze an author's word choice by looking deeply at the meaning of words. Why does an author choose one particular word? To understand a word's effect, look at the word from three different angles:

- **Denotation:** What's the meaning of the word?
- **Connotation:** What associations does the word have?
- **Comparison:** How does the word compare to similar words?

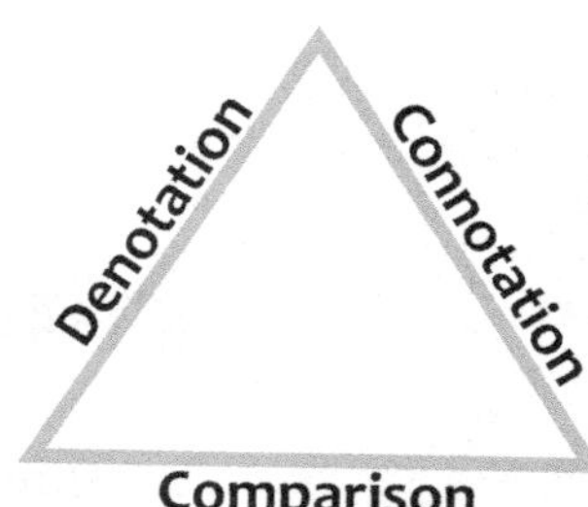

From this information, you can determine the word's purpose.

The story "A Respectable Woman" by Kate Chopin is about a woman who is attracted to her husband's friend.

Use this passage for the exercises that follow.

This was a man she had heard much of but never seen. He had been her husband's college friend; was now a journalist, and in no sense a society man or "a man about town," which were, perhaps, some of the reasons she had never met him. But she had unconsciously formed an image of him in her mind. She pictured him tall, slim, cynical; with eye-glasses, and his hands in his pockets; and she did not like him. Gouvernail was slim enough, but he wasn't very tall nor very cynical; neither did he wear eyeglasses nor carry his hands in his pockets. And she rather liked him when he first presented himself.

But why she liked him she could not explain satisfactorily to herself when she partly attempted to do so. She could discover in him none of those brilliant and promising traits which Gaston, her husband, had often assured her that he possessed. On the contrary, he sat rather mute and receptive before her chatty eagerness to make him feel at home and in face of Gaston's frank and wordy hospitality. His manner was as courteous toward her as the most exacting woman could require; but he made no direct appeal to her approval or even esteem.

From "A Respectable Woman" by Kate Chopin, 1894

Identify Significant Words

An author selects words that will be meaningful and will enhance the reading experience. As you read, find words that seem distinctive and noticeable. Does the text include unusual words? Are words used in an unusual way? Are they interesting words? Are they repeated often?

Word Choice

1. Read the passage. List three significant words.

Significant Words	Denotation	Connotation
	Comparison	
	Comparison	
	Comparison	

You might select words like *society, cynical, brilliant, chatty,* or *courteous.*

Define the Word

Words can have complex meanings. The literal meaning of a word is its denotation. Use your prior knowledge, the word's context, and a dictionary to define the words. Remember that words may have more than one meaning. Make sure that your definition fits the context.

2. Write the definitions of the words in the second column of the chart.

Significant Words	Denotation	Connotation
Society		
	Comparison	
Cynical		
	Comparison	
Courteous		
	Comparison	

Determine the Connotations

A **connotation** is what the word suggests or implies. A word might have a negative connotation or be considered insulting. It might be associated with a particular idea or context.

3. Write the connotation of each word in the second column of the chart.

Significant Words	Denotation	Connotation
Society	A self-defined leisure class that defines fashion and manners	
	Comparison	
Cynical	Distrustful of human sincerity or integrity	
	Comparison	
Courteous	Polite, respectful, considerate	
	Comparison	

Compare to Similar Words

Try a synonym in the same text. How does it change the meaning or feeling of the text?

4. Try a similar word in the same sentence. How does it change the passage?

Significant Words	Denotation	Connotation
Society	A self-defined leisure class that defines fashion and manners	High class or snooty
	Comparison	
Cynical	Distrustful of human sincerity or integrity	Used as an insult or value judgment
	Comparison	
Courteous	Polite, respectful, considerate	Formally polite, but not warm or welcoming
	Comparison	

Connect to Literary Elements

Evaluate the three aspects of the words. What effect do the words have on the text? What is the purpose of each word? Do they help show a particular point of view or voice? Do they communicate a tone or a theme? Do they enhance character development or the setting?

Significant Words	Denotation	Connotation
Society	A self-defined leisure class that defines fashion and manners	High class or snooty
	Comparison "in no sense a *society* man or 'a man about town'" "In no sense an *upper-class* man . . ." puts emphasis on wealth instead of socializing.	
Cynical	Distrustful of human sincerity or integrity	Used as an insult or value judgment
	Comparison "She pictured him tall, slim, *cynical*; with eye-glasses, and his hands in his pockets" "She pictured him tall, slim, *skeptical* . . ." makes him seem disbelieving of ideas instead of people's motives.	
Courteous	Polite, respectful, considerate	Formally polite, but not warm or welcoming
	Comparison "His manner was as *courteous* toward her as the most exacting woman could require" "His manner was as *polite* toward her . . ." emphasizes good manners, but seems to suggest a less friendly relationship, as one might be polite to a waiter.	

5. What is the effect of the words in the passage?

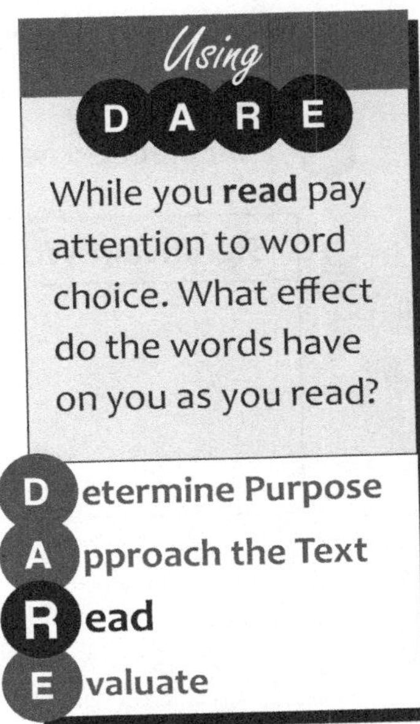

All together, the words in context paint a picture of someone who is not out to impress and is neither a warm nor a critical person. The narrator appears to like male attention and is put off by the fact that Gouvernail doesn't try to impress her in any way.

"The Purloined Letter" is a detective story by Edgar Allan Poe. In it, the detective C. Auguste Dupin recovers a stolen letter.

Read the passage and answer the questions that follow.

At Paris, just after dark one gusty evening in the autumn of 18—, I was enjoying the twofold luxury of meditation and a meerschaum, in company with my friend C. Auguste Dupin, in his little back library, or book-closet, au troisieme, No. 33, Rue Dunot, Faubourg St. Germain. For one hour at least we had maintained a profound silence; while each, to any casual observer, might have seemed intently and exclusively occupied with the curling eddies of smoke that oppressed the atmosphere of the chamber. For myself, however, I was mentally discussing certain topics which had formed matter for conversation between us at an earlier period of the evening; I mean the affair of the Rue Morgue, and the mystery attending the murder of Marie Roget. I looked upon it, therefore, as something of a coincidence, when the door of our apartment was thrown open and admitted our old acquaintance, Monsieur G—, the Prefect of the Parisian police.

We gave him a hearty welcome; for there was nearly half as much of the entertaining as of the contemptible about the man, and we had not seen him for several years. We had been sitting in the dark, and Dupin now arose for the purpose of lighting a lamp, but sat down again, without doing so, upon G.'s saying that he had called to consult us, or rather to ask the opinion of my friend, about some official business which had occasioned a great deal of trouble.

From the "The Purloined Letter" by Edgar Allan Poe, 1844

1. Select three words in the first paragraph, and use them to complete the chart.

Significant Words	Denotation	Connotation
	Comparison	

Word Choice

Significant Words	Denotation	Connotation
	Comparison	
	Comparison	

 **2.** In the second half of the passage, the author uses the following phrases to describe the events and characters:

> "door of our apartment was thrown open"
>
> "We gave him a hearty welcome"
>
> "for there was nearly half as much of the entertaining as of the contemptible about the man"

How does the word choice affect the meaning and the tone?

3. How does the narrator feel about Monseiur G? How do you know?

In this passage from "The Yellow Wallpaper" by Charlotte Perkins Gilman, the narrator is describing the yellow wallpaper in her bedroom.

Read the passage and answer the questions that follow.

It is dull enough to confuse the eye in following, pronounced enough to constantly irritate and provoke study, and when you follow the lame uncertain curves for a little distance they suddenly commit suicide—plunge off at outrageous angles, destroy themselves in unheard of contradictions.

The color is repellent, almost revolting; a smouldering unclean yellow, strangely faded by the slow-turning sunlight.

It is a dull yet lurid orange in some places, a sickly sulphur tint in others.

No wonder the children hated it! I should hate it myself if I had to live in this room long.

There comes John, and I must put this away,—he hates to have me write a word.

From "The Yellow Wallpaper" by Charlotte Perkins Gilman, 1892

 **4.** Select three words that show how the narrator feels about the wallpaper, and use them to complete the chart.

<table>
<tr><th>Significant Words</th><th>Denotation</th><th>Connotation</th></tr>
<tr><td rowspan="2"></td><td></td><td></td></tr>
<tr><td colspan="2">Comparison</td></tr>
<tr><td rowspan="2"></td><td></td><td></td></tr>
<tr><td colspan="2">Comparison</td></tr>
<tr><td rowspan="2"></td><td></td><td></td></tr>
<tr><td colspan="2">Comparison</td></tr>
</table>

 **5.** What does the word choice tell you about the overall purpose of language in the passage?

Check Your Skills

The novel *The Jungle* by Upton Sinclair is about immigrants working in the meatpacking industry in the 1900s.

Read the passage and answer the questions that follow.

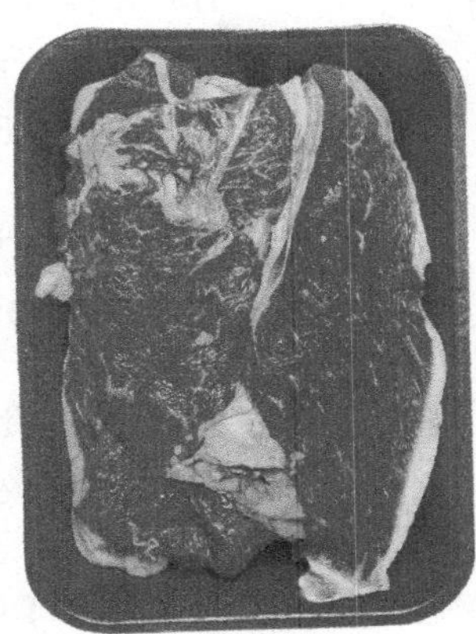

The meat would be shoveled into carts, and the man who did the shoveling would not trouble to lift out a rat even when he saw one—there were things that went into the sausage in comparison with which a poisoned rat was a tidbit. There was no place for the men to wash their hands before they ate their dinner, and so they made a practice of washing them in the water that was to be ladled into the sausage. There were the butt-ends of smoked meat, and the scraps of corned beef, and all the odds and ends of the waste of the plants, that would be dumped into old barrels in the cellar and left there. Under the system of rigid economy which the packers enforced, there were some jobs that it only paid to do once in a long time, and among these was the cleaning out of the waste barrels. Every spring they did it; and in the barrels would be dirt and rust and old nails and stale water—and cartload after cartload of it would be taken up and dumped into the hoppers with fresh meat, and sent out to the public's breakfast.

From *The Jungle* by Upton Sinclair, 1906

1. Which of the following is the best synonym for "tidbit" in the passage?
   - **a.** Delicacy
   - **b.** Snack
   - **c.** Hors d'oeuvre
   - **d.** Crumb

2. What is the effect of the word "dumped" in the passage?
   - **a.** It conveys carelessness in disposing of the waste.
   - **b.** It has the same effect as "placed" or "put."
   - **c.** It conveys a sense of urgency in getting rid of the waste.
   - **d.** It makes the disposal of the waste seem past and forgotten.

The short story "The Curious Case of Benjamin Button" by F. Scott Fitzgerald is about a man who is born old and ages backwards throughout his life.

Read the passage and answer the questions that follow.

Wrapped in a voluminous white blanket, and partly crammed into one of the cribs, there sat an old man apparently about seventy years of age. His sparse hair was almost white, and from his chin dripped a long smoke-coloured beard, which waved absurdly back and forth, fanned by the breeze coming in at the window. He looked up at Mr. Button with dim, faded eyes in which lurked a puzzled question.

"Am I mad?" thundered Mr. Button, his terror resolving into rage. "Is this some ghastly hospital joke?"

"It doesn't seem like a joke to us," replied the nurse severely. "And I don't know whether you're mad or not—but that is most certainly your child."

The cool perspiration redoubled on Mr. Button's forehead. He closed his eyes, and then, opening them, looked again. There was no mistake—he was gazing at a man of threescore and ten—a *baby* of threescore and ten, a baby whose feet hung over the sides of the crib in which it was reposing.

From "The Curious Case of Benjamin Button" by F. Scott Fitzgerald, 1922

3. Choose the best words to complete this quotation from the story.

A ______________ picture formed itself with dreadful clarity before the eyes of the ______________ man—a picture of himself walking through the crowded streets of the city with this ______________ apparition stalking by his side.

   a. Grotesque, tortured, appalling

   b. Unusual, confused, interesting

   c. Wonderful, delighted, amazing

   d. Faded, gleeful, dragging

4. Which of the following is the best synonym for "crammed" in the passage?

   a. Placed

   b. Deposited

   c. Situated

   d. Stuffed

Remember the Concept

To understand a word choice, look at it in three ways:

- Denotation
- Connotation
- Comparison

Figurative Language

Connections

While reading, have you ever . . .

- Enjoyed a vivid description of something familiar?
- Found an interesting comparison?
- Seen a vivid picture of the events in your mind?

Chances are you were reading **figurative language.** Figurative language uses words not for their literal definitions, but to paint a picture, make a comparison, or evoke an emotion.

Authors use many types of figurative language. Figurative language can be used for the way it sounds, the image it evokes, or the feeling it brings to a text.

Examples of Figurative Language

Metaphor	A comparison stating *something* is or has qualities of *something else* ***Example:*** The night was a pitch-black cavern.
Simile	A comparison between two things, using a word such as *like* or *as* ***Example:*** The night was like a pitch-black cavern.
Hyperbole	An extreme exaggeration ***Example:*** My boss is so rich that he could buy the moon.
Understatement	An extreme under-exaggeration ***Example:*** Bill Gates has a couple bucks to his name.
Oxymoron	A self-contradictory statement; two opposites together ***Example:*** The room filled with a thundering silence.
Alliteration	The repetition of sounds at the beginning of words or syllables ***Example:*** The west wind whistled.
Personification	Applying human qualities to animals or non-living things ***Example:*** The computer screen stared at me mockingly.

Words → Meaning → Purpose for Figurative Language

A **Words → Meaning → Purpose** chart will help you understand figurative language and get more out of the text.

"The Legend of Sleepy Hollow" is a short story by Washington Irving about Ichabod Crane, the headless horseman.

Use this passage for the exercises that follow.

In this by-place of nature there abode, in a remote period of American history, that is to say, some thirty years since, a worthy wight of the name of Ichabod Crane, who sojourned, or, as he expressed it, "tarried," in Sleepy Hollow, for the purpose of instructing the children of the vicinity. He was a native of Connecticut, a State which supplies the Union with pioneers for the mind as well as for the forest, and sends forth yearly its legions of frontier woodmen and country schoolmasters. The cognomen of Crane was not inapplicable to his person. He was tall, but exceedingly lank, with narrow shoulders, long arms and legs, hands that dangled a mile out of his sleeves, feet that might have served for shovels, and his whole frame most loosely hung together. His head was small, and flat at top, with huge ears, large green glassy eyes, and a long snipe nose, so that it looked like a weather-cock perched upon his spindle neck to tell which way the wind blew. To see him striding along the profile of a hill on a windy day, with his clothes bagging and fluttering about him, one might have mistaken him for the genius of famine descending upon the earth, or some scarecrow eloped from a cornfield.

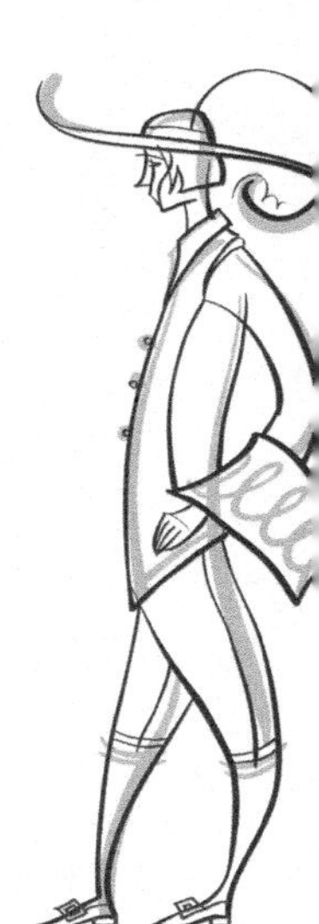

From "The Legend of Sleepy Hollow" by Washington Irving, 1917

Identify the Figurative Language

Find words and phrases that aren't used for their literal meaning.

?

1. Write an example of figurative language from the passage in the first column.

Words	Meaning	Purpose

One example is: "with his clothes bagging and fluttering about him, one might have mistaken him for the genius of famine descending upon the earth, or some scarecrow eloped from a cornfield."

Identify the Meaning

Identify the type of figurative language and the meaning. If it is alliteration, what is the effect of the repeated sound? If it is a metaphor, simile, or personification, what is it comparing?

?

2. Write the meaning of the figurative language in the second column of the chart.

Words	Meaning	Purpose
"mistaken him for the genius of famine descending upon the earth, or some scarecrow eloped from a cornfield."		

This simile compares Ichabod Crane to a starving person or a scarecrow that escaped from a cornfield. Even though the phrase "one might have mistaken him for" does not use the words *like* or *as*, it makes a direct comparison.

Determine the Purpose

Figurative language provides meaning and evokes emotion for the reader. What effect does the figurative language have? What connections will the reader make?

?

3. Write the author's purpose in the third column.

Words	Meaning	Purpose
"mistaken him for the genius of famine descending upon the earth, or some scarecrow eloped from a cornfield."	Compares Ichabod Crane to a starving person or a scarecrow that escaped from a cornfield	

The author shows how thin and gawky Crane is by comparing him to very thin figures: a starving man and a scarecrow.

?

4. Identify another piece of figurative language and its meaning and purpose.

Words	Meaning	Purpose
"mistaken him for the genius of famine descending upon the earth, or some scarecrow eloped from a cornfield."	Compares Ichabod Crane to a starving person or a scarecrow that escaped from a cornfield	The simile shows how thin and gawky Crane is.

The novel *Desert Gold* by Zane Grey is the story of Dick Gale, who travels to the border town of Casita looking for adventure. He finds gambling, corruption, and revenge.

Read the passage and answer the questions that follow.

A sound disturbed Cameron's reflections. He bent his head listening. A soft wind fanned the paling embers, blew sparks and white ashes and thin smoke away into the enshrouding circle of blackness. His burro did not appear to be moving about. The quiet split to the cry of a coyote. It rose strange, wild, mournful—not the howl of a prowling upland beast baying the campfire or barking at a lonely prospector, but the wail of a wolf, full-voiced, crying out the meaning of the desert and the night. Hunger throbbed in it—hunger for a mate, for offspring, for life. When it ceased, the terrible desert silence smote Cameron, and the cry echoed in his soul. He and that wandering wolf were brothers.

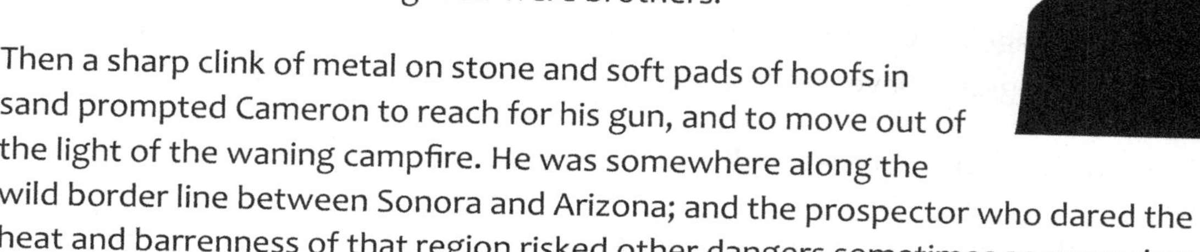

Then a sharp clink of metal on stone and soft pads of hoofs in sand prompted Cameron to reach for his gun, and to move out of the light of the waning campfire. He was somewhere along the wild border line between Sonora and Arizona; and the prospector who dared the heat and barrenness of that region risked other dangers sometimes as menacing.

Figures darker than the gloom approached and took shape, and in the light turned out to be those of a white man and a heavily packed burro.

From *Desert Gold* by Zane Grey, 1913

1. Find three examples of figurative language in the passage, and complete the Words → Meaning → Purpose chart.

Words	Meaning	Purpose

 2. What does figurative language add to this passage?

> **Reading for Understanding**
>
> Figurative language can let you know how the author feels about a person, setting, or event. The author might make a comparison to something wonderful, dangerous, ugly, or nostalgic.

The poem "Song of Myself" by Walt Whitman is a celebration of self and the connection between each person and the universe.

Read the passage and answer the questions that follow.

I CELEBRATE myself, and sing myself,
And what I assume you shall assume,
For every atom belonging to me as good belongs to you.

I loafe and invite my soul,
I lean and loafe at my ease observing a spear of summer grass.

My tongue, every atom of my blood, form'd from this soil, this air,
Born here of parents born here from parents the same, and their parents the same,
I, now thirty-seven years old in perfect health begin,
Hoping to cease not till death.

Creeds and schools in abeyance,
Retiring back a while sufficed at what they are, but never forgotten,
I harbor for good or bad, I permit to speak at every hazard,
Nature without check with original energy.

From "Song of Myself" by Walt Whitman, 1855

 3. Complete the chart using two different kinds of figurative language from the passage.

Words	Meaning	Purpose

 4. What does figurative language add to this passage?

White Fang by Jack London is set in the Yukon Territory during the Klondike Gold Rush.

Read the passage and answer the questions that follow.

But at front and rear, unawed and indomitable, toiled the two men who were not yet dead. Their bodies were covered with fur and soft-tanned leather. Eyelashes and cheeks and lips were so coated with the crystals from their frozen breath that their faces were not discernible. This gave them the seeming of ghostly masques, undertakers in a spectral world at the funeral of some ghost. But under it all they were men, penetrating the land of desolation and mockery and silence, puny adventurers bent on colossal adventure, pitting themselves against the might of a world as remote and alien and pulseless as the abysses of space.

They travelled on without speech, saving their breath for the work of their bodies. On every side was the silence, pressing upon them with a tangible presence. It affected their minds as the many atmospheres of deep water affect the body of the diver. It crushed them with the weight of unending vastness and unalterable decree. It crushed them into the remotest recesses of their own minds, pressing out of them, like juices from the grape, all the false ardours and exaltations and undue self-values of the human soul, until they perceived themselves finite and small, specks and motes, moving with weak cunning and little wisdom amidst the play and inter-play of the great blind elements and forces.

From *White Fang* by Jack London, 1906

5. Find two examples in figurative language in the passage, and complete the Words → Meaning → Purpose chart.

Words	Meaning	Purpose

6. Identify one similarity and one difference between the figurative language in the passages from *White Fang* and *Desert Gold*.

Check Your Skills

The novel *A Tale of Two Cities* by Charles Dickens depicts the conflict between French peasants and the French aristocracy before and during the French Revolution.

Read the passage and answer the questions that follow.

With drooping heads and tremulous tails, they mashed their way through the thick mud, floundering and stumbling between whiles, as if they were falling to pieces at the larger joints. As often as the driver rested them and brought them to a stand, with a wary "Wo-ho! so-ho-then!" the near leader violently shook his head and everything upon it—like an unusually emphatic horse, denying that the coach could be got up the hill. Whenever the leader made this rattle, the passenger started, as a nervous passenger might, and was disturbed in mind.

There was a steaming mist in all the hollows, and it had roamed in its forlornness up the hill, like an evil spirit, seeking rest and finding none. A clammy and intensely cold mist, it made its slow way through the air in ripples that visibly followed and overspread one another, as the waves of an unwholesome sea might do. It was dense enough to shut out everything from the light of the coach-lamps but these its own workings, and a few yards of road; and the reek of the labouring horses steamed into it, as if they had made it all.

From *A Tale of Two Cities* by Charles Dickens, 1859

1. The passage states that the horses moved "as if they were falling to pieces at the larger joints." What does this show about the horses?
   - **a.** The horses are falling apart.
   - **b.** The horses are moving clumsily.
   - **c.** The horses are trying to escape the driver.
   - **d.** The horses are moving in all directions.

If your **purpose** is to immerse yourself in a book or story, understanding figurative language will help you build a picture in your mind.

Determine Purpose
Approach the Text
Read
Evaluate

2. What is the effect of the phrase "tremulous tails" in the passage?
   - **a.** It emphasizes the horses' nervousness.
   - **b.** It emphasizes the horses' beautiful long tails.
   - **c.** It emphasizes the length of the journey.
   - **d.** It emphasizes the discomfort of the passengers.

3. Which word best describes the horses in the passage?
   - **a.** Sleepy
   - **b.** Energetic
   - **c.** Passionate
   - **d.** Willful

4. Which word best describes the setting in the passage?
   - **a.** Gloomy
   - **b.** Hopeful
   - **c.** Frightening
   - **d.** Bustling

5. Which is the best interpretation of the statement that the mist "had roamed in its forlornness up the hill, like an evil spirit, seeking rest and finding none"?
   - **a.** The mist is bad-smelling and sulfurous.
   - **b.** The mist is black and gray.
   - **c.** The mist is caused by an evil spirit.
   - **d.** The mist is ominous.

6. Which of the following best describes the mist?
   - **a.** Gushing through the air
   - **b.** Invisible in the dark night
   - **c.** So thick nothing can be seen
   - **d.** Unexpected, sudden, and unusual

Remember the Concept

Figurative language creates a vivid picture. A **Words** → **Meaning** → **Purpose** chart can help you understand how figurative language is used.

Characters

Connections

Have you ever...

- Questioned the motives of a character on your favorite television show?
- Felt a connection with the lead character in a movie?
- Suspected a relationship between two characters in a story wouldn't last?

Readers form personal connections and attachments to characters. The characters often determine how you feel about a novel or story.

Is the main character sympathetic? Do you love to hate the antagonist? Are you annoyed or frustrated by the characters' actions?

Analyzing characters helps you get more from a novel or story. Understanding characters in fiction can reveal themes. You can even learn about yourself and human nature from interesting characters.

You can learn about characters from how they talk, act, think, and look. Authors also reveal characters' qualities through their relationships with other characters.

Making Inferences about Characters

In a fictional text, the author will rarely tell you directly about a character's personality. You have to make inferences about characters through their words and actions.

In the Sherlock Holmes novel *The Hound of the Baskervilles* by Sir Arthur Conan Doyle, Holmes and his friend Dr. John Watson investigate an attempted murder in Dartmoor, an area of moorland in Devon, England.

Use the passage for the exercises that follow.

Mr. Sherlock Holmes, who was usually very late in the mornings, save upon those not infrequent occasions when he was up all night, was seated at the breakfast table. I stood upon the hearth-rug and picked up the stick which our visitor had left behind him the night before. It was a fine, thick piece of wood, bulbous-headed, of the sort which is known as a "Penang lawyer." Just under the head was a broad silver band nearly an inch across. "To James Mortimer, M.R.C.S., from his friends of the C.C.H.," was engraved upon it, with the date "1884." It was just such a stick as the old-fashioned family practitioner used to carry—dignified, solid, and reassuring.

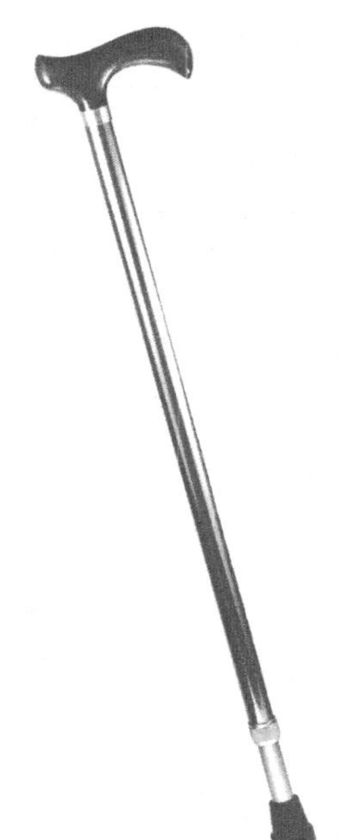

"Well, Watson, what do you make of it?" Holmes was sitting with his back to me, and I had given him no sign of my occupation.

"How did you know what I was doing? I believe you have eyes in the back of your head."

"I have, at least, a well-polished, silver-plated coffee-pot in front of me," said he. "But, tell me, Watson, what do you make of our visitor's stick? Since we have been so unfortunate as to miss him and have no notion of his errand, this accidental souvenir becomes of importance. Let me hear you reconstruct the man by an examination of it."

"I think," said I, following as far as I could the methods of my companion, "that Dr. Mortimer is a successful, elderly medical man, well-esteemed since those who know him give him this mark of their appreciation."

"Good!" said Holmes. "Excellent!"

From *The Hounds of the Baskervilles* by Sir Arthur Conan Doyle, 1902

Choose a Detail

First, identify character actions or dialogue in the text that seem significant.

1. Select a detail that seems significant about Sherlock Holmes, and write it in the inference chart.

Detail from the Text	What I Already Know	Character Inference

You might choose the following detail: "'Well, Watson, what do you make of it?' Holmes was sitting with his back to me, and I had given him no sign of my occupation."

Review What You Already Know

Identify what you know already that can help you make an inference.

2. What do you know that can help you make an inference about the character? Write it in the inference chart.

Detail from the Text	What I Already Know	Character Inference
"'Well, Watson, what do you make of it?' Holmes was sitting with his back to me, and I had given him no sign of my occupation."		

You already know that it's hard to tell what someone is doing if your back is turned. You can use that knowledge to make an inference.

Reading for Understanding

Based on your knowledge of the characters, try to predict what they will do next as you read.

Make an Inference

Make your inference based on the character's actions and dialogue, along with your own prior knowledge.

? **3.** What inference can you make about Holmes?

Detail from the Text	What I Already Know	Character Inference
"'Well, Watson, what do you make of it?' Holmes was sitting with his back to me, and I had given him no sign of my occupation."	It's hard to tell what someone is doing if your back is turned.	

You can infer that Holmes is very perceptive.

Synthesize Inferences

You can make a series of inferences about a character to improve your picture of that character as a whole. Put together the inferences. What conclusion can you draw about the character?

? **4.** Add one more inference to this inference chart. What can you say about Holmes as a character based on the inferences?

Detail from the Text	What I Already Know	Character Inference
"'Well, Watson, what do you make of it?' Holmes was sitting with his back to me, and I had given him no sign of my occupation."	It's hard to tell what someone is doing if your back is turned.	Holmes is very perceptive.

Your inferences might vary, but you'll probably conclude that Holmes is logical and intelligent and that he enjoys showing off his intelligence. Holmes knows that small details can lead to big answers.

The novel *Ethan Frome* by Edith Wharton tells the story of Ethan Frome, a man who wrecks his life in a suicide attempt.

Read the passage and answer the questions that follow.

Frome turned away again, and taking up his razor stooped to catch the reflection of his stretched cheek in the blotched looking-glass above the wash-stand.

"Why on earth should Mattie go?"

"Well, when she gets married, I mean," his wife's drawl came from behind him.

"Oh, she'd never leave us as long as you needed her," he returned, scraping hard at his chin.

"I wouldn't ever have it said that I stood in the way of a poor girl like Mattie marrying a smart fellow like Denis Eady," Zeena answered in a tone of plaintive self-effacement.

Ethan, glaring at his face in the glass, threw his head back to draw the razor from ear to chin. His hand was steady, but the attitude was an excuse for not making an immediate reply.

"And the doctor don't want I should be left without anybody," Zeena continued. "He wanted I should speak to you about a girl he's heard about, that might come—"

Ethan laid down the razor and straightened himself with a laugh.

"Denis Eady! If that's all, I guess there's no such hurry to look round for a girl."

"Well, I'd like to talk to you about it," said Zeena obstinately.

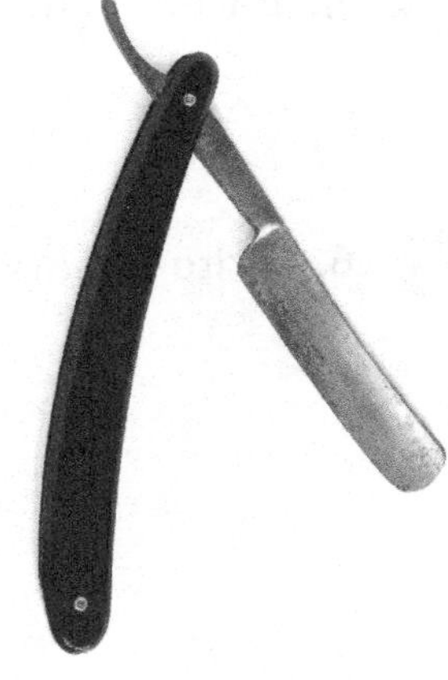

He was getting into his clothes in fumbling haste. "All right. But I haven't got the time now; I'm late as it is," he returned, holding his old silver turnip-watch to the candle.

Zeena, apparently accepting this as final, lay watching him in silence while he pulled his suspenders over his shoulders and jerked his arms into his coat; but as he went toward the door she said, suddenly and incisively: "I guess you're always late, now you shave every morning."

From *Ethan Frome* by Edith Wharton, 1911

1. Select two significant details about Ethan Frome, and complete the inference chart.

Detail from the Text	What I Already Know	Character Inference

2. Based on the inference chart, what can you say about Ethan as a character?

3. How do you think Ethan feels about Mattie? How do you know?

4. Select two significant details about Zeena, and complete the inference chart.

Detail from the Text	What I Already Know	Character Inference

5. Based on the inference chart, what can you conclude about Zeena as a character?

6. Write a short paragraph comparing Ethan and Zeena.

Comparing Two Characters

You can use a Comparison Alley graphic organizer to visually compare characters or discover how a character changes throughout the book.

Summary of *Pride and Prejudice* by Jane Austen

The novel Pride and Prejudice tells the story of the Bennet family and their five unmarried daughters. Mrs. Bennet is set on marrying her daughters into wealth. When Charles Bingley, an eligible wealthy bachelor, arrives at neighboring Netherfield Park, Mrs. Bennet plans to introduce her daughters to him.

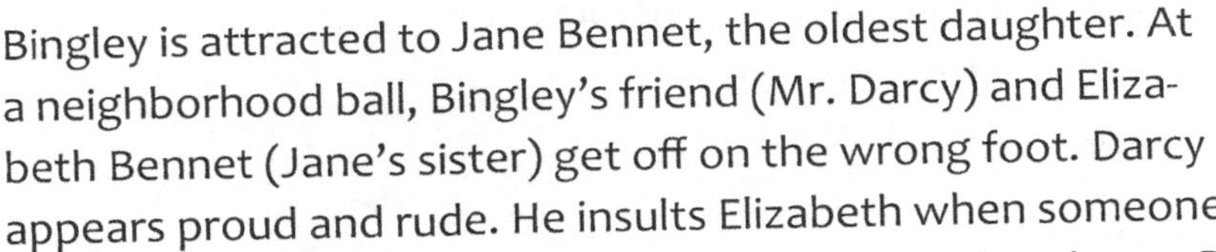

Bingley is attracted to Jane Bennet, the oldest daughter. At a neighborhood ball, Bingley's friend (Mr. Darcy) and Elizabeth Bennet (Jane's sister) get off on the wrong foot. Darcy appears proud and rude. He insults Elizabeth when someone suggests that he ask her to dance. Later, at another dance, Darcy witnesses the sharpness of Elizabeth's mind. He shows his attraction to Elizabeth, but she refuses him because of his former insults.

Soon after, Bingley and Darcy leave for London with no intentions of returning to Netherfield anytime soon. Jane hears that Bingley will likely marry another woman—Mr. Darcy's sister. Meanwhile, Elizabeth meets Mr. Wickham, who tells her lies about Darcy's character.

Elizabeth runs into Darcy again, and he is so in love with her that he proposes. She refuses. Darcy gives her a letter explaining that Wickham lied and that Darcy only opposed the marriage between Bingley and Jane because Jane seemed only interested in Bingley's money. Elizabeth begins to believe Darcy, but he has already left for London again.

Elizabeth once again runs into Darcy at his estate. She finds that Darcy is much more agreeable than before, but she is called back home quickly when she hears her younger sister Lydia has run off with Wickham. Darcy saves the day when he helps pay Lydia's dowry, which impresses Elizabeth.

Bingley reappears in Netherfield Park for a short while and resumes courting Jane. They become engaged. A few days later, Darcy returns and proposes to Elizabeth again. She now accepts. The two couples are married on the same day.

D Determine the Purpose

Imagine you are reading *Pride and Prejudice* for your next book club meeting. The club will be comparing Mr. Darcy and Mr. Bingley.

A Approach the Text

To compare the characters, you need to be able to identify character traits and analyze character actions and interactions. Before you read, it can be helpful to decide what aspects you will compare.

1. Which of the following would be most helpful to compare? Select all correct answers.
   - ❑ Character traits
   - ❑ Your opinion of the characters
   - ❑ Character feelings and reactions to other characters
   - ❑ How the characters know other characters
   - ❑ Changes in a character
   - ❑ Character backgrounds

You could compare many aspects of the characters. Character traits, feelings and reactions, changes, and backgrounds are all possibilities. Your opinion is a conclusion you would draw based on your comparison. How the characters know other characters is a minor detail that may not be important when comparing characters.

R Read

As you read, make notes of character traits and examples of character behavior. Determine similarities and differences, and add them to the Comparison Alley.

2. Read through the passage, and complete the graphic organizer.

Similarities

Differences

Differences

E Evaluate

Evaluating is an important step when you're using a graphic organizer. Interpreting the results of a graphic organizer helps you draw conclusions about what you read. It allows you to think of information in a new way. What conclusions can you draw?

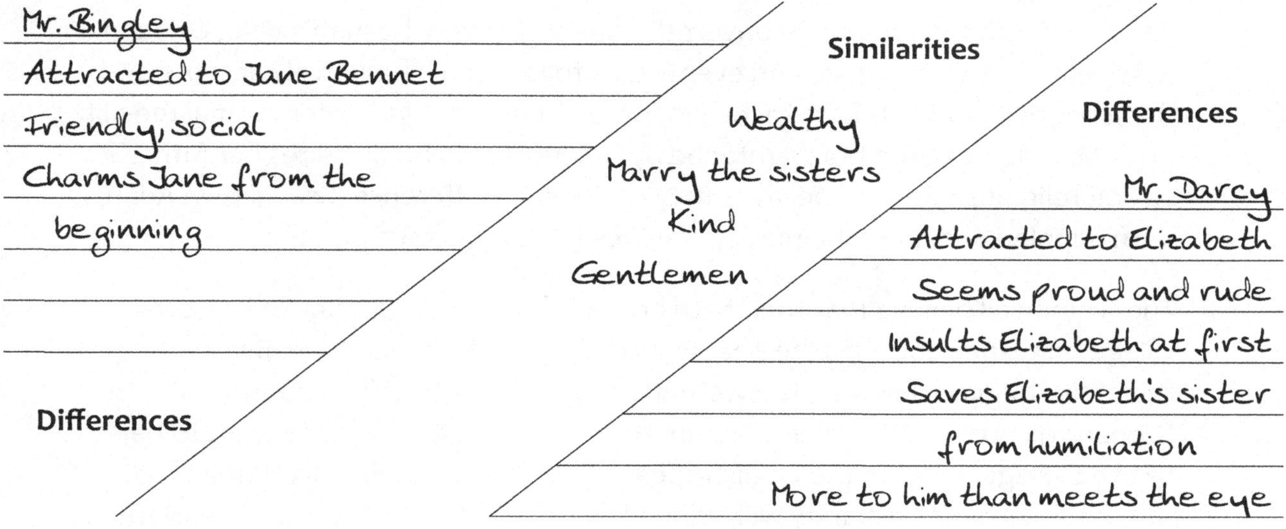

3. What can you conclude about Darcy and Bingley, based on the graphic organizer?

Bingley is loved from the beginning. His personality shows no surprises. Darcy is more of a complex character. He appears to be rude and proud at the beginning but later proves to be a gentleman.

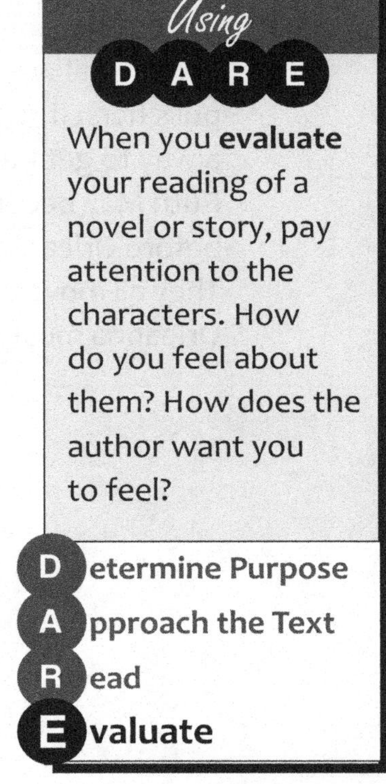

Read the passage and answer the questions that follow.

Summary of *The Poisonwood Bible* by Barbara Kingsolver

In 1959, Nathan Price, an overzealous Baptist minister, takes his wife and four daughters into the Congo to convert the unenlightened. Nathan's wife, Orleanna, passively accepts the move and events that follow, as she passively accepts everything her husband tells her. Rachel, 15, resents having to leave her normal teen life. Ruth May, 5, is excited but frightened by the move. Leah, 14, shares her father's strong religious faith and believes they can make a difference. Leah's twin Adah, born crippled and mute, helplessly watches the events take place.

The women all believe that their faith and culture are far superior to those in the village of Kilanga and that the people will follow without question. Before long, their faith begins to waver. The women are slowly affected by what they see, but Nathan will not stray from his mission. He refuses to give up his attempt to baptize the villagers. When the English-speaking teacher Anatole tells Nathan that the chief worries Christianity will result in the moral decline of his people, Nathan refuses to listen to reason.

The family learns that they must leave the country to remain safe from a revolution. Though his wife and daughters plead with him to take action, Nathan refuses to leave. The day that the evacuation plane arrives, Nathan forbids his family from fleeing. Orleanna is upset, and retreats to her room. She is unable or unwilling to get out of bed.

For several weeks, the three older girls care for the family. When Orleanna finally pulls herself together, she speaks her mind to Nathan and begins to search for a way to get her daughters out of Africa. However, Ruth May becomes ill with malaria and eventually dies before Orleanna finally takes her daughters away. They all move on to follow different paths, and Orleanna must deal with her guilt.

Characters

1. Compare the character traits of Nathan and Orleanna, using the Comparison Alley.

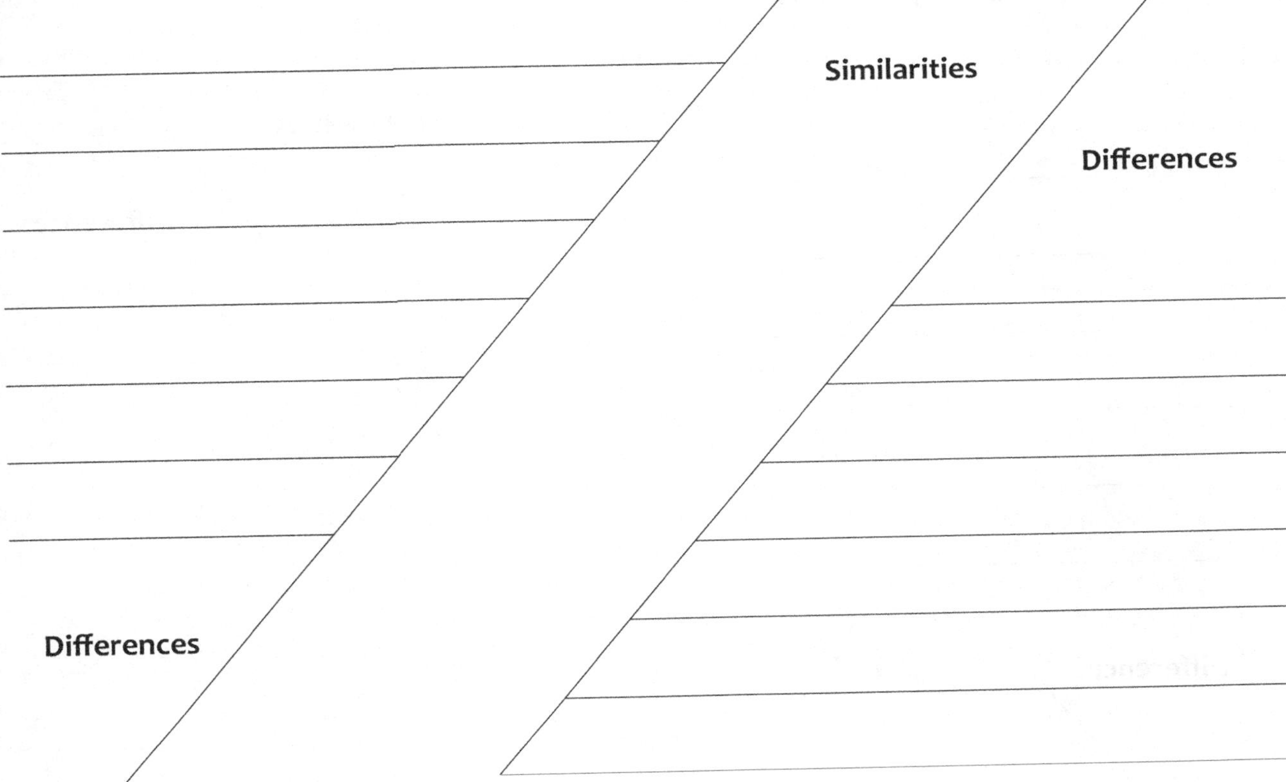

2. What can you conclude about Nathan and Orleanna based on the Comparison Alley?

3. What do the characters reveal about culture and religion?

 4. Using a character from *Pride and Prejudice* and a character from *The Poisonwood Bible*, complete the Comparison Alley.

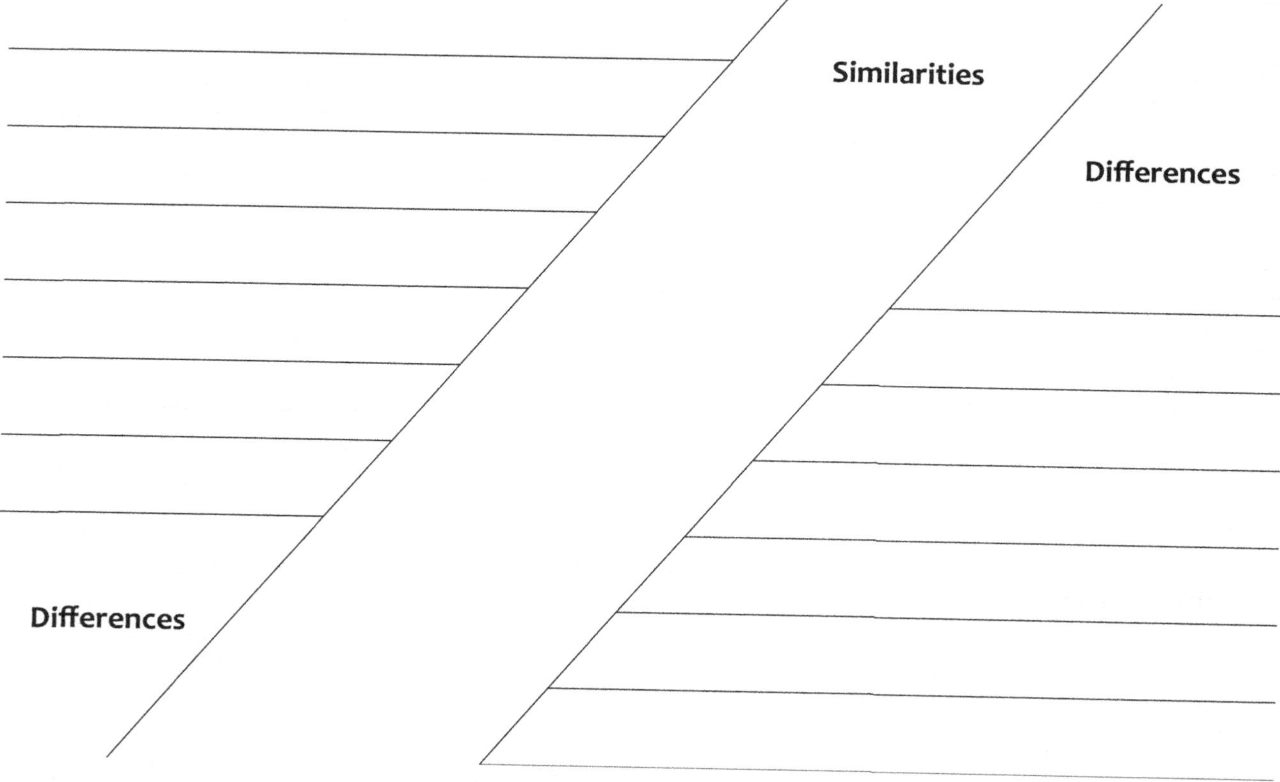

 5. Compare the two characters based on the Comparison Alley.

Check Your Skills

F. Scott Fitzgerald's novel *The Great Gatsby* tells the story of young millionaire Jay Gatsby, who is in love with Daisy Buchanan. In this passage, the narrator describes two women sitting on a couch at a party.

Read the passage and answer the questions that follow.

The younger of the two was a stranger to me. She was extended full length at her end of the divan, completely motionless, and with her chin raised a little, as if she were balancing something on it which was quite likely to fall. If she saw me out of the corner of her eyes she gave no hint of it—indeed, I was almost surprised into murmuring an apology for having disturbed her by coming in.

The other girl, Daisy, made an attempt to rise—she leaned slightly forward with a conscientious expression—then she laughed, an absurd, charming little laugh, and I laughed too and came forward into the room.

"I'm p-paralyzed with happiness." She laughed again, as if she said something very witty, and held my hand for a moment, looking up into my face, promising that there was no one in the world she so much wanted to see. That was a way she had. She hinted in a murmur that the surname of the balancing girl was Baker. (I've heard it said that Daisy's murmur was only to make people lean toward her; an irrelevant criticism that made it no less charming.)

At any rate, Miss Baker's lips fluttered, she nodded at me almost imperceptibly, and then quickly tipped her head back again—the object she was balancing had obviously tottered a little and given her something of a fright. Again a sort of apology arose to my lips. Almost any exhibition of complete self-sufficiency draws a stunned tribute from me.

I looked back at my cousin, who began to ask me questions in her low, thrilling voice. It was the kind of voice that the ear follows up and down, as if each speech is an arrangement of notes that will never be played again. Her face was sad and lovely with bright things in it, bright eyes and a bright passionate mouth, but there was an excitement in her voice that men who had cared for her found difficult to forget: a singing compulsion, a whispered "Listen," a promise that she had done gay, exciting things just a while since and that there were gay, exciting things hovering in the next hour.

From *The Great Gatsby* by F. Scott Fitzgerald, 1925

1. Organize the similarities and differences listed below in the Comparison Alley to compare Jordan Baker, the "balancing girl," with Daisy Buchanan.

Privileged	Is aware of her charming effect on men	Independent
Low, thrilling voice	Might be covering up unhappiness	Self-sufficient
Intimidating	Is aware of her beauty	Appears confident

Similarities

Differences

Differences

2. How does the narrator feel about Jordan Baker?
   - a. He is amused by her.
   - b. He is in awe of her.
   - c. He is frightened of her.
   - d. He is bored by her.

3. The author states, "Her face was sad and lovely with bright things in it, bright eyes and a bright passionate mouth." Based on this passage, which statement about Daisy is most accurate?
   - a. Daisy is not aware of her effect on men.
   - b. Daisy often finds herself overshadowed by others.
   - c. Daisy might not be as happy as she appears.
   - d. Daisy is carefree and wants nothing.

4. How does the narrator feel about Daisy?
   - a. He is amused by Daisy's behavior.
   - b. He sees Daisy for who she is.
   - c. He is unaware of the power of Daisy's charm.
   - d. He feels sorry for Daisy.

Remember the Concept

Look for significant details in a character's:

- Actions
- Dialogue
- Interactions
- Appearance
- Thoughts

Story Structure and Conflict

Connections

Have you ever...

- Wondered why a book had to end the way it did?
- Been frustrated when a character got caught in a bad situation?
- Felt thrilled at the final confrontation between a hero and villain?

The events and conflicts in a book or story follow a structure. Understanding the story's structure can help you identify what's important.

Fictional texts usually follow a particular story structure. The characters, setting, and conflict are introduced and a series of events take place. Through the different events, the character or characters resolve a problem or conflict.

A conflict is a problem or challenge that a character faces and deals with through the course of events. There are four general categories of conflict:

- Person versus nature
- Person versus person
- Person versus society
- Person versus self

Using a Plot Triangle

A plot triangle illustrates a story's structure. Mapping out significant events helps you understand how they contribute to the story's conflict and meaning.

Summary of *The Princess Bride* by William Goldman

Beautiful Buttercup lives on a farm in the country of Florin with her parents and Westley, the farm boy. After years of treating Westley cruelly, she finally realizes that she loves him. After she tells him, he leaves for America in search of a fortune so the two can wed. It isn't long before she is distraught to hear that he has been murdered by the Dread Pirate Roberts.

In her grief, the evil Prince Humperdinck forces Buttercup to agree to marry him. Then, Buttercup is kidnapped by a group of criminals—Vizzini, Fezzik, and Inigo. As they travel across the sea, they are followed, and each of the men is defeated by the pursuer, a man in black. Inigo and Fezzik are left alive and unconscious, but Vizzini is killed. Buttercup discovers the man in black is actually her beloved Westley, who has taken over the role of the Dread Pirate Roberts. With Prince Humperdinck pursuing them, the lovers travel through the treacherous Fireswamp. Humperdinck finds them, and Buttercup agrees to return with the prince to Florin as long as he promises to return Westley safely to his ship.

Humperdinck is planning to murder Buttercup on their wedding night in order to start a war. He lies to Buttercup and tortures Westley in the Zoo of Death, but Inigo and Fezzik hear Westley's screams and come to his rescue. When they finally find Westley's body, they seek help from Miracle Max, Humperdinck's former magician. Max creates a successful miracle pill that revives Westley. Then, Westley and his new allies plan to break into the castle and rescue Buttercup.

Buttercup marries Humperdinck. She plans to kill herself until she sees Westley, alive on the prince's bed. When Humperdinck finds them, Westley intimidates Humperdink and Buttercup ties him to a chair. Fezzik appears with the prince's four white horses, and Buttercup rides away with the rescuers. The prince's men pursue them, but the riders escape to a happy if not perfect ending.

D *Determine the Purpose*

Imagine you are writing an essay about *The Princess Bride*. You aren't sure which events are important and how they are related to the meaning of the book.

A Approach the Text

You can use a plot triangle graphic organizer to identify and connect important events in a text. Skim the text to determine the setting, important characters, and conflicts that take place in the story.

? **1.** List three conflicts in the passage, and identify the category of each conflict.

You might identify these three conflicts:

- Buttercup must decide to give herself up to the Prince to try to save Westley: person versus self.
- The man in black fights the band of criminals: person versus person.
- Buttercup and Westley must defeat the Prince to be with each other: person versus person.

R Read

Read the text, and note significant events throughout the plot:

- **Introduction:** What events set up the story and main conflict?
- **Rising action:** What events escalate the conflict?
- **Climax:** What event brings the conflict to its final confrontation?
- **Falling action:** What events happen during the final confrontation?
- **Resolution:** What events finish resolving the conflict and end the story?

? **2.** Complete the plot triangle based on the passage.

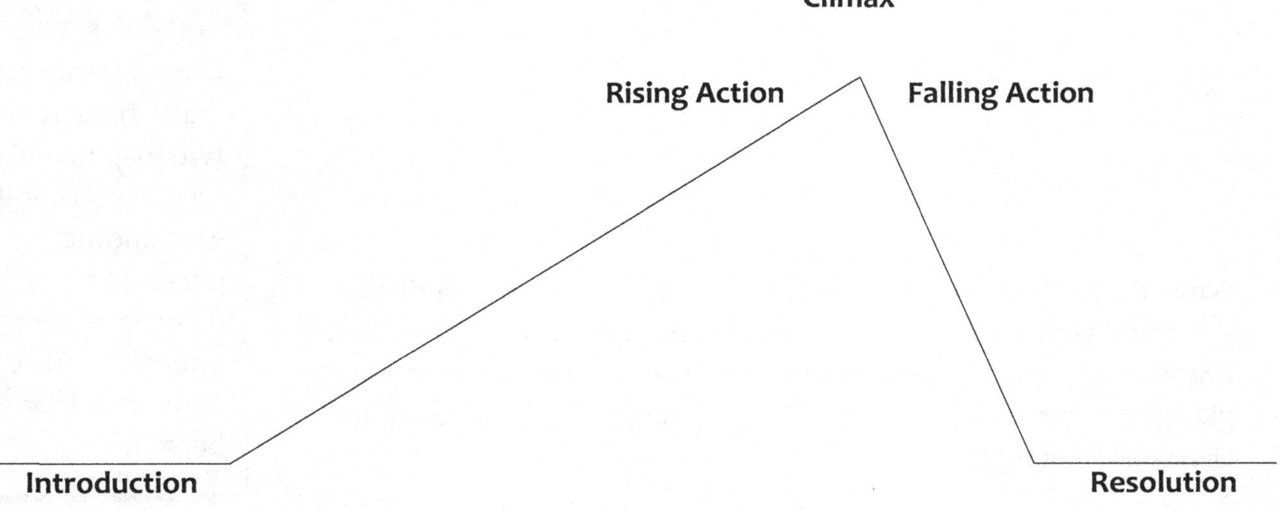

E Evaluate

A story is about more than isolated events, characters, and setting. The way the events come together and the meaning they produce is what makes a story. Evaluate the graphic organizer to draw conclusions about the story and its meaning.

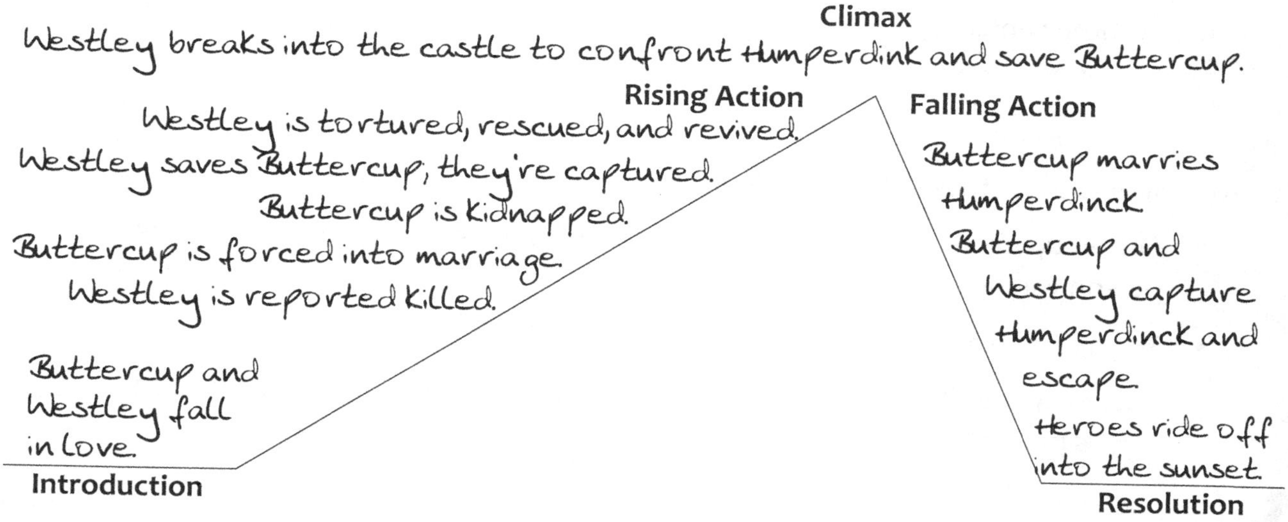

Climax
Westley breaks into the castle to confront Humperdink and save Buttercup.

Rising Action
Westley is tortured, rescued, and revived.
Westley saves Buttercup; they're captured.
Buttercup is kidnapped.
Buttercup is forced into marriage.
Westley is reported killed.

Introduction
Buttercup and Westley fall in love.

Falling Action
Buttercup marries Humperdinck.
Buttercup and Westley capture Humperdinck and escape.

Resolution
Heroes ride off into the sunset.

?

3. Connect specific events in the story to one of the conflicts you listed. How does the story structure develop the conflict?

When Buttercup thinks she has lost Westley, the central conflict of the book is introduced. The two must fight many outside forces to be together. Their main opponent is the Prince, and the characters struggle against him until they finally confront and defeat him during the climax and falling action.

> ***Reading for Understanding***
>
> In many stories, the main character has two major conflicts: an external conflict with another person, nature, or society and an internal conflict with himself or herself.

Read the passage and answer the questions that follow.

Summary of *The Blind Side* by Michael Lewis

Michael Oher, 17, moves from one foster home to the next over the years. Unable to cope with the instability, he runs away each time he has to move. Eventually he catches a break. The football coach of a prestigious private Christian school helps Mike get admitted to the school because of his size and athletic talents. At his new school, Michael makes friends with SJ.

One night, SJ's mother, Leigh Anne Tuohy, sees Michael walking down the street. When he tells her he plans to spend the night outside the school gym, she offers her house for the night. Michael finds a home and family in the Tuohys. Eventually, Leigh Anne tries to become Michael's legal guardian and learns he was taken away from his drug-addicted mother as a young child.

When his grades improve, Michael is allowed to join the football team. After a shaky start and support from his adopted family, he eventually becomes a star player. His family sees his talent, and they contact college coaches around the country. Leigh Anne hires a tutor to help Michael to raise his grades. Michael is courted by many schools, but he eventually commits to play for the University of Mississippi, known as Ole Miss. The university is Leigh Anne and her husband's alma mater. After Michael's coach receives a job at Ole Miss, Michael, Leigh Anne, and her husband become the subject of an NCAA investigation. The Tuohys are Mississippi boosters and authorities are suspicious about their connections with the Ole Miss. Michael confronts Leigh Anne, asking her if she only took him in so he would play football for her alma mater. Michael then runs away to his birth mother's apartment in the projects.

When Michael finally reconciles with Leigh Anne, she tells him she will support any decision he makes. Michael eventually tells the NCAA investigator that he chose Ole Miss because it is his family's school, and that ends the investigation. When it is time for Michael to begin college, Leigh Anne and her family take him to campus. He eventually is drafted by the Baltimore Ravens.

1. List three conflicts in the passage. Name the category of each conflict.

2. Complete the graphic organizer based on the passage.

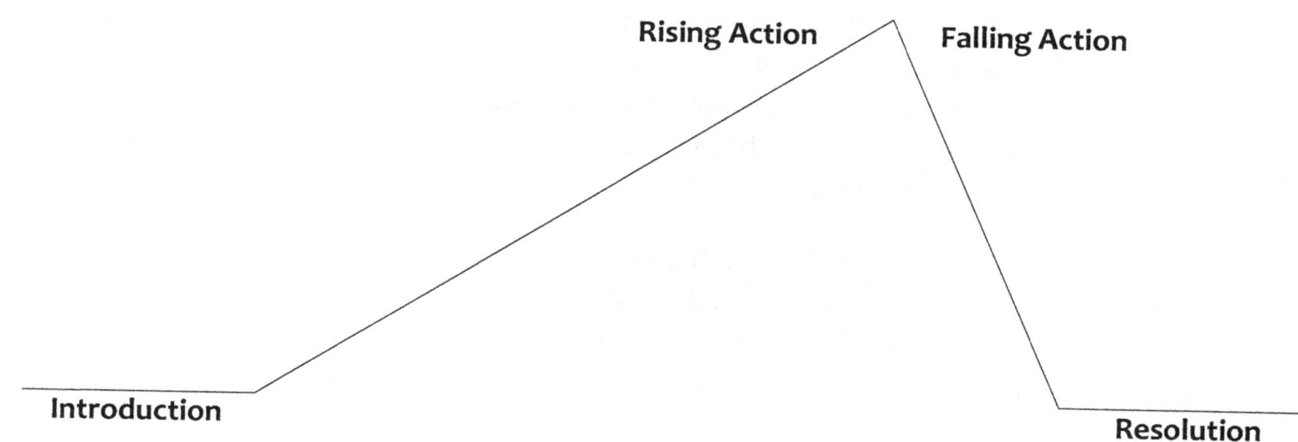

3. Connect specific events in the story to one of the conflicts you listed. How does the story structure develop the conflict?

4. How does the climax and resolution relate to the conflict in the story?

Reading for Understanding

The main conflict drives the story forward, and the resolution of the conflict is the story's ending.

Check Your Skills

Read the passage and answer the questions that follow.

Summary of *The Art of Racing in the Rain* by Garth Stein

Enzo, a dog and the story's narrator, is nearing his life's end. As he prepares for the end, he recounts his life and memories. Enzo's fierce love and loyalty for his owner, Denny, fuels the story. Enzo begins with his first memory of Denny. Denny picks Enzo out of a litter of puppies on a country farm and takes him to live in his Seattle apartment. Enzo is a country dog at heart but endures city life for Denny. He is very protective and is critical of Denny's romantic attachments. Eventually one woman, Eve, wins his heart and Denny's. Denny marries Eve, and the two start a family. When Denny, an aspiring race car driver, is racing in Daytona, Florida, Eve gives birth to his daughter Zoe with Enzo at her side. Enzo's protective nature deepens with the birth of Zoe. Eve asks Enzo to promise to protect Zoe, and he faithfully watches over them and does what he can to take care of them.

All this happens on the same day as Denny experiences a major professional setback. A driver on his team has an accident, taking them out of the running. Denny is forced to go back to working at an auto shop.

Back at home, life is settling down, but Enzo can see that Eve is not well. He can smell a decaying odor coming from her head. When Denny is away from home at his next race, Eve wakes up in excruciating pain. She takes Zoe and leaves Enzo alone for days.

Denny's racing team wins first place, but he must turn down the offer of a lifetime to take care of his family. Eve is in extreme pain and suffering from mood swings, vertigo, and nausea, but she refuses to go to the doctor. When she learns she is dying of cancer, Denny's world continues to crumble. Eve moves in with her parents, leaving Denny alone and sad. After Eve dies, her parents seek custody of Zoe, and a custody battle follows. Eventually Denny receives custody of Zoe, but Enzo is dying. Enzo focuses on the memories of his life and those he has loved. He hopes to be reincarnated as a human.

1. Which of the following is a conflict in the story?
   - **a.** Enzo watches the birth of Zoe.
   - **b.** Enzo looks back on memories in his life.
   - **c.** Denny fights for custody of Zoe.
   - **d.** Denny picks Enzo out of a litter of puppies.

2. What happens at the climax of the story?
   - **a.** Enzo discovers Eve has cancer.
   - **b.** Enzo watches the birth of Zoe.
   - **c.** Denny loses his race.
   - **d.** Eve moves in with her parents.

3. Organize the events into the plot triangle graphic organizer.

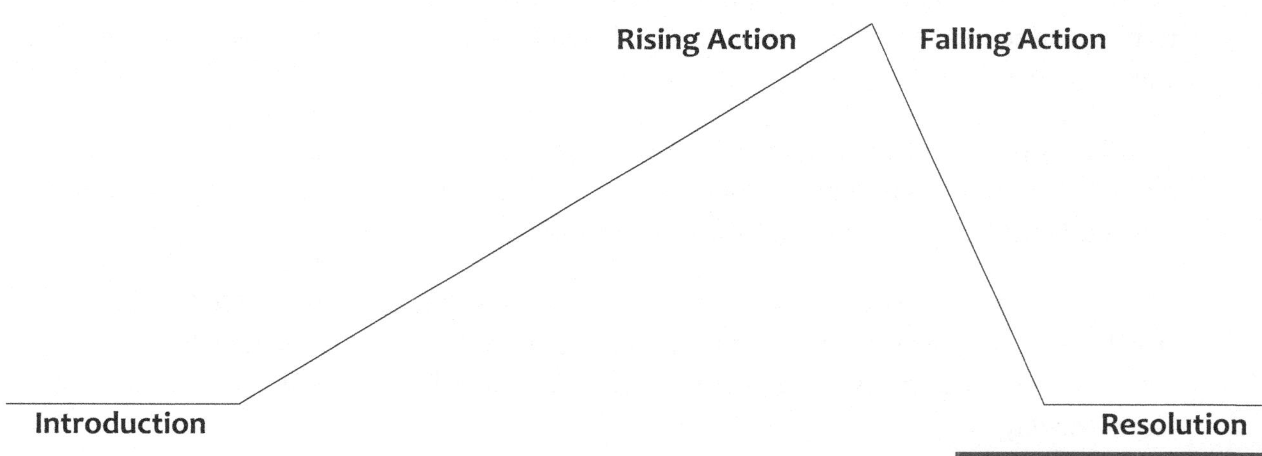

Denny gets custody of Zoe.
Denny loses a race and his racing career.
Denny picks Enzo out of a litter.
Eve gives birth to Zoe.
Enzo passes away.
Enzo accepts and loves Eve.
Denny misses the birth.
Eve gets cancer and moves home.
Eve passes away.

Remember the Concept

Stories follow a basic structure:

- Introduction
- Rising Action
- Climax
- Falling Action
- Resolution

Setting, Tone, Genre, and Style

Connections

Have you ever...

- Been unable to put down an engrossing book?
- Decided not to see a movie because you dislike horror?
- Read a book that made you sad?

When you read, you react to what you're reading. Maybe you enjoy it or dislike it. Maybe you don't understand it. Maybe you're on the edge of your seat with excitement and anticipation.

Stylistic elements like setting, tone, and genre affect your understanding and enjoyment of a text.

Setting is the time, place, and circumstance where a story takes place. A book's setting might be a small town in New England, on a winter's evening in 1964. The upcoming race for mayor, the German heritage of the town, and the local logging industry would all contribute to the setting.

Tone is the author's attitude. In fiction, tone is often related to mood, the atmosphere of the work or the feeling that you get while reading it. The tone of a coming of age novel might be hopeful or regretful. The tone of a story about a lost love might be wistful or sentimental.

A **genre** is a category or type of story. Genres are defined by what they have in common: their subject, style, and form. Genres are often general categories, like comedy or drama. A story's specific genre can fall into a smaller sub-group and contain elements from multiple genres, like a historical coming-of-age romantic comedy.

An author's **style** is a broad term. It includes how the author uses words, constructs sentences, and approaches the story. Setting, tone, and genre are just a few elements of style.

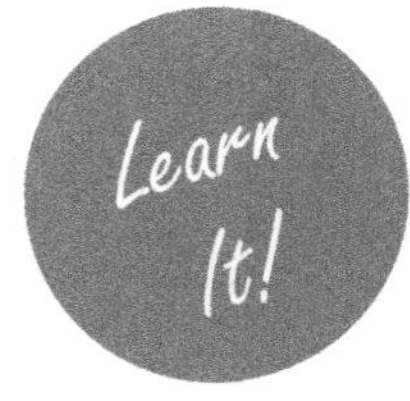

Words → Meaning → Purpose Chart for Style Elements

Understanding elements of style will help you get more out of what you read. You can use a Words → Meaning → Purpose chart to understand an author's style.

The Secret Adversary is a novel by Agatha Christie about important papers that go missing during World War I and the search for them after the war.

Use the passage for the exercises that follow.

Prologue

It was 2 P.M. on the afternoon of May 7, 1915. The Lusitania had been struck by two torpedoes in succession and was sinking rapidly, while the boats were being launched with all possible speed. The women and children were being lined up awaiting their turn. Some still clung desperately to husbands and fathers; others clutched their children closely to their breasts. One girl stood alone, slightly apart from the rest. She was quite young, not more than eighteen. She did not seem afraid, and her grave, steadfast eyes looked straight ahead.

"I beg your pardon."

A man's voice beside her made her start and turn. She had noticed the speaker more than once amongst the first-class passengers. There had been a hint of mystery about him which had appealed to her imagination. He spoke to no one. If anyone spoke to him he was quick to rebuff the overture. Also he had a nervous way of looking over his shoulder with a swift, suspicious glance.

She noticed now that he was greatly agitated. There were beads of perspiration on his brow. He was evidently in a state of overmastering fear. And yet he did not strike her as the kind of man who would be afraid to meet death!

"Yes?" Her grave eyes met his inquiringly.

He stood looking at her with a kind of desperate irresolution.

"It must be!" he muttered to himself. "Yes—it is the only way." Then aloud he said abruptly: "You are an American?"

"Yes."

"A patriotic one?"

The girl flushed.

"I guess you've no right to ask such a thing! Of course I am!"

"Don't be offended. You wouldn't be if you knew how much there was at stake. But I've got to trust someone—and it must be a woman."

"Why?"

"Because of 'women and children first.'" He looked round and lowered his voice. "I'm carrying papers—vitally important papers. They may make all the difference to the Allies in the war. You understand? These papers have GOT to be saved! They've more chance with you than with me. Will you take them?"

From *The Secret Adversary* by Agatha Christie, 1922

D Determine the Purpose

Imagine you are looking at books in the library with a friend. You show her *The Secret Adversary* by Agatha Christie and open to the first pages. She isn't sure if she's interested in reading it. She is curious about the genre of the book and the author's style. You aren't sure what to say.

A Approach the Text

Elements of style like the setting, tone, and genre affect your reaction to fiction. You might be thrilled or excited. You might be saddened or intrigued. When you approach a text, thinking about style elements can help you get more meaning from the text and understand what you enjoy. Before you read, you can preview the text to get clues to genre, setting, and other elements of the work.

?

1. Skim the passage. What can you tell about the genre and setting? What do you expect based on the genre and setting?

You might identify the genre as a mystery or spy novel because of the important papers and mention of patriotism. You also might recognize the author as a mystery writer and associate the words secret and adversary with mystery. The setting is a sinking ship in 1915, before the U.S. entered World War I. The torpedoes are a result of the war. You might expect romance, danger, and international intrigue.

R *Read*

As you read, pay attention to the characters, dialogue, and description. How do they express the work's style? How are they related to other works in the same genre or setting? What is familiar, and what is new? What descriptive words can you use to express the style and tone? How do these elements help you understand or enjoy what you read?

Using a Words → Meaning → Purpose chart can help you link details to their meaning and effect on style.

Setting

You can understand the effect of setting better by identifying quotations that relate to the setting and evaluating their meaning and purpose.

? **2.** Complete the following chart. What is the author saying about the setting? What is the purpose of this passage?

Words	Meaning	Purpose
"The Lusitania had been struck by two torpedoes in succession and was sinking rapidly, while the boats were being launched with all possible speed."		

The setting is a sinking ship, the Lusitania, which has been hit by torpedoes. The presence of torpedoes indicates a war. Passengers are escaping by lifeboat.

The author's purpose is to give a dramatic and exciting reason for the man to pass off important papers to the woman. The setting creates an air of urgency and suspense.

Tone

Evaluate tone by identifying details that show emotion or perspective.

? **3.** Complete the following chart. List a detail that the author uses to set the tone. What does the detail mean?

Words	Meaning	Purpose
"The Lusitania had been struck by two torpedoes in succession and was sinking rapidly, while the boats were being launched with all possible speed."	The setting is a sinking ship, the Lusitania, which has been hit by torpedoes. The presence of torpedoes indicates a war. Passengers are escaping by lifeboat.	The author's purpose is to give a dramatic and exciting reason for the man to pass off important papers to the woman. The setting creates an air of urgency and suspense.

You might choose a detail like, "Her grave, steadfast eyes looked straight ahead." Considering the setting, the woman is especially calm and collected. You might conclude that the tone is one of calm amid intense danger.

Words	Meaning	Purpose
"The Lusitania had been struck by two torpedoes in succession and was sinking rapidly, while the boats were being launched with all possible speed."	The setting is a sinking ship, the Lusitania, which has been hit by torpedoes. The presence of torpedoes indicates a war. Passengers are escaping by lifeboat.	The author's purpose is to give a dramatic and exciting reason for the man to pass off important papers to the woman. The setting creates an air of urgency and suspense.
"Her grave, steadfast eyes looked straight ahead."	The woman is calm and collected.	The tone is one of calm amid intense danger.

E *Evaluate*

Think about the author's style. What is the overall feeling you get from the work? What is your reaction to genre, tone, setting, and other elements of style?

? **5.** Describe the author's style. How does the style affect your reading experience?

The setting, tone, and genre set up a mysterious scene and make the reader curious. An element of danger is introduced through the dialogue and description.

The novel *A Connecticut Yankee in King Arthur's Court* by Mark Twain tells the story of a man who travels back in time to the days of King Arthur.

Read the passage and answer the questions that follow.

". . . Now tell me, honest and true, where am I?"

"IN KING ARTHUR'S COURT."

I waited a minute, to let that idea shudder its way home, and then said:

"And according to your notions, what year is it now?"

"528—nineteenth of June." . . .

I seemed to believe the boy, I didn't know why. *Something* in me seemed to believe him—my consciousness, as you may say; but my reason didn't. My reason straightway began to clamor; that was natural. I didn't know how to go about satisfying it, because I knew that the testimony of men wouldn't serve—my reason would say they were lunatics, and throw out their evidence. But all of a sudden I stumbled on the very thing, just by luck. I knew that the only total eclipse of the sun in the first half of the sixth century occurred on the 21st of June, A.D. 528, O.S., and began at 3 minutes after 12 noon. I also knew that no total eclipse of the sun was due in what to *me* was the present year—i.e., 1879. So, if I could keep my anxiety and curiosity from eating the heart out of me for forty-eight hours, I should then find out for certain whether this boy was telling me the truth or not.

Wherefore, being a practical Connecticut man, I now shoved this whole problem clear out of my mind till its appointed day and hour should come, in order that I might turn all my attention to the circumstances of the present moment, and be alert and ready to make the most out of them that could be made. One thing at a time, is my motto—and just play that thing for all it is worth, even if it's only two pair and a jack. I made up my mind to two things: if it was still the nineteenth century and I was among lunatics and couldn't get away, I would presently boss that asylum or know the reason why; and if, on the other hand, it was really the sixth century, all right, I didn't want any softer thing: I would boss the whole country inside of three months; for I judged I would have the start of the best-educated man in the kingdom by a matter of thirteen hundred years and upward.

From *A Connecticut Yankee in King Arthur's Court* by Mark Twain, 1889

1. Select three words or phrases that help set the tone. Fill in the chart below.

Words	Meaning	Purpose

2. Which details give you information about the setting of the passage?

3. What does the setting add to the passage?

4. Which of the following genres describes the passage?
   a. Comedy
   b. Historical fiction
   c. Suspense
   d. Drama

5. Explain how you identified the genre.

6. What other genre or genre elements are present in the passage?

7. How does the style of the passage affect you as a reader?

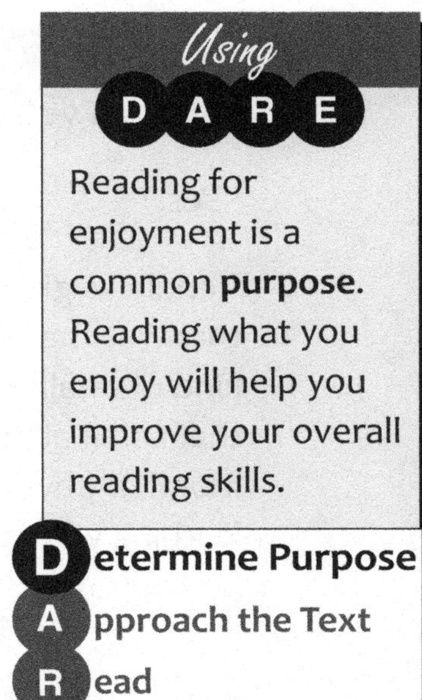

Check Your Skills

The short story "Second Variety" by Philip K. Dick takes place after nuclear war has turned the world into a wasteland.

Read the passage and answer the questions that follow.

The boy fell in beside him. Hendricks strode along. The boy walked silently, clutching his teddy bear.

"What's your name?" Hendricks said, after a time.

"David Edward Derring."

"David? What—what happened to your mother and father?"

"They died."

"How?"

"In the blast."

"How long ago?"

"Six years."

Hendricks slowed down. "You've been alone six years?"

"No. There were other people for awhile. They went away."

"And you've been alone since?"

"Yes."

Hendricks glanced down. The boy was strange, saying very little. Withdrawn. But that was the way they were, the children who had survived. Quiet. Stoic. A strange kind of fatalism gripped them. Nothing came as a surprise. They accepted anything that came along. There was no longer any normal, any natural course of things, moral or physical, for them to expect. Custom, habit, all the determining forces of learning were gone; only brute experience remained.

"Am I walking too fast?" Hendricks said.

"No."

"How did you happen to see me?"

"I was waiting."

"Waiting?" Hendricks was puzzled. "What were you waiting for?"

"To catch things."

"What kind of things?"

"Things to eat."

"Oh." Hendricks set his lips grimly. A thirteen year old boy, living on rats and gophers and half-rotten canned food. Down in a hole under the ruins of a town. With radiation pools and claws, and Russian dive-mines up above, coasting around in the sky.

"Where are we going?" David asked.

"To the Russian lines."

"Russian?"

"The enemy. The people who started the war. They dropped the first radiation bombs. They began all this."

The boy nodded. His face showed no expression.

"I'm an American," Hendricks said.

There was no comment. On they went, the two of them, Hendricks walking a little ahead, David trailing behind him, hugging his dirty teddy bear against his chest.

From "Second Variety" by Philip K. Dick, 1953

Reading for Understanding

A **genre** (such as comedy, science fiction, or romance) refers to general qualities of a work and how it fits into a group of similar works. You can understand a genre best by comparing many works in that genre.

1. Which genre is this passage?
   a. Historical fiction
   b. Science fiction
   c. Comedy
   d. Romance

2. The passage states, "A thirteen year old boy, living on rats and gophers and half-rotten canned food. Down in a hole under the ruins of a town." What can you conclude based on this detail?
   - **a.** The boy is a runaway living in the wilds.
   - **b.** Human civilization has been devastated.
   - **c.** Only rats and gophers have survived.
   - **d.** The town is the main setting of the story.

3. What can you expect the story to be about based on the genre and the setting?
   - **a.** A struggle for survival in a post-apocalyptic society
   - **b.** A recount of historical battles and outcomes
   - **c.** A heartwarming story of the rescue of a young boy
   - **d.** The power struggle between different forms of evil

4. What is the tone of the passage?
   - **a.** Hopeful, heartening
   - **b.** Dark, hopeless
   - **c.** Angry, vengeful
   - **d.** Cynical, sarcastic

5. Which detail most directly expresses the tone of the passage?
   - **a.** "'I'm an American,' Hendricks said."
   - **b.** "On they went, the two of them, Hendricks walking a little ahead."
   - **c.** "But that was the way they were, the children who had survived."
   - **d.** "Custom, habit, all the determining forces of learning were gone; only brute experience remained."

> **Remember the Concept**
>
> Elements of style like setting, tone, and genre affect your understanding and enjoyment of a text. Identify the **Words** → **Meaning** → **Purpose** to understand how the author communicates.

Point of View

Connections

Have you ever…

- Felt the narrator in a movie wasn't telling the whole story?
- Argued with your friend about what they actually said?
- Wondered what a character was thinking?

When you read, the author tells the story from a specific point of view. No two people will tell the same story the same way. How a character, place, or situation is described will affect your understanding of the story.

Point of view is the perspective of the story. Who tells it? What do (and don't) you know? The perspective will be different depending on who is telling the story. Be aware that some writers may switch between different points of view.

Types of Point of View

First Person	*I* thought the man was lying. *I* looked at Tom, but his face was blank.	Shows only what the narrator sees, hears, feels, and thinks
Second Person	*You* thought the man was lying. *You* looked at Tom, but his face was blank.	Addresses the reader directly
Third Person	*John* listened to the man. *He* looked at Tom, but Tom's face was blank.	Observes characters objectively, may or may not reveal thoughts
Third Person, Omniscient	John *thought* the man was lying, but *in Tom's mind*, the stranger was the only one telling the truth.	Can show you any character's thoughts and feelings, and anything that's happening
Third Person, Limited	John *thought* the man was lying. He looked at Tom, but Tom's face was blank.	Shows you only one character's thoughts and feelings

A Process for Evaluating Point of View

To evaluate point of view:

- Look for **pronouns** (who the narrator is)
- Look for **thoughts** (what the narrator knows)
- Evaluate **words** (what the narrator says)
- Synthesize **viewpoint** (what the narrator is like)

The narrator can add a lot to a book or story. Is the narration objective? Does it give commentary on the story? Does the narrator crack jokes or emphasize the story's sadness? How does the narrator change your thoughts, impressions, and feelings about the story?

The short story "2BR02B" by Kurt Vonnegut is about a society where natural death has been obliterated and the government offers assisted suicide to those who want to die.

Use the passage for the following exercises.

Everything was perfectly swell.

There were no prisons, no slums, no insane asylums, no cripples, no poverty, no wars.

All diseases were conquered. So was old age.

Death, barring accidents, was an adventure for volunteers.

The population of the United States was stabilized at forty-million souls.

One bright morning in the Chicago Lying-in Hospital, a man named Edward K. Wehling, Jr., waited for his wife to give birth. He was the only man waiting. Not many people were born a day any more.

Wehling was fifty-six, a mere stripling in a population whose average age was one hundred and twenty-nine.

X-rays had revealed that his wife was going to have triplets. The children would be his first.

Young Wehling was hunched in his chair, his head in his hand. He was so rumpled, so still and colorless as to be virtually invisible. His camouflage was perfect, since the waiting room had a disorderly and demoralized air, too. Chairs and ashtrays had been moved away from the walls. The floor was paved with spattered dropcloths.

The room was being redecorated. It was being redecorated as a memorial to a man who had volunteered to die.

A sardonic old man, about two hundred years old, sat on a stepladder, painting a mural he did not like. Back in the days when people aged visibly, his age would have been guessed at thirty-five or so. Aging had touched him that much before the cure for aging was found.

The mural he was working on depicted a very neat garden. Men and women in white, doctors and nurses, turned the soil, planted seedlings, sprayed bugs, spread fertilizer.

From "2BR02B" by Kurt Vonngeut, 1962

Identify Pronouns

The pronouns an author uses will help you determine the point of view of the story.

- **First person** uses first person pronouns: *I, me, us, we.*
- **Second person** uses second pronoun pronouns: *you, your.*
- **Third person** uses only third person pronouns: *he, she, they, them.*

?

1. What is the point of view of the passage?

a. First person
b. Second person
c. Third person

The point of view is third person.

Look for Thoughts

Do you get to see inside any characters' minds? Whose thoughts does the narrator know?

?

2. Which characters' thoughts does the narrator know?

In this passage, you don't know any of the characters' thoughts. You have to infer the characters' thoughts and feelings.

Examine Word Choice and Details

The narrator is not a character in this passage, but the narrator still has a viewpoint. What words does the narrator choose? What effect do those words have?

To evaluate point of view in a story, you can use a Words → Meaning → Purpose chart. The chart will help you identify details and their effect.

? **3.** Select three powerful words or phrases that help you understand the narrator's viewpoint, and complete the chart with their meaning and purpose. Look for the words' effect to identify purpose.

Words	Meaning	Purpose

Some of the most powerful words the narrator uses are: *swell, demoralized,* and *sardonic.* You might complete the chart like this:

Words	Meaning	Purpose
Swell	Excellent	Shows on the surface, everything is going great; seems ironic in context
Demoralized	Losing confidence or hope	Describes the depressing nature of a waiting room, normally a happy place
Sardonic	Grimly mocking or cynical	Shows that even though man now lives forever, life wears people down

Evaluate Viewpoint

Put together what you know about the narrator. What is the point of view?

? **4.** Think about the narrative point of view in this passage. What is the narrator like? What does the narration add to the story?

The third-person narrator in this passage stands outside society and comments subtly on what's happening, using ironic and contrasting words. On the surface in this passage, humans seem to have it made. They don't age and don't have to die unless they volunteer. The narrator's word choice implies that the people aren't actually happy and that the society, which seems ideal on the surface, is not ideal at all.

The novel *The War of the Worlds* by H.G. Wells tells the story of a Martian invasion of Earth.

Read the passage and answer the questions that follow.

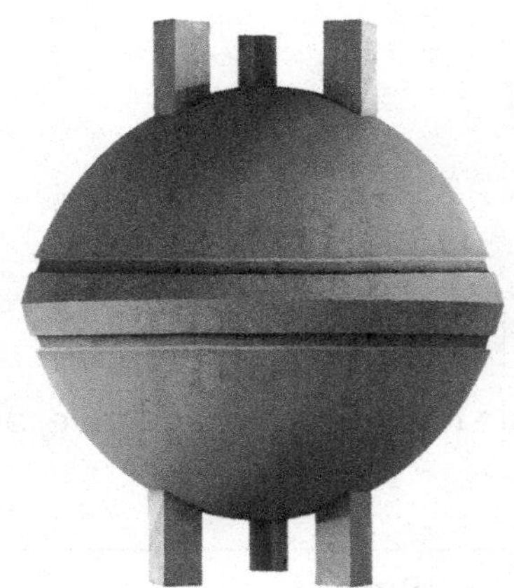

And then he perceived that, very slowly, the circular top of the cylinder was rotating on its body. It was such a gradual movement that he discovered it only through noticing that a black mark that had been near him five minutes ago was now at the other side of the circumference. Even then he scarcely understood what this indicated, until he heard a muffled grating sound and saw the black mark jerk forward an inch or so. Then the thing came upon him in a flash. The cylinder was artificial—hollow—with an end that screwed out! Something within the cylinder was unscrewing the top!

"Good heavens!" said Ogilvy. "There's a man in it—men in it! Half roasted to death! Trying to escape!"

At once, with a quick mental leap, he linked the Thing with the flash upon Mars.

The thought of the confined creature was so dreadful to him that he forgot the heat and went forward to the cylinder to help turn. But luckily the dull radiation arrested him before he could burn his hands on the still-glowing metal. At that he stood irresolute for a moment, then turned, scrambled out of the pit, and set off running wildly into Woking. The time then must have been somewhere about six o'clock. He met a waggoner and tried to make him understand, but the tale he told and his appearance were so wild—his hat had fallen off in the pit—that the man simply drove on. He was equally unsuccessful with the potman who was just unlocking the doors of the public-house by Horsell Bridge. The fellow thought he was a lunatic at large and made an unsuccessful attempt to shut him into the taproom. That sobered him a little; and when he saw Henderson, the London journalist, in his garden, he called over the palings and made himself understood.

From *The War of the Worlds* by H.G. Wells, 1898

Reading for Understanding

The narrator isn't always reliable. Occasionally, the narrator's point of view is so subjective that you can't trust what the narrator says.

1. What is the point of view of the passage?
    a. First person
    b. Second person
    c. Third person

2. Whose thoughts does the narrator communicate?

3. Identify three powerful words in the passage that show the narrator's perspective, and use them to complete the chart.

Words	Meaning	Purpose

4. How does Ogilvy feel about what he sees?

5. How does the narrator's point of view affect your thoughts about events in the passage?

6. Compare Ogilvy's point of view to the narrator's point of view.

When you **evaluate** fiction, try to understand the difference between the narrator's viewpoint and the author's viewpoint. Sometimes they are similar, but they can also be very different.

Determine Purpose
Approach the Text
Read
Evaluate

Check Your Skills

The story "The Pit and the Pendulum" by Edgar Allan Poe is set during the Spanish Inquisition, an institution of the Catholic government in 15th- and 16th-century Spain which tried people accused of breaking the rules of the religion.

Read the passage and answer the questions that follow.

I WAS sick—sick unto death with that long agony; and when they at length unbound me, and I was permitted to sit, I felt that my senses were leaving me. The sentence—the dread sentence of death—was the last of distinct accentuation which reached my ears. After that, the sound of the inquisitorial voices seemed merged in one dreamy indeterminate hum. It conveyed to my soul the idea of revolution—perhaps from its association in fancy with the burr of a mill wheel. This only for a brief period; for presently I heard no more. Yet, for a while, I saw; but with how terrible an exaggeration! I saw the lips of the black-robed judges. They appeared to me white—whiter than the sheet upon which I trace these words—and thin even to grotesqueness; thin with the intensity of their expression of firmness—of immovable resolution—of stern contempt of human torture. I saw that the decrees of what to me was Fate, were still issuing from those lips. I saw them writhe with a deadly locution. I saw them fashion the syllables of my name; and I shuddered because no sound succeeded. I saw, too, for a few moments of delirious horror, the soft and nearly imperceptible waving of the sable draperies which enwrapped the walls of the apartment.

And then my vision fell upon the seven tall candles upon the table. At first they wore the aspect of charity, and seemed white and slender angels who would save me; but then, all at once, there came a most deadly nausea over my spirit, and I felt every fibre in my frame thrill as if I had touched the wire of a galvanic battery, while the angel forms became meaningless spectres, with heads of flame, and I saw that from them there would be no help. And then there stole into my fancy, like a rich musical note, the thought of what sweet rest there must be in the grave. The thought came gently and stealthily, and it seemed long before it attained full appreciation; but just as my spirit came at length properly to feel and entertain it, the figures of the judges vanished, as if magically, from before me; the tall candles sank into nothingness; their flames went out utterly; the blackness of darkness supervened; all sensations appeared swallowed up in a mad rushing descent as of the soul into Hades. Then silence, and stillness, night were the universe. I had swooned; but still will not say that all of consciousness was lost. What of it there remained I will not attempt to define, or even to describe; yet all was not lost.

From "The Pit and the Pendulum" by Edgar Allan Poe, 1842

1. Who is the narrator?
   - a. An insane man who does not know where he is
   - b. An executioner at a prison who must end a man's life
   - c. A prisoner who plans to escape
   - d. A prisoner who has been sentenced to death

2. What is the narrator describing in the passage?
   - a. Losing consciousness
   - b. Trying to escape
   - c. Having a mental breakdown
   - d. Wrestling with his conscience

3. Which word best describes the narrator's feelings in the passage?
   - a. Hopeless
   - b. Angry
   - c. Delirious
   - d. Hopeful

4. In the passage, the narrator says, "the sound of the inquisitorial voices seemed merged in one dreamy indeterminate hum." What effect does this have?
   - a. It makes the sounds in the courtroom seem very loud.
   - b. It allows the reader to imagine sounds of the scene more objectively.
   - c. It shows the narrator's experience, drifting in and out of reality.
   - d. It indicates to the reader that the whole scene is a dream.

5. What do the candles indicate?
   - a. The narrator's changing perspective on hope
   - b. The narrator's light in a time of darkness
   - c. The narrator's illness that comes over him
   - d. The narrator's desire to die

Remember the Concept

Evaluate point of view with four steps.

- Look for **pronouns.** Pronouns tell who the narrator is.
- Look for **thoughts.** Thoughts tell what the narrator knows.
- Evaluate **words.** Words tell what the narrator says.
- Synthesize **viewpoint.** Viewpoint tells the narrator's perspective.

Comparing Fiction

Connections

Have you ever...

- Read a story that reminded you of a character in another book?
- Needed to decide which book to recommend to a friend?
- Seen a new movie that had a twist on a familiar genre?

It's natural to compare books, movies, and stories. You can gain a better understanding of both stories and discover similarities and differences you never knew existed.

Comparing fiction can help you learn more about genre. It can help you make connections between stories written at different times and in different cultures, and it can expand your understanding of thematic idea.

When you compare, you look for similarities and differences. First, decide what you will compare and why. Choose:

- **A frame of reference:** What qualities are you comparing? You could compare an idea, theme, purpose, tone, character, genre, setting, or something else.
- **Grounds for comparison:** Why are you comparing these particular things? What can you learn?

Using a Comparison Alley to Compare Fiction

Comparing fictional texts can give you a bigger picture about themes, ideas, genres, and trends in literature. You can learn:

- How authors' styles are related.
- How a genre is reflected across different texts.
- How different authors treat similar time periods, themes, or characters.

Use these passages for the exercises that follow.

The Metamorphosis by Franz Kafka is a novella about a man who wakes up to find he has transformed into an insect.

One morning, when Gregor Samsa woke from troubled dreams, he found himself transformed in his bed into a horrible vermin. He lay on his armour-like back, and if he lifted his head a little he could see his brown belly, slightly domed and divided by arches into stiff sections. The bedding was hardly able to cover it and seemed ready to slide off any moment. His many legs, pitifully thin compared with the size of the rest of him, waved about helplessly as he looked.

"What's happened to me?" he thought. It wasn't a dream. His room, a proper human room although a little too small, lay peacefully between its four familiar walls. A collection of textile samples lay spread out on the table—Samsa was a travelling salesman—and above it there hung a picture that he had recently cut out of an illustrated magazine and housed in a nice, gilded frame. It showed a lady fitted out with a fur hat and fur boa who sat upright, raising a heavy fur muff that covered the whole of her lower arm towards the viewer.

Gregor then turned to look out the window at the dull weather. Drops of rain could be heard hitting the pane, which made him feel quite sad. "How about if I sleep a little bit longer and forget all this nonsense," he thought, but that was something he was unable to do because he was used to sleeping on his right, and in his present state couldn't get into that position. However hard he threw himself onto his right, he always rolled back to where he was. He must have tried it a hundred times, shut his eyes so that he wouldn't have to look at the floundering legs, and only stopped when he began to feel a mild, dull pain there that he had never felt before.

From *The Metamorphosis* by Franz Kafka, 1915

The "Piper in the Woods" by Philip K. Dick is a short story about a soldier who claims he is a plant.

"Well, Corporal Westerburg," Doctor Henry Harris said gently, "just why do you think you're a plant?"

As he spoke, Harris glanced down again at the card on his desk. It was from the Base Commander himself, made out in Cox's heavy scrawl: *Doc, this is the lad I told you about. Talk to him and try to find out how he got this delusion. He's from the new Garrison, the new check-station on Asteroid Y-3, and we don't want anything to go wrong there. Especially a silly damn thing like this!*

Harris pushed the card aside and stared back up at the youth across the desk from him. The young man seemed ill at ease and appeared to be avoiding answering the question Harris had put to him. Harris frowned. Westerburg was a good-looking chap, actually handsome in his Patrol uniform, a shock of blond hair over one eye. He was tall, almost six feet, a fine healthy lad, just two years out of Training, according to the card. Born in Detroit. Had measles when he was nine. Interested in jet engines, tennis, and girls. Twenty-six years old.

"Well, Corporal Westerburg," Doctor Harris said again. "Why do you think you're a plant?"

The Corporal looked up shyly. He cleared his throat. "Sir, I am a plant, I don't just think so. I've been a plant for several days, now."

"I see." The Doctor nodded. "You mean that you weren't always a plant?"

"No, sir. I just became a plant recently."

"And what were you before you became a plant?"

"Well, sir, I was just like the rest of you."

There was silence. Doctor Harris took up his pen and scratched a few lines, but nothing of importance came. A plant? And such a healthy-looking lad! Harris removed his steel-rimmed glasses and polished them with his handkerchief. He put them on again and leaned back in his chair. "Care for a cigarette, Corporal?"

"No, sir."

From "Piper in the Woods" by Philip K. Dick, 1952

D Determine the Purpose

You are reading *The Metamorphosis* and "Piper in the Woods" in your literature class. Both texts contain a strange transformation. Your teacher asks you to compare the idea of transformation in the two works.

A Approach the Text

A Comparison Alley provides a visual way to analyze the similarities and differences. Before you read, decide what you will compare.

?

1. Which of the following would be helpful to compare to evaluate transformation in the two passages? Select all correct answers.
   - ☐ Character
   - ☐ Length
   - ☐ Tone
   - ☐ Point of View
   - ☐ Date Written
   - ☐ Predictability

You could compare many aspects of the passages, but comparing character, tone, and point of view will be most relevant to how they treat transformation.

The similarities and differences should help you gain a deeper understanding. The length, date written, and predictability will not help.

R Read

As you read, make notes about the characters, point of view, and tone. Determine similarities and differences, and add them to the Comparison Alley.

?

2. Read the passage, and complete the graphic organizer.

Similarities

Differences

Differences

Your finished graphic organizer might look like this:

Metamorphosis
Gregor is transformed into a beetle
Physical transformation
Gregor is confused by the transformation
Tone is troubled, sad
See transformed man's thoughts
Differences

Similarities
Topic transformation
Neither are really disturbed by transformation
Third person point of view
Some humor

Differences
Piper in the Woods
Transformed into a plant
Mental transformation
Westburg is matter-of-fact
Tone is light
See the nontransformed character's thoughts

E Evaluate

Comparing texts allows you to draw conclusions and evaluate the information to gain a deeper understanding of the texts that you read. What did you learn from comparing the texts?

?

3. Compare how the passages treat the idea of transformation.

Gregor and Westburg have both undergone bizarre transformations but seem undisturbed by them. Gregor's transformation is physical, since he has actually turned into a beetle. Westburg's is mental; he believes he has turned into a plant. The reader sees Gregor's thoughts, and while Gregor regards his transformation with confusion, he doesn't react emotionally, with the fear or horror the reader might expect. In "Piper in the Woods," the reader only sees the doctor's thoughts, and like Gregor, the doctor is confused. However, Westburg seems to have accepted his transformation, showing even less emotion than Gregor. Both passages have an element of humor because of the strangeness of the transformations, but The Metamorphosis is more melancholy than "Piper in the Woods." Gregor's transformation is a burden, which he accepts stoically; Westburg's transformation seems to burden only his commanders.

Read these passages, which both deal with characters trying to better themselves, and answer the questions that follow.

Summary of *The House on Mango Street* by Sandra Cisernos

When Esperanza is 12, her family buys a house of their own on Mango Street. It is rundown and small, and located in a poor Latino neighborhood in Chicago. Esperanza has no privacy, and she resolves that she will someday leave Mango Street and have a house all her own.

Esperanza begins writing as a way to escape. She is ashamed of her heritage and her family's lack of money. Esperanza makes friends with the girls across the street, Lucy and Rachel. The three have adventures around the neighborhood. Throughout the year, the girls start to cross over from childhood to the adult world. Esperanza starts to notice boys. She must deal with the deaths of her grandfather and Aunt Lupe. She tries to learn from the mistakes of the other women in her neighborhood and prays that she doesn't end up like them.

When one of the girls on the street is assaulted, Esperanza becomes more determined to leave Mango Street. She realizes that even after she leaves, she will always be connected to the neighborhood and the women she is leaving. Esperanza decides that writing will be a vehicle to help her escape figuratively and literally.

Summary of *The Bean Trees* by Barbara Kingsolver

Taylor Greer lives in rural Kentucky. She watches those who stay there lead dead-end lives and is determined not to end up like them. Five years after she graduates from high school, she has finally saved enough money to head out on her own.

She heads out without a destination in mind and has car trouble in the middle of the Cherokee Nation in Oklahoma. A woman approaches her car and puts a baby in the front seat for Taylor to have. Taylor decides to leave with the baby, and she later finds out the child has been abused. She names the baby Turtle. In Tucson, Arizona, Taylor gets two flat tires. She goes to a tire store to replace them and befriends the owner, Mattie. Taylor decides to stay, and she eventually finds a room for rent listed in the paper. The room is being rented out by a woman named Lou Ann, another native Kentuckian and single mother. Taylor ends up working for Mattie at the shop. One day Taylor discovers that two of Mattie's friends, Estevan and Esperanza, are illegal aliens living in Mattie's home above the tire shop.

Comparing Fiction

Estevan and Esperanza had to leave a child behind in Guatemala. The government took away their daughter to force information from them, but they chose to save seventeen lives. They fled their country without their daughter.

One day, Taylor leaves Turtle in the care of a blind babysitter, and at the park, a man attempts to take Turtle. The babysitter stops him, but Taylor is shaken. When police investigate, they learn that Taylor is not a legal guardian and attempt to take Turtle away. At the same time, Estevan and Esperanza are in danger after a recent crackdown on illegal immigration. Taylor tells authorities that Turtle is Estevan and Esperanza's daughter so she can receive custody. Estevan and Esperanza move to Oklahoma, where the immigration laws are different, and Taylor and Turtle return to Tuscan.

---

1. After reading the passages, which qualities would you compare to help you understand their meaning? Select all correct answers.
   - ❑ Theme
   - ❑ Character backgrounds
   - ❑ Character descriptions
   - ❑ Setting
   - ❑ Point of view
   - ❑ Character motivations

2. Use the categories you selected to find similarities and differences, and complete the Comparison Alley graphic organizer.

Similarities

Differences

Differences

 3. Compare Taylor and Esperanza's attitudes about the places they lived as children.

 4. Compare the role of friends and families in Taylor and Esperanza's lives.

 5. Compare the elements that force Taylor and Esperanza to grow up or mature.

Reading for Understanding

While you read, relate the text to other things you've read and seen. Comparing while you read can help you better comprehend the text.

Check **Your Skills**

Read the passages and answer the questions that follow.

In *The Mysterious Affair at Styles* by Agatha Christie, Detective Hercule Poirot investigates the death of Emily Inglethorp, a recently remarried wealthy widow.

"This is a very pleasant meeting for me, Miss Cynthia. This is my old friend, Monsieur Poirot, whom I have not seen for years."

"Oh, we know Monsieur Poirot," said Cynthia gaily. "But I had no idea he was a friend of yours."

"Yes, indeed," said Poirot seriously. "I know Mademoiselle Cynthia. It is by the charity of that good Mrs. Inglethorp that I am here." Then, as I looked at him inquiringly: "Yes, my friend, she had kindly extended hospitality to seven of my country people who, alas, are refugees from their native land. We Belgians will always remember her with gratitude."

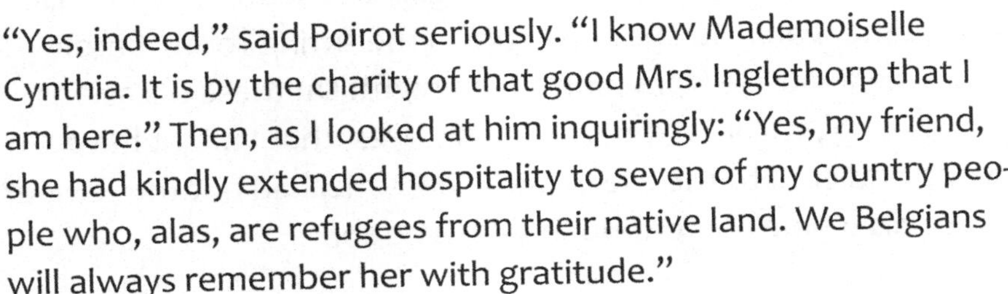

Poirot was an extraordinary looking little man. He was hardly more than five feet, four inches, but carried himself with great dignity. His head was exactly the shape of an egg, and he always perched it a little on one side. His moustache was very stiff and military. The neatness of his attire was almost incredible. I believe a speck of dust would have caused him more pain than a bullet wound. Yet this quaint dandified little man who, I was sorry to see, now limped badly, had been in his time one of the most celebrated members of the Belgian police. As a detective, his flair had been extraordinary, and he had achieved triumphs by unravelling some of the most baffling cases of the day.

He pointed out to me the little house inhabited by him and his fellow Belgians, and I promised to go and see him at an early date. Then he raised his hat with a flourish to Cynthia, and we drove away.

"He's a dear little man," said Cynthia. "I'd no idea you knew him."

"You've been entertaining a celebrity unawares," I replied.

And, for the rest of the way home, I recited to them the various exploits and triumphs of Hercule Poirot.

From *The Mysterious Affair at Styles* by Agatha Christie, 1916

In *A Study in Scarlet* by Sir Arthur Conan Doyle, Sherlock Holmes investigates the murder of Enoch Drebber.

[Sherlock] Holmes was certainly not a difficult man to live with. He was quiet in his ways, and his habits were regular.

It was rare for him to be up after ten at night, and he had invariably breakfasted and gone out before I rose in the morning. Sometimes he spent his day at the chemical laboratory, sometimes in the dissecting-rooms, and occasionally in long walks, which appeared to take him into the lowest portions of the City. Nothing could exceed his energy when the working fit was upon him; but now and again a reaction would seize him, and for days on end he would lie upon the sofa in the sitting-room, hardly uttering a word or moving a muscle from morning to night. On these occasions, I have noticed such a dreamy, vacant expression in his eyes, that I might have suspected him of being addicted to the use of some narcotic, had not the temperance and cleanliness of his whole life forbidden such a notion.

As the weeks went by, my interest in him and my curiosity as to his aims in life, gradually deepened and increased.

His very person and appearance were such as to strike the attention of the most casual observer. In height he was rather over six feet, and so excessively lean that he seemed to be considerably taller. His eyes were sharp and piercing, save during those intervals of torpor to which I have alluded; and his thin, hawk-like nose gave his whole expression an air of alertness and decision. His chin, too, had the prominence and squareness which mark the man of determination. His hands were invariably blotted with ink and stained with chemicals, yet he was possessed of extraordinary delicacy of touch, as I frequently had occasion to observe when I watched him manipulating his fragile philosophical instruments."

From *A Study in Scarlet* by Sir Arthur Conan Doyle, 1886

Evaluating what you've read doesn't mean only thinking about one text. You can compare a text to other texts, find information about the author and the time it was written, and bring your own knowledge and experience to your evaluation.

Determine Purpose
Approach the Text
Read
Evaluate

1. Compare these two statements:

   "Poirot was an extraordinary looking little man."

   "His very person and appearance were such as to strike the attention of the most casual observer."

   Why do both authors emphasize the strangeness of the characters' appearances?

   a. To make the narrators seem out-of-touch
   b. To make the reader embarrassed for the characters
   c. To make the characters stand out as unique people
   d. To make the novels seem believable

2. In the first passage, the narrator says: "I believe a speck of dust would have caused him more pain than a bullet wound." What does this indicate about Poirot?

   a. He is troubled by the injury that makes him limp.
   b. He is meticulous about his personal appearance.
   c. He is a hypochondriac.
   d. He is apt to overreact to simple problems.

3. What do Holmes and Poirot have in common?

   a. Appearance
   b. Carefulness
   c. Nationality
   d. Sense of humor

4. What is a significant difference between Holmes and Poirot?

   a. Holmes's fits of energy and malaise
   b. Poirot's situation of sharing a home
   c. Holmes's regular habits
   d. Poirot's impressive past cases

 5. Use the following list of words and phrases to complete the comparison alley graphic organizer to compare narrative point of view in the passages.

First person	Describes the detective physically	Admiring
Curious	Describes the detective's activities	Likes the detective
Sociable	Knows the detective's history well	Notices details

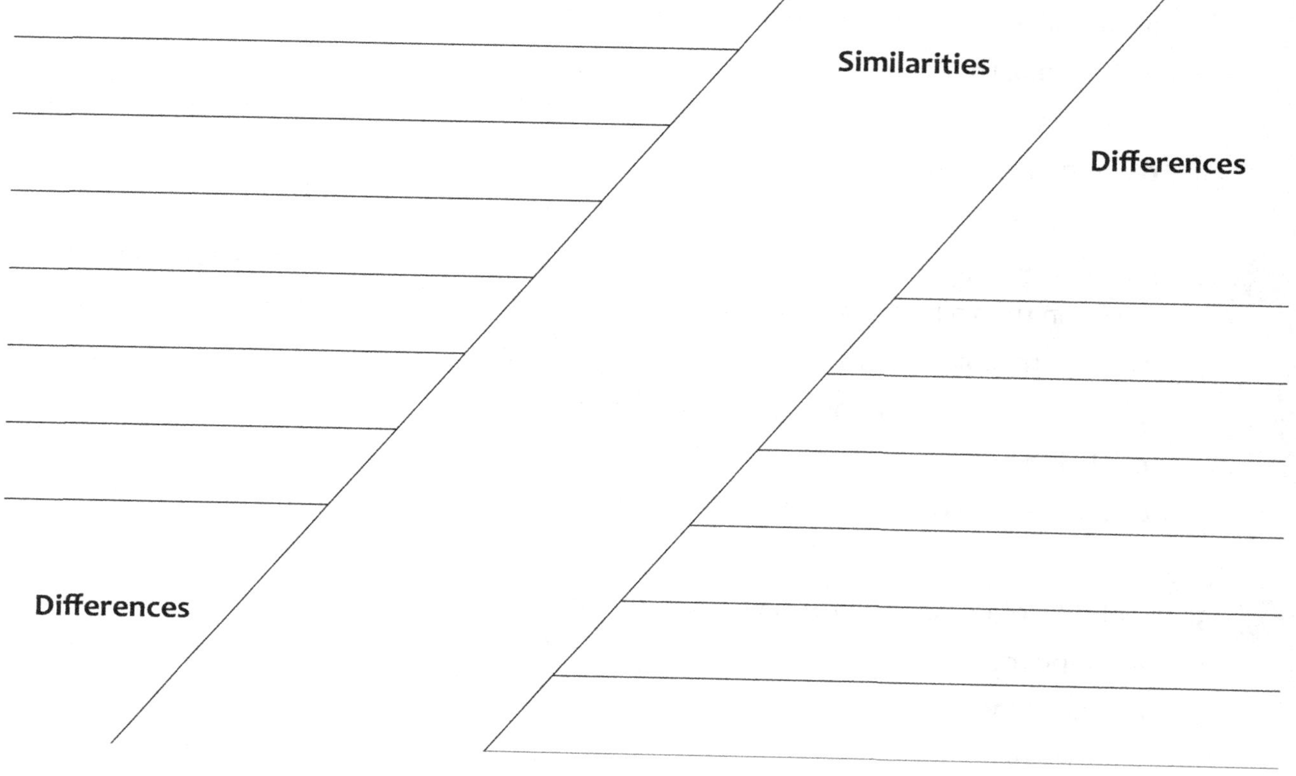

6. How does genre affect the two passages?

Remember the Concept

To compare:

- Decide what to compare.
- Find details that are similar or different.
- Draw conclusions.

Answers and Explanations

The Answers and Explanations section provides sample answers and brief explanations for the Practice It! and Learn It! exercises in this workbook. Keep in mind that many questions have more than one possible answer, especially questions that involve complex tasks such as comparing and evaluating. Refer to the sample answers for examples of good responses.

Reading Strategically *page 3*

The DARE Process *page 5*

Using DARE

Practice It! *pages 8–10*

1. a. Read the subheads of the warranty and then read sections related to viruses

   With this approach, Tom avoids reading unnecessary text and skims to find the location of the information.

2. b. Read, take notes, and then read the text again while doing the experiment

   Sarah needs to understand the details and order of the steps in the experiment so she knows exactly what to do and when to do it.

3. c. Write down her questions and read through each editorial looking for answers and taking notes

   Hillary needs to identify what she needs to know to understand the issue to take a position.

4. Joe is reading the whole text, which is long and time consuming. He may find it difficult to find what he needs if he's also reading material that's irrelevant.

5. Taking notes is an effective strategy to help Joe remember what he read. Note-taking helps Joe set aside the information that is important.

6. Sally isn't remembering anything she reads because she isn't reading actively and identifying important information. The important information may not stand out to her. She could take notes to help her remember key points.

7. Sally is reading the whole manual, which is important because she needs to be ready to answer a question about anything in the manual.

8. Nate should first determine what he needs to know. Then he can write down questions or have them in mind. Reading the heads will help him determine which sections would likely lead him to the answers. He should read those sections carefully to find the information he needs.

9. Nate should be somewhat concerned because hunters are at a higher risk of infection by mosquitoes. He can take protective measures to prevent mosquito exposure while hunting, and he can properly cook his meat.

Check Your Skills

pages 11–12

1. d. Taking a brief call from your daughter's school at your desk

   Employees are asked to limit personal calls, but a brief personal call is allowable.

2. b. A wife who is going into labor

   This is the only answer that describes a situation that requires immediate attention.

3. Situations that are not addressed include phone calls at your desk during lunch hour and the specific limits of personal calls at your desk.

4. a. The company is concerned about employees' safety and avoiding accidents.

5. One approach would be try to find out more about the situation. You might ask her about the age of her children, the illness, and the situation. Chances are that she can wait until after the meeting to check her messages and make a call.

Questioning

page 13

Asking and Answering Questions

Practice It!

pages 16–18

1. Possible questions are: Does Alice explain why she hardly knows who she is? Why might a person say they hardly know who they are?

2. Tran can write questions that will lead him to what he wants to know. Tran might ask: What does the interaction make me see about Alice? Why might the caterpillar behave the way he does? How can I relate the behavior to my own life? He can then go back and look for details, dialogue, or description that help him answer the questions.

3. Maria could ask: What can I do to prevent dementia? What impact does diet have on memory and thinking skills?

4. You can prevent dementia by starting to eat a Mediterranean diet. The Mediterranean diet may help you retain your thinking skills. If you can't find the answers to your questions, you could do additional research from other sources.

5. What are the guidelines for the Mediterranean diet?

6a. Why does the Mediterranean diet help prevent dementia?

6b. The omega-3 fatty acids benefit the mind.

7a. What kinds of food are included in the Mediterranean diet?

7b. Foods rich in omega-3 fatty acids, such as fish, chicken, and olives.

8. What can I do to prevent dementia?

Check Your Skills

pages 19–20

1. a. Warmer spring temperatures are causing a lack of snow cover in the Rocky Mountains.

2. a. A USGS survey each April since 1980 showed that warmer temperatures melted the snow earlier than in previous years.

3. b. A large portion of the people and environment in the western U.S. will be severely affected.

   The answer encapsulates the specific environmental impacts mentioned in the passage.

4. The runoff from the snow provides a major percentage of the water supply for more than 70 million people living in the western United States and also affects irrigation, dams, and wildfires. It will have a significant effect on the ecosystem in the western United States.

Skimming and Scanning

page 21

A Process for Skimming

Practice It!

pages 24–25

1. U.S. businesses are showing the first rise in unemployment since 2008, a sign that the economy is recovering.

   Clues from the text:

   "The growth in employment combined with the increase in annual payroll is another indication of a recovering economy."

   "This year's County Business Patterns report is the first since the most recent recession to show a reversal in the downward trend of employment."

   "This year is the first since 2008 in which U.S. businesses reported an increase in employment over the prior year."

2. The central idea is that U.S. businesses are showing the first increase in unemployment since 2008. The passage breaks down results by state and industry. Skimming the title and heads will help you identify the central idea.

3. Climate change is expected to make droughts and wildfires across the western United States more severe.

4. Trees already stressed by drought may be more likely to die from fires.

A Process for Scanning

Practice It!

page 28

1. The number of businesses in North Dakota increased by 2.5 percent since 2010.

2. Educational services had a 3.4 percent increase in employment.

3a. The mining, quarrying, and oil and gas extraction industry had a 12 percent increase in employment between 2010 and 2011.

3b. You can scan for numbers and words like *industry* or *increase* to locate this information in the first paragraph.

4. The growth in employment along with the increase in annual payroll shows that the economy is recovering.

   You can find this information by scanning for the name *William Bostic*.

5. Mary should identify the specific questions that she needs to answer. Then, she should look for heads and subheads in the manual to identify sections that might have the answers. She should let her eyes run over several lines of text at once looking for keywords to help her find what she is looking for more quickly. She can read the text in the area around the keywords to find the answers to her questions.

Check Your Skills *pages 29–30*

1. a. Migratory elk are coming back from Yellowstone National Park with fewer calves due to drought and increased numbers of big predators.
2. b. Only 70 percent of migratory elk were pregnant, compared to 90 percent of residents.
3. a. They are often lethally removed by wildlife managers and ranchers.
4. c. Wildlife are migrating more and more infrequently.

Note-taking and Summarizing *page 31*

Taking Notes through Preview → Note → Review

Practice It! *pages 34–35*

1. You might ask:

   How can vitamin C help my baby stay healthy?

   What effects will vitamin C have on my baby?

   How long will the effects last?

   How often should I take vitamin C?

2. Possible notes:

   Taking vitamin C may help protect a baby's lungs.

   Wheezing was also lower in children whose mothers who took vitamin C.

   The healthy lung function continued during the first year.

   The women in the study took one 500-milligram capsule per day.

3. Possible reviewed and organized notes:

   In women who took one 500-milligram capsule a day, vitamin C improved lung function and reduced wheezing in babies. In the study, the positive results continued throughout the first year.

4. To keep the baby as healthy as possible, a pregnant woman should try to quit smoking. In the meantime, she should start taking vitamin C every day. Even if she does not succeed in quitting smoking, vitamin C will be beneficial to her and the baby.

5a. Eva should preview the article and read the title as well as any heads or subheads. Before she starts reading, she should decide what information she needs. Does she have any questions? Should she focus on any specific historical figures or on any particular parts of the American Revolution? Based on this information, she can limit the parts of the text she reads, take notes on main ideas, and write down important examples. She should review and reorganize her notes to decide what information to include in the paper and how to include it.

5b. Looking at statistics is a good idea. Frequently, statistics provide you with hard facts that allow you to put information in perspective. Make sure the statistics relate to the information you are seeking and take complete notes that you can understand. If you write down numbers, write down what they mean.

6a. Ron should preview the table of contents, chapters, and heads to locate the important information. He should write down his specific questions to focus his note-taking. Then he can read through the relevant sections and note answers to his questions, important ideas, and examples. He can then review and organize the information.

6b. Words in bold are often important to note and understand. Many books include bold words that are key to understanding the concepts in the text.

Using the 5Ws and H to Summarize

Practice It!

page 38

1. **Who?** Parents

   What? Sucking on infants' pacifiers

   When? While their children are infants

   Where? A study

   Why? To protect infants from developing allergies

   How? Helps train the immune system to ignore germs that aren't a threat to the body

2. A study shows parents can suck on their infants' pacifiers to help train the infants' immune systems to ignore germs that aren't a threat.

3. You could skim the text and then answer the questions:

   Who? Pregnant smokers

   What? Should take vitamin C

When? While they are pregnant

Where? A study

Why? To protect their babies' lungs

How? By giving the babies healthier lungs at birth and a year after birth

You can use the information from the questions to write a one-sentence summary.

Check Your Skills

pages 39–40

1. c. The earthquake was an aftershock from a 5.8 earthquake in 2011.
2. a. Earthquakes can damage a larger area on the East Coast.
3. b. It was one of 50 aftershocks large enough to be felt.
4. d. On May 15, 2013, one of many aftershocks of a widespread 2011 earthquake was felt in Louisa, Virginia, a town in the Central Virginia seismic zone.

   This summary answers: who? (the town of Louisa), what? (an aftershock), when? (May 15, 2013), where? (Louisa, Virginia in the Central Virginia seismic zone), why? (a widespread 2011 earthquake), and how? (as part of many aftershocks).

Graphic Organizers

page 41

Using a Graphic Organizer

Practice It!

pages 44–45

1.

Fast food isn't much healthier than 14 years ago.

The score for restaurants increased from 45 to 48.	Scores for fast food are low nutritionally, promoting bad diets.	The small increase is surprising.
No change for fruit, vegetables, legumes, grains, oils	Experts say restaurants can improve U.S. diet quality.	Fast food restaurants have added healthy menu options.
Improved for meat, saturated fat, and calories from solid fats and added sugars	More than one-quarter of U.S. adults eat fast food two times a week.	Restaurants switched to healthier cooking fats and reduced sodium.
Milk/dairy and sodium got worse	Score of 48 below average U.S. diet	Legislative efforts have been made to improve menu options.

2. The overall idea is the central idea, the main point the author is trying to make. The smaller ideas are supporting ideas that give more information and explanation about the central idea, such as explaining what a score of 48 means. Details break down the supporting ideas, providing further information, examples, and statistics.

3. Fast food plays a large role in Americans' health because they eat out so often. Because of all the talk about improving nutrition, it's surprising the quality hasn't increased more. A reader might ask the following questions in response to the article: Why is the fast food industry being targeted? Aren't Americans responsible for their own actions? Shouldn't they be accountable for what they eat?

4.

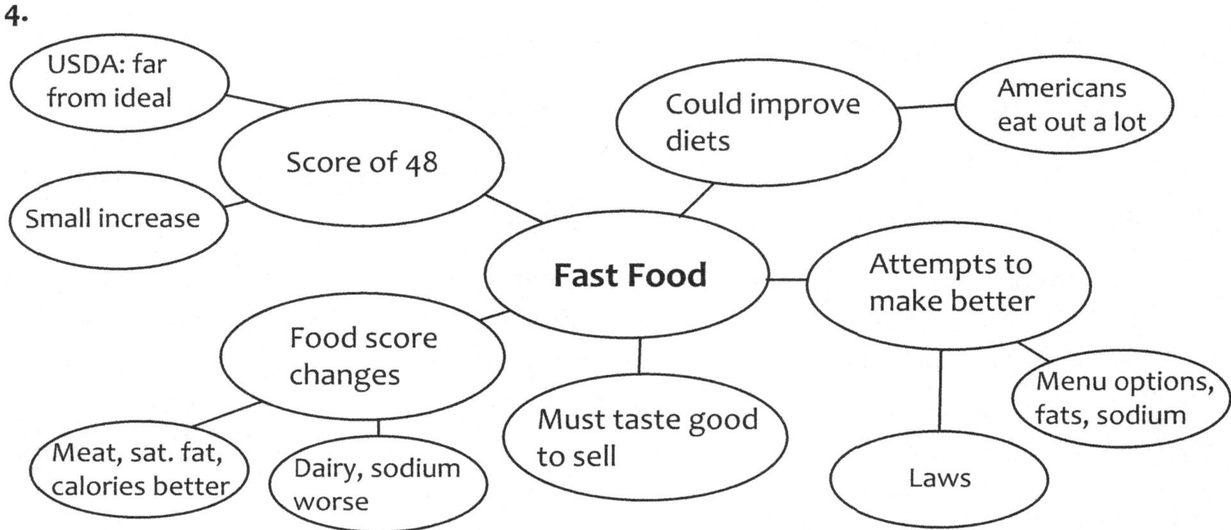

The organizer helps the reader figure out which ideas are important and which details support those ideas. The information is similar to a structural overview, but not as structured. The web is more informal and contains related words or phrases to help you understand the concept.

Answers and Explanations

Evaluating Information in a Graphic Organizer

Practice It!

page 48

1.

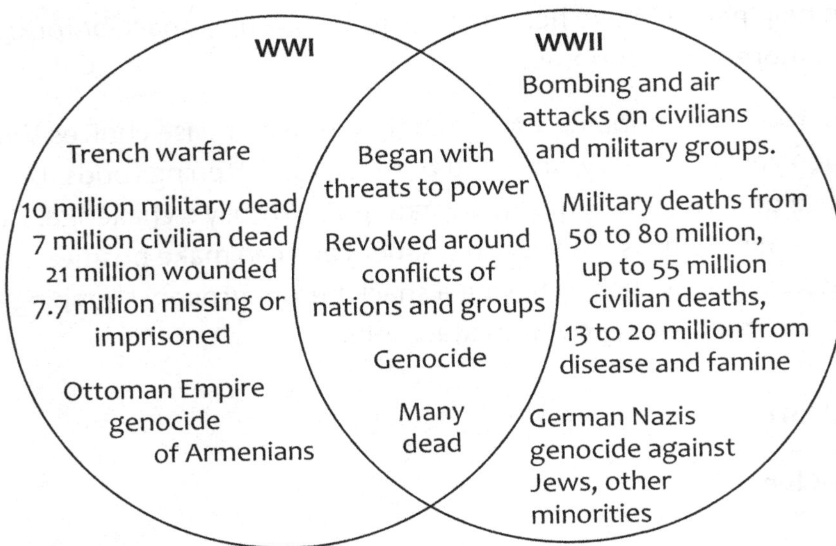

2. The different methods that the military used in combat in World War II, including bombing and air attacks, resulted in more deaths.

3. Both wars began with threats to power and revolved around conflicts between nations and groups of people. Political leaders in both wars committed genocide.

Check Your Skills

pages 49–50

1.

Fast Food

Fast food hasn't gotten healthier.

A lot of talk about healthier options

Some Americans eat out at least twice a week

Groceries

People who shop hungry buy more fattening foods.

Affects meals throughout the week.

The body goes into survival mode when hungry and wants highest calorie foods.

eat healthy foods regularly, monitor portions

Both

Two unwise choices Americans make

When hungry, you may make unwise food choices

Healthy diet means making choices

2. After reading the passages, Becca might realize that eating fast food and shopping while hungry are two unwise choices that many Americans make. Both articles show that when you are hungry, you don't always reach for the healthiest option.

3. Becca can help herself make healthy choices by having a snack before grocery shopping and eating more meals at home.

4. Eating fast food and shopping while hungry are two unwise choices that Americans make. When you are hungry, you tend to reach for fattening foods. Busy lives and the convenience of unhealthy foods make eating healthfully a challenge. Having a healthy diet involves mindfulness while eating. Americans can make positive choices by making small lifestyle changes such as having a snack before grocery shopping or making meals at home rather than eating out at restaurants.

Unfamiliar Words *page 51*

Using Context Clues

Practice It! *pages 54–55*

1. A non-living or unmoving object

2. There are several examples of inanimate objects in the passage such as doorknobs, money, and tabletops. If you think about what they have in common, they are all non-living things. *In-* is also a prefix that means *not*. *Animate*, as in *animated movie*, means that something moves. *Inanimate* means non-moving and non-living.

3. She was startled when she ran into something, but she was relieved to find that it was an *inanimate* object.

4. A fight or argument that often results in a disturbance

5. By using context clues in the sentence, you can tell that *fight* is a synonym for *altercation*.

6. She was fired from the store after she had an *altercation* with an impatient customer.

7. You might have a sister with *impeccable* taste in clothing who looks well put together and gets compliments on everything she wears.

8. You might have *balked* at an advertisement promising that you would drop 10 pounds in a week if you took a particular supplement. It doesn't sound healthy or possible.

9. Have you ever *balked* at something your mom told you?

   Yes! I *balked* when I was visiting her and she told me I had to be home by midnight. I'm 25 years old and don't need to be treated like a child.

10. How do you know when someone has *impeccable* taste?

Everything they like or recommend is the best of the best.

Using Word Parts

Practice It!

page 58

1.

	Word	Prefix	Root	Suffix
Word Parts	Ex: Amorphous	a-	-morph-	-ous
Definitions	Having the quality of no shape	None, without	Shape	Having a quality
Word Parts	Ambidextrous	ambi-	-dex-	-trous
Definitions	Able to use both hands equally	Both	Hands	Having a quality
Word Parts	Transformation	trans-	-form-	-ation
Definitions	Process of turning into something else	Change	Appearance, form	In a state or process
Word Parts	Nonconformity	non-	-conform-	-ity
Definitions	Not following expected rules or standards	Not; absence of	Following rules or standards	Showing a state or condition

2a. in- Not

-suffi- Enough

-cient A quality or state

2b. Not enough

3a. pyro- Fire

-mania- Craze or desire

-ac Person

3b. A person who has a craze for fire

Check Your Skills

pages 59–60

1. b. To use your head to hit a ball
2. a. Observing over long periods of time
3. c. "observes people over a period of decades"
4. a. Speeds

5. b. "of 50 miles per hour or more"

6. b. Irregularities

7. c. Normal

Career and College Vocabulary *page 61*

Using a Word Web

Practice It! *pages 66–67*

1. The following are possible correct answers. Select answers that will help you understand the meaning of the word *research*.

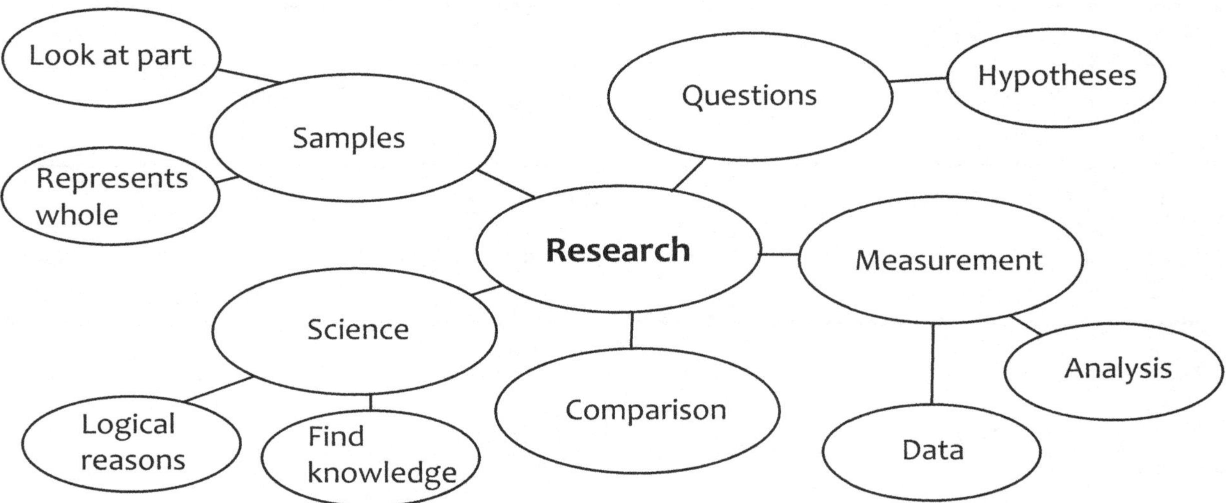

2. As I decided how to perform my *research*, I selected a *sample* population from which to make comparisons.

   To find an answer to the *research question*, I set up a *science* experiment.

3. a. Study

   When you research something, you are performing a study to find answers.

4. Research is connected to measurement because the results of research are measured as scientists analyze and draw conclusions.

   Research is connected to samples because researchers sample the population when they find participants for their studies.

   Research is connected to science because research is often a scientific study or experiment.

5. Your sample must be representative of a whole population. If it isn't, the experiment will not be valid.

   You should start the experiment with a research question. In other words, you should know what you want to learn.

6. The downturn of the **economy** a few years ago affected many families' **income**. A **section** of the population who once **occupied** expensive housing had to move to apartments. **Data** shows that the economy is improving, but not as quickly as many hoped. We need a **method** of developing **policy** that will prevent something like this from happening again.

Check Your Skills

pages 68–70

1. b. By recalling his date's reactions
2. a. Procedure

   Procedure and *method* each describe a series of steps to perform a task.

3. c. Witnessing the birth of your first child

   This is a memorable and important event, so it fits the definition of *significant.*

4. b. Advance

   Advance and *proceed* both mean to move forward.

5. Mark is very excited about the date. He wants to know how it went because he wants another date. He doesn't usually act this way and normally wouldn't care whether his date was interested in him.
6. a. To find a cure for a disease that affects her family
7. c. Set up

   Structured and *set up* both mean constructed or put together.

8. She started to mark off a part of the lab to do her experiment.

   Mark and *experiment* are synonyms that make sense in this context.

9. b. Differed

   Differed and *varied* both mean showed different characteristics.

10. d. Procedure

    Procedure and *process* both mean a set of steps to achieve an end result.

Inferences

page 71

Making Inferences Using an Inference Chart

Practice It!

pages 74–76

1.

Detail or Clue	What I Already Know	Inference
"you could download a virus or spyware that would damage the system and allow people outside the company to access private information"	Damaging the system and allowing others to access private information can be very harmful.	Avoid websites that may have viruses or spyware.
"Any emails that discriminate against employees based on race, gender, nationality, or religion will be dealt with according to the harassment policy."	Emails sometimes contain jokes based on race, gender, nationality, or religion.	Using email to make fun of a woman's clothes or looks could get you into serious trouble.
"Keep in mind that the company owns any email sent through the company email account and any document stored on a company computer."	In some companies, management monitors the email.	Management may see any email you send or receive.

2. The guidelines say email is for business use only. For more serious offenses, the passage says the employee can possibly be fired. Since this is probably not a serious offence, Curtis might receive a warning for his behavior.

3. Becca could be given a warning or receive disciplinary action. Her company would also find out she was looking for other work if they found the application, which could have negative consequences. For example, the company might not consider her for promotion, since she wants to leave the company. She should have kept the file on a personal computer, and she should move the file off her computer immediately. The passage says that the company owns all content on the computers and that management can check employee computers at anytime.

4. Websites that belong to the company's competitors

   Google, to perform company research

   Twitter, to see what your company and its competition are posting in their business accounts

5. The company would not allow Dwayne to check on a personal order. The company allows Internet use for "only business-related purposes."

6. Sarah's palms are sweaty, and she is jittery. She was up all night studying, but she doesn't think she can remember anything. As the teacher passes out the papers, she takes a deep breath.

Using a Chart to Support Your Inference

Practice It! *pages 79–80*

1.

Detail or Clue	What I Already Know	Inference
"a smile of pleasure passed across his face"	Things that you like make you smile.	Basil likes the painting he's just finished.
"Yes, I knew you would"	You can predict the behavior of people you know well.	Basil and Lord Henry are friends.
"You do anything in the world to gain a reputation. As soon as you have one, you seem to want to throw it away."	Sometimes you talk in general to make a point about one person in particular.	Basil is a successful artist.

2. Basil and Lord Henry have a comfortable, friendly relationship. Lord Henry jokes around Basil. He is enthusiastic about Basil's work, though he doesn't necessarily understand Basil's feelings about the painting.

3. Lord Henry shows that he's a social person through this comment and the comment that it's worse to have so many pictures at an art show that you can't see the people. He means that it is bad for people to gossip about you, but it's worse to be ignored.

4. Basil likes the painting, but it also seems to make him uncomfortable. He feels that he's put his own emotions and personal thoughts into the painting. Lord Henry only admires the painting as a work of art, and he sees it as an opportunity for Basil to improve his reputation as an artist.

Check Your Skills

pages 81–82

1. a. A child with autism is more likely to have ADHD than other children.

2. Lack of concentration

   Interrupting

   Trouble sitting still

3. d. Symptoms of the two conditions resemble each other.

   There is not enough information to say both conditions have the same cause, but both have similar symptoms. The director is likely familiar with symptoms of both conditions and wouldn't be surprised that the conditions are related.

4. c. The symptoms of autism can be similar to those of ADHD.

   A quote from an official source and details in the text show that because the symptoms of autism can be similar to those of ADHD, it's harder to tell in extreme cases.

5. d. A child is more helpful with chores.

   A child with autism and ADHD is not likely to be more helpful with chores.

Central Ideas *page 83*

Finding a Central Idea

Practice It! *pages 86–88*

1. c. Garbage pickup

   The other possible answers are mentioned in the passage, but the author is arguing about garbage pickup.

2. Answers will vary, but the following are important ideas:

   Some people say that less frequent service is unfair for larger families or those with infants and toddlers.

   If families were not as wasteful, less frequent garbage pickup would not be an issue.

   Households could make many changes to reduce the amount of waste they produce.

3. If people would change their wasteful habits, every-other-week garbage pickup would not be a problem.

4. Some 1999 Volkswagen Jettas manufactured between February and April of 1999 may have defective driver's side air bags and are being recalled for repair.

5. Use paragraph structure to locate information. The first sentence tells what central idea of the passage is. The rest of the paragraph gives more explanation and examples, or supporting details. Identify the topic: defective airbags. Next, identify the author's ideas. Note that the passage calls on people to get their airbags repaired, so that is part of the central idea.

6. Example detail: "In several instances, the airbag did not deploy properly during a collision, resulting in unnecessary injuries and trauma." This detail relates to the central idea by describing how the air bags may be defective.

7. Rose should skim the text and pay attention to the title, heads, and photo. These structural elements usually reflect the topic and central idea of the story. She should ask herself: "What do they say, and what do they all have in common?"

   Based on the answer to question, she should identify the topic of the article. To locate the central idea, she should answer the question: "What is the author trying to say about the topic?" She can make a list of the important ideas and figure out what they have in common. The central idea is a one-sentence summary of the important ideas about the topic.

8. To find the topic, Sarah should look for words that are repeated throughout the section. Once she finds the topic, she can figure out what the author is trying to say about the subject. Sarah should make a list of the important ideas in the text. She can then figure out what the important ideas have in common. By writing a one-sentence summary of the important ideas, she can locate the central idea.

Check Your Skills *pages 89–90*

1. a. Objections to fluoridation of water are unscientific and incorrect.

2. b. Chemicals are not necessarily harmful.

   The author supports this idea by mentioning that iron, calcium, potassium, and even water are chemicals.

3. b. To compare fluoride to other commonly accepted substances

   By applying the word *chemical* to common, safe substances, the author tries to alleviate the worry associated with the word.

4. a. Scientists are looking for habitable planets.

5. Scientists want to find planets similar to Earth.

   Planets at the right distance from a star are more likely to support life.

   NASA's Kepler telescope helps scientists find planets.

Reading Nonfiction Texts *page 91*

Text Structure *page 93*

Using Structure to Find Meaning

Practice It! *pages 96–98*

1. c. Problem and solution
2. The first paragraph introduces the problem of the declining amphibian species. The last paragraph introduces the solution: we should make an effort to conserve the endangered animals.
3. a. Frogs, salamanders, and toads are quickly disappearing from their habitats.
4. c. We need to confront the problem and take action on conservation.
5. a. Descriptive

   This paragraph describes the decline of the amphibian population.
6. The study showed that U.S. amphibian declines may be more widespread and severe than previously believed.

7a. The text is about historical events, and it starts in the past and ends in the present. It likely uses a chronological order structure. It also likely uses a cause and effect structure because it discusses the causes and effects of the Great Depression.

7b. Shae can identify when the New Deal took place and use the chronological structure to find the information.

8a. This text likely uses a problem and solution structure and a chronological structure. The process is probably set out in steps, which is a chronological structure. Because the text describes how the process resolves problem, it also probably uses a problem and solution structure.

8b. Because the order of the steps would logically be chronological, the information about how to initiate contact with a client is likely towards the beginning of the text.

9a. This text likely uses a cause and effect structure because the article is looking at the effects new high schools had on their communities.

9b. Mary can use the cause and effect structure to identify effects of new high schools.

Check Your Skills *pages 99–100*

1. a. The formation of an after-school program

2. a. To reduce the dropout rate

3. **Pro:** Students would be able to pursue new interests. Students would be able to receive homework help. The dropout rate would likely be reduced.

   Con: Costs are unknown. Costs could be high. There is no location yet.

4. More information is needed. The results of the cost analysis should be considered, and potential locations should be identified. It would be beneficial to seek out input from community members.

5. This proposal has unanswered questions about costs and expenses. The program proposal is too vague; it is unclear how the program will attract at-risk youth in order to target the dropout rate. The program needs quality instructors, but its creators don't want to spend much money.

Text Features

page 101

PPL: Preview → Predict → Learn with Text Features

Practice It!

pages 105–106

1. The topic of the passage is population growth.

2. The author uses the subheads to make it easier for the reader to find information and predict what they will read in the section.

3. The author wants to set aside and draw attention to the bulleted facts. The list makes the text stand out and makes it easier to read.

4. The article is about population growth and gives details using specific numbers and facts.

5. b. "The Earliest Settlers"

   This chapter title refers to the first Europeans in America, often referred to as settlers.

6. d. A recent tornado

   All the titles could relate to a recent tornado. Only one of the titles relates to disaster victims, and none directly relate to preventing disasters or first aid.

Check Your Skills

pages 107–108

1. a. Try to extinguish the fire with a fire extinguisher.

   The passage states that if you discover a small fire, you should try to extinguish it with a fire extinguisher.

2. PASS

    This acronym refers to Pull, Aim, Squeeze, and Sweep. It gives instructions on how to use a fire extinguisher, and it can be identified in the passage by the large letters.

3. A fire evacuation map on the first floor does not help people who are on higher floors and need to evacuate. A possible solution is to post a map on each floor.

4. b. Employees are in contact with some chemicals.

    The text states that the company does use a limited number of chemicals and that employees will have a separate orientation for chemical safety.

Visual Elements *page 109*

Previewing Visual Elements

Practice It! *pages 113–116*

1. a. International migration versus increase in population from births between 2012 and 2060

2. a. To compare information

    The graph shows the increase in international migration compared with the natural increase in population from births and deaths.

3. The graph shows that net international migration is projected to overtake natural increase in population in 2027. The amount of population increase from migration is rising, while the amount of population increase from births is decreasing.

4. The graph summarizes the most important ideas in the passage. The passage explains that international migration is expected to exceed the natural increase in population. In other words, more people will migrate to the U.S. each year than will be born in the U.S. that year (accounting for deaths). The passage further develops the central idea by explaining the reasons for the shift. It also explains how the shift would affect the United States population.

5. A doctor is inserting a syringe labeled "Prohibition" into a patient labeled "American People." Two others watch. The man wears a suit. You can identify him as a government representative, and you might recognize him as Herbert Hoover, the President at the time. The nurse is helping with the experiment. If you look closely, she is labeled WCTU, which stands for the Women's Christian Temperance Union, an organization that lobbied for the prohibition of alcohol.

6. The caption says "Yes, it's a noble experiment," but the cartoonist does not think this procedure is noble. The man representing the American people is forcibly undergoing a frightening-looking shot, so it seems that the cartoonist thinks Prohibition is an unethical and potentially dangerous experiment.

7. The caption introduces a contradiction. Because of the way the American people are portrayed, as helpless and resistant, the label "Noble Experiment" is ironic. The cartoonist portrays Prohibition as the opposite of noble.

8. The introductory text helps to clarify the meaning of the cartoon by defining Prohibition and explaining the term "The Noble Experiment." The cartoon shows the irony of the term "Noble Experiment" defined in the text.

9. Prohibition increases crime and becomes problematic for the government to enforce. The author shows Prohibition as a dangerous wildcat, implying that Prohibition causes more problems than it solves.

10. You can think through the cartoon's meaning by considering what you know about Prohibition and its effects, examining the cartoon and its labels, and reading the introductory text. Since one government agency is trying to hand the dangerous wildcat to another, you can infer that neither government agency wanted to deal with Prohibition. It was probably difficult and costly to enforce.

11. Both cartoons are opposed to Prohibition, but the authors focus on different reasons why. The first cartoon portrays Prohibition as taking away the rights of the people and enforcing something against the will of the people. It shows Prohibition as unethical. The second cartoon looks at Prohibition from a more practical perspective. It focuses on the difficulty of enforcing the law. Instead of showing the harm Prohibition might do to the American people, it shows the harm Prohibition does to the government agency trying to enforce it.

Check Your Skills

pages 117–118

1. d. The percentage of people of different races who voted in Presidential elections between 1996 and 2012

2. a. Black voter turnout has climbed steadily since 1996.

3. One central idea is that a higher percentage of Black voters participated in 2012 election than any other ethnicity. You might emphasize the fact that the percentage of Black voters surpassed the percentage of non-Hispanic white voters for the first time and that Black voter turnout has been increasing since 1996. The article could also focus on the fact that Hispanic and Asian voters are less likely to vote in Presidential elections than Black and non-Hispanic white voters.

4. a. A woman is begging on the streets.

   The woman is sitting by the sidewalk with a container in her hand. Her posture, dress, and the bag she is carrying all indicate that she is probably begging.

5. A newspaper article about homelessness

   A social studies text about life in a foreign country

Author's Purpose *page 119*

Big Picture & Details to Find Purpose

Practice It! *pages 123–125*

1. a. Kemp's ridley sea turtles are endangered.

2. b. Inform the reader

   No opinion or bias is shown in the details, and the author doesn't try to entertain or question.

3a. The author's purpose is to inform the reader about the state of Kemp's ridley turtles. Information is presented in a factual, straightforward way, so the intent is to convey information.

3b. This passage could be found in an environmental or wildlife magazine or website. People who are interested in wildlife, ecology, or the environment might read this article.

4.

Big Picture & Details

Big Picture: Skim and use your background knowledge to get an overview. What's the big picture?

The proposed ballot measure includes an unfair tax.

Details: Look for details to expand and support your ideas.

Detail: Raises money for schools Meaning: Most people view this as a good thing.	Detail: Taxes gross income. Meaning: Taxes money that pays for the business's expenses
Detail: Where will businesses get the money? Meaning: There is no money to pay the tax.	Detail: Prices will go up. Meaning: Raising prices is bad for business and consumers.

5. The author's purpose is to argue against the proposed ballot measure.

Check Your Skills *pages 126–128*

1. b. To explain why the people are separating from the government
2. The author says that when it is necessary to separate politically from another entity, it is respectful and decent to explain why.
3. The author probably hopes to get world opinion on his side, as well as the opinions of the people of the colonies. It is unlikely that the author seeks to influence the British government through this document.
4. b. To add constitutional amendments that protect the rights of the American people
5. To prevent abuse of powers and to protect rights, specific amendments should be added to guarantee certain important rights. The Bill of Rights includes the Ninth Amendment, which states: "The enumeration in the Constitution, of certain rights, shall not be construed to deny or disparage others retained by the people." In other words, though the Bill of Rights explicitly affirms specific rights, those are not the only rights of the people.
6. b. "in order to prevent misconstruction or abuse of its powers, that further declaratory and restrictive clauses should be added"

Reading in Science *page 129*

Diagramming Scientific Systems and Processes

Practice It! *pages 132–134*

1. **Beginning:** Magma forms from intense heat.

   Ending: A volcano is formed.

2.

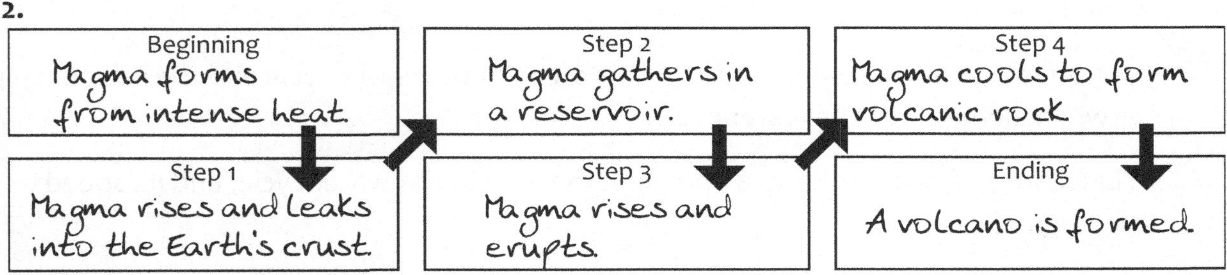

3. Magma may come from the Earth's crust or further down inside the Earth. The gases and minerals in magma cause variations, as does the amount of pressure in the magma.

4. Questions could include:

   What differences are there between fully formed volcanoes?

   What causes a volcano to become inactive?

   What factors determine whether magma will erupt?

   What causes a magma chamber to form?

5.

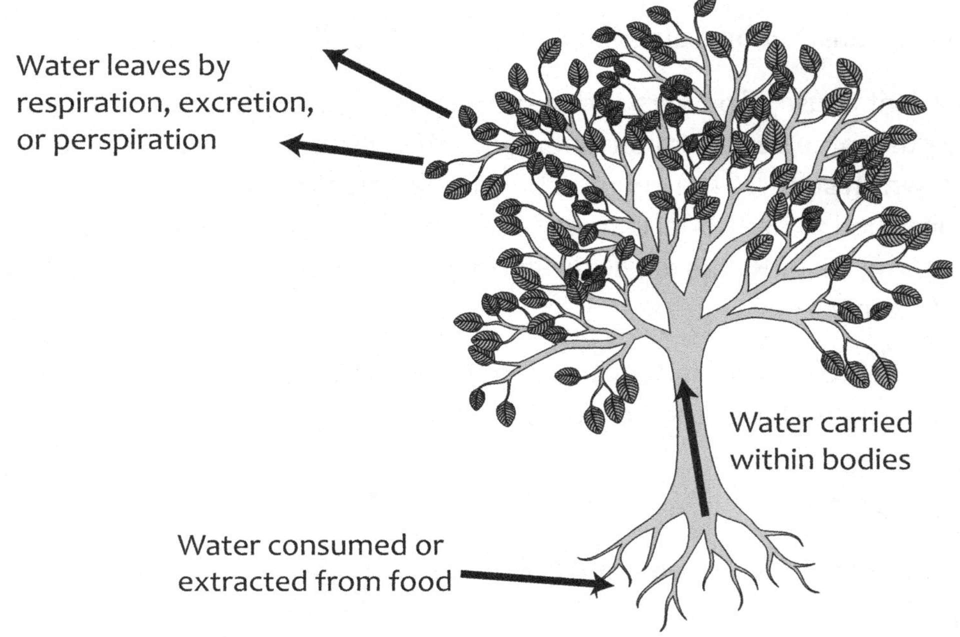

6. The water cycle is very simplistic and only shows major ways water moves. The actual path of any given water molecule can be varied and complex. Water cycle diagrams do not show the amount of time that a water molecule may take as it travels through the water cycle.

7. Diagramming helps you think through the steps of the water cycle and the relationships between elements of the water cycle.

8. b. Each drop of water follows a unique path through the water cycle, and its speed may vary.

9. You might add more detail to the water cycle, such as showing animals, underground water reserves, or snowmelt. You might also add information about when water changes state between a gas, a liquid, and a solid.

Distinguishing Fact from Opinion

Practice It!

pages 137–138

1. a. To persuade that countries should collaborate on space exploration
2. It is an opinion. The statement cannot be proven, since there is no measure of how unifying space exploration is. This sentence explains the author's personal beliefs about space exploration.
3. The author is stating that people from different countries across the earth are part of the same world. People of Earth need to work together for space exploration. This opinion is supported by quotations about space exploration. The author also refers to Obama's policies and facts about the Earth's place in the universe.
4. The author's purpose is to inform readers about the effect of pesticides on amphibian populations.
5. The sentence is a fact. It can be shown to be true by reading the study that is discussed in this passage.
6. The facts in the passage further elaborate the results of the study, giving specific examples of pesticides that have been found in frogs for the first time. The author suggests the hypothesis that frogs might serve as indicators that pesticides are negatively impacting the environment.

Check Your Skills

pages 139–140

1. b. Digestive juices dissolve and break down food that moves through the system.
2. d. The mucus layer is unable to fully protect the stomach.
3. a. Different digestive juices break down food in different ways as it moves through the digestive system.
4. d. "much like detergents that dissolve grease from a frying pan."

   The statement "much like detergents that dissolve grease from a frying pan" is making a comparison. It is not stating a fact.
5. b. Breaking down food requires multiple stages.
6. c. Starch

Reading in Social Studies

page 141

Determining Author's Perspective

Practice It! *pages 145–148*

1.

Big Picture & Details

Big Picture: Skim and use your background knowledge to get an overview. What's the big picture?

The Supreme Court ruled to desegregate schools because segregation negatively impacts the education of children

Details: Look for details to expand and support your ideas.

Detail: Sense of inferior status Meaning: Segregation make minorities feel others look down on them	Detail: Lifelong inner wounds Meaning: Problems from segregation last a lifetime
Detail: "separate but equal" has no place Meaning: Education cannot be separate & equal	Detail: "hearts and minds" Meaning: Shows court's empathy for students

2. Chief Justice Warren has reviewed examples where students were negatively impacted by segregation. He has determined that, legally and emotionally, segregation deprives students of equal educational opportunities. He believes that segregation itself makes students feel unequally valued and separates them emotionally from the community.

3. b. Separate schools don't provide equal education.

4. c. Children's psychological well-being

5. Susan B. Anthony sees voting as her right as a United States citizen. She sees women as being equal to men and included in the Constitution through the phrase "We, the people." She believes that any country that would not recognize a woman's vote is not a democracy.

6. **Example 1:** "I not only committed no crime, but, instead, simply exercised my citizen's rights, guaranteed to me and all United States citizens by the National Constitution, beyond the power of any State to deny." With these words, Anthony claims that her decision to vote is justified by the U.S. Constitution because it refers to "We, the people," not just "the white male citizens."

   Example 2: "And it is a downright mockery to talk to women of their enjoyment of the blessings of liberty while they are denied the use of the only means of securing them provided by this democratic-republican government—the ballot." Anthony strongly rejects the idea that liberty can be separated from the ballot, the right to vote. She uses the word mockery, which shows her strong emotion.

7. Anthony is stating that to women, the government's powers are unjustified because women have no representation in the government. Without the right to vote, women cannot be justly ruled over by a government.

8. You might use the information in this passage to learn more about the American women's rights movement and the core beliefs and arguments of its leaders.

Check Your Skills *pages 149–150*

1. a. President Roosevelt is explaining why the banks have closed.

2. d. He wants the listeners to be supportive of his policies.

3. a. The American people

4. b. To calm the public's fears about the bank failure

5. d. He wants to work with the banks to reconstruct the economy.

Tone *page 151*

Determining Tone through Word Choice

Practice It! *pages 154–156*

1a. Self-pitying

1b. Angry

1c. Cautious

2. a. Upbeat, positive

   Compared with the other answers, this tone is more likely impress people reviewing job applicants, who want upbeat and positive employees.

3. b. To persuade Julie's company to bring him or her in for a job interview

4. An author's tone will usually match his or her purpose. If the author wants to inform, the tone will likely be factual and neutral. A persuasive letter might be filled with strong beliefs, opinions, or emotions.

5. An angry letter to the editor might make the reader feel uncomfortable and defensive. It might make the author seem unreasonable. A reasoning, persuasive tone is more likely to persuade the reader.

6.

Words	Meaning	Purpose
Important	Having great significance or value	Shows that having a large-scale emergency plan is a positive measure
Kindness	Friendly, generous	Shows that the author is appreciative
Devastating	Highly destructive	Shows how bad the tornado was

7. Appreciative

8. Possible examples include "the kindness of friends, family, neighbors, and strangers is helping us through this difficult time" and "thank everyone who has donated time and money for those families struggling to put their lives back together."

9. The author is appreciative of individual efforts but also thinks that the response would have been more effective if the community had been better prepared.

10.

Words	Meaning	Purpose
Concern	Worry	Shows the management is serious the security of their employees but is not overly emotional
Safety	Protected against danger	Shows that an unsafe situation must be addressed
Seriously	Solemn, grave	Shows that management is not taking the situation lightly

11. Cautious

    The tone is concerned, but it is not emotional. It could be described as *official* or *prudent*.

12. The author shows tone through the selection of details and examples. The author gives specific guidelines for security and issues orders to employees.

Check Your Skills *pages 157–158*

1. b. To persuade listeners that the author is against the war but supports his country and Europe

2. b. Basing policy on pure emotion is a bad idea.

3. d. Defensive

   Kennedy is defending himself against those who criticize him for his opinion on the war.

4. Kennedy thinks that some members of the press are biased and forcing their views on the nation. He says "a few ruthless and irresponsible Washington columnists have claimed for themselves the right to speak for the nation. The reputation of the American press for fairness is being compromised by the tactics of these men."

5. a. Supportive

   Kennedy refers to press coverage in favor of the war and criticism against him for opposing America's involvement. This implies that the public, or at least the media, was generally supportive of the war.

Details in Nonfiction

page 159

Creating an Outline

Practice It!

pages 163–166

1. Diversity is critical to the success of the CIA.

2.

   I. Central Idea
   Diversity is critical to the success of the CIA.

   a. Supporting Idea The CIA must hire a diverse workforce with broad cultural expertise.

      1. Detail
      a broad range of ethnic and cultural backgrounds

      2. Detail
      language expertise

      3. Detail
      a broad range of educational and life experiences

   b. Supporting Idea
   The CIA must create a dynamic and engaged "culture of inclusion"

      1. Detail
      Engaged employees are more productive.

      2. Detail Diverse hiring practices bring workers to the CIA with varied ideas, perspectives, and talents.

      3. Detail Diverse hiring practices shows the CIA's commitment to equality of opportunity.

3. Brennan uses details to show the benefits of diversity for the CIA. He includes examples of benefits of diverse employees. He also argues that equality of opportunity is important and that a diverse CIA will attract better employees. He could add details about the diversity of the CIA's workforce, such as the current opportunities for women and minorities.

4. Brennan says the CIA's employees make the agency great because they bring a broad range of skills, experiences, and viewpoints to the workplace.

5. a. The CIA is committed to hiring a diverse workforce and creating a culture of inclusion.

6. I. NASA is backing a study to explore using a 3D printer to make food on spaceflights.

    A. Systems and Materials Research Consultancy will study feasibility.

        1. Small Business Innovation Research Phase I contract, an early stage of research

        2. Research for long-duration space flights

    B. Deep space flight requires new technology for foods.

        1. Need nutritionally balanced food

        2. Need five-year shelf live and maintained nutrients

        3. Need to use few resources

    C. Astronauts need variety and personal choice over long periods.

        1. Current foods are pre-selected.

        2. Variety ensures that crew members eat enough and get enough nutrients.

7. 3D printing technology layers materials to create 3D objects. This is useful for creating variety, as noted in the article about 3D printed foods. Since 3D printers can create a variety of different objects with few resources, they could be good for other purposes besides printing foods. For example, 3D printing could create replacement parts or leisure items for astronauts. It seems like a promising technology for space travel.

Check Your Skills *pages 167–168*

1. b. Researchers analyzed 13 years of satellite data to find the feeding grounds of the sea turtles.

2. a. For the first time, researchers have found the endangered Kemp's ridley sea turtles' feeding grounds in the Gulf of Mexico, an area that is known for commercial fishing, oil spills, and oxygen depletion.

3. d. It is important for recovery of the Kemp's ridley species.

4. a. It is the first information of its kind.

5. The sea turtle population in 2012 was 22,000. The population can be increased by protecting feeding grounds and increasing conservation of the water and environment where the sea turtles live.

Arguments

page 169

Identifying an Argument

Practice It!

pages 172–174

1. The central idea is that working on commission is bad for clients and therefore bad for the business.

   The author states the central idea near the beginning of the email, beginning with the phrase "I strongly believe." This wording shows that the author is stating a claim.

2. The author's purpose is to try to change the commission policy at the workplace.

3. The author's tone can be described as *concerned* or *frustrated*.

4. The text uses a cause and effect structure. The author explains that the effect of working on commission is to work against the best interests of the customers. The text also could be described as using a problem and solution structure, since the author outlines the problem with commissions and then proposes to raise wages as a solution.

5. The author's argument is that, by paying employees on commission, the company is alienating its clients. The author presents the logical argument that employees on commission will try to sell clients items or services they don't need. The clients will then be upset. The author uses an example of a phone call from an angry client. The author's solution is to raise wages and eliminate commissions.

6. The central idea tells you what the author is trying to say. The purpose and tone show you the author's attitude. The text structure can help you identify how the author organizes details and evidence to persuade you.

7. The author attempts to persuade voters to support the President's plan to cut interest rates on student loans. The author explains what the plan would do and why it would improve interest rates.

8. The passage uses a problem and solution structure. The author begins by describing the problem, that student loan rates will soon double. Then, the author describes the President's proposal as a solution.

9. Opponents might argue that student loan rates should increase so that the student loan program is affordable. Opponents might also argue that aligning student borrowing costs to government borrowing costs is not reasonable, since students are more of a risk to lenders.

10. Sofia is reading an email from a client who complains that her bill was inaccurate and explains why.

    Jin is reading a scientific journal article stating that earlier studies are inaccurate and a recent study should be taken more seriously.

11. Molly can first determine the central idea of the text and then the author's purpose. She can skim the text to identify what text structures the author uses. Particular structures, like problem and solution, are more common in arguments. By examining the central idea, the author's purpose, and the text structure, she can draw a conclusion about whether the essay is making an argument.

Check Your Skills *pages 175–176*

1. c. The U.S. must step in to save Greece.

2. Helpless

   Hard-working

   Peaceful

3. d. Truman's portrayal of Greece evokes sympathy to gain support for aiding the Greeks.

   When this speech was given, the German army had been defeated. The new threat to Greeks came from armed minorities taking advantage of the turmoil in Greece. These minorities were backed by the Soviet Union.

4. d. To maintain control over the area

5. Opponents to Truman's argument could include those who did not want to enter into another military action following World War II and those who supported the Soviet Union.

Claims and Evidence *page 177*

The Claims and Evidence Pyramid

Practice It! *pages 180–182*

1. C: Everyone should try to eat as healthily as possible.

   S: A healthy diet will help you feel better and lose weight.

   S: A healthy diet is linked to fewer health problems and a longer life.

2. S: Affordable daycare centers often lack trained staff and adequate safety procedures.

   C: It's hard for working parents to find quality, affordable day care.

   S: Quality day care can cost $15,000 to $20,000 a year per child.

   S: Not all parents have a relative or family friend nearby who can lend a hand.

3. We are understaffed, and employees are working overtime to make it work.

   Our profits have been growing, and if we make cuts, we will have enough in the budget for more employees.

   With overtime pay, we waste money and overwork staff.

4. Corporations need stricter regulation to control waste disposal and stricter consequences for violations.

   All three statements support this claim.

5.

CLAIM: The new tax on bicycles should not be implemented.

CONNECTION	EVIDENCE	EVIDENCE	CONNECTION
Tax would discourage biking, cause traffic.	biking = less car traffic	biking = healthy	Tax would discourage biking, discourage good health.
Tax would discourage biking, cause road repairs.	biking = fewer road repairs	bike shops = money in economy	Tax would discourage biking, hurt bike shops.
Tax would discourage biking, cause need for parking.	biking = fewer parking spaces		

6. The argument provides ample support for biking. It gives examples of how biking is good for individuals and the community. The argument against the tax depends on the connection that a tax will discourage bicycling, and this is a reasonable assumption.

7. Bicyclists use the road but don't pay gas taxes for road maintenance. A tax on bicycles could contribute to road repair.

8.

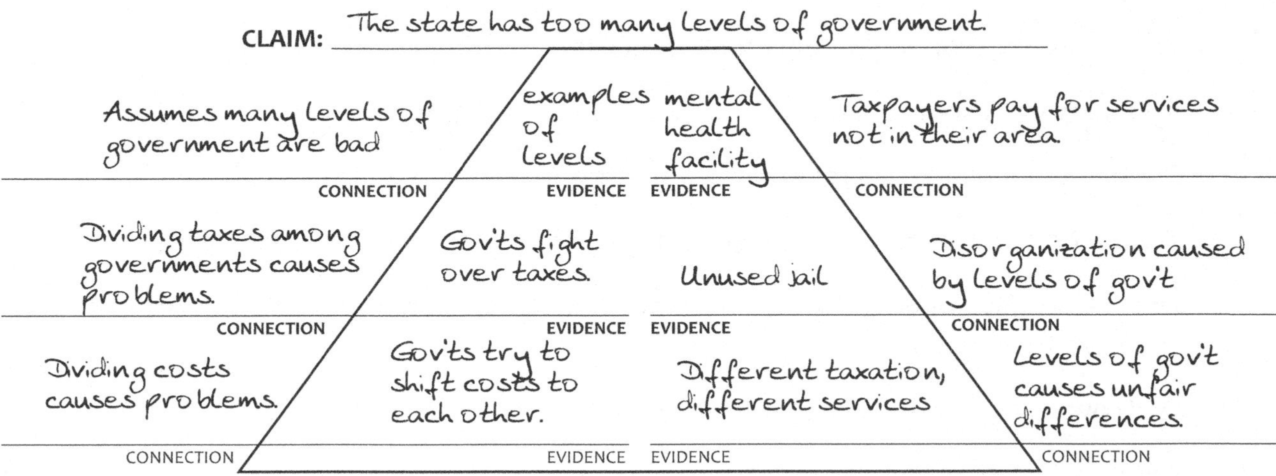

9. The author gives support to show that overlapping governments are negatively effecting the taxpayers. There may be examples of the benefits of levels of government that the author doesn't address. The author should propose possible solutions to the problem and ways to keep the benefits of government structure while eliminating problems.

Check Your Skills *pages 183–184*

1. a. Nonviolence defeats the opponent without humiliation and through love.
2. b. Violence creates bitterness.
3. c. It is a nonviolent approach that promotes eventual unity.
4. d. He says non-violent protest means to love your opposition as fellow humans.
5. Opponents might argue that governments can simply ignore nonviolent protesters, rendering nonviolence ineffective. Opponents could also argue that nonviolence gets less attention in the media than violence.

Fallacies *page 185*

Is the Evidence PALE?

Practice It! *pages 188–190*

1. Herbert's argument is a personal attack. He says opponents are lazy and unconcerned about the environment instead of making an argument about the issue.
2. Raymond's argument is a straw man. He says that opponents think the local paper is the only news source, which is unlikely. He bases his own argument on a poor opposing argument.

3. Allie's argument is a slippery slope. It assumes that smoking will be made illegal in other places besides bars without evidence.

4. Sonia's argument does not contain a fallacy. It's logical that if money is spent in one place, it then can't be spend in another place.

5. Van's argument is a bandwagon argument. He argues that the best candidate is the one who is most popular, which is not necessarily true.

6. The second argument is sounder. It gives an example of why Sanchez is tough on crime. The first argument uses fallacious reasoning. The fact that the mayor's son was arrested for disturbing the peace has nothing to do with whether or not the mayor is tough on crime.

7. The second argument is sounder. It provides valid reasons why swimming is good; it provides exercise and recreation. The first argument lacks evidence. Just because children go to a swimming pool doesn't mean that they will neglect their studies.

8. The first argument is sounder. The author gives an example why the apartment manager is doing a bad job. The second argument connects two unrelated events. There is no reason to believe the manager is responsible for the elevator problems.

9. The second argument is sounder. The author gives statistics on crime and the number of police officers. The first argument relies on a personal observation of one street. It doesn't necessarily indicate that the police department is understaffed.

10. The claim is that children need an at-home parent. The evidence is the father's personal experience. He gives examples of how he supervises his children and gives them attention. He also says that if you aren't willing to sacrifice income for your children, you're making a wrong choice.

11. The author assumes that children don't get supervision or opportunities for play if both parents work. He doesn't consider that two-parent households may share time supervising their children or that children may benefit from experiences at day care. The author also makes a personal attack by saying that couples who don't have a stay-at-home parent are spending their money on expensive vacations and other luxuries instead of choosing to make sacrifices for their children.

12. The argument clearly explains benefits of a child having supervision, but it fails to show that having one parent stay home is the only way to get these benefits. It is only superficially convincing.

Check Your Skills

pages 191–192

1. d. The U.S. Conference of Mayors in 2005 stated that 30% of homeless people suffer from addiction.

   This statement supports the idea that homeless people might spend handouts on their addictions.

2. b. A 1996 study concluded that 40% of homeless men served in the armed forces.

   This statement supports the idea that many homeless people are mentally ill veterans.

3. d. That panhandlers are addicted to drugs, alcohol, or cigarettes

4. b. That people who complain about aggressive panhandlers don't consider them human

Persuasive Appeals

page 193

Understanding a Persuasive Appeal

Practice It!

pages 196–198

1. This scenario uses pathos. Lia appeals to the boss's empathy and values to help her in a bad situation.

2. This scenario uses ethos. The mayor is relying on her past experience as mayor and her voting record to gain trust and credibility with voters.

3. c. A specific example of a person who couldn't afford organic produce otherwise

   This appeal is pathos. It uses an emotional appeal to illustrate to the audience the benefits of the produce stand.

4. Eisenhower's claim is that government needs to be balanced and that no one program should outweigh the others.

5. Eisenhower uses logos to argue that a large investment in a seemingly promising new program could cause imbalance and frustration.

6. Eisenhower uses pathos to appeal to Americans' pride in their country. He calls America the "strongest, most influential and most productive nation in the world" to appeal to national pride and patriotism. He says that to do less than strive for peace, progress, and liberty would be "unworthy of a free and religious people." He is appealing to Americans' image of themselves as free and religious.

7. Eisenhower uses ethos when he reminds the audience of his 50 years of service to the country, which includes his time in the military as well as his time as President. This establishes his credibility and prominence at the beginning of the speech.

8. This passage is fairly persuasive. Eisenhower's arguments don't seem overly controversial. The passage argues for balance, and it contains strong appeals to patriotism and a call to promote peace, progress, and freedom. Few would argue against Eisenhower's claims, but many would argue about the details of how to achieve them. The appeals to patriotism might seem somewhat exaggerated, casting America in an almost all-powerful light.

9. A possible counterargument is: America is capable of doing great good in the world, but it must first accomplish great good at home. Eisenhower argues against investment in a "miraculous solution," but he could scarcely foresee the opportunities of technology. Today, America has powerful technology that has changed all our lives: the Internet an instantaneous access to information. America should invest in this miracle and bring high-speed Internet to every corner of our great land. Knowledge will lift up all our citizens, and our country will become stronger than ever.

   This argument uses pathos to appeal to patriotism and logos to explain the benefits of investing in high-speed Internet access.

Check Your Skills

pages 199–200

1. b. His shared values with other Americans

   This quotation is an example of pathos.

2. d. "... a policy based on constant decency in its values and on optimism in our historical vision."

   The description of Carter's policy is vague, but the other quotations do not describe the foreign policy that Carter backs.

3. b. He speaks about the freedom that draws Americans and the human race together.

4. a. That Americans can spread their values through foreign policy

5. b. Carter shows that he believes in the people.

   Carter states that Americans want the world to know they stand for more than prosperity. He refers to their decency, optimism, and belief in human freedom.

Evaluating Arguments and Evidence

page 201

Evaluating an Argument

Practice It!

pages 204–206

1. The author's claim is that diets are unhealthy and that to lose weight, you should make sensible nutrition changes and start exercising.
2. The author gives the example of friends, coworkers, and acquaintances who have dieted and then gained back all the weight and more. The author also reasons that because diets have rigid rules, they are too hard to follow. Then, the author states that diets slow your metabolism, but the author does not give details such as scientific studies to confirm this information.
3. The author generalizes about diets by saying that all diets give you too few calories and too rigid rules. The author also mentions friends' experiences and the idea that diets slow your metabolism without backing up either idea with data or scientific studies.
4. The author uses pathos to appeal to the common goal of losing weight and not wanting to struggle and starve in vain. The author uses logos to argue that rigid, stringent diets cause people to break their diets. The author uses ethos by establishing himself or herself as an overweight person who is trying to avoid the pitfalls of dieting.
5. The author should qualify that the argument refers to overly stringent diets, since not all diets are the same. The argument also needs additional support to prove that diets do lower the dieter's metabolism. If those changes were made, the argument would be effective.
6. The author's claim is that we should reduce the length of the work week while maintaining pay levels.
7. The author's argument states that new technology is changing the amount of workers needed in the economy. The author gives two examples: self-driving cars which will disrupt the transportation industry and 3D printers which will disrupt the manufacturing industry.
8. The author sets up a false dilemma by claiming that, if nothing is done, thousands of workers will be cast into poverty. This is not necessarily the case. The author seems to ignore the possibility of new jobs arising in new industries and doesn't give evidence that the total number of jobs will be reduced.

9. The author uses pathos to evoke fear that thousands of people will become impoverished. The author uses logos to explain how self-driving cars and 3D printing will disrupt shipping and manufacturing industries. The author does not use ethos.

10. The argument is somewhat effective but has several flaws. It does not give enough information on the total number of jobs that may be lost due to technology versus the total number of jobs that might be gained in fields such as engineering, design, and computer programming.

Check Your Skills

pages 207–208

1. d. Freedom

2. b. To emphasize that Khrushchev was wrong

3. a. To question the sincerity of the actions of the Soviet Union

4. c. Part of a logical argument that Soviet Communism is inferior

5. d. China has a growing economy under a Communist government.

Comparing Nonfiction

page 209

Comparing with a Graphic Organizer

Practice It!

pages 213–216

1. b. The information and visuals in the advertisements

2. The first advertisement contains specific arguments for using the sunscreen. The second advertisement focuses on the visual and uses the image to sell the product.

3. Both advertisements contain attractive visuals.

4. The first advertisement would benefit from having less text and directing the advertisement to focus on one benefit. The second advertisement could use an argument that shows a benefit of the sunscreen.

5. The first advertisement contains more reasons to buy SafeScreen, so it might be the better choice based only on the advertisements.

6.

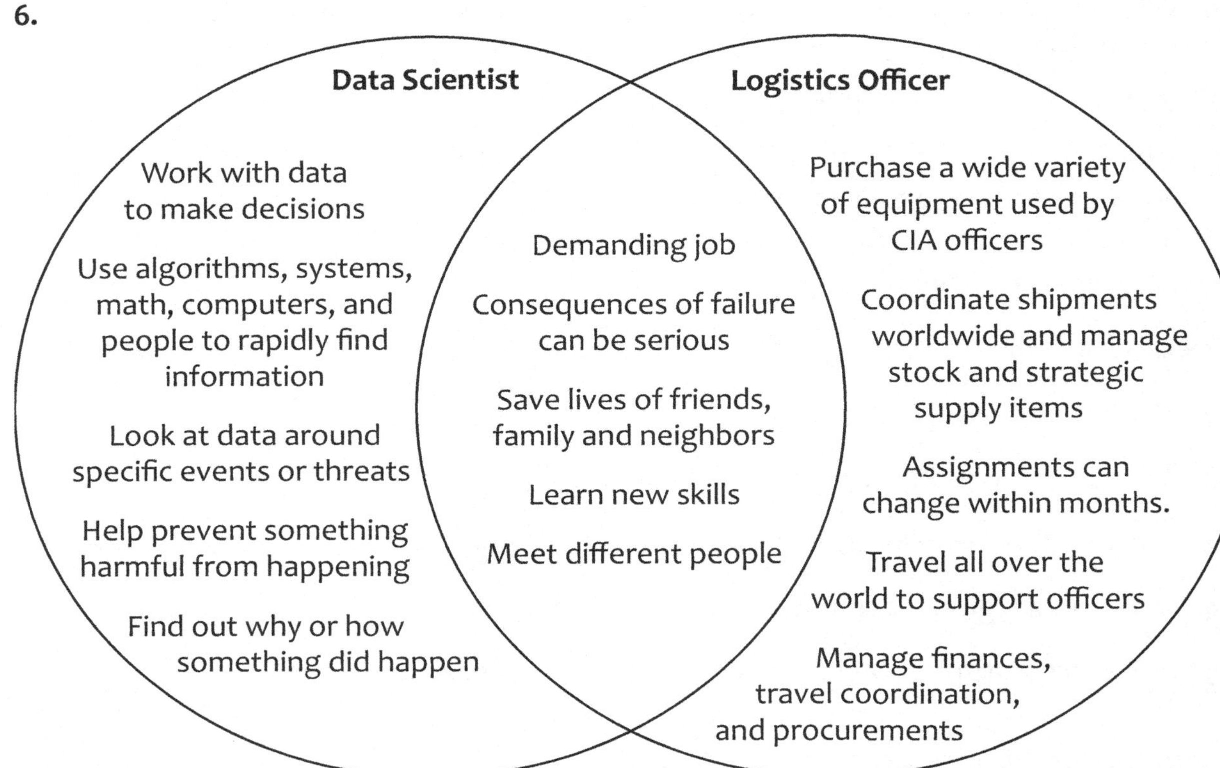

7. Molly is more qualified to be a logistics officer. She is detail-oriented, and her executive assistant experience will prepare her for booking travel. Her accounting experience will prepare her for managing money.

8. The data scientist is likely a higher pressure position. The data scientist helps identify threats and affects the lives of coworkers and the American people.

9. Cameron made more money in the private sector, but he finds working for the CIA much more rewarding. He gets to see the information he finds play out in world events. Cameron knows that what he does matters.

10. The logistics officer prepares CIA officers for their jobs by making sure all the small details are handled. It is an organizational and administrative role. Data scientists have a more direct impact on missions. They locate information that will guides the mission.

11. Both positions need extreme attention to detail and math skills. Both need to be able to succeed in a high pressure environment. Both must work efficiently with rigid time restraints.

Check Your Skills

pages 217–218

1. a. The school system should train teachers to mentor students and help at-risk students.
2. c. Teachers already go above and beyond without receiving recognition.
3. Both writers believe that a teacher's role isn't just limited to the classroom, and both want teachers to mentor students. However, Hines believes that few teachers do this, while Vasquez claims that many teachers go "above and beyond" without recognition. Hines's claim is that teachers should receive training to help students outside of the classroom. She supports this claim with the example from a news story about Miss Orowitz. Because Miss Orowitz helped her students, Hines reasons that more teachers can be trained to help their students as well. Vasquez uses his personal experience as a teacher to argue that teachers already mentor students but go unrewarded. He uses ethos, since his information comes from his experience as a teacher. Since Hines has no information about how many teachers help their students outside of the classroom, Vasquez seems to have the stronger argument.

Reading Fiction Texts page 219

Theme and Author's Purpose page 221

What the Characters Learn

Practice It! pages 224–228

1. b. The narrator realizes he has created a monster.

   The narrator has completed his difficult task. When he sees the result, he recoils in horror: "the beauty of the dream vanished, and breathless horror and disgust filled my heart."

2. d. The narrator wanted to bring a man back to life and now must deal with the consequences.

3. a. He should have considered the consequences of bringing something dead back to life.

   Considering the narrator's horrified reaction to his creation, this is the most likely lesson.

4. c. The pursuit of knowledge can be destructive.

   Frankenstein pursues knowledge without thinking about the consequences. If you expand this idea to the world in general, the unthinking pursuit of knowledge can lead to destructive consequences.

5. Sometimes, the pursuit of knowledge brings with it destructive power. An example is the creation of the nuclear bomb. The destruction in Hiroshima and Nagasaki was horrific. Today, we live in a world where weapons of mass destruction, including chemical and biological weapons as well as nuclear bombs, pose a significant threat to mankind.

6. The problem Maria faces is that she left the plum cake on the train because she was distracted by the older man. She has wasted her time and money selecting the perfect cake for Joe.

7. You can infer that Maria is a lonely woman. She blushes when the woman behind the counter compares the plum cake to a wedding cake. The young men on the tram do not notice her, since she is older and a working woman. She does not have youth or beauty, and she does not have a family of her own.

8. The story resolves with Joe's compassion for Maria's predicament. Joe tells her not to worry and asks her to sit comfortably by the fire. Joe and the children are a family for Maria, and Joe does not want anything from her.

9. Maria might learn that good friends can provide love, support, and happiness, even though she doesn't have her own family.

10. One theme you can infer from the passage is that your friends can provide love, support, and happiness, even through troubled times.

11. When you make a mistake, like losing your wallet or forgetting a friend's birthday, you might become anxious and angry. You could relate the theme of the passage to these moments and realize that your friends are more important than these small problems.

12. In the passage from The Red Badge of Courage, the theme is that to find courage you must know yourself. In the passage from "Clay," the theme is that friends can provide love, support, and happiness, even through troubled times. Both themes relate to knowing yourself. If you know and are confident in yourself, you can have courage and be happy with a community of friends. Maria and Henry both could benefit from self-examination. Henry is aware that he needs to learn about himself so that he can deal with the reality of war. Maria seems less self-aware. She hasn't come to terms with the idea that she may not marry; she is still bewildered by the man on the train. Maria could benefit from Henry's sense of self-examination to develop her own courage and be truly happy with her friends.

Check Your Skills

pages 229–230

1. d. Jim is a troublemaker who doesn't get caught.

2. b. George never does anything wrong but gets punished unfairly.

3. a. Stories portray unrealistic ideas of justice and good versus evil.

   When Twain imagines a judge appearing and pointing out the innocence of the boy, he portrays a stereotypical story where good wins over evil. He contrasts this caricature with his more realistic portrayal of events, where Jim isn't punished. Jim has a different idea of justice than the unrealistic storybook justice, since he wants to misbehave and not be punished. He is also annoyed with George, who always follows the rules.

4. d. "And then Jim didn't get whaled, and the venerable justice didn't read the tearful school a homily."

   At the end of the story, Jim's mischief prevails over George's honesty. Unapologetically, Jim delights in his triumph. "The model boy George got thrashed," Twain writes, "and Jim was glad of it because, you know, Jim hated moral boys." There is no stereotypical justice in real life, and the definition of a "good" boy isn't clear.

5. b. George blushes because he realizes he looks guilty.

Support for a Theme

page 231

Connecting Support with a Theme

Practice It!

pages 235–238

1. You might choose any of the following words: *good heart, cold, hunger, eyes, sapphires, pluck, appreciated,* or *admire.*

2.

Evidence	Explanation
"I will wait with you one night longer," said the Swallow, who really had a good heart. "Shall I take him another ruby?"	This quotation shows that the Swallow is kind and generous.
"My eyes are all that I have left."	This quotation shows that the prince is willing to give up everything he has for someone else.
"I am beginning to be appreciated," he cried; "this is from some great admirer. Now I can finish my play," and he looked quite happy.	This quotation shows how unselfish love can make someone else happy.

3. The theme in "The Happy Prince" involves unselfish love and devotion. The author's message also speaks of sacrifice as the narrator describes the way the prince gives away his valuable sapphire eye for the sake of the poor. You might state the theme as: "Unselfish giving and sacrifice have their own rewards."

4. Depending on your thought process, you could choose any of the following words: *unhappy, bond, trial, hindered, tied, nearness, blessedness, murders, curse,* or *death.*

5.

Evidence	Explanation
"I mean, marriage drinks up all our power of giving or getting any blessedness in that sort of love."	The quotation shows that Dorothea believes that when you're married, love outside that marriage is corrupted.
"I know it may be very dear—but it murders our marriage—and then the marriage stays with us like a murder—and everything else is gone."	The quotation shows that a deep attachment outside of marriage can destroy the marriage.
"And then our husband—if he loved and trusted us, and we have not helped him, but made a curse in his life—."	The quotation shows that a woman must help her husband and not make his life difficult. Love and trust is not enough.
"It is so hard, it may seem like death to part with it—and we are weak—I am weak—."	The quotation shows that Dorothea herself is "weak" and attracted to someone outside of her marriage.

6. The information in the table shows that Dorothea is torn. She feels a strong attraction outside of her marriage but believes it would "murder" her marriage. Her advice is to abandon all attractions outside of marriage, but she is "weak" and parting with an attraction is "like death." You might expand your idea of the theme to state: The constrictions of marriage lead to inner turmoil when a person is attracted to someone besides his or her spouse.

Check Your Skills *pages 239–240*

1. a. "They think of the word only as connected with ragged clothes, scanty food, fireless grates, rude manners, and debasing vices."

2. b. The narrator associates kindness with material possessions.

   Poor people lack material possessions. The narrator associates kindness with providing clothes, food, and other possessions. She believes that kindness is difficult if you don't have money.

3. d. Undesirable

   The narrator associates poverty with begging and degradation. She believes her impoverished relatives are undesirable.

4. a. Being uneducated and ill-mannered

5. c. You can be hard-working but still be poor.

Details in Fiction

page 241

Using Details to Make Inferences

Practice It!

pages 245–246

1. Meg, Jo, Amy, and Beth are the major characters in the passage. They are sisters.
2. Meg tells her sister Jo that she knows better than to misbehave and be a tomboy. Jo refuses to behave like a "lady." Meg also scolds her sister Amy for being too prim, the opposite of Jo. Everyone agrees that Beth is a dear, since she is everyone's favorite.
3.

Detail	What I Already Know	Inference
"If turning up my hair makes me one, I'll wear it in two tails till I'm twenty."	Wearing your hair up was a sign of being a lady, not a girl.	Jo does not want to be a lady.
"Stroking the rough head with a hand that all the dish washing and dusting in the world could not make ungentle in its touch"	Washing dishes can dry out your hands and make them rough.	Beth's hands are gentle, despite hard work, because of her gentle nature.
"I like your nice manners and refined ways of speaking, when you don't try to be elegant. "	People who try too hard to be proper or elegant can be seen as stuck up.	Amy tries too hard to be elegant and seems stuck up.

4. Jo will fight society's expectations of women throughout the novel. Her personality will conflict with Amy's, since Amy is concerned with what people think of her and what is accepted by society.
5. Scott can plan to watch for details relating to the setting. He might start by watching a trailer for the movie and writing down some questions about the setting. What different settings are used during the movie? What is the importance of the time, as well as the place? How do the settings affect the characters? How would the movie change if the setting was different? Scott will be able to find more significant details by thinking about his questions.
6. While Susie is reading, she should think about Ender's character. She could write down adjectives that describe Ender. She should also identify passages in the novel that relate to Ender's character. She can underline or highlight passages, or she can write them down in her notes. Then, she should make notes about what the details mean.

7. Walter can first identify a problem and lesson a character learned. He can then identify which details led him to that conclusion. He can explain the connection of each detail to the theme and the inferences he makes based on those details. With that information he can look at what the details as a whole say about the theme.

Check Your Skills

pages 247–248

1. Rude

   Stuck up

   Bossy

   Disdainful

   The girl calls the narrator "boy" and is scornful. The adjectives *rude, stuck up, bossy,* and *disdainful* describe her best.

2. c. The house is big but unwelcoming.

   The chains on the door make the house appear unwelcoming.

3. c. "I answered, more in shyness than politeness."

   This quotation tells about the character's motivation and feelings.

4. b. Timid

5. c. He is frightened by the strange woman.

Word Choice *page 249*

Three Sides of Word Meaning

Practice It! *pages 254–256*

1.

<table>
<tr><th>Significant Words</th><th>Denotation</th><th>Connotation</th></tr>
<tr><td rowspan="2">Luxury</td><td>State of great comfort and abundance</td><td>Riches; pleasure over need</td></tr>
<tr><td colspan="2">Comparison "I was enjoying the twofold luxury of meditation and a meerschaum"

"I was enjoying the twofold lavishness . . ." would emphasize richness more than comfort.</td></tr>
<tr><td rowspan="2">Profound</td><td>Very great or intense</td><td>Something significant or life changing</td></tr>
<tr><td colspan="2">Comparison "we had maintained a profound silence"

"We had maintained an intense silence . . ." would emphasize how strong the silence was more than how significant or thoughtful it was.</td></tr>
<tr><td rowspan="2">Exclusively</td><td>Excluding others</td><td>Elite</td></tr>
<tr><td colspan="2">Comparison "intently and exclusively occupied"

"Intently and uniquely occupied . . ." would imply that it was strange that the smoke occupied his attention, rather than the smoke took up all his attention and focus.</td></tr>
</table>

2. The tone changes from contemplative and relaxed to more energetic and amusing. The words signal that action is beginning to build. The passages show that Monseiur G has energy and that the narrator and his companion like Monseiur G.

3. The narrator is amused by Monseiur G and friendly toward him but also looks down on him. He describes him as "entertaining" but also "contemptible." The narrator likely enjoys the drama Monseiur G brings with him.

4.

<table>
<tr><th>Significant Words</th><th>Denotation</th><th>Connotation</th></tr>
<tr><td rowspan="2">Suicide</td><td>To take your own life</td><td>Depression, sadness, loneliness, violence</td></tr>
<tr><td colspan="2">Comparison “they suddenly commit suicide”

“They suddenly end…” would not have the same violent and depressive connotations. The word “suicide” also gives the wallpaper human characteristics, making it seem more than just wallpaper.</td></tr>
<tr><td rowspan="2">Repellent</td><td>To be repulsive or disgusting</td><td>To feel emotionally propelled away from something</td></tr>
<tr><td colspan="2">Comparison “The color is repellent”

“The color is terrible…” would not have the same idea of violent disgust.</td></tr>
<tr><td rowspan="2">Sickly</td><td>Unpleasant or nauseating</td><td>Unhealthy</td></tr>
<tr><td colspan="2">Comparison “a sickly sulphur tint in others”

“An unpleasant sulphur tint in others…” would not include the alliteration which emphasizes the nauseating color. It also would not have the connotations of being pale and unhealthy, again giving the wallpaper human characteristics.</td></tr>
</table>

5. The word choice shows that the narrator hates the wallpaper, but more than that, it shows that the narrator is frustrated and feels trapped. The wallpaper takes on a significance greater than just a colorful pattern on the wall. The wallpaper seems almost like a living thing that surrounds the narrator, sickening her. The narrator's intense disgust with the wallpaper creates a disgusted, unhappy tone and narrative point of view. The narrator is desperate to be free, and the narrator's feelings about the wallpaper are a reflection of that desperation.

Check Your Skills

pages 257–258

1. d. Crumb

2. a. It conveys carelessness in disposing of the waste.

3. a. Grotesque, tortured, appalling

4. d. Stuffed

Figurative Language

page 259

Words → Meaning → Purpose for Figurative Language

Practice It!

pages 262–264

1.

Words	Meaning	Purpose
"crying out the meaning of the desert"	This personifies the wolf, which seems to be explaining the meaning of the desert with its cry.	The description shows the connection between the wolf's cry and the desert.
"Hunger throbbed in it—hunger for a mate, for offspring, for life."	"Hunger throbbed" is a metaphor. Hunger cannot throb. The wolf's cry seems desperate, full of desire.	The description shows the importance of survival in the harsh desert. The narrator interprets the wolf's cry as a deep desire to survive.
"desert silence smote Cameron"	This is personification. Silence "smote" Cameron, like a hand hitting him.	The description shows how much Cameron was disturbed by the silence at the end of the wolf's cry.

2. The figurative language shows Cameron's connection to the wolf and the desert. It also contributes to the tone of dreariness as Cameron struggles to survive in the lonely desert.

3.

Words	Meaning	Purpose
"every atom belonging to me as good belongs to you"	This is a simile, stating that every part of the narrator is just like the reader.	The simile shows the similarities and links between all people.
"I loafe and invite my soul"	This personifies the soul as something separate from you. The narrator is calling out to himself.	This quotation emphasizes that the narrator is consciously bringing himself to relaxation and peace.

4. The figurative language reinforces that idea that we all share human origins, regardless of time and place. It makes the passage pensive and focuses on unity and peace.

5.

Words	Meaning	Purpose
"This gave them the seeming of ghostly masques, undertakers in a spectral world at the funeral of some ghost."	This is a simile, comparing the men to ghostly undertakers because of their white, deathly appearances.	The description shows the reader that the men may be alive, but they are a shell of their former selves. It shows how close to death they are.
"Pitting themselves against the might of a world as remote and alien and pulseless as the abysses of space"	This is a simile, comparing the frozen North to outer space because of its emptiness and strangeness.	The description shows the unforgiving nature of their surroundings and emphasizes how far away from civilization they are.

6. Figurative language is used in both passages to connect the setting and the tone. In *Desert Gold*, figurative language helps the connect the main character, Cameron, to the sadness and loneliness of the desert. In *White Fang*, the figurative language shows the obstacles the men face in the wilderness and the hopelessness of their chances of survival.

Check Your Skills *pages 265–266*

1. b. The horses are moving clumsily.

   The horses are "floundering" and "stumbling." The idea that they seem "falling to pieces" means that they are moving clumsily.

2. a. It emphasizes the horses' nervousness.

3. d. Willful

4. a. Gloomy

5. d. The mist is ominous.

6. c. So thick nothing can be seen

Characters

page 267

Making Inferences about Characters

Practice It!

pages 271–272

1.

Detail	What I Already Know	Character Inference
"His hand was steady, but the attitude was an excuse for not making an immediate reply."	You might delay replying if you're not sure what to say.	Ethan is bothered by the possibility of Mattie leaving to get married and doesn't want to agree with his wife.
"I guess you're always late, now you shave every morning."	Men often shave when they care about their appearance.	Ethan is shaving because he wants to impress Mattie.

2. Ethan is not honest with his wife, and he is attracted to Mattie. He is careful about what he says to his wife and tries not to let his feelings show. Still, he wants to make sure Mattie stays with them.

3. Ethan appears to love Mattie. He is bothered when his wife talks about Mattie marrying someone else. He dismisses talk of hiring someone else. Ethan shaves every day now, a departure from his past habits, which shows that he is trying to impress Mattie.

4.

Detail	What I Already Know	Character Inference
"Zeena answered in a tone of plaintive self-effacement."	People who sound sad and humble often are not.	Zeena is trying to appear kind and humble, but she may actually realize her statement will upset Ethan.
"And the doctor don't want I should be left without anybody," Zeena continued.	If a doctor says you shouldn't be alone, you're likely seriously ill.	Zeena is not well.

5. Zeena is a needy person and is seems jealous and manipulative. She is trying to get a reaction from Ethan through her passive aggressive words.

6. Ethan and Zeena are not honest with each other. Ethan hides his feelings toward Mattie and is cautious about what he says to his wife. Zeena also seems to choose her words carefully. She mentions Ethan shaving every day and pushes Ethan to talk about Mattie leaving to get married. Zeena also focuses attention on her illness. She seems manipulative, while Ethan seems defensive.

Comparing Two Characters

Practice It!

pages 276–278

1.

Nathan

Differences

- Strong faith
- Will not give up on baptizing the unenlightened
- Values his faith over his family or own life

Similarities

- Baptist
- Mssionaries
- Believe their faith and culture are superior to others

Differences

Orleanna

- At first, passive about husband's decisions
- Faith not as strong
- Stands up to Nathan when her family's life is at stake

2. Nathan seems unchanged by events around him and refuses to take other perspectives into account. His faith is more important than anything to him, and he will not be shaken. Orleanna grows throughout the novel and changes from passive to assertive. She realizes her family's safety is more important to her than being a missionary.

3. Through Orleanna's growth, she recognizes that she cannot enforce her culture and religion on others without consequences. She begins to accept that others may consider their culture and religion superior to hers. Nathan cannot see another perspective besides his own. He only believes in his own culture and religion and does not see value in other cultures. The characters reveal that to relate to another culture successfully, you must learn to see the world from the perspective of that other culture.

4.

Mrs. Bennet

Differences

- Thinks she knows what's best for her daughters always
- Wants daughters to marry into wealth
- Believes her daughters deserve wealth

Similarities

- End up doing what they think is best for their daughters
- Exhibit qualities of strong women
- Have different values than their families

Differences

Orleanna

- Passively accepts husband's decisions at first
- Does not stand up for her daughters at first
- Lives in regret
- Believes her faith is best

5. Orleanna grows throughout *The Poisonwood Bible*, becoming active and taking her children away from harm. Mrs. Bennet stays the same in *Pride and Prejudice*, learning nothing from the events of the plot. She wants her daughters to marry well, and she is single-minded in working toward this. Orleanna is passive at first, letting her husband make decisions, while Mrs. Bennet is active, trying to arrange marriages for her daughters. The mothers might not make the best decisions for their daughters, but they both do what they think is right.

Check Your Skills

pages 279–280

1.

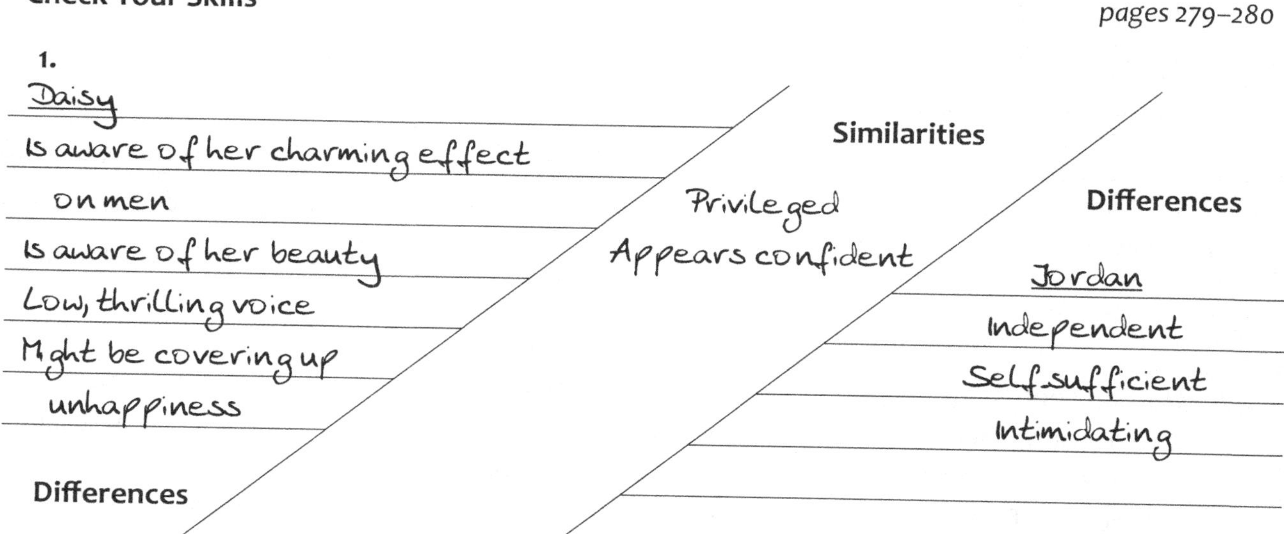

2. b. He is in awe of her.

3. c. Daisy might not be as happy as she appears.

4. b. He sees Daisy for who she is.

Story Structure and Conflict

page 281

Using a Plot Triangle

Practice It!

pages 285–286

1. One conflict is Michael's struggle with the foster system growing up. (person versus society)

   A second conflict occurs when Michael believes his adopted family might be using him. (person versus person)

   A third conflict is between the NCAA investigators and Michael's family. (person versus person)

2.

Climax
Mchael confronts Leigh Anne and runs away to the projects.

Rising Action
Mchael's family is investigated by the NCAA.
Mchael gets his grades up and is recruited to Ole Mss.
Mchael becomes a star player.
Leigh Anne takes in Mchael.

Mchael, a foster child, enrolls in Wngate.
Introduction

Falling Action
Mchael and Leigh Anne reunite.
Leigh Anne says she will support any decision
Mchael satisfies the NCAA.

Mchael begins college.
Resolution

3. One conflict revolves around the fact that Michael believes his family is using him. When the investigator tells Michael about Leigh Anne and her husband's Ole Miss connections, Michael starts to doubts his family's motives. After the climax, this conflict is resolved when Leigh Anne says she will support any decision he makes.

4. The climax occurs when Michael runs away, the height of Michael's conflict with his adopted family. The conflict is finally resolved during the falling action, when Michael accepts that Leigh Anne is not using him. Michael goes to Ole Miss and is then drafted by the Baltimore Ravens, showing that he has overcome his mistrust. He has successfully turned his life around. He grew up struggling to survive, and he is now successful.

Check Your Skills *pages 287–288*

1. c. Denny fights for custody of Zoe.
2. a. Enzo discovers Eve has cancer.

3.

Climax
Eve gets cancer and moves home.

Rising Action
Denny loses a race and his racing career.
Denny misses the birth.
Eve gives birth to Zoe.
Enzo accepts and loves Eve.

Denny picks Enzo out of a litter.
Introduction

Falling Action
Eve passes away.
Denny gets custody of Zoe.

Enzo passes away.
Resolution

Setting, Tone, Genre, and Style

page 289

Words → Meaning → Purpose Chart for Style Elements

Practice It!

pages 294–295

1.

Words	Meaning	Purpose
"Now tell me, honest and true, where am I?"	The narrator questions the reality of where he is.	The casual way the narrator reacts to his situation sets up a humorous tone.
"if, on the other hand, it was really the sixth century, all right, I didn't want any softer thing: I would boss the whole country inside of three months."	The narrator plans to use his situation to his advantage to gain power.	The narrator has a carefree and self-aggrandizing perspective. His first thought is to get into a powerful position
"I now shoved this whole problem clear out of my mind till its appointed day and hour should come"	The narrator isn't too worried about the situation. He is able to compartmentalize.	This quotation sets up a casual, carefree tone in a potentially stressful situation.

2. Details that give you information about the setting include:

   "IN KING ARTHUR'S COURT."

   "528—nineteenth of June."

   "I shall never see my friends again—never, never again. They will not be born for more than thirteen hundred years yet."

   "I knew that the only total eclipse of the sun in the first half of the sixth century occurred on the 21st of June, A.D. 528, O.S., and began at 3 minutes after 12 noon. I also knew that no total eclipse of the sun was due in what to me was the present year—i.e., 1879."

3. The setting is far-fetched and ridiculous, adding to the humor of the passage, as well as setting up the central problem.

4. a. Comedy

5. The narrator has a lighthearted tone, and his reaction to the absurd situation is humorous. The premise of the story is also playful and unrealistic.

6. Because this story is set in the past, it has elements of historical fiction. Because of its imaginative aspect, the story has elements of fantasy.

7. You might be drawn to the passage through the humorous attitude of the narrator. His story seems unpredictable and far-fetched, so you might be curious to see what happens next.

Check Your Skills

pages 296–298

1. b. Science fiction
2. b. Human civilization has been devastated.
3. a. A struggle for survival in a post-apocalyptic society
4. b. Dark, hopeless
5. d. "Custom, habit, all the determining forces of learning were gone; only brute experience remained."

Point of View

page 299

A Process for Evaluating Point of View

Practice It!

pages 303–304

1. c. Third person

   The narrator uses third person pronouns such as *he* and *him* to describe all the characters. Since first or second person pronouns are never used, the passage is in third person.

2. The narrator knows Ogilvy's thoughts. The narrator says that "he perceived" the top of the capsule was opening and "he scarcely understood" what was happening.

3.

Words	Meaning	Purpose
Dreadful	Terrible, horrifying	The word shows how affected Ogilvy is by watching the men trapped in the cylinder.
Irresolute	Uncertain	The word shows that Ogilvy takes a moment to decide what to do. He thinks through his actions.
Wildly	Uncontrolled or unrestrained	The word describes the strong emotions that motivate Ogilvy to run.

4. Ogilvy is horrified by the idea of men trapped in the capsule. Ogilvy is wild with emotion, since the capsule from Mars is so startling.

5. The narrator describes Ogilvy's thoughts and feelings, so you see the story through his point of view. If Ogilvy is terrified, you are more likely to see the situation as terrifying. You know Ogilvy isn't actually crazy as he runs for help. You understand the situation and his reaction.

6. The narrator in this text is a third-person limited narrator, who has a knowledge of events and Ogilvy's thoughts and perspective. While Ogilvy is filled with fear and alarm, the narrator still calmly describes Ogilvy's actions.

Check Your Skills *pages 305–306*

1. d. A prisoner who has been sentenced to death

2. a. Losing consciousness

3. c. Delirious

4. c. It shows the narrator's experience, drifting in and out of reality.

5. a. The narrator's changing perspective on hope

Comparing Fiction *page 307*

Using a Comparison Alley to Compare Fiction

Practice It! *pages 312–314*

1. Theme

   Setting

   Point of view

   Character motivations

   Comparing theme allows you to compare the messages of the authors. Point of view affects how a story is told and the way a reader understands it, so it is a good quality to compare. Character motivations can drive the plot and meaning of a text. Setting can be beneficial to compare because it is often directly affects why and how something happens. Character backgrounds and descriptions can be interesting to compare, but will not likely directly lead you to the meaning of a text.

2.

The Bean Trees: Taylor
Young woman who has left home for the first time
Takes in a child
Finds a new home and family
Protects those she loves.
Differences

Similarities
Want to escape
Grow up poor and
Learn from choices of others.
Live their lives in a conscientious way to change their situations

Differences
House on Mango Street: Esperanza
Young girl living with family
Lives at home, wants to escape.
Turns to writing.
Starts becoming an adult when she must deal with adult issues.

3. Both Taylor and Esperanza see the places they grew up as places to be escaped. They both have support from friends and family but don't want to make the same choices. They want better lives for themselves, so they work hard to leave their childhood homes.

4. Taylor and Esperanza both learn from the people around them. They both have support from friends and family. Esperanza learns from her friends and family what she can become. Taylor finds a new family in the friends she makes during her travels. She fights for them as if they are her family.

5. Esperanza must endure a death in the family and an assault in the community. These events make the adult world a reality to Esperanza, so she must grow up. Taylor similarly finds herself facing adult situations. In Taylor's case, she must care for a child. She matures as she tries to support and protect the child.

Check Your Skills

pages 315–318

1. c. To make the characters stand out as unique people.

2. b. He is meticulous about his personal appearance.

3. b. Carefulness

4. a. Holmes's fits of energy and malaise

   Poirot's situation of sharing a home is not significant. Both characters share regular habits and impressive past cases.

5.

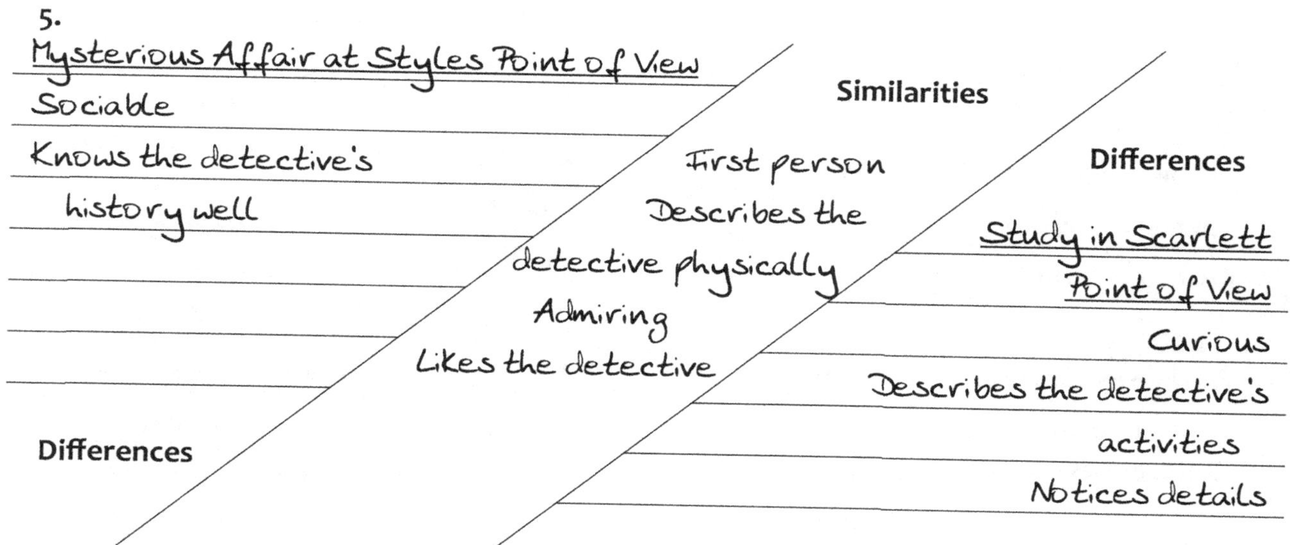

6. Both passages are from the detective fiction genre, and each passage introduces the detective who will solve a mystery. Because of the genre, you predict that each of the detectives will investigate and then solve a crime. You know that the characters' eccentricities will be questioned by others at first, but their quirks, in the end, will work in their favor.

Resources

Use the following resources to continue practicing and improving your reading. Reading every day is important. Find topics and authors that interest you, and read for pleasure. You'll expand your knowledge and improve your reading skills at the same time.

Free Online eBooks

Project Gutenberg offers over 42,000 free ebooks to read on your computer, Kindle, or smartphone. The collection includes both fiction and nonfiction.
http://www.gutenberg.org/

Forgotten Books offers over 1,000,000 free ebooks, including fiction, drama, folklore and mythology, self-help, philosophy, history, science, art, music, and language.
http://www.forgottenbooks.org/

Gizmo's Freeware blog lists 862 sites offering free ebooks, including biographies, textbooks, modern fiction by new authors, business books, philosophy books, and more.
http://www.techsupportalert.com/best-free-ebooks-online.htm

Your local library likely offers free ebooks if you have a library card. Use OverDrive to access the titles at your public library with your library card and PIN. Ask your library for details.
http://search.overdrive.com/

Online News and Magazines

Google News compiles news stories from across the web. News is updated throughout the day, and you can search for news stories on particular topics.
https://news.google.com/

The Internet Public Library (IPL) has a directory of newspapers and magazines available online, including local newspapers worldwide and magazines covering a wide range of topics.
http://www.ipl.org/div/news/

Time magazine has political, world, business, health, technology, and entertainment news. Most magazines have websites where you can read stories online.
http://www.time.com/time/

Made in the USA
Las Vegas, NV
17 October 2023

79240391R00214

Animal Bodies UP CLOSE

An[illegible]g EYES Up Close

Enslow Elementary
an imprint of

Enslow Publishers, Inc.
40 Industrial Road
Box 398
Berkeley Heights, NJ 07922
USA
http://www.enslow.com

Melissa Stewart

CONTENTS

WORDS TO KNOW

haw (HAW)—A clear eyelid that protects the eyes of some animals.

predator (PREH duh tur)—An animal that hunts and kills other animals for food.

tarsier (TAR see ur)—A small furry animal that lives in Asia. It jumps from tree to tree and eats mostly insects.

HONEY BEE

Animals use their *eyes* to see the world. A bee has five *eyes*! Three small eyes are on top of its head. These eyes can only tell if it is light or dark. Two large eyes are on the sides of its head. These eyes can see objects.

EAGLE

UP CLOSE

An eagle sees eight times better than you do. It uses its eyes to hunt. It can spot a rabbit from a mile away.

An eagle's eye has three eyelids. Two of them work just like yours. The inner eyelid is called a **haw**. It is clear. The bird can see through it. A haw protects an eagle's eyes.

PANTHER CHAMELEON

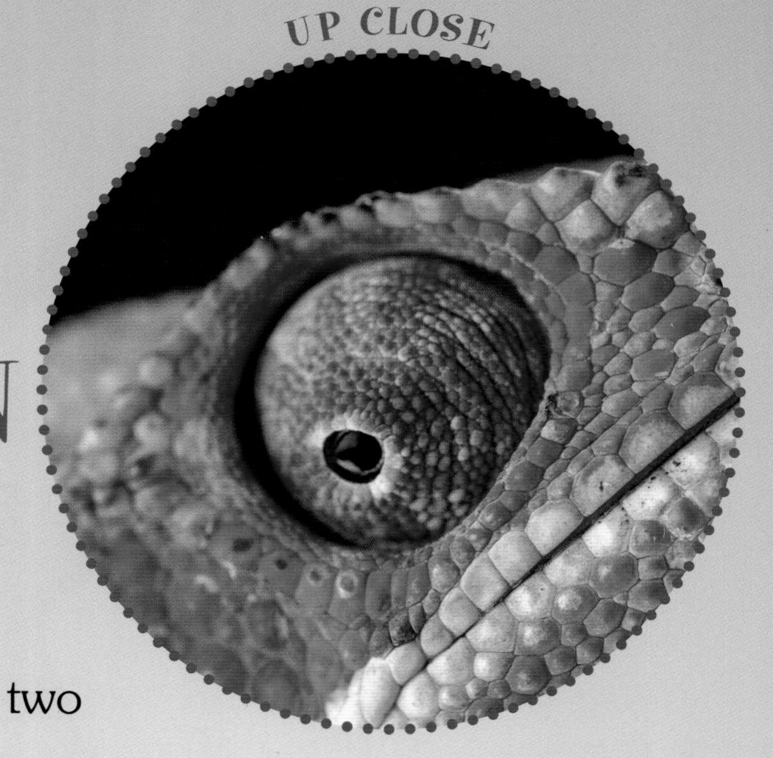

This lizard can move its *eyes* two ways at once. One *eye* looks up. The other looks down. One *eye* can look left. The other can look right. That makes it easier to find food and stay safe.

TARSIER

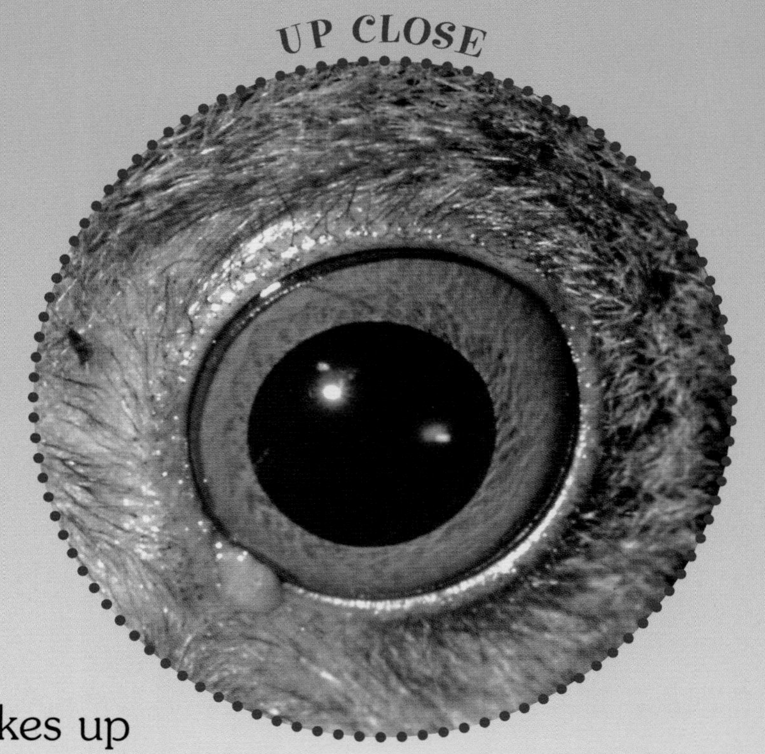

A **tarsier** (TAR see ur) wakes up as the sun sets. It hunts for insects and lizards all night long. Its huge eyes let in lots of light, so it can see in the dark.

RED-EYED TREE FROG

These big red eyes surprise **predators**. That gives the frog time to jump out of sight.

The frog's huge eyes stick out of its head. That means it can sit still and see far to the right and left.

FOUR-EYED FISH

UP CLOSE

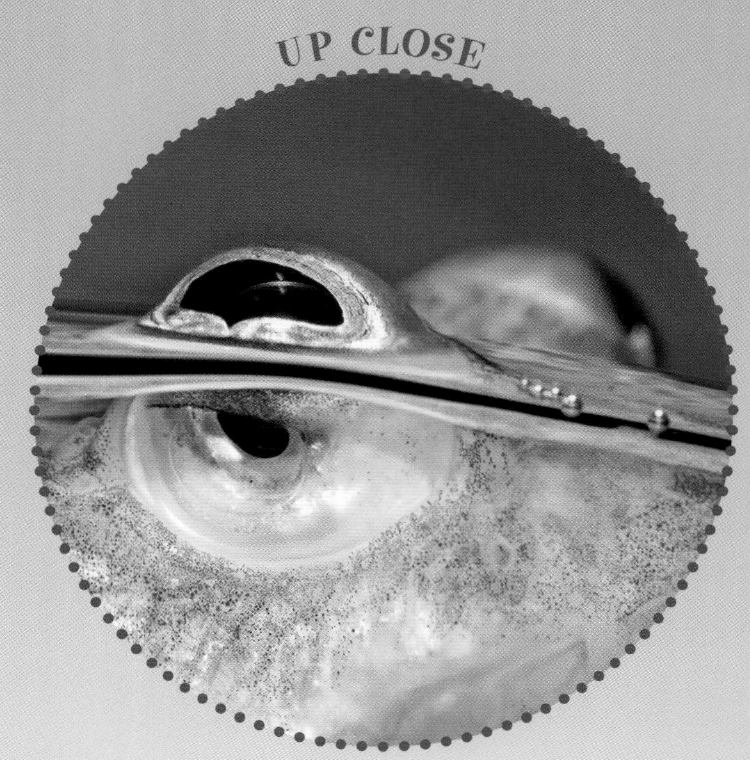

This fish doesn't really have four eyes. But each eye works in two different ways. The top half of each eye can watch what is happening above the water. The bottom half sees what is going on below the water at the same time. What a great trick!

GIANT SQUID

A giant squid has the largest eyes on Earth. They are twice as big as a dinner plate!

Giant squid live in the deep ocean. Their huge eyes help them see in the dark water.

YOUR EYES

UP CLOSE

You are an animal too. And you have eyes. They spot friends and watch for cars when you cross the street. They help you catch a baseball and read the words in this book. Thank goodness for eyes!

1. **How many eyes do some scallops have?**
2. **How many eyes does a giant clam have?**
3. **How many eyes does a snail have?**
4. **How many eyes does a tarantula have?**

A. **more than 1,000**
B. **8**
C. **2**
D. **more than 100**

(Do not write in this book! Write your answers on a piece of paper.)

See answers on page 24.

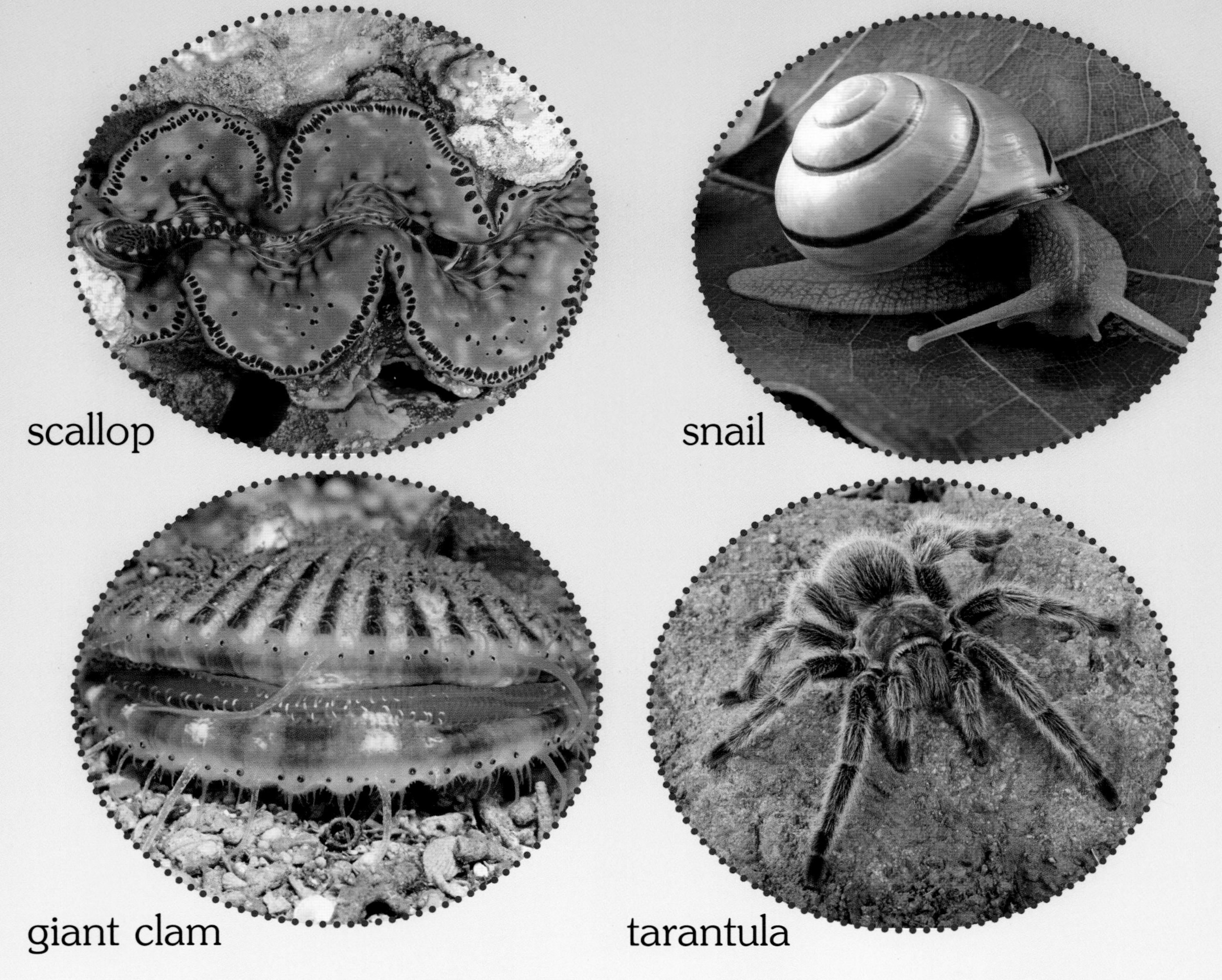
scallop

snail

giant clam

tarantula

LEARN MORE

Books

Barnhill, Kelly Regan. *Animals With No Eyes.* Mankato, Minn.: Capstone Press, 2008.

Hall, Peg. *Whose Eyes Are These?* Mankato, Minn.: Picture Window Books, 2007.

Jenkins, Steve, and Robin Page. *What Do You Do With a Tail Like This?* Boston: Houghton Mifflin, 2003.

Lynch, Wayne. *Whose Eyes Are These?* Toronto: Whitecap Books, 2009.

Stone, Lynn M. *How Do Animals Use Their Eyes?* Vero Beach, Fla.: Rourke, 2008.

WEB SITES

Animal Eyes Quiz

http://kids.aol.com/quizzes/animal-eyes-quiz

KidsHealth: Your Eyes

http://kidshealth.org/kid/htbw/eyes.html

INDEX

Note to Parents and Teachers: The **Animal Bodies Up Close** series supports the National Science Education Standards for K–4 science. The Words to Know section introduces subject-specific vocabulary words, including pronunciation and definitions. Early readers may need help with these new words.

Enslow Elementary, an imprint of Enslow Publishers, Inc.
Enslow Elementary® is a registered trademark of Enslow Publishers, Inc.

Library of Congress Cataloging-in-Publication Data
Stewart, Melissa.
Amazing eyes up close / Melissa Stewart.
p. cm. — (Animal bodies up close)
Includes bibliographical references and index.
Summary: "Discover how different animals use their eyes to hunt, scare other animals, or stay safe"—Provided by publisher.
ISBN 978-0-7660-3889-9 (alk. paper)
1. Eye—Juvenile literature. I. Title.
QL949.S743 2011
591.4'4—dc22
2011003336

Future editions:
Paperback ISBN 978-1-4644-0080-3
ePUB ISBN 978-1-4645-0987-2
PDF ISBN 978-1-4646-0987-9

Printed in China

012012 Leo Paper Group, Heshan City, Guangdong, China

10 9 8 7 6 5 4 3 2 1

To Our Readers: We have done our best to make sure all Internet Addresses in this book were active and appropriate when we went to press. However, the author and the publisher have no control over and assume no liability for the material available on those Internet sites or on other Web sites they may link to. Any comments or suggestions can be sent by e-mail to comments@enslow.com or to the address on the back cover.

Photo Credits: Albert Lleal/Minden Pictures, p. 8; © Andreas Werth, p. 14; © Bob Cranston/Animals Animals, p. 16; Brian J. Skerry/National Geographic Stock, p. 17; Gerry van der Walt/Photo-Africa Stock Library, pp. 2, 9; © GoSeeFoto/Alamy, p. 15; © Graham Eaton/naturepl.com, pp. 3 (haw), 6; © iStockphoto.com/Miodrag Gajic, p. 18; © Michael Dick/Animals Animals - Earth Scenes, pp. 3 (tarsier), 11; Photolibrary: Age fotostock, p. 4, Imagebroker.net, p. 5, Michael L Peck, pp. 3 (predator), 7, Andre Seale, p. 21 (giant clam), OSF, p. 10, Paul Kay, p. 21 (scallop); Shutterstock.com, pp. 1, 12, 13, 19, 21 (snail, tarantula), 23.

Cover Photo: Shutterstock.com

Series Literacy Consultant:
Allan A. De Fina, PhD
Dean, College of Education
Professor of Literacy Education
New Jersey City University
Past President of the New Jersey Reading Association

Science Consultant:
Helen Hess, PhD
Professor of Biology
College of the Atlantic
Bar Harbor, Maine

Answers to the Guessing Game

1. Scallops: more than 100
2. Giant clam: more than 1,000
3. Snail: 2
4. Tarantula: 8